The Game Cookery Book

To The Vandervorts —

Thank you for everything

(babysitting)!

Merry Christmas 1976

Cec & Don

Padre & Banjo

The Game Cookery Book

Compiled for The Game Conservancy by Julia Drysdale

Collins · Glasgow and London

First Published 1975
Published by William Collins Sons and Company Limited
Glasgow and London
Printed in Great Britain

ISBN 0 00 435165 7

Acknowledgements

I have tried throughout the book to be as honest as I possibly could as to where I have found my recipes. Unfortunately I have collected clippings from papers and magazines for years and never thinking that I would use them to inspire anyone other than myself, I have not kept track of what I clipped them from. I know that this is particularly true of *The Field*, *Country Life* and *The Shooting Times*. Members of the Game Conservancy and other friends have been incredibly generous with their contributions.

It will be obvious that I am deeply influenced by Elizabeth David, and I hope that I have done justice to all I have learnt from her. Jane Grigson in *The Observer* and in her books has taught me much about game. The Gourmet Cookbooks have also been by my side, and when I could not think of how to describe a method I consulted *Mastering the Art of French Cooking* by Simone Beck, Louisette Bertholde and Julia Child.

Apart from these pros I thank my long-suffering family and close friends who have lived through all the moans and groans, have been fed game with hardly a break and then been asked to discuss every mouthful. My daughter Anne and her friends from Winkfield and the Cordon Bleu know more about cooking than I do, and have given much help and advice and criticism; and my daughter Penny has typed the entire manuscript from my handwriting. Finally, a special thanks to our keeper Ken Dakers for all his enthusiasm and help.

The Author wishes to thank the following for permission
to use their recipes in this book:

James Beard (pages 58, 94, 122)
Elizabeth David (pages 38–9, 50, 53, 54, 93, 113, 128,
    143, 192)
Jane Grigson (pages 96, 105, 124)
Club National des Bécassiers (pages 83–6)
The Women's Institute for recipes from *The Women's
Institute Cookbook* (pages 93, 95)

F. J. Taylor Page, The British Deer Society, Forge
Cottage, Askham via Penrith for the information
on deer (pages 215–16)

Contents

Illustrations by Anne Knight

Introduction

It was a sunny day and we were lying in the heather eating our lunch. Charles Coles mentioned the Conservancy's plan to publish a cook book, I said that I would quite like to help, and Douglas Hutchison suggested that I should go ahead and organize it myself as I had a sympathetic knowledge of the subject. By the time we were back in the butts, I was more or less committed and wondering once again why I always had to join in everyone else's conversation. As if that wasn't enough, it then seemed a good idea to ask Collins to publish it for the Game Conservancy as many of their directors have similar interests. Suddenly I was committed to two very professional concerns knowing I was a total amateur. Together they have dragged this from me.

My original idea of what the book should be called was *The Game Bag*, in other words the gallant female who managed to make the most of and enjoy the seven months when game is in season. The 11th of August is a day when I sway between the happy joy of knowing that tomorrow I will be back on the hill, and that before the first of February there will be days when irritation and gloom will engulf me. It is seven months of exhilaration, friendship and fun, it is also a long hard struggle of pre-planned food, lists everywhere. There are shooting lunches, house parties, dinner-parties to entertain the house parties. A week's walking up grouse teaches you as quickly as anything the art of simplifying a picnic, particularly if you are responsible for breakfast and dinner as well. Lunches in the house produce more mess and chaos, more exhausted dailies and less thanks than anything except possibly the Hunt Ball. It is difficult to find the balance between giving the maximum hospitality and still being around to enjoy the day thoroughly yourself.

Then there is the problem of the Game Larder. Ours groans from the middle of August until the middle of February. Each year when I see the first brace of grouse hanging there, I promise myself that this year I really will keep it in perfect order, but, like a new puppy, if you don't watch it continually it tends to get out of hand very quickly. You open the door and out of nowhere have arrived seven pigeons, three woodcock, one snipe, two mallard, one teal, and six pheasants, two badly shot. If it was a mirage in May you could be inspired, but in the chaos of November a sight such as that can make me long for a plate of fish fingers. I have even sneaked out with a spade and buried half of it, promising myself that if my husband or our keeper didn't notice, I would really try to be a better wife in the future. This was before the enormous rise in the price of meat: now we who are lucky enough to have game, even in odd quantities, can eat far better than city dwellers to whom it is a luxury instead of a way of life.

Julia Drysdale

Game Cookery and Conservation

The Game Conservancy, whose idea it was to publish this book and whose members have contributed many of the recipes, has been in existence for about forty years. The staff comprises both scientists and field consultants, whose normal job is not associated with such things as preparing a Terrine de Lièvre. They are concerned with investigating day-to-day game problems on farms and estates, and applying practical remedies to improve the shooting.

Our countryside is shrinking: our farming has become more intensive with chemicals, machines and unsympathetic cropping patterns, which create heavy pressures on game and other wildlife. Hazel coppices with oak and other attractive hardwood mixtures have largely disappeared, to be replaced by sombre conifers, which by and large do not encourage the same density or variety of game. It is to the Game Conservancy – an independent private organization supported by members from many countries – that people turn for assistance.

From the serious job of a laboratory post-mortem on a partridge, or tracking the peregrinations of a wild pheasant brood to record its survival pattern, we have taken time off to think about cooking. There is probably no *less* game reaching the table today than there was a generation ago, but the diversity has certainly diminished and some of the expertise of the old country house kitchen is being lost. The regular appearance every Saturday evening of the brace of reared pheasants from the stockbroker syndicate may have something to do with it. ('Roast it, casserole it with Supermarket Spanish Red – or give it to cousin Mary?')

Certainly today's shooting man is far more careless about the condition of the game when it reaches the table. Not everyone can tell an old from a young bird. Few people appreciate the 'butter duck' – in fact, few know which one it is. Not so long ago Uncle Charlie would have been greatly concerned with the fate of his brace of golden plover all the way through from his game bag to their appearance at his breakfast table. Less so today: however one hopes that these interests will be rekindled.

In compiling this book we were not only concerned with cooking game, but also in providing recipes for the sportsman – whether a simple 'piece for the hill' or a traditional hot pot for a shooting luncheon. It has naturally been a question not of what to include, but what to leave out.

We have been lucky with our competent author, Julia Drysdale, wife of one of our council members and an enthusiastic cook who has also had invaluable practical experience of frequently having to cope with a house full of shooting guests, uninvited labradors and hungry young people. To Julia Drysdale we are sincerely grateful.

The Game Conservancy is devoting all its time and funds to ensuring that shooting will continue as a sport, that our countryside be enriched by partridges or woodcock or roe deer. We need more members and more donations to support our research work. If you feel you can assist us we hope you will get in touch. If not, *bon appétit* nevertheless – we are being granted royalties from this book.

The Game Conservancy,
Fordingbridge,
Hampshire

Charles Coles.

Director

Note on Metrication

Metric equivalents and oven temperatures have been included in all the recipes throughout this book.
Conversions based on 25 g = 1 oz, 500 ml = 1 pint, and 2.5 cm = 1 inch, are in accordance with Standard British Practice. With larger amounts, quantities have been rounded up or down, and have been appropriately balanced.

Game Cooking

If your bird or beast is young and in prime condition then it is a pity to do anything other than to roast it. This does not mean putting it in an oven, forgetting about it, and expecting perfection to reappear 45 minutes later. This means careful preparation, trussing it well, barding and larding then basting and basting. Basting makes far more difference than whether or not you mix a little lemon juice with the butter which you have placed inside the bird or put a few juniper berries on the venison. These are nice subtleties, but the fat and the basting are what produce the final moist juicy offering. No two birds are quite alike, and often when you are given a brace you will find a considerable variance in the weight which will mean slightly longer cooking for one than for the other.

Later in the season when the game is a little older, it will need braising or stewing. It then becomes more docile, allowing you to trust it to a dinner-party without the same fuss and bother. It still needs careful preparation but often you don't even have to pluck it as skinning will do. Most of the recipes in this book are easily interchangeable. There is no reason why grouse and pheasants, pigeons and partridge, venison and hare cannot exchange recipes. It is flexible as long as you bear in mind the size and age of the bird or roast, enabling you to have an idea of how long to cook it.

Try experimenting with winter vegetables and salads. They are much more interesting than frozen peas and can be prepared hours early. Who wants to stand watching a pea melt while your friends drink by the fire? I haven't suggested which vegetables go with what because in the country the shops are so unpredictable. As soon as you get your confidence back from your last disappointment you go off with the week's list and return home shattered again. Even the simple classic instructions 'sprinkle with finely chopped parsley' can become ridiculous if you forgot to plant the parsley in the greenhouse during the summer.

By choice I would have been far less dogmatic over most of the ingredients, but my publishers are exacting task masters. Just because I've let them bully me, do not feel that you must do precisely as I say. The recipes are suggestions to be adapted by each person to their own taste.

How to Tell the Age of a Bird

There are only two tests which apply to most species throughout the whole of the season. At the start of each variety I will have any other tips, but these two are general.

All young gamebirds have a small blind-ended passage opening on the upper side of the vent. This passage, commonly known as the Bursa, is believed to play some part in disease control. In all species it becomes much reduced or may close completely when the bird reaches sexual maturity, and the presence of a normal bursa is a certain test for a young bird. Insert a matchstick which is burnt at one end so that it is narrow but not too sharp.

The second method (which unfortunately cannot be applied to the pheasant) is to examine the two outer primaries or flight feathers. In the partridge the pointed, lance-shaped tips of these feathers distinguish the young bird from the old, which has blunt-ended outer primaries. It should be mentioned that when feathers are wet, even blunt-ended ones can look pointed.

This I quote, and many other facts too, from *The Complete Book of Game Conservation*, edited by Charles Coles who is the director of the Game Conservancy. Charts and other useful information may be found on pages 211 to 216.

How to Pluck

You can pluck twice as quickly if you do it outdoors as it doesn't matter where the feathers and down go. Otherwise use as large and deep a box or garbage can as possible in the hopes that it will catch most of the feathers. Pluck towards the head, against the way the feathers lie, using your thumb against your bent first finger. Try all the time to avoid tearing the skin: sometimes when the skin is torn you will have to pluck around it, pulling the feathers out the way they grow. Use tweezers for the pin feathers. If it's of any help, working at leisure, I allow 20 minutes per grouse taken from the larder to being completely oven ready.

Americans dip their feathered game in hot paraffin wax, let cool and just pull it off. They think we are mad to do it as we do, but I have never remembered to try to buy the paraffin wax.

How to Clean

Cut off the head so that the neck is as long as possible. Pull back the skin and cut the neck close to the body. Try to ease out the crop without breaking it, but if it is punctured clean out the cavity and pull out the skin of the crop. Most directions tell you to cut around the vent to get at the entrails, but I use the vent for keeping the legs down when the bird is trussed, so I make an incision just above the vent. Remove the entrails gently but completely, take hold of the gizzard, pull, and most of the contents will come with it. If you have not removed the vent, cut the intestine close to it. Feel around to make sure there is nothing left. Wipe well with a clean damp cloth. Retain liver, heart and gizzard. Be careful to discard the gall bladder without puncturing it. If the liver has any discolouration cut that out immediately. If you wish to remove the tendons from the legs, cut carefully around the skin just at the joint where the scaly bit begins, being careful not to cut the tendons, snap the joint and pull away – the tendons should come, but if not force a skewer under them and pull them out separately.

How to Truss

Trussing game birds is not just as easy as trussing a domestic bird which has had its neck wrung. You come across wobbly legs and missing joints which won't hold or fit where you wish them to. The point of trussing a bird is to keep it as compact as possible: the legs and wings don't dry out, it looks more attractive and is easier to carve. Use either a trussing needle and thick thread, wooden cocktail sticks or skewers and string to close the hole near the vent. If the legs will fit place the ends into the vent or into a slit made in that region. With a perfect bird you should be able to fold the skin of the neck down over the back and secure it with the wing tips which you bend backwards, but this isn't always possible and you will have to improvise with some of the above-mentioned equipment.

How to Singe

Hold the bird over a gas flame, candle, taper or burning methylated spirits. I use methylated spirits, but you must be careful not to get black fumes on the bird.

How to Sour Cream

As sour cream is almost impossible for me to buy where we live, I sour my own. All I do is to put approximately 2 teaspoons lemon juice or vinegar in 125 ml ($\frac{1}{4}$ pint) of cream which is at room temperature, stir it and leave it until it thickens. It needs a little practice to get it right as you want as little acid as possible. It is hard to say just how long it will take as it turns quicker when it is older – sometimes it goes immediately, other times it takes an hour.

How to Keep Blood

Mix the blood (the amount you would get from a hare) with 1 tablespoon vinegar and keep in the refrigerator. This will also freeze.

Grouse

A French friend staying with us one August remarked: 'How typically British to have a most superb bird to cook and then create bread sauce as the ideal accompaniment.' Every time I've seen bread sauce I have thought of Edouard and I have seldom made it since.

I'm surprised at how hard it is to find original ways of cooking grouse. Maybe it's because during the grouse season cooking doesn't seem as important as at other times of the year. Everyone is busy, hopefully outside, and this doesn't lend itself to being creative in the kitchen. Also, at the end of a day a good plain meal seems enough with so many people to be catered for. Young grouse are easy, for as long as they are properly cooked they must be delicious. Then there are pâtés, terrines, pies and stews, but all fairly classical stuff. Grouse seem to be aristocrats and it is hard to picture them surrounded by cabbage or bedded down in potatoes, but I don't see why, if you have a glut of them, they shouldn't adapt themselves to some of the more plebeian partridge or pheasant dishes.

Hanging Grouse

Young grouse can manage to be over ripe in a day or two if the weather is warm or damp. They need careful watching as it is a pity to spoil the flavour by letting them get high. Young birds shot and eaten on the 12th August (the opening day of the grouse season) are delicious – either don't hang them at all, or hang them for 2–4 days. This of course depends on the weather – they will keep far longer if it is cool. Hang them where the air can circulate, and preferably not touching each other.

When I first read that if your birds had become clammy from travelling in parcels or cars, or had become a bit high, then all you had to do was to dip them in Milton (what they use for babies' bottles), I couldn't believe it and I was sure you would notice the taste. You don't – it's marvellous, and has saved me many anxious moments.

Telling the Age of a Grouse (extract from *The Complete Book of Game Conservation*)

The infallible way to tell the age of a grouse, as with all other birds, is the bursa test (see page 15). A matchstick or quill can be inserted into it for a distance of 1 cm ($\frac{1}{2}$ in) if it is a young bird. Other less reliable methods are to compare the two outer primaries with that of the rest. If they are all of a kind with rounded tips, then it is an old bird. If the tips of the two most outer feathers are pointed and clearly differ in shape from the others, it will be a young bird. However, a bird of the previous year, which has not yet moulted these two primaries, will exhibit the same feathers, except that the two primaries will look tattered and faded in colour.

Another guide is that adult grouse shed their toenails between July and September. When a nail is seen in the process of becoming detached it is a sure sign of an old bird. A transverse ridge or scar across the top of the nail, where the old nail was attached, may persist for a month or more after it has been shed and so is indicative of an old bird.

The traditional methods are not as reliable. The lower beak of a young grouse can fail to break as early as 12th August if the bird is well developed, and is thoroughly misleading by mid-September. Testing the strength of a bird's skull by trying to crush it with the thumb will, if it succeeds, be indicative of a young bird, but it too can be misleading.

Mollie's Roast Young Grouse

brace of grouse
50 g (2 oz) seasoned butter
2 slices bacon
2 slices white bread, sautéed in additional butter

Anyone who has been lucky enough to have grouse roasted by Mollie, Douglas Hutchison's housekeeper at Bolfracks, knows that Mollie's way must be the best. Her grouse is always done to perfection, so I nearly wept when I saw her ordinary, mundane recipe – no secret at all. She has since admitted that it's difficult to say, when writing down a recipe, just how much watching and basting and time you have to give a grouse. That is her secret. I think some of the kudos must also go to Mr Chalmers, the headkeeper, who knowing both grouse and Mollie has never given her anything but perfect birds to start with!

Prepare grouse. Insert piece of seasoned butter into each bird. Cover breast of birds with bacon. Place on slice of well-buttered bread. Put into roasting tin in a moderately hot oven (190°C, 375°F, Mark 5) for 35–40 minutes, depending on size of grouse.

Remove bacon 10 minutes before the bird is ready, to allow the breast to brown. Serve with bread sauce, fried breadcrumbs and gravy, green salad and crisps.

Grouse are often served on a croûton of bread fried in butter on which the mashed and sautéed liver of the bird has been spread. This may be put under the bird during part of the cooking to catch the juices, or merely when you serve it.

Grilled Grouse

1 grouse
1 tablespoon butter
pepper and salt
2–3 juniper berries, crushed

Only the best grouse should be grilled.

Heat grill. Split the grouse down the back and force halves apart until they are flat. Then skewer them open. Rub them well with softened butter and season with plenty of pepper and salt and a few crushed juniper berries if you wish. Grill under a hot heat, turning occasionally, and brushing with more butter if necessary. Do not overcook.

You may, of course, cut the birds completely in half, but this is more inclined to let the juices run out of the breasts.

Barbecued Grouse

During August and September I use our barbecue all the time for chickens, hamburgers, chops and all the usual things, but several years ago when the Laird suggested we barbecued grouse I was shocked. By all means stew them, pot them, turn them into pâtés or soup – but to barbecue them seemed rather sacrilegious. In the end, however, we had a go and they are delicious.

grouse
oil
salt and pepper

Either split the birds in half or cut them down the back and force them apart until they are flat, and then run a skewer or two through them to keep them open. Cover them well with oil and season with salt and pepper. It is difficult to say how long they should take to cook – about 15 minutes depending on the fire. Try not to get them too black on the outside. Baste them as often as possible.

Fried Grouse (Willow Grouse)

From Mrs Bo Thelander (Sweden).

brace of grouse
2 tablespoons butter or margarine
salt and pepper
5 slices carrot
1 small onion
5 juniper berries, crushed
125 ml (¼ pint) red wine
125 ml (¼ pint) beef broth or water
125 ml (¼ pint) cream
2 tablespoons arrowroot
1 teaspoon blackcurrant jelly
1 tablespoon brandy (optional)

Clean and truss the birds, heat butter or margarine in a pan and fry the birds. Add salt, pepper, carrot, onion cut into four, and juniper berries. Add wine and beef broth, then cover, and let simmer slowly until birds are tender. Take out the birds and keep them hot while you make the sauce. Strain the gravy, add cream and bring to boil. Add arrowroot dissolved in a little water, blackcurrant jelly and the brandy. Cut birds into halves and put them on a serving plate. Serve with small fried potato cubes, blackcurrant jelly, sauce and salad.

Grouse Stewed in Butter

If you think your grouse isn't quite young enough to roast or grill – but still good – try cooking it, covered, in butter. I use this recipe for all good game birds – they vary slightly in cooking time but 35–45 minutes usually is enough. Grouse seem to like brandy and red wine best, pheasants and partridges are not so particular.

25 g (1 oz) butter
2–3 slices streaky bacon, diced
1 grouse
2 tablespoons brandy
75 ml (3 oz) red wine

Melt butter in a casserole just large enough to hold the grouse. Add diced bacon (a little chopped onion if you like), and lightly brown the bird all over. Pour over a little brandy, shake well, put the bird on one side, cover tightly, and simmer gently for 40 minutes, turning the bird once during the cooking. Remove bird, add red wine, cook, thicken slightly, and serve as gravy.

Duntreath Roast Grouse

1 grouse
¼ tablespoon butter
¼–½ apple
5–6 slices streaky bacon

This is another way of roasting grouse which Juliet Edmonstone says is used by many people in the west of Scotland and always produces a perfectly cooked bird.

Place a knob of butter and piece of apple inside the bird. Completely wrap bird in streaky bacon, stand it in 1 cm (½ in) water in a roasting pan, cover with greaseproof paper, then with a lid or foil, and cook in a slow oven (150°C, 300°F, Mark 2) for ¾–1 hour.

Cold Roast Grouse

Cold roast grouse can be just as good as hot and yet one seldom sees them except in a picnic lunch, and then it is inclined to be overcooked as it is usually leftovers.

Undercook the grouse by about 5 minutes as they will continue to cook a little as they cool. If you can, keep them in a cool larder instead of the refrigerator, and eat them within a day of being cooked.

Potted Grouse

1 grouse, pre-cooked
ham, pre-cooked or ¾ ham to ¼ tongue
200 g (8 oz) clarified butter or 200 g
   (8 oz) softened butter
few drops lemon juice
salt
cayenne
tabasco sauce (optional)
extra clarified butter

Potting game is a personal thing and it also depends on how much time you have. I like pounding in my mortar, and there is usually someone in the kitchen talking to me who might as well be pounding at the same time! I think it does make for a better consistency, but in a rush the liquidizer is adequate. If the birds are young you can roast them or stew them in butter, but if they are old they need longer gentle cooking and careful draining. The longer the bird has been cooked the more ham you need to add to it.

Chop the cooked flesh of the grouse and add about a quarter of its weight of chopped mild cooked ham, or ham and tongue. Then either put this in the liquidizer with the clarified butter and blend, or pound with softened butter in a mortar. Add the lemon juice, salt if necessary, a few grains of cayenne, and a drop of tabasco if you like. Pour into small pots with clarified butter which is just warm enough to pour, in order to seal the pot.

Grouse with Rösti

I've used this recipe under pheasant (see page 60). It is advisable to use a young grouse. This is a quick dish to prepare.

Eggleston Grouse

This was kindly donated by Eggleston Hall Finishing School, Barnard Castle, Co. Durham.

1 brace roasting grouse
2 rashers bacon
50 g (2 oz) butter

Place the bacon on the birds' breasts and a quarter of the butter inside each; put the rest of the butter in the roasting tin with the birds. Roast in a pre-set hot oven (200°C, 400°F, Mark 6) for about 40 minutes or until cooked. Allow to cool. Meanwhile prepare the sauces:

Hollandaise Place the vinegar, peppercorns, bayleaf and mace in a small saucepan and reduce to two teaspoonfuls; set aside. Work the butter until slightly soft. Cream the egg yolk in a small bowl with a nut of butter and a small pinch of salt. Strain on the vinegar. Set the bowl in a bain Marie on a gentle heat and stir the mixture until thick with a sauce whisk or a wooden spatula. Add the rest of the butter in small pieces about the size of a hazelnut, stirring continuously. When all the butter has been added, season delicately – if too sharp add a little extra butter. Set the sauce aside but still keep it in the bain Marie while making the Béchamel sauce.

Hollandaise Sauce
3 tablespoons wine vinegar
6 peppercorns
½ bayleaf
1 blade mace
50 g (2 oz) fresh butter
1 egg yolk
salt and pepper

Béchamel Sauce
250 ml (½ pint) milk
½ bayleaf
1 blade mace
1 slice of onion
6 peppercorns
15 g (½ oz) butter
15 g (½ oz) flour

Béchamel Infuse the milk with the bayleaf, mace, onion and peppercorns. Melt the butter, blend in the flour and blend in the infused milk, stir until boiling. Add a little of the Béchamel sauce to the Hollandaise and then add this to the main bulk of Béchamel and beat until cool. Season the sauce and set aside.

Accompanying Salad
100 g (4 oz) boiled rice
1 carrot, diced
2 sticks celery, diced
8 walnuts, quartered
French dressing

Skin and shred the grouse and arrange at one end of an oval serving dish. Coat with the sauce and reserve the rest to serve separately. At the other end of the dish arrange the salad, which is made by mixing all the ingredients together and binding with a little French dressing. Garnish the dish with a dusting of paprika pepper.

Mollie's Old Grouse Stewed in Cider

Place butter and oil in a thick-bottomed saucepan and froth. Brown grouse all over. Add bacon or ham and cook for a few minutes, then take out birds and ham. Add vegetables and turn in saucepan for a few seconds. Return birds and ham. Add bayleaf and peppercorns, stock and cider, and cook slowly for 2–2½ hours. Remove birds, and split them in two. Place in a serving dish. Remove bacon and put in dish with grouse. Strain sauce, return to the pan, season well, bring to boil, then pour over grouse. Serve hot.

25 g (1 oz) butter
1 tablespoon oil
1 brace grouse
100 g (4 oz) ham or bacon
4 carrots, sliced
2 onions, sliced
1 bayleaf
4 peppercorns
500 ml (1 pint) stock
500 ml (1 pint) cider
salt and pepper

Grouse (Ryper) Norwegian Style

2 young grouse
1½ teaspoons salt
2 thin slices pork fat or bacon
2 tablespoons butter
375–500 ml (¾–1 pint) good stock or stock cube and water
75 ml (3 oz) cream or sour cream

Sauce
2 tablespoons flour
250 ml (½ pint) stock
375 ml (¾ pint) cream or preferably sour cream
minced liver of birds
salt and pepper

This is one of Mary Jakhelln's super Norwegian recipes (you must try her duck pâté). Poor Mary, she spent ages converting them from the metric for me, only to find out we had to be metric too! It is a delicious way of cooking grouse. We like it served with rice.

Prepare birds: put salt on one side of the pork fat, place on breasts of birds, then heat up butter in a heavy pot and brown birds all over, turning with a wooden spoon. Add stock and cream; baste well. Put lid half over pot and let birds simmer over low heat, basting occasionally. Add more liquid during cooking if necessary. Remove fat slices or bacon halfway through cooking so breast is nicely browned. The birds are cooked when a skewer goes easily through breast or thigh. Do not overcook as birds will be dry. Cooking time 45–60 minutes.

Sauce Mix flour with a little cold stock, and when blended add rest of stock and cream gradually. Add finely chopped or minced livers of bird and boil for at least 5 minutes. Cut birds in half, put some sauce over them and serve rest separately. Serve with cranberry sauce or rowan jelly.

My note – if you use bacon and a stock cube, be careful not to over-salt.

Grouse à la Crème

2 young grouse
salt and pepper
50 g (2 oz) butter
250 ml (½ pint) cream
2 tablespoons brandy

Thanks to Ginny Fairfax.

Season the grouse, cover with half of the butter, truss, and cook in a heavy saucepan in a moderate oven (180°C, 350°F, Mark 4). When the grouse is cooked – about 35–40 minutes – remove from pan, pour out surplus butter, add brandy and bring to the boil. Add the cream and bring to the boil once more. Stir in remainder of butter and season to taste. Remove string from grouse, cut in halves if desired, and pour over sauce. Serve hot.

Mushrooms can also be added to this dish.

Grouse or Game Soufflé

This is based on a recipe from *Lady Hindlip's Cookery Book* and was kindly recommended to me by Jill Dixon.

Take the breasts of the grouse or equivalent quantity of other game that has been cooked and pound them in a mortar with the butter and onion. When you have rubbed these through a sieve, add the yolks of the eggs, then stir in the whites which must be whipped up to a froth. Season lightly with salt and cayenne. 20 minutes in a quick oven will bake this. To be served as hot as possible.

the breasts of 2 grouse or equivalent quantity of any other game
50 g (2 oz) best quality butter
heart of 1 small onion
4 eggs, separated
salt and cayenne

Alma's Salmis of Grouse

As the sauce is responsible for the character of this dish, the stock is most important.

Rub birds in softened butter and roast until about half cooked. Then you may either cut them into serving pieces, remembering to catch all the juices on a plate, or remove the legs and then gently pull the rest of the meat away from the carcass. Crush the carcass and simmer in the stock.

Place meat in a shallow, heatproof oven dish. Sauté the onions, carrots and garlic in butter, stir in flour, then slowly add red wine (dregs are fine), stock, tomato purée, thyme, bayleaf, salt and pepper, and simmer all this for about an hour. Thicken a little more if necessary. Meanwhile sauté a few sliced mushrooms and croûtons of bread. Place mushrooms over grouse and then strain the sauce over the meat. Heat very slowly, never allowing it to bubble, until the grouse is heated through, about 15 minutes. Surround with chopped parsley and croûtons.

2 young grouse
2 tablespoons softened butter
250 ml (½ pint) stock
2 onions, chopped
2 carrots, chopped
1 clove garlic, mashed
2 tablespoons butter
1 tablespoon flour
75 ml (3 oz) red wine
1 tablespoon tomato purée
thyme
1 bayleaf
salt and pepper
5–10 mushrooms, sliced
5–10 small white onions (optional)
croûtons
1 tablespoon chopped parsley

Grouse au Vin

Cut grouse into serving pieces. Remove rind, cut bacon into small squares and simmer for 10 minutes in plenty of water. Rinse in cold water and dry, then fry in butter till golden and remove to a plate. Fry grouse in remaining butter and when brown return bacon to pan; season, cover, and cook slowly for 10 minutes. Add brandy, ignite, and shake the pan until the flames die out. Add wine, stock, tomato paste, garlic and herbs. Cover, and simmer slowly for 30–50 minutes depending on the age of your grouse.

Meanwhile sauté onions and then mushrooms in butter until golden. Remove grouse, skim off fat from liquid and then reduce liquid to 500 ml (1 pint). Check for seasoning. Thicken sauce with cornflour mixed with 75 ml (3 oz) water. Serve from casserole, placing mushrooms, onions and triangles of fried bread around it. Sprinkle the top with the parsley.

1 brace grouse
100 g (4 oz) piece of lean bacon
2 tablespoons butter
salt and pepper
100 ml (4 oz) brandy
500 ml (1 pint) red wine
250 ml (½ pint) grouse stock, chicken stock or tinned consommé
½ tablespoon tomato paste
1 clove garlic, crushed
¼ teaspoon thyme
1 bayleaf
1 packet frozen onions in white sauce (remove sauce before unfreezing)
200 g (8 oz) mushrooms
butter
1 tablespoon cornflour
12 small bread triangles, fried in butter
1 tablespoon chopped parsley

Very, Very Old Grouse

One of the best ways of using up very old grouse other than turning it into soup or stock is to cut it into quarters and cook it in a steak and kidney pie or pudding, using it for flavour only, and remove it when the pie is opened. It gives the pie a wonderful extra something.

Grouse and Hare Pie

400 g (1 lb) beef skirt or venison
black pepper
1 brace grouse
2 pigeons (optional)
best parts of one hare
2 sheep's kidneys, skinned
2 hard-boiled eggs (optional)
1 small onion, finely chopped
100 g (4 oz) mushrooms, chopped
200 g (8 oz) piece of streaky bacon, blanched and diced
a few forcemeat balls (optional)
250 ml ($\frac{1}{2}$ pint) good strong stock, made from leftover bones, and cuttings of hare, birds and meat
70 ml (1 gill) port (optional)
150 g (6 oz) rich shortcrust pastry

I love this recipe because it's so very Scottish, but you may leave out many of the ingredients and turn it into a plain grouse, steak and kidney pie, or else leave off the pastry and just use forcemeat balls, or have neither. You can have more mushrooms or use red wine instead of port. It's really just a rough guide to how you might make a grouse pie.

Cut beef or venison into strips, season with black pepper, and place in a deep pie dish. Cut up grouse, pigeons, hare and kidneys, quarter eggs and place in layers on top of the meat, filling gaps with onion, mushrooms and bacon. Place forcemeat balls on the top, pour in stock and port, cover tightly, and cook for $1\frac{1}{2}$ hours. Remove lid and cover with rich short crust pastry, then finish cooking.

Blackgame, Capercaillie and Ptarmigan

These are all difficult birds to cook, and it is the exception when you can honestly say that they were anything more exciting than just edible. They are all lean and dry and require as much larding and basting as you can give them.

Sharp sauces go well with these birds, rowanberry or cranberry jelly. An orange salad is a good accompaniment and so is red cabbage. As they are all fairly rare no one has had much chance to experiment with more exotic recipes, but you can easily adapt some of the wild goose and venison recipes if you have a plentiful supply of these normally unyielding birds.

All these birds can be skinned and used in stock, and if one appears a hopeless case you may just nick out the breasts, put it in a stew or meat pie for flavour, and then discard them before serving the dish.

Blackgame

It is far easier to write about Blackgame than to write about how to cook them! At the Tower, above Kenmore, where we spend our autumns, we are surrounded by Blackcocks and are always rather surprised if we can't point one out to a friend. They seldom bring their ladies, the Greyhen – it's more like a man's club where you drop in for an hour in the evening. Who decides whether it will be the hillock, the old birch wood or the bracken behind the dyke I don't know, but it's all highly organized with opening and closing times and very alert sentries to keep us where we belong – behind our binoculars. They are so lovely that it seems unjust to call them the poor relations of grouse, but when it comes to cooking them, they certainly are.

Our son shot two young cocks on the 20th August (the day they came into season). They were barely feathered. We hung them for five days and then plain roasted them. They were good, much better than I'd expected.

Unless they are very very young like that, I think a day or two in a marinade help. You can hang them up to three weeks (or more if shot later in the year), but even then I've had some very tough ones. The first one I ever cooked I hung for a month, marinated it for four days, cooked it slowly for three hours, and you still couldn't get a knife through him, so I've learnt not to be bothered with old Blackgame, but young are possible. It is very important, as with venison and geese, to make sure the plates are very hot.

Roast Blackgame

1 blackgame
25 g (1 oz) butter
6 slices bacon

At the end of August you sometimes get blackgame which are very young, in fact barely feathered, and these are worth roasting. Lard the bird if you wish, place a large knob of butter inside, rub it well in butter and then cover well with bacon. Place in a moderately hot oven (190°C, 375°F, Mark 5) and cook, basting as often as possible for 40–50 minutes. If it is a very young small greyhen then this time might be reduced. Serve with a sharp sauce.

1 young bird either blackcock 900 g
    (2¼ lb) or greyhen 700–800 g (1¾–2
    lb)
1½–2 teaspoons salt
pepper
slice of pork fat or bacon
1½–2 tablespoons butter
375–500 ml (¾–1 pint) stock or stock
    cube and water
cream or sour cream

Blackgame Norwegian Style

Cook as for Grouse Norwegian Style (see page 24). Cooking time 1–1½ hours. Carve, then return slices to breast bone. Sauce as for Norwegian grouse.

Capercaillie, Capercailzie, Capercailye

'Caper' were originally indigenous to the north of England, Scotland and Ireland, but for some reason they died out in the eighteenth century and were re-introduced into Scotland from Sweden, at Taymouth, near Aberfeldy, by Lord Breadalbane, from where they have spread as far as north of Ross-shire and south as Wigtownshire. There are various translations as to what the original Gaelic meant, the one that describes its culinary possibility is best, I think, 'horse of the woods!' Old keepers say the only thing to do with a caper if you shoot one is to bury it for three weeks, dig it up, look at it, and then bury it again for good. Now our friends say: 'Give it to Julia Drysdale and see what she can do with it for her book.'

What I will say in their favour is that people are curious to taste them, so if you can manage to make them edible they are quite a success, and any small boy who has just shot one for the first time will gnaw away manfully rather than have his prize quietly disposed of when he isn't around. Take the crop out as soon as possible (Scottish keepers say to put an onion in the cavity) and hang it for several weeks or up to a month depending on the age of the bird and the weather. If the crop shows that the bird has been living on pine shoots there is a chance that it will taste of resin. The only thing you can do for this is to soak it in milk at room temperature overnight before cooking it.

I once cooked a very young hen caper which was so good that everyone asked for second helpings, but by that time it had turned to leather with no taste at all. They must be carved on to very hot plates and eaten immediately.

Braised Caper

1 young caper
3 tablespoons olive oil
stock
2 tablespoons redcurrant jelly
sour cream (optional)

Hang the caper for about 1 month depending on its age and the weather.

Marinate bird for 2–3 days depending on how high it is after hanging. Turn several times a day. Take bird from marinade and dry well.

Truss. Heat the olive oil in a heavy casserole, as close to the shape of the bird as possible. Brown the bird all over, strain over the marinade and add a little stock so that the bird is covered to about halfway up. Put bird on its breast, bring to simmer, cover tightly and place in a slow oven (150°C, 300°F, Mark 2) for about 2 hours. When the bird is cooked, pour off the juices, skim off fat, add about 2 tablespoons redcurrant jelly, and if you like some sour cream.

Marinade
100 ml (4 oz) olive oil
½ bottle red wine
6 juniper berries, crushed
1 onion, sliced
1 clove garlic, mashed
1 bayleaf

Capercaillie

Cook as for Grouse Norwegian Style (see page 24). Cooking time 1½ hours.

Sauce 3 tablespoons flour, 375 ml (¾ pint) cream or sour cream, 375 ml (¾ pint) stock or stock cube and water, a little black or redcurrant jelly, minced or finely chopped liver of bird.

1 young male bird about 1.6 kg (4 lb) or female bird about 1.1 kg (2½ lb)
2–3 teaspoons salt
pinch pepper
1 slice pork fat or bacon
1½–2 tablespoons butter
375–500 ml (¾–1 pint) stock or stock cube and water
cream

Mountain Cock (Caper)

This was sent to us by Baroness Josefine Rosenfeld, Schloss Pfannberg, Steiermark, and, I hope, properly translated by us.

Place a handful of parsley, salt and pepper and half of the bacon inside the mountain cock. Bard the bird with the rest of the bacon tied on with string. Brown the bird all over in 50 g (2 oz) of the butter and remove. Brown the vegetables and then add lemon rind, bayleaves, juniper berries, fir or spruce sprouts and red wine; place bird on top. Cover tightly and cook for 3–4 hours for a young bird or 4–5 hours for an old one. Baste it frequently and turn the bird from side to side. When the bird is tender remove from pot, take off the breasts, carve them and keep warm. Mince the remaining meat.

Strain juices and skim off fat. Add to mince and keep warm in double boiler.

Make a cream sauce. Melt remaining butter for 5 minutes but do not allow to colour, whisk in the cream and cook until the sauce is smooth and boiling. Season with salt and pepper and about 1 teaspoon Worcestershire sauce. Fry croûtons.

In a serving dish make a bed of the mince, place on it the thinly carved breast, arrange croûtons around the edge and pour over some of the cream sauce. The rest of the sauce may be served separately. Sprinkle with finely chopped parsley.

1 mountain cock
small handful of parsley
salt and pepper
200 g (8 oz) bacon, diced
75 g (3 oz) butter
3 carrots, sliced
4 sticks celery, sliced
rind of a lemon cut in thin strips
2 bayleaves
2–3 juniper berries, crushed
a few sprouts of fir or spruce
250 ml (½ pint) red wine
250 ml (½ pint) cream
1 tablespoon flour
Worcestershire sauce to taste
croûtons
finely chopped parsley

Swedish Braised Caper or Blackgame

1 caper or blackgame
100 g (4 oz) fat pork
3–4 tablespoons butter
2 teaspoons salt
250 ml (½ pint) stock
500 ml (1 pint) cream
beurre manié: 25 g (1 oz) flour combined with 20 g (¾ oz) butter
1 tablespoon redcurrant jelly

Wipe bird well and lard with thin strips of fat pork. Truss, brown in butter, add salt, boiling stock and cream. Cover and cook slowly until tender – 2–3 hours for caper, 1½–2 hours for blackgame.

Remove bird from pot, skim off any excess fat, thicken juices with beurre manié and add redcurrant jelly.

Ptarmigan

Ptarmigan are dear little birds which you are more likely to come across while stalking on high ground than when you are shooting grouse. They are continually changing their plumage, from ash grey in summer to pure white in very cold seasons. I have never seen them shot but have watched them on the North Beat in Angus when suddenly you see what looks like a group of stones, get up and run or fly away. They are smaller than a grouse, weighing about 500 g (1¼ lb), but this does not turn them into a baby poussin. They should be cooked as you would an old grouse or a Norwegian Ryper. They eat much the same food as the ryper.

Swedish Grouse (Ptarmigan)

100 g (4 oz) fat pork in 3 slices
3 grouse and giblets
3 tablespoons butter
2 teaspoons salt
250 ml (½ pint) stock
500 ml (1 pint) cream

Tie the pork over the breasts. Brown in butter together with giblets, add salt, boiling stock and then cream. Simmer, covered, until quite tender – about 1¼–1½ hours or longer, basting frequently. Serve with the gravy either reduced by boiling or slightly thickened with flour.

Partridge

Possibly if you live in Lincolnshire partridges might not be your favourite bird as you have so many, but I think most people consider that the partridge is their favourite game bird. Sadly, due to modern farming methods, there are fewer and fewer game larders filled with partridges and wives wondering how next to cook them. As a result of the hard work being done by Dr Potts and his team on behalf of the Game Conservancy, we hope that we can look forward to having more of them throughout the country in the future.

I think without exception everyone I have asked for an idea or recipe for partridges has said that they prefer them plain roasted. People seem to presume that all partridges are young and tender, which they certainly aren't. They can be as tough as an old goose, quite useless except for flavour. The flavour of a partridge is very subtle, so try to use fat salt pork instead of bacon when larding the bird; when braising or stewing it always use stock, as a chicken cube will smother the taste.

To Tell the Age of a Partridge   (extract from *The Complete Book of Game Conservation*)
With a grey partridge, in September and early October, the familiar dark beak, yellowish legs and relatively soft bones of the young birds will readily differentiate them from the grey-beaked, grey-legged, hard-boned adults, but later in the season the simple flight feathers test is to be recommended – the pointed primaries (two outer feathers) indicating a young bird. In September a few partridges in their second year may not have moulted these sharply pointed primaries of the juvenile plumage, but the feathers will be faded and abraded to such an extent that the bird will be easily recognized as old.

The Bursa test (see page 15) may be applied with a matchstick which should go up to about 1 cm ($\frac{1}{2}$ in) in a young bird. In a red-legged partridge the bursa is approximately the same. Another method of ageing redlegs is to inspect the two outer primaries – not for shape but for colour markings. The young bird has these two flight feathers tipped with a cream colour; sometimes other primaries not yet moulted will also show this cream colouration.

Hanging a Partridge
A young partridge shot in September will not need to be hung for very long, as you don't want to cover its flavour with too strong a taste of game. Three to five days should be adequate. Later in the season, and with older birds, they may hang for ten days or more. Watch for a discolouration around the vent, and with a young bird you don't want more than a whiff of a gamey smell.

Roast Partridge

5–10 g (¼ oz) butter, seasoned
1 partridge
1 thin strip pork fat or streaky bacon

There is the usual question as to whether partridges should be roasted on their backs or on their sides and turned. I think, so long as you are going to give them plenty of basting with plenty of butter, the back is best; but if you aren't going to be in the kitchen all the time, then the side method is better, as at least each side is sitting in butter for half its cooking time. A trivet is also very satisfactory and mine holds three in it in a row.

Place the knob of seasoned butter inside the bird, truss bird well and tie preferably pork fat rather than bacon over the breast. Cook in a very hot oven (220°C, 425°F, Mark 7), basting frequently with melted butter, for about 30 minutes. Towards the end, remove fat to allow breast to brown.

Partridge, or any Small Bird wrapped in Vine Leaves

5–10 g (¼ oz) butter, seasoned
1 partridge
1 thin strip pork fat or streaky bacon
1–2 vine leaves

For years I presumed vine leaves were exotic, Mediterranean-type food, and never the ordinary vine growing in the garden or greenhouse. Having eventually discovered that my vine leaves were vine leaves I now think they are very chic and love wrapping food in them. It is also very good.

Follow the method for roasting that you prefer best. After you have placed the pork fat over the breast, wrap the bird completely in one or two leaves. Baste just as often.

Grilled Partridge

1 tender young partridge
1 tablespoon butter
salt and pepper

I can't remember where I read it but I think it was Norman Douglas who wrote: 'Turn on the grill before you hang up your hat!' Even if you feel that you are being recklessly extravagant, always make sure your grill has had plenty of time to get hot.

Turn on your grill. Only tender young partridges should be grilled. Split the partridge down the back and force the halves apart until they are flat. Skewer them open or cut them in half if you wish. Rub them all over very well with the softened butter and season with salt and pepper. Grill under a hot grill, being careful not to let them burn, and turn them several times, brushing with more butter. Do not overcook them – about 10–15 minutes should be long enough.

Partridge with Cabbage I

This is my recipe but Mary Impey sent me one almost the same. She cuts her birds in half after they have been browned, therefore they don't need as long to cook. She also adds her sausages about an hour after the partridges have been in, which would sound a good idea as it stops them occasionally turning to mush. Sometimes she adds two sliced sweet apples.

Cut cabbage into fine slices and parboil in boiling salted water for 7 minutes. Drain carefully and press out all water. Blanch bacon or ham if salty and cut into slices.

Brown birds in butter or (better still) bacon fat, and place a small onion, with a clove stuck into it, inside each bird. Put a layer of cabbage in a deep casserole, lay the partridges on top, then the ham, sliced carrots, sausages, juniper berries, salt, pepper and nutmeg. Cover with the rest of the cabbage, pour over stock to about halfway up, cover with paper and the lid and cook in a cool oven (140°C, 275°F, Mark 1) for 3–4 hours or longer. The gravy may need to be thickened slightly or reduced.

1 goodish size hard cabbage
100 g (4 oz) piece ham or lean bacon
1 brace partridge
3 tablespoons butter or bacon fat
2 small onions
2 cloves
2 carrots
2 small smoked sausages (or cocktail frankfurters or 100 g (4 oz) garlic sausage)
2–3 crushed juniper berries
salt and pepper
a scraping of nutmeg
375 ml (¾ pint) well-flavoured stock

Partridge with Cabbage II

Cook as Sautéed Pheasant with Cabbage. See page 58.

Mollie's Casseroled Partridge with Red Wine and Mushrooms

Dice bacon, reserving half. Heat remainder in heavy saucepan until fat runs, add partridges. Brown all over. Draw pan from heat, add whole onions and whole mushrooms. Pour over red wine and 250 ml (½ pint) of the stock and add bouquet garni. Place in centre of moderately slow oven (170°C, 325°F, Mark 3) for 2–2½ hours.

Meanwhile heat remaining pieces of bacon in saucepan in vegetable fat. Add onion and cook gently until soft. Add flour, continue to cook gently until roux is dark brown colour (15 minutes). Stir in remaining stock, bring to boil, stirring. Add mushroom trimmings. Simmer for 30 minutes, thinning with stock if necessary. When partridge is cooked, remove from casserole and strain liquid off. Cut birds in half, remove breast and leg section from carcass. Replace these in casserole. Pour seasoned sauce over birds. Sprinkle with parsley and serve. Serves 6.

200 g (8 oz) streaky bacon
3 partridges and seasoning
200 g (8 oz) little whole onions
200 g (8 oz) whole button mushrooms (reserve trimmings)
125 ml (¼ pint) red wine
750 ml (1½ pints) stock
bouquet garni
25 g (1 oz) vegetable fat
1 small onion, finely chopped
1 tablespoon flour
1 tablespoon chopped parsley

Mollie's Casseroled Partridge with Onions

2 partridges for casseroling
2 large onions
125 ml (¼ pint) stock
50 g (2 oz) butter
seasoning
4 tablespoons double cream

Place partridges in deep casserole. Surround with sliced onions, stock, butter and seasonings. Cover, and put in moderately slow oven (170°C, 325°F, Mark 3) for 1½–2 hours. Lift birds and split in two down the back bone. Pass onions and rest of casserole contents through liquidizer. Add cream. Reheat, spoon over birds, then serve. Serves 4.

Partridge with Lentils

I have had a hang-up about lentils ever since my year in Paris when every Tuesday evening we had a particularly revolting lentil soup. Just to look at the word brings back the feeling of standing in the Métro knowing what was waiting when we got back chez Madame. But partridges with lentils is a great classic dish, so what more can I do than to quote Elizabeth David which must be delicious.

Perdrix à la Purèe de Lentilles

Clean and truss the partridges in the ordinary way: put them into a pan just large enough to hold them with 75–100 g (3–4 oz) butter, a large onion, sliced, and 2 carrots cut in rounds. When the birds have taken colour pour over them a glass of white wine and let it reduce by half; then add seasoning and a glass of good stock, cover the pan, and finish cooking over a very small flame. The exact time depends upon the age of the partridge.

In the meantime you will have prepared a purée with 400 g (1 lb) of brown lentils, an onion stuck with 2 cloves, 2 cloves of garlic, 2 carrots, and salt. Cover with water, simmer for 2 hours, and when the lentils are quite soft put them through a sieve. In a saucepan mix the purée with half the sauce from the partridges, and work it over the fire until the purée is smooth and of the right consistency.

Serve the partridges on a dish, with the purée all round and the rest of the sauce poured over. Quantities for six birds.

Perdrix à la Catalane

This is another of Elizabeth David's recipes. She said that she thought I could write a book without her help – I am rapidly proving to her that I can't.

You don't, of course, use the tenderest little roasting partridges for this dish. More elderly birds, so long as they are nice and plump, will do very well.

Truss four partridges as for roasting and put them into a thick pan, just large enough to hold them, in which you have melted two good tablespoons of pork or bacon fat. Season them with salt and pepper, and brown them all over. Sprinkle them with 2 tablespoons of flour, and stir until the flour and the fat are amalgamated and turning golden.

Now pour over them 2 glasses of white wine – in the Roussillon they use the Rancio wine – but an ordinary, not too dry white wine can be used, with a small glass of port added. Add a little water until the liquid comes a little over halfway to covering the partridges. Cover the pan and simmer over a low fire. Halfway through the cooking add 2 sweet red peppers cut into strips.

In the meantime peel 24 cloves of garlic and cut a Seville orange into slices, rind included. Throw these into a pint of water and cook until the water boils. This operation is to remove the bitterness from the orange and the garlic, which are then strained and put into a second lot of water and cooked for another 8–10 minutes. The garlic will now taste very mild; anyone who likes their garlic strong can omit this second cooking.

By this time the liquid will be considerably reduced and the whole mixture is added to the partridges, together with the juice of a second orange, and all cooked together for another 10–15 minutes, until the partridges are tender.

If the sauce is not thick enough, take the partridges out and keep them hot, turn up the flame and let the sauce bubble until it is sufficiently reduced.

Serve the partridges surrounded with the sauce, the sweet peppers, the orange and the garlic, very hot.

The partridges will take from 2–3 hours to cook, according to how old and tough they are.

Partridge with Red Cabbage and Chestnuts

Melt fat in casserole, brown bacon pieces, remove, then brown partridges all over. Wash the cabbage, shred it, place half in the bottom of the casserole, put in partridges, then the bacon and chestnuts, salt and pepper. Cover with remaining cabbage and pour over cider. Cover casserole tightly and place in a moderately slow oven (170°C, 325°F, Mark 3) for 1½–2 hours.

25 g (1 oz) bacon fat, dripping or butter
50 g (2 oz) streaky bacon, cut into small pieces
2 partridges
1 small red cabbage
200 g (8 oz) chestnuts (peeled)
salt and pepper
200 ml (8 oz) still cider

Partridge Stewed in White Wine

25 g (1 oz) butter
50 g (2 oz) streaky bacon, cut into
    small pieces
2 partridges
3 tablespoons brandy (optional)
100 ml (4 oz) white wine
75 ml (3 oz) white or game stock
bouquet garni

There are various other things you can add to change this dish slightly each time. A few juniper berries placed inside each bird before it is put in the casserole, or a generous handful of seedless grapes or sautéed mushrooms warmed in the gravy before you pour it over the birds, and it is greatly improved by flaming the birds in brandy before you put in the white wine.

Melt butter in a casserole just big enough to hold the birds. Start to brown bacon, then add partridges and brown lightly all over. Add brandy if you wish, then add wine, stock and bouquet garni. Cover very tightly and bring to boil, then place in moderately slow oven (170°C, 325°F, Mark 3) for about 1¾ hours. When cooked, reduce sauce until it just coats a spoon, then pour over birds.

Young Partridge with White Wine and Seedless Grapes

3 partridges
4 tablespoons butter
salt and pepper
3 slices fat salt pork or streaky bacon
3 or 6 croûtons
100 ml (4 oz) dry white wine
75 ml (3 oz) game stock
200 g (8 oz) seedless grapes (about)

Truss partridges, spread 1 tablespoon butter over each bird, sprinkle with salt and pepper, place a slice of pork or bacon over each breast and roast birds in a hot oven (200°C, 400°F, Mark 6) for about 30 minutes, basting occasionally. Remove pork or bacon slices and set aside, then place birds back in the oven until breasts are browned, about 5 minutes. If you wish to serve one bird per person then place each bird on a croûton, or if you wish to serve half a bird per person then cut the birds in half and place each half on a separate croûton. Place on a warm serving dish and keep warm. Pour off any fat from the roasting pan, then add wine, stock and about half the grapes to the pan, and cook for 4 minutes, stirring all the crusty bits up off the bottom of the pan. Add remaining butter and cook for a minute. Put the slices of bacon or pork back on the birds and place a few small bunches of grapes around the platter. Serve sauce in a sauce boat.

Swedish Fried Partridge

7 partridges
7 vine leaves
7 thin slices larding pork
40 g (1½ oz) butter
1 tablespoon salt
white bread and cooking fat
125 ml (¼ pint) stock (if necessary)
125 ml (¼ pint) cream (if necessary)

Wrap each bird in a vine leaf (if available) and over this place a thin slice of larding pork. Bind and truss into shape, brown on all sides in butter and salt and continue to fry for about 25–35 minutes, or until tender. To keep from browning too much, baste with a little stock. Old birds must be cooked longer (1–1½ hours) and basted with stock and cream.

Cut bread into triangles and fry in deep fat. Remove string and pork from birds, cut birds in half and arrange on a platter with bread. Stir the pan juices well and pour over meat. If cream has been used for basting and the birds have been cooked for a long time, serve the gravy from the pan separately.

Greek Partridge

Brush birds with olive oil, rub with garlic and dust with salt and cayenne. Place a pinch of rosemary in each. Wrap them in one or two vine leaves, securing them with wooden toothpicks. Chop livers and giblets with equal amounts of mushrooms, sauté the lot in butter until half done. Stir in dry white wine to make enough basting liquid. Butter casserole, put in birds and liquid, cover very well with tinfoil and lid, and cook for 45 minutes in a moderate oven (180°C, 350°F, Mark 4). When done reduce gravy.

Quantity of the following ingredients depends on how many birds you are cooking

partridges
olive oil
garlic
salt
cayenne
rosemary
vine leaves
livers
giblets
mushrooms
butter
dry white wine

Hungarian Partridge

Rub the birds inside and out with salt, brush with olive oil and place juniper berries in them.

Make a basting liquid by mixing the red wine, grated onion, salt, cayenne, almonds and grapes or raisins. Put the birds in a hot oven (200°C, 400°F, Mark 6). Baste frequently until cooked, about 40 minutes. Reduce liquid and thicken slightly. Pour over birds.

partridges
salt
olive oil
2–3 crushed juniper berries per bird
75 ml (3 oz) red wine
1½ teaspoons finely grated onion
cayenne
40 g (1½ oz) chopped almonds
50 g (2 oz) halved Muscat grapes or
    fat raisins

Partridge with Apples

Truss partridges, cover them with 1 tablespoon butter each and season with salt and pepper. Place in a pan with enough water in it to cover the bottom, and roast in a moderate oven (180°C, 350°F, Mark 4) for 30 minutes.

Peel the apples, remove cores and cut in half. Place them on a buttered baking dish, flat side down. Dot them with butter and place in oven until they are just cooked. Keep warm.

Sauté bread in 1 tablespoon butter and spread with a paste made of the sautéed partridge livers and ½ tablespoon butter (or a small amount of liver pâté if you have some). Arrange partridges on the toast on a hot platter. Blend the juices in the pan with Calvados or whisky (whisky is supposed to be a better substitute for Calvados than brandy), ignite, and shake pan until the flame goes out. Pour this over the partridges and surround with the apples and watercress.

You may also cook partridges in the same way as the Pheasant with Cream, Calvados and Apples. They will take less cooking, about 30 minutes.

2 young partridges (retain livers when
    cleaning)
4½ tablespoons butter
salt and pepper
2 sweet hard apples
2 slices bread
4 tablespoons Calvados or whisky
1 bunch watercress

Bentley Cold Partridge

25 g (1 oz) butter
1 partridge
500 ml (1 pint) jellied stock, depending
   on size of the bird
2 tablespoons sherry

Put butter inside the partridge. Place in a casserole and cover with jellied stock. Add sherry and cook very slowly for about two hours. It is important that the casserole has a very tight-fitting lid. Leave to cool and set. Don't remove the butter on top until ready to eat.

Serve with a salad of lettuce, and pears stuffed with cream cheese.

Bentley Partridge with Oysters

1 partridge
oysters (these may be tinned)
1 slice bacon
1 tablespoon bacon fat
375 ml ($\frac{3}{4}$ pint) milk

Stuff partridge with cooking oysters. Cover breast with bacon, tied on well. Place in casserole lined with bacon fat. Cook very slowly in milk for $1\frac{1}{2}$ hours. Make cream sauce with the liquid. Pour over cooked partridge and serve with pastry strips.

Pheasant

More people become bored with cooking or eating pheasant than with any other game bird; in fact, they get to the stage where they just can't be bothered. Maybe a roasted young pheasant lacks the touch of magic that a little partridge has, but it's still a good dish. There are so many other ways of cooking it, often making a far better dish than chicken. Almost any robust chicken recipe will adapt to pheasant, which is especially useful now that it is difficult to find a tasty chicken with a good flavour.

If you are in doubt as to whether a bird is young or not then take it that it's not; you may be wrong, but the dish will still be edible, which is more than a middle-aged, under-cooked pheasant will be. All our pheasants are tagged with numbers so not only do I know their age, but also how far they have wandered; yet, even if you take two hens from the same rearing pen, clean shot in the same drive, one always seems to have a slightly better flavour than the other, particularly when they are roasted.

I don't know which are my favourite of the following recipes – probably the pheasant dishes cooked with potatoes or cabbage. They have such a wonderful aroma and flavour and make ideal winter dishes and shooting lunches.

Hanging a Pheasant

As with all other game it is practically impossible to define how long you should hang your bird. When they are young the weather is warmer so they require less hanging than in winter when they are older. I would put my average at about ten days, but a young bird shot during a hot spell in October will only need about three days, or else you lose the flavour of having a tender young bird. I usually prowl around below its breast bone to see when it is beginning to go blueish and have a slight smell. One other point – a weekend in the boot of the car, because your husband forgot to take them out and hang them up, does a brace of birds no good at all, especially if they are wet. Birds should be hung with air circulating freely around them and preferably not touching each other, but it is very difficult to stop people from hanging them up in pairs.

To Tell the Age of a Pheasant (extract from *The Complete Book of Game Conservation*)

The bursa test (see page 15) can be applied to both cock and hen relatively easily. In young birds the depth of the bursa will be approximately 2.5 cm (1 in). (This is tested by inserting a match.) In old birds it may be closed completely. The site of the opening is often marked by a slight bump, which remains open for about 5 mm ($\frac{1}{4}$ in) and very rarely up to 1 cm ($\frac{1}{2}$ in).

This is the only method of distinguishing young hen pheasants from old ones. Early in the season young cocks may be separated from old by their blunt and relatively short spurs. Later in the season the spurs of early-hatched young birds can be as long and as sharply pointed as some old birds.

Roasting Pheasants

Roasting pheasants is a little unreliable, and there are many theories and ideas on the best way to do it. At the beginning of last season, a friend telephoned to tell me that she had discovered that if you roasted your pheasant breast down it was perfect – she had just done it once, and she and her husband agreed that it was the best ever. Later on I asked her if she had found this consistent throughout the season, and she admitted that she had not. She still thought it was the best way to roast pheasant, but even so, some she had cooked had been fairly ordinary.

Last year a chicken brick was my great discovery. I think it is a very good way to cook a pheasant if you aren't quite sure how young it is, and if you are feeding your family and have better things to do than stand around basting a pheasant for them. Once in the oven it is out of sight and out of mind, and you don't even have to remember to pre-heat the oven.

This year was the year for my trivet. I bought it at David Mellors on Sloane Square, and until some other idea appears, I think it is a winner. It is a metal rack with two adjustable sides, rather like a book stand for two books who want to read each other! Being adjustable, you can use it for anything from a large cockerel to several snipe, and they clean very easily.

You roast the birds upside down, which makes sense as the juices are running over the breast instead of off it.

Roast Pheasant

1 young pheasant
2 tablespoons butter
salt and pepper
3 slices streaky bacon or fat salt pork

optional
1 apple, cored and chopped
½ onion, chopped
or
juice of ½ lemon worked into the 2
  tablespoons butter

(If you wish to do so, place the apple and onion or a mixture of butter and lemon inside the bird.) Place 1 tablespoon of the butter inside the bird and a good screw of pepper and salt. Truss bird very well and rub it all over with remaining butter. Cover the breast with streaky bacon or fat salt pork, and place in oven preheated at a moderately hot temperature (190°C, 375°F, Mark 5) for about 45 minutes. Baste as often as possible, taking the bacon or fat off during the last 10 minutes to allow the breast to brown, or place the bird breast down in small pan, turning at half time.

When using a trivet, I put the bacon over the back of the bird (the bird being upside down) which still keeps the fat running over the breast.

Roast Pheasant Filled with Petit Suisse and Herbs or Fruit

Neil Ramsay of Farleyer very kindly wrote to La Marquise de Brantes asking if she could give us any ideas. She replied

46

with a charming letter saying that she never really used a recipe at all, she just played it by ear using whatever was at hand, but practically always put Petit Suisse (a kind of cream or cottage cheese) inside a pheasant or a duck, with herbs or raisins or any other fruit, including cherries, apples, spiced peaches and mirabelles.

Several other people have also said they used Petit Suisse with all kinds of game birds and it is delicious.

Pheasant in a Chicken Brick

A chicken brick (obtainable from Habitat and other good kitchen shops) is an easy and unmessy way of roasting a bird that is of questionable age. Any kind of game bird will do, and depending on its size, you may fill the brick with as many as it will hold. Always be sure to follow the directions which come with your brick, both for preparing and cleaning. As the birds need to be well oiled, I keep bottles of herb-flavoured olive oil. You can buy thyme, rosemary, fennel, basil and tarragon olive oil – just use whichever you feel like. It is better not to mix herbs in a brick – you get a better flavour if they are single. You may put a few vegetables under the bird – onions, carrots, celery and some peppercorns. If the birds look very dry, lay some bacon over them. Always season them, inside and out, with salt and pepper.

2 small pheasants
2 tablespoons olive oil
4–5 juniper berries
salt and pepper
2 slices streaky bacon

Rub the pheasants with the olive oil. Place the juniper berries inside the birds with salt and pepper. Season the outside as well, place the bacon over the breast and put in the brick. Place brick in a cold oven, set very hot (230°C, 450°F, Mark 8), and bake for 1½ hours.

Braised Pheasant

Brown the pheasant all over in the butter. In the bottom of the casserole make a bed of the vegetables and place the pheasant on it with salt and pepper. Pour over the stock and red wine, cover, and cook in a moderate oven (180°C, 350°F, Mark 4) for about 1 hour. Baste occasionally. Strain off gravy, thicken if you like with cornflour, and add the redcurrant jelly. Simmer until jelly has dissolved, and pour back over bird. I've liquidized the vegetables with the stock and thought this better.

1 pheasant
2 tablespoons butter
2 carrots, sliced
1 onion, sliced
4 sticks of celery, chopped
4 sprigs of parsley, chopped
salt and pepper
185 ml (⅜ pint) stock
250 ml (½ pint) red wine
2 tablespoons redcurrant jelly

Pheasant in Butter

50 g (2 oz butter)
1 pheasant

optional
a few slices of diced streaky bacon
brandy, whisky or Calvados
white wine
or
game stock and Marsala

This is the basic method of many of the recipes here. It can be varied by adding different ingredients for a change. If you are going to cook pheasants often, it is essential to own a small casserole into which the bird will just fit with the cover on.

Melt butter in the casserole (adding bacon if you wish). Brown pheasant all over until it is just golden and leave it on one side. (You may add some spirit at this stage.) Cover very tightly and cook gently for about 45 minutes, turning once at half time. You may increase the gravy by adding a little white wine or a little stock and Marsala.

This recipe goes very well with the winter vegetables you can braise such as lettuce, chicory (Belgian endive), celery or leeks. You may add some of the juices from the bird to the vegetables for their last 10–15 minutes of cooking.

Pheasant in Sour Cream

1 young pheasant, cut into quarters
2 tablespoons olive oil
2 tablespoons butter
seasoned flour
500 ml (1 pint) sour cream
1 tablespoon paprika
2 tablespoons chopped parsley

If you wish to skin the pheasant rather than pluck it, wrap the pieces in bacon secured with wooden toothpicks.

Heat oil and butter in heavy casserole. Dredge pheasant pieces in seasoned flour, and cook them carefully in the fat so that they remain just golden. Pour over the sour cream, paprika and parsley, bring to simmer, cover casserole, and cook gently for about 45 minutes. Serve with new potatoes added to the dish just before serving, or with noodles.

Mollie's Casseroled Pheasant with Chestnuts

1 pheasant
25 g (1 oz) butter or 1 tablespoon oil
300 g (12 oz) good chestnuts, shelled
200 g (8 oz) little white onions
25 g (1 oz) flour
500 ml (1 pint) good stock
grated rind and juice of 1 small orange
2 teaspoons redcurrant jelly
100 ml (4 oz) red wine
bouquet garni
salt and pepper
1 tablespoon chopped parsley

Mollie, Douglas Hutchison's cook, has appeared in every chapter, which proves, as we all know, how very well the Chairman of the Game Conservancy lives.

Brown pheasant all over in hot butter or oil. Remove from pan. Sauté chestnuts and onions briskly until they begin to turn brown, shaking the pan frequently. Remove from pan and add enough flour to pan to take up remaining fat. Mix well, add remaining ingredients except parsley, and bring to the boil. Put in pheasant, surround with chestnuts and onions, and cover tightly. Cook in a moderately slow oven (170°C, 325°F, Mark 3) for 1–1½ hours. Take up and joint bird and place in a fresh casserole or deep dish with chestnuts and onions. Remove bouquet garni, skim liquid, add seasoning and pour over pheasant. Sprinkle with parsley.

Pheasant in Red Wine

This is just Coq au Vin made with pheasant instead of chicken. If you use your common sense you can vary it between a young pheasant cut into serving pieces and gently cooked, and the damaged ones which you skin and cut up as neatly as possible. Sometimes it is easier to remove all the flesh from the carcass and end up with a dish that looks more like a stew. This then gives you more bones for stock which you can keep to use another time. Stew-type dishes make a wonderful shooting lunch, but you may wish to stretch it with more vegetables as it is rather expensive if your friends are hungry.

Remove rind from bacon and cut bacon into small cubes. Brown cubes lightly in 2 tablespoons of the butter in a heavy casserole. Remove. Brown pheasant pieces, a few at a time. Put all pheasant pieces and bacon back into casserole; cover and heat for a few minutes, then pour over brandy and ignite. Pour over wine and the strained stock to cover pheasant. Stir in tomato paste and cook until the pheasant is tender. It is quite impossible to say how long this will take – probably 1–2 hours.

While the birds are cooking, sauté the mushrooms. Braise the onions by rolling them around in a pan in the rest of the butter and the oil until they are brown, then add the stock or wine, cover the pot, and simmer very slowly until they are tender but not squishy, about 40 minutes. Make croûtons. When the birds are ready, pour off liquid, skim the fat from it, and reduce it to about 500 ml (1 pint) by rapid boiling. Beat in most of the soft butter and flour mixture, a little at a time, until the sauce is thick enough. Simmer for a couple of minutes.

Arrange the pheasants, mushrooms and onions in the casserole, pour over the sauce, simmer again until you are sure it is hot, and place the croûtons around the edge.

100 g (4 oz) piece of lean bacon
3 tablespoons butter
2 pheasants, cut into serving pieces
50 ml (2 oz) brandy
¾ bottle red wine – preferably Burgundy or Beaujolais. Make sure that if you are using dregs they haven't been around too long!
250 ml (½ pint) stock, made from the backs, necks and other leftover bones of the pheasants, plus a cut up onion and carrot, a bayleaf and ¼ teaspoon thyme
½ tablespoon tomato paste
1 clove garlic, mashed
salt and pepper
200 g (8 oz) mushrooms
15–20 little white onions (you can buy frozen ones, but remove the white sauce before unfreezing as it is not needed)
1 tablespoon oil
100 ml (4 oz) stock or wine
3 tablespoons flour worked into 2 tablespoons softened butter
croûtons fried in butter, if you wish

Duntreath Pheasant

Fry pheasant in butter for 10 minutes, turning frequently. Remove and keep warm, then add onions and green pepper or celery. Fry gently, add wine and seasonings and bring to the boil. Remove from heat, stir in cream, return pheasant to the pan and heat very gently for 30 minutes. If sauce looks a little curdled you may beat in more cream off the heat, and this should smooth it out.

1 pheasant, jointed
100 g (4 oz) butter
2 large onions, chopped
¾ green pepper or 1 large stick of celery, chopped
300 ml (1 cup) white wine

pinch of
mixed herbs
cinnamon
thyme
nutmeg
cloves

250 ml (½ pint) cream

Faisan à la Cauchoise (Pheasant with Cream, Calvados and Apple)

This is the first of several of Elizabeth David's recipes which I feel I must include in this section. As I'm only trying to compile a book I don't think they can be left out as they are so often just what is wanted, perfect as they are. This recipe is so simple and straightforward, and pleases me enormously.

I have never managed to cook two pheasants in this way, even in separate cocottes, and make them equally good. They seem to like individual attention – but then no two pheasants are the same, even when you are only roasting them.

Cook a tender roasting pheasant in butter in a heavy iron or earthenware cocotte on top of the stove, turning it over once or twice so that each side is nicely browned. It will take about 40–45 minutes to cook. Carve it, transfer it to the serving dish and keep it warm. Pour off the juices into a shallow pan, let them bubble; pour in a small glass of warmed Calvados (or brandy, marc or whisky), set light to it, shake the pan, and when the flames have burnt out add a good measure, 200–250 ml (8–10 oz), of thick cream. Shake the pan, lifting and stirring the cream until it thickens. Season with a very little salt and pepper. Pour the sauce over the pheasant. Serve separately a little dish of diced sweet apple, previously fried golden in butter and kept warm in the oven: 2 apples will be sufficient for one pheasant.

This is, I think, the best of the many versions of pheasant with apples and Calvados, usually called Faisan Normand.

Sautéed Pheasant

1 young pheasant
2 tablespoons seasoned flour
4 tablespoons butter or 2 tablespoons butter and 2 tablespoons oil

Cut pheasant into two to four pieces, depending on how greedy you feel and how big the pheasant is. Dip the pieces in seasoned flour. Melt butter or butter and oil, but be careful not to burn it. Add pheasant and brown quickly all over. Turn down heat, cover, and cook slowly until tender, about 25 minutes.

This is a basic recipe from which you can make an endless variety of dishes. After you reduce the heat you can add finely chopped onion, garlic, tomatoes or mushrooms. You can cook some streaky bacon very slowly first to get out all the fat, and then brown the bird in the bacon fat and at the end sprinkle it with crispy bacon. After you have removed the pheasant from the pan you can add some flour to blend with the fat, and then milk, tinned tomatoes or stock, in order to make any sort of gravy you wish. It is very popular with children with a barbecue sauce on it.

Curried Pheasant

My brother claims he takes a gun in the curry as well as in the shoot. He is inclined to be disappointed about other things, when all the birds fly over his neighbours and not himself, or when all the birds fly over him and he misses them, or when my poodle convinces his impeccable labrador that chasing hares is enormous fun. Incidents like these are inclined to bring on gloom, but none more so than not getting curry when he expects it.

Curried pheasant is a good way of using up older birds or badly shot ones. If it is easier, you can skin the pheasant without plucking it. It is easier to get the flesh off the carcass if you partially roast it in a moderate oven (180°C, 350°F, Mark 4) for approximately 20 minutes. If they are skinned, wrap them in foil to prevent the outer layer of flesh going hard. As it is very extravagant for a large number of people, you may have to stretch it indefinitely with more apples, onions, carrots, celery, or several packages of frozen casserole vegetables. I usually thaw these first and then sauté them. You may add raisins, but as they aren't always popular I have them as a side dish. One Christmas we threw in the leftover cranberry sauce and it was very good and looked most colourful.

In order to taste the pheasant flavour, try to keep the curry mixture cool. If you remember in time, do make the ghee first – it keeps for ages in the refrigerator. I didn't use to bother about nut milk either, but now I do. Curry is best made a day or two before and kept in a cool larder in a covered earthenware bowl. If you do keep it, add the nut milk and thicken it when you re-heat it. Curry does not freeze.

4 tablespoons ghee or butter
2 teaspoons ground coriander
½ teaspoon ground chillies
1½ teaspoons ground cummin
1 teaspoon ground cardamon
½ teaspoon ground tumeric
½ teaspoon ground pepper
1 teaspoon salt
½ teaspoon mixed spice
1 large onion
1 clove garlic, mashed
2 crisp apples
2 pheasants, partially roasted with meat taken off the bone and the bones turned into stock; or cut into serving pieces and the backs used for stock
500 ml (1 pint) stock
1 bayleaf
3–4 cm (1½ in) cinnamon stick
juice of ½ lemon
2 teaspoons redcurrant jelly
250 ml (½ pint) nut milk

Heat ghee or butter in large pan. Add all dried spices and fry gently for a few minutes. Add onion, garlic, apple and fry until soft. Add pheasant cut into pieces, and keep turning until well coated and brown. Add stock, bayleaf, cinnamon stick, lemon juice and redcurrant jelly. Simmer for 1–1½ hours. Add nut milk for the last 10 minutes and thicken if necessary with a little cornflour mixed with water.

Serve with masses of sweet mango chutney. Young & Saunders in Edinburgh have an excellent one, though they are given to running out, which produces total panic on both sides of the Forth! The recipe for Raita is also very popular as a side dish, particularly with the young.

To make Ghee
Simmer butter very slowly for 1½ hours, when it will be brown and have a sweet nutty smell. Strain it through muslin.

Ghee
200 g (8 oz) butter

To make Nut Milk

Nut Milk
3 tablespoons desiccated coconut or ground almonds
125 ml (¼ pint) milk (optional)

Infuse desiccated coconut or ground almonds in 250 ml (½ pint) freshly boiled water or 125 ml (¼ pint) water plus 125 ml (¼ pint) milk for 30 minutes, then strain through muslin.

I use my husband's port strainer for both these jobs. It is probably not quite as good as muslin, but it is handy and easy – just be careful to make sure it is very clean afterwards, as ghee in the port is unpopular!

Raita

1 large cucumber
salt
125 ml (¼ pint) carton of plain, fat-free yoghurt
black pepper
sugar to taste

Peel the cucumber and grate coarsely onto a plate. Sprinkle with salt, cover, and stand the plate in the refrigerator or in a cold place for 30 minutes. Drain the cucumber thoroughly. Mix it with the yoghurt in a bowl and add black pepper and a little sugar to taste.

Cold Curried Pheasant

2 pheasants
375 ml (¾ pint) stock or 1 chicken stock cube

Mayonnaise
1 egg
1 egg yolk
salt
pepper
½ teaspoon dry mustard
4 teaspoons sugar
50 g (2 oz) sugar
50 ml (2 oz) vinegar
250 ml (10 oz) oil

125 ml (¼ pint) cream
curry powder to taste
25 g (1 oz) raisins
1 small bunch white grapes
tomatoes to decorate

Veronica Phayre-Mudge, whose husband is on the Council of the Game Conservancy, has very kindly sent us several good recipes.

Roast pheasants in stock. When cold, carve and joint, remove skin.

Mayonnaise Put the egg and egg yolk, salt, pepper, dry mustard, sugar and vinegar in the liquidizer; gradually add the oil.

Add cream to the mayonnaise and curry powder to taste. Mix in the raisins and the peeled and pipped grapes. Arrange pheasant on dish, spoon over the sauce and decorate with quarters of tomatoes.

Drizzle and PCH's Very Quick Curry

1 pheasant
2 185 g (7½ oz) tins Veeraswamy's curry (can be bought in any reasonable supermarket)

I was fooled. I really thought they'd spent all day in the kitchen and this is all they did.

Cut up the pheasant into serving pieces and follow the instructions on the tin implicitly. It will take about an hour to cook. Serve with suitable accompaniments.

Pheasant with Green Peppercorns

Elizabeth David was one of the first people in this country to experiment with these tinned soft peppercorns from Madagascar. I first met them in Switzerland, and coming home full of enthusiasm nearly blew a dinner-party out of the dining-room. I don't think her recipe is quite strong enough so I've added a few more peppers and some to the final sauce, but you can reduce them if you have a more sensitive palate, as she has.

4 heaped teaspoons green peppercorns
1 slither garlic
40 g (1½ oz) butter
½ teaspoon cinnamon or coriander
½ teaspoon ground cummin and/or ginger
1 pheasant
salt

Make a paste of 2 heaped teaspoons green peppercorns, garlic, butter and spices, and a little salt if you have used unsalted butter.

Lift the skin off the pheasant, and rub first the salt and then the paste well over the flesh, making a few gashes with a sharp knife in the legs so that the spices penetrate. Put a lump of the paste inside the pheasant and, if possible, leave for an hour or two before cooking. Wrap the bird well in buttered paper or foil and place in a moderate oven (180°C, 350°F, Mark 4) for 45 minutes. Uncover the bird, add the remaining peppercorns to the juices, and baste frequently until the skin is golden brown. Serve with juices in a sauce-boat.

Pheasant with Celery and Walnuts

This recipe and the following one have been given to me by Sue Deptford, who besides helping to find new ideas has been an enormous help both by encouraging me and trying out ideas on her extremely lucky and pampered directors at the Bank of America Limited.

1 pheasant
4 strips bacon
3 tablespoons butter
juice and rind of 2 oranges
75 ml (3 oz) Madeira or port
salt and pepper
75 ml (3 oz) stock
1 head celery
75 g (3 oz) shelled walnuts

Cover pheasant with bacon, and brown in 2 tablespoons of the butter in a casserole. Add orange juice and Madeira or port, salt, pepper and stock. Cover with a lid and simmer gently for 45 minutes or cook in a moderate oven (180°C, 350°F, Mark 4). Meanwhile trim celery and cut into slices crossways. Heat rest of butter in a frying pan, add the walnuts and celery, and toss over the heat with a pinch of salt, keeping celery crisp. Shred and cook orange rinds in boiling water until tender, then drain and rinse. Dish up pheasant, boil up the sauce it has cooked in, and thicken if necessary with a little cornflour mixed with water.

Serve with the celery and walnuts scattered on the top with the orange rind.

Pheasant in Cider and Apples

1 pheasant
3 tablespoons butter
½ lemon
rosemary
6 Cox's apples
½ teaspoon cinnamon
½ teaspoon celery salt
ground pepper
250 ml (½ pint) cider
2 tablespoons cream

Brown the pheasant in 2 tablespoons of the butter in a casserole, turning it over all the time. Take out and fill the inside with the lemon and a sprinkling of rosemary, together with the remaining juice and butter left in the casserole.

Wipe out casserole, add the rest of the butter, and fry the peeled and sliced apples. When slightly soft, sprinkle with cinnamon and return the pheasant to the casserole, breast side down. Add celery salt and pepper, pour over cider and cream. Cover, and cook in a moderate oven (180°C, 350°F, Mark 4) for 50 minutes, or until pheasant is cooked.

Joint pheasant and serve, pouring over boiled-up sauce.

This is straight from Elizabeth David's *French Provincial Cooking*, and as she says, a wonderful winter dish.

Faisan au Riz Basquais (Pheasant with Spiced Rice)

A highly seasoned and highly colourful dish, which makes a most cheering sight on a chilly winter evening.

A large pheasant weighing 1–1¼ kg (2–2½ lb), 4 Spanish or Basque sausages (chorizos) or 300 g (12 oz) of the type of coarsely cut boiling sausage sold in delicatessen shops, 150–200 g (6–8 oz) streaky bacon, a carrot, an onion, a bouquet of herbs plus a small strip of orange peel, a clove of garlic; pork, goose or duck dripping for frying, 400 g (1 lb) of ripe tomatoes, 3 or 4 sweet red peppers or the contents of a 100 g (4 oz) tin of Spanish sweet peppers or pimientos in oil, 300 g (12 oz) of rice, veal stock or water, paprika pepper.

Melt 2 tablespoons of the dripping (failing either pork, goose or duck dripping, olive oil will do) in a heavy saucepan large enough to hold the pheasant. Brown the sliced onion and carrot, then the pheasant, turning it over two or three times, so that it colours evenly. Cover with half stock and half water, or all water. Put in the bacon in one piece, the bouquet, orange peel and the garlic; cover the pan. Simmer gently for 20 minutes before adding the sausages. Cook another 20 minutes if the pheasant is a roasting one, 1¼ to 1½ hours if an old bird, but in this case add the sausages only 20 minutes before the end.

Put the rice into a large saucepan of boiling salted water and boil for 10 to 12 minutes. Strain it very carefully. Put it, with a little more dripping, into the top half of a double saucepan. Pour over it, through a strainer, a ladle of the stock from the pheasant. Put a folded tea cloth on top, then the lid of the saucepan, and steam for about 20 minutes, until the rice is tender.

In the meantime prepare the following tomato and sweet pepper mixture. Skin and chop the tomatoes, remove the seeds and cores of the peppers, wash them and cut them into strips. If tinned ones are being used, drain off the liquid and rinse them before slicing them. Heat another tablespoon of dripping in a small saucepan or frying pan, put in the tomatoes and sweet peppers and cook fairly briskly for about 10 minutes. Season with salt, pepper and a dessertspoon of paprika, which is the nearest approach we can get here to the coarsely ground red pepper called piment basquais, which they use in the Basque country. This tomato and pepper mixture must be thick but not a purée.

To serve, turn the rice on to a heated dish. Extract the sausages and the bacon from the saucepan. Cut each sausage into three slices; remove the rind from the bacon, cut into squares. The pheasant may be either carved and arranged in the centre of the rice, or brought to table whole and then carved. The sausages and bacon are arranged round the pheasant, and the tomato and sweet pepper mixture in a ring round the rice.

A chicken may be cooked in the same way, allowing 45 minutes for an average-size roaster, 2 to 3 hours' very slow cooking for a boiler.

The Spanish sausages can be bought in Soho shops and in quite a few delicatessens.

Pheasant with Wild Rice, Cream and Horseradish

This was my first big pheasant dish and in those days wild rice, though expensive, was not astronomical and no one in Britain knew what it was, so I was always sure that I was being fairly unique. Now when I do use wild rice I usually stretch it with ordinary white rice. Wild rice is a grass seed which grows in the Northern American States and Canada, and I believe it is so expensive because it is difficult to harvest. You can buy it in most luxury food shops.

Skin and quarter the pheasants, reserving the backs and necks. Place the backs and necks in stock, or water and chicken cube, and add the onion, celery, bayleaf and carrot. Simmer fairly hard until it is reduced to about half.

2 pheasants
375 ml (¾ pint) chicken stock or a chicken cube dissolved in water
1 onion
1 stick celery
1 bayleaf
1 carrot
8 slices streaky bacon
2 tablespoons butter
6–8 salad onions depending on their size
50 ml (2 oz) brandy
salt and pepper
100 ml (4 oz) pickled horseradish sauce
750 ml (1½ pints) double cream
150 g (6 oz) wild rice

Wrap pheasant pieces in bacon strips, secure with wooden toothpicks, then brown in butter with the chopped salad onions. The onions become a bit black but this doesn't matter. When the pieces are brown, pour over brandy and ignite. Put all this in a deep casserole, pour over strained broth, season with salt and pepper, cover casserole and place in a moderate oven (180°C, 350°F, Mark 4) until the pheasant is tender – this could take up to 2 hours, but less if the pheasant is young. Pull out toothpicks. Before serving, warm up casserole, add horseradish, cream and previously cooked rice. I've always found this recipe was even better the next day provided the rice doesn't become too solid. The greater the proportion you have in it, the less it is inclined to congeal.

Pheasant à la Me!

1 pheasant
375 ml (¾ pint) stock
1 onion, finely chopped
2 tablespoons butter
200 g (8 oz) mushrooms, finely chopped
25–50 g (1–2 oz) raisins
100 g (4 oz) cooked rice
mixed herbs
300 g (12 oz) puff pastry

From Veronica Phayre-Mudge.

Cook pheasant in stock, then take off all the meat in large chunks. Soften onion in butter, add mushrooms and cook well. Add raisins, cooked rice and mixed herbs; season well.

Arrange slices of pheasant, with stuffing sandwiched in between them, on rolled out puff pastry. Fold up pastry in a fat sausage roll and decorate with leftover pastry pieces. Brush with beaten egg and bake for 30 minutes in hot oven (200°C, 400°F, Mark 6). Serve with rich gravy, to which you may add wine and redcurrant jelly if desired.

2 pheasants
2 tablespoons butter
1 tablespoon oil
75 ml (⅓ cup) minced shallots or green onions
250 ml (½ pint) tinned tomatoes
1 clove garlic
¼ teaspoon salt
¾ teaspoon pepper
½ teaspoon thyme
bouquet garni, consisting of 4 sprigs parsley, 1 celery top, 1 large bayleaf
2 large strips lemon peel
125 ml (¼ pint) white wine or less vermouth
250 ml (½ pint) brown stock or tinned consommé

Garnish
200 g (8 oz) mushrooms, sliced
a few white onions
2 tablespoons finely chopped parsley

Pheasant in Tomatoes

Cut up pheasant into serving pieces and brown a few at a time in butter and oil. Keep warm. Cook shallots in remaining butter and oil, then stir in tomatoes, garlic, salt, pepper, thyme, bouquet garni and lemon peel. Pour in wine and stock. Replace pheasant in pan and cook slowly for 30 minutes, basting occasionally. While this is cooking, sauté mushrooms and also some small white onions if you wish.

When pheasant is cooked, remove any surplus fat from the sauce and remove bouquet garni and lemon peel. Thicken sauce if necessary with 1 tablespoon arrowroot mixed with 2 tablespoons water. Reheat for 5 minutes, then serve on a hot platter. Surround pheasant with mushrooms and onions, and sprinkle with parsley.

Cold Game Soufflé

From Lt. Col. C. G. Austin, a Conservancy member.

Mince cold game very finely. Dissolve gelatine in consommé over very low heat. Mix mince and mayonnaise into the consommé. Stir in the cream lightly. Add sherry, sauce and seasoning to taste. Fold in the whites of eggs and put the whole mixture in a soufflé dish. Place in refrigerator for 1 hour or in a cool larder for 2 hours.

200–300 g (8–12 oz) cold cooked pheasant (or partridge)
15 g (½ oz) gelatine
125 ml (¼ pint) tinned consommé
125 ml (¼ pint) mayonnaise
125 ml (¼ pint) cream, lightly whipped
1 tablespoon sherry
1 tablespoon Harvey's sauce
salt and pepper (Lawry's seasoned, if possible)
3 egg whites

Pheasants as in Saint-Éminié

Mrs Nina Fiske very kindly sent this in to the Game Conservancy when she heard that we were trying to compile a book. It is a Danish recipe.

2 pheasants
3 tablespoons butter

Casserole or brown in the oven the pheasants in 2 tablespoons of the butter – nothing else. When done, take them out and scrape the meat off the legs. Mince this meat, and mix with the butter in the pan. Mix in remaining cold butter, bring to the boil, and when boiling take off the heat. This minced meat is divided on four plates, nicely served breast laid on top. Serve small potatoes and unsweetened apple sauce with this dish.

Duntreath Devilled Pheasant

Juliet Edmonstone telephoned me as soon as she heard that I needed help and offered me this recipe for pheasant, which was more than kind, realizing how many people she and Archie entertain at Duntreath who must be longing to know her secrets.

Dry Sauce
2 teaspoons sugar
1 teaspoon ground pepper
1 teaspoon ginger
½ teaspoon curry powder
½ teaspoon mustard

2 jointed pheasants

Mix the dry ingredients, rub them well into two jointed pheasants, and leave for 1 hour.

Brush the pheasant pieces in the butter and grill gently until brown and crisp, 10 minutes each side, then put them on the bottom of the grill pan. Mix the sauces with the remaining butter, heat, and spoon over the pheasants. Continue cooking the birds under the grill, basting frequently, then arrange them in a dish. Dilute sauce with stock if necessary and pour over pheasants. Serve with long grain rice and onions.

Wet Sauce
50 g (2 oz) melted butter
3 tablespoons tomato chutney
1 tablespoon Worcestershire sauce
1 tablespoon soya sauce
2 dashes tabasco
1 tablespoon H.P. sauce

stock if necessary

Guinea fowl and chicken can also be cooked the same way.

Sautéed Pheasant with Cabbage

1 pheasant
4 tablespoons fat (lard, butter, bacon fat)
1 medium cabbage
salt and pepper
250 ml ($\frac{1}{2}$ pint) cream
$\frac{1}{4}$ teaspoon paprika

From James Beard. I have used this recipe so often for every kind of bird that I have forgotten that it really isn't mine. If you would rather skin the pheasant, I think it is better to wrap the pieces in streaky bacon secured with a toothpick before you sauté them.

Singe, clean and cut pheasant in convenient serving pieces. Brown pheasant in fat. Reduce the heat, cover and cook for 20 minutes.

Shred the cabbage finely and parboil in salted water for 10 minutes. Salt to taste and drain. Add the cabbage to the pheasant in pan and allow to cook for 10 minutes, covered. Add lots of salt and pepper to taste, and the cream, and simmer for 5 minutes. Sprinkle with paprika and serve with boiled potatoes. A few juniper berries added to this dish gives a really fine flavour.

This recipe is also good with guinea fowl or pigeon.

Pheasant à la Gaybird

2 onions, sliced
50 g (2 oz) sultanas
2 pheasants – breasts only are used (keep legs and wings for vol au vents or risotto later)
500 ml (1 pint) red wine
salt and pepper
25 g (1 oz) butter
250 ml ($\frac{1}{2}$ pint) double cream

Served with sultanas, onion and cream sauce.

As Graham Harvey-Evers supplies so many of us with pheasant eggs and chicks, it is very kind of his wife Mollie to tell us what she does when they are finally in the bag.

Lay sliced onions on a large piece of transparent cooking film in a baking tin (or foil – but allow extra time, as foil is a good insulator). Sprinkle over the sultanas and lay the pheasants on this bed. Pour over the wine, season, add a little butter to each breast, and wrap into an airtight parcel. Cook in a very hot oven (230°C, 450°F, Mark 8) for 20–25 minutes, depending on size of pheasants. This will heat them right through and brown the breasts if transparent film has been used. Now move the dish to a very cool oven (110°C, 225°F, Mark $\frac{1}{4}$) for 1–1$\frac{1}{4}$ hours. This section can be done the previous day if required.

Unwrap and remove the birds. Tip the rest of the ingredients (except cream) into a saucepan or frying pan and cook until the liquid is reduced to 125 ml ($\frac{1}{4}$ pint). Season to taste. Meanwhile slice the breasts, lay them in a dish, and cover to stop them getting dry. When sauce is reduced, stir in the cream and allow to boil for a few minutes until it becomes thick. Pour sauce over meat, cover tightly. Keep warm or serve at once.

This recipe is equally delicious with grouse. Use four old birds.

Pheasant 'Guidwife' (Old Birds)

From Mrs P. Coats.

Brown onions in butter then remove to casserole. Brown pheasant in remaining fat, then place on top of onions. Spread breast thickly with chutney, season, then pour in stock to come halfway up bird and put in a hot oven (200°C, 400°F, Mark 6) for 1½ hours. If a thick sauce is required, thicken it with a little beurre manié (butter and flour in equal quantities kneaded together) about half an hour before the end of cooking time. This recipe is equally good for pigeons.

800 g (2 lb) onions cut in thick rings
2 tablespoons butter (beurre manié optional)
1 old cock pheasant
2 tablespoons sweet fruit or mango chutney
seasoning
1 pint stock

Pheasant with Peppers and Oranges

This is adapted from a chicken recipe which I cut out of an American magazine. It is a colourful pheasant dish which makes a change from the more usual mushroom, onion and bacon ones.

Brown pheasants in butter or bacon fat; pour over Madeira or sherry. Remove pheasants, then add the tomato paste, Bovril and potato flour to the pan. Stir very well and gradually pour in stock. Stir till mixture comes to a boil, put pheasants back in pan, then add bouquet garni, salt and pepper. Cover, and cook slowly for about 40 minutes. Arrange on warm platter, removing bouquet garni.

Heat olive oil, add garlic, and cook for a minute, then add peppers, tomatoes and orange rind. Cook gently for several minutes, then add the sliced oranges, and as soon as they are warm, pour sauce over pheasants.

2 respectable pheasants cut into serving pieces
3 tablespoons butter or preferably bacon fat
2 tablespoons Madeira or sherry
1 teaspoon tomato paste
½ teaspoon Bovril
1 tablespoon potato flour
generous 250 ml (½ pint) stock
bouquet garni of parsley, bayleaf and thyme
salt and pepper
2 tablespoons olive oil
1 clove garlic, mashed
100 g (4 oz) mushrooms, sliced
½ red pepper, diced
½ green pepper, diced
3 tomatoes, skinned, seeded and coarsely chopped
grated rind of 1 orange
2 oranges, peeled, skinned and sliced ery thin

Steamed Pheasant

Bianca Muratori sent this recipe from Italy.

Prepare the pheasant with sage, streaky bacon, salt and pepper. Place it in a saucepan with a quarter of an onion sliced fine, a clove of garlic and sufficient olive oil.

Brown slowly, then add a ladle of stock (or water). Turn over the pheasant, taking care it does not stick to the pan, in which case add more stock or water until the bird is cooked, keeping the saucepan covered.

Remove the pheasant from the pan and carve it. Add a little dry white wine (or red wine) to the sauce left in the pan. Return the sliced pheasant to the sauce and reheat until the sauce simmers.

A Way of Tackling Old Tough Birds

2 old birds
100 g (4 oz) seasoned flour
3 tablespoons olive oil
375 ml (¾ pint) boiling water
375 ml (¾ pint) milk
185 ml (⅜ pint) fresh or sour cream
1 tin mushrooms
1 small onion or 3 shallots, minced
Worcestershire sauce
1 tablespoon flour
1 tablespoon finely chopped parsley

Cut birds into serving pieces, dip in seasoned flour and fry in oil until brown. Add boiling water and simmer, uncovered, until tender. Add milk and cream, and tinned mushrooms previously sautéed with finely minced onions, and Worcestershire sauce to taste. Stir in flour mixed with a little water. Cook for 15 minutes. Arrange in serving dish, pour over sauce, and sprinkle with finely chopped parsley.

Pheasant and Rösti

1 pheasant
2 slices bacon
2 tablespoons lard or bacon fat
1 small onion, chopped
2–3 potatoes, coarsely grated
freshly ground pepper
2–3 juniper berries, crushed

Caroline Stroyan suggested this dish which is a great success and very easy. One of my favourites.

Skin pheasant, cut into serving pieces, and wrap in bacon, securing with toothpicks. Brown pheasant in lard or bacon fat. Remove pieces from pan and sauté onion in remaining fat. When onion is slightly brown add potatoes as well as lots of pepper and the juniper berries. Place mixture in a shallow casserole and put the pheasant pieces on top. Place in moderate oven (180°C, 350°F, Mark 4) for 30 minutes.

Pheasant Bonne Femme

200 g (8 oz) bacon
6 tablespoons butter
1 teaspoon thyme
juice of ½ lemon
salt
2 pheasants
20 white onions or 1 packet little onions in white sauce. (Remove sauce before unfreezing as it is not needed)
600 g (1½ lb) potatoes, diced or ball-like, 3 cm (1¼ in) in diameter
12 carrots cut in 5 cm (2 in) pieces (optional)
1 bouquet garni of 4 sprigs parsley, 2 celery tops, thyme and 1 bayleaf

Remove rind from bacon, cut into 5 mm (¼ in) squares and simmer for 10 minutes in plenty of water, then rinse in cold water and dry. Sauté the bacon in 1 tablespoon of the butter until light brown, then remove.

Mix thyme, lemon juice and salt with 2 tablespoons butter and put half inside each bird. Truss birds. Brown the pheasants in the remaining fat from bacon, turning and making sure that it doesn't burn. This will take about 15 minutes. Remove and pour out fat.

Boil fresh onions in salted water slowly for 5 minutes. Drain. Cover potatoes with cold water, bring to the boil, and drain. Heat remaining butter in a casserole, add potatoes and carrots and roll them around for a minute, then push them to the sides and place pheasants in the middle. Put bacon, onions and bouquet garni on top of all of this, baste with the melted butter, cover with foil, and place the lid on the casserole. Heat casserole until sizzling, then put in a moderately slow oven (170°C, 325°F, Mark 3) for an hour. Baste occasionally.

Instead of the onions and potatoes you may add 200 g (8 oz) sautéed chipolata sausages and 300 g (12 oz) sautéed mushrooms for the last 10 minutes of cooking, but put finely chopped onion in the casserole with the bacon.

Pheasant in Red Wine Sauce

We had guinea fowl cooked this way one time when we were driving through France. It was so delicious that when the waiter appeared to prepare it for the people at the next table we tore all the wrappers off the sugarlumps so I could write down exactly what he did. By the time pheasants were in season again and I consulted my wrappers, the instructions were somewhat confusing, but it is very good and works wonderfully well with pheasant.

1 young pheasant
150 ml (6 oz) red wine
375 ml (¾ pint) strong game stock
1 tablespoon redcurrant jelly
5 tablespoons brandy
2 tablespoons Dijon mustard
juice of ½ lemon
200 g (8 oz) chicken livers lightly sautéed and served whole or liquidized

Roast pheasant in moderate oven (180°C, 350°F, Mark 4), basting as often as possible, for 45 minutes. Carve into serving pieces and keep warm.

In frying pan reduce red wine and stock to about 125 ml (¼ pint). Whisk in redcurrant jelly until melted, add brandy and mustard, whisking all the time, then add lemon juice and finally chicken livers. When the sauce is smooth and bubbling, place pheasant in pan and heat in the sauce for 5 minutes.

Un Régal de Faisan

These next two recipes were sent by a member from France· They are very good and beautifully simple.

½ teaspoon paprika
1 pheasant (reserve liver)
1 tablespoon bacon fat
3 tablespoons oil
1½ tablespoons Cognac
1 cube instant stock
salt and pepper
1 tablespoon flour
40 g (1½ oz) butter
½ teaspoon strong mustard

Sprinkle the inside of the pheasant with paprika and cover with bacon fat. Brown the pheasant in the oil. Flame it with Cognac. Prepare half of the stock and pour it on the pheasant. Add very little salt as the stock is already salty. Add pepper. Cook very gently in a covered dish. During this time work flour and butter in a bowl. Add chopped raw liver and the mustard. When the pheasant is cooked, about 1½ hours depending on its age, take it out and keep warm.

Sauce Pour the rest of the stock into the pan, warm it thoroughly and add the mixture from the bowl, thoroughly whisking it in. Keep stirring without stopping so that the sauce is smooth and runny. At the last moment stir in the fresh cream. Remove from the heat. Carve the pheasant. Serve with croûtons and cover with the sauce.

Faisan aux Noix

Wrap the pheasant with bacon strips, secured with toothpicks. Brown in a heavy casserole, then add walnuts, orange juice, Madeira, salt and pepper. Cook for 45 minutes. Add stock and allow to simmer for a few minutes. Serve the pheasant garnished with the nuts separately from the sauce.

1 pheasant
2 strips bacon
12 walnuts (about)
juice of 1–2 oranges
5 tablespoons Madeira
salt and pepper
5 tablespoons stock

Pheasant Pie

2 goodish pheasants
3 tablespoons butter
200 g (8 oz) unsweetened pie crust
500 ml (1 pint) stock
250 ml (½ pint) red or white wine
12 small white onions
200 g (8 oz) mushrooms
2 carrots, sliced
1 small packet frozen peas
1 small packet broad beans
1 tin new potatoes

This is very easy and looks rather more colourful than most pies of this type.

Roast pheasants in butter for 45 minutes. Make pie crust. Cut birds into serving pieces. Remove as many of the body bones as possible, add them to the stock and wine, and simmer for 30 minutes. Strain the liquid and thicken with a little corn-flour mixed with water, if necessary.

While this is happening cook onions, mushrooms, carrots, peas and broad beans. Open tinned potatoes, cut them in half and sauté them until brown.

Put the pheasants and all the vegetables in a deep casserole, pour over gravy, cover with pie crust and bake in hot oven (200°C, 400°F, Mark 6) for 30 minutes.

Pheasants with Apple Purée

100 g (4 oz) unsmoked gammon, diced
1 onion, finely chopped
1 clove garlic, mashed
2 tablespoons butter
2 tablespoons oil
1 pheasant
300 g (12 oz) hard cooking apples
2 tablespoons Calvados, brandy or whisky
250 ml (½ pint) cream
salt and pepper

Lightly fry gammon, onion and garlic in butter and oil in a heavy casserole. Remove from fat. Brown pheasant all over in the fat, turning frequently, then remove and keep warm. Peel, core and slice apples and add them to the fat. Cook until they start to turn golden. Pour over spirit and skim fat from pan juices. Put pheasant back in casserole and surround with apples, gammon and vegetables. Bring to simmer, stir in cream, salt and pepper, then cover casserole and cook in a very cool oven (130°C, 250°F, Mark ½) until tender, about 1½ hours. When ready, remove pheasant with bits of gammon, purée the remaining sauce, and taste for seasoning.

Pheasant with Pineapple and Sauerkraut

2 young pheasants
salt and pepper
2 thin slices bacon
2 tablespoons butter
600 g (1½ lb) sauerkraut
125 ml (¼ pint) white wine
250 g (10 oz) fresh pineapple, diced

Wipe birds, season inside and out with salt and pepper. Place bacon on breast of each bird and secure with toothpicks, then brown in butter for 15 minutes. Place in casserole.

Drain sauerkraut a little, mix with wine and pineapple and surround birds. Cover, and cook slowly for an hour. When done, take out the pheasants, remove toothpicks, and place birds on a warm serving dish. Stir flour into sauerkraut and cook for a few minutes, place it around birds.

Partridges may be done the same way, only substitute 2 peeled, cored and chopped apples for the sauerkraut.

'To deal with an Old Cock Pheasant with spurs like hob nails and as tough as old boots'

Pluck and dress as usual and then put the aged warrior in a colander over a pan of gently boiling water for 15–20 minutes. Have ready a heavy iron casserole, melt butter in it and brown him on all sides.

Take two large cooking apples (preferably Bramleys), peel, core and slice them and lay them under and around the bird. Cover the casserole and cook in a medium oven (180°C, 350°F, Mark 4) for 30–40 minutes according to size of the bird. Take out the bird and keep hot, and pour into the casserole containing the apples, butter and cooking juices, the Calvados and cream. Stir well with a wooden spoon to a smooth consistency (do not boil – the residual heat of the heavy iron pan is enough).

Carve the bird and serve the sauce separately. This dish is even better with a young bird in which case the tenderizing by steaming is unnecessary.

1 old pheasant
50 g (2 oz) butter
2 large cooking apples
50 ml (2 oz) Calvados
100 ml (4 oz) single cream

Pheasant in Gin

I'd always heard that gin was the thing to cook pheasant in as juniper berries were good with pheasant and gin was flavoured with juniper berries, so they ought to go together. It all sounds so obvious that I'm surprised we don't meet gin more often in game cooking.

Prepare pheasants for roasting in the normal way and place 2–3 crushed juniper berries inside each bird. Put the birds in a very hot oven (230°C, 450°F, Mark 4) and baste frequently with gin and hot water. When cooked – about another 35 minutes – serve with strained juices as gravy.

2 pheasants
4–6 juniper berries
75 ml (¼ cup) gin
75 ml (¼ cup) water

Breast of Pheasant with Ham and Rice

Sometimes you can afford to be extravagant and just use the breasts of the pheasants, leaving the rest for stock or pâté.

Cook ham in hot butter until brown, remove and keep hot. Sauté pheasant breasts in the butter, add salt, pepper and mushrooms, and cook for 15 minutes, turning frequently and basting with pan juices.

In a serving dish, place ham on toast, pheasant on ham and top with mushrooms. Stir flour into pan juices, let boil, add Madeira or sherry, stir, and when boiling pour over pheasant.

Serve this with rice cooked with a little sautéed onion.

1 thin slice of uncooked ham *per serving*
2 tablespoons butter
1 pheasant breast
salt and pepper
2 mushroom caps
1 slice toast
½ teaspoon flour
4 tablespoons sherry or Madeira

1 thin slice Gruyère cheese
    per serving

Variation You may place a thin slice of Gruyère cheese on the ham, and after pouring over the sauce, place the dish under the grill until the cheese melts and bubbles.

Capitaine à la Campagne

300 g (12 oz) leftover roast pheasant
    or other game
15 g ($\frac{1}{2}$ oz) flour
40 g (1$\frac{1}{2}$ oz) butter
2 teaspoons curry powder
salt and pepper
$\frac{1}{2}$ teaspoon paprika
3 tomatoes, peeled and diced
200 ml (8 oz) tomato sauce
4 onions, thinly sliced
2 tablespoons salad oil
75 g (3 oz) croûtons (bread cubes)
4 tablespoons chopped parsley

From Madame Benoît.

In the Victorian days it was a mark of savoir-faire to use the French name for a dish. The recipe for the capitaine usually started with, 'Take any piece of cold game.'

Slice pheasant into pieces as even in size as possible. Dip each piece in flour. Melt butter in a saucepan, add curry powder, salt, pepper and paprika. Stir over medium heat until blended. Add pheasant pieces and brown on each side over low heat. Add tomatoes and tomato sauce and bring to the boil. Place pheasant on a hot platter, pour over sauce and keep warm.

Fry onions in the same saucepan with oil. When brown, remove and place on top of pheasant. Brown the croûtons (bread cubes) in the same pan and place on platter to form a border. Sprinkle middle with parsley.

January Pheasant

2 pheasants
1 tablespoon hot dripping
2 tablespoons flour
1 swede
1 turnip
1 parsnip
200 g (8 oz) carrots
200 g (8 oz) onions
200 g (8 oz) tomatoes
1 clove garlic
2 chicken stock cubes
salt, pepper, bayleaves, etc.
90 ml (3$\frac{3}{4}$ oz) sherry
250 ml ($\frac{1}{2}$ pint) cream

From Miss June Gray.

Joint and skin pheasants as with chicken (i.e. into four). If badly shot in any part, discard that part. Brown pheasants in dripping, remove and place in a casserole dish, add flour to the fat and brown, then add to the casserole. Roughly chop all vegetables and add stock cubes, seasoning and half of the sherry. The stock should be sufficient to just cover the game and vegetables. Place lid on casserole and cook for an hour, or until pheasant and vegetables are tender, in a moderate oven (180°C, 350°F, Mark 4). Remove from oven and separate the game and the stock and vegetables. Liquidize the vegetables and add the remainder of the sherry and the cream. The pheasant can either be replaced in the dish on the bone, or if desired it can be stripped from the bone (often goes farther in an emergency). Add the liquidized stock and vegetables, and replace in the oven until ready to serve. This will also keep in the deep freeze.

Instead of sherry, for a change redcurrant jelly can be added. This gives a sweet taste and should be used in moderation.

Devilled Pheasant

The Hon. Mrs James Ogilvy's recipe.

Put the pheasants in a casserole with carrot, onion, garlic, parsley and herbs. Cover birds with water and cover casserole. Bring to boil and simmer gently until tender. Remove meat from bones and put back in juices in which it was cooked. Heat very slowly in these juices so that the meat does not become dry. Meanwhile whip double cream stiff and leave in refrigerator for approximately 1 hour until it becomes quite hard, then beat the chutney and Worcestershire sauce into it and keep cool in refrigerator until ready to use. Place meat, thoroughly drained of cooking juices, in the dish in which it is to be served. Cover with the cream mixture and put in the oven for 10 minutes to heat through. You can do devilled chicken in the same way.

Hint The birds can be cooked in the morning and the rest of the preparation done about 1½ hours before dinner, but remember to keep the stock in which the birds were first cooked for reheating.

2 pheasants
1 large carrot
1 large onion
1 clove garlic
1 sprig parsley
1 sprig thyme
2 bayleaves
250 ml (½ pint) double cream
1 large jar Green Label chutney
4 tablespoons Worcestershire sauce

Midi Pheasant

From Stuart Wilson.

A big pheasant, no longer young, is a fine bird: it will make a good dish for six people.

Take any good sized oven pot, with a lid – I prefer the unglazed pottery which is rubbed from time to time inside and out with raw cloves of garlic – and into this put a generous bed of onions, nicely fried, but not browned, in olive oil. Lay the pheasant into this, breast downwards, and add all around and sliced, not too fine, tomatoes, a red and a green pepper, courgettes, aubergines, cucumber, and anything else of that sort you happen to have about, adding in what proportions the whim of the moment dictates. Season with sea-salt and pepper from the mill – I have half black and half white corns in mine – and as many cloves of garlic through the presser as your guests will bear. Moisten with only a little water or suitable stock – the vegetables supply a good deal of moisture – and cook slowly in the oven, with the lid on the pot, for 3 hours, (150°C, 300°F, Mark 2). For the last hour place breasts upward, high and dry; the bird will thus be nicely browned all over, tender enough to cut with a spoon, though still moist all through the breast, and with a delicious flavour.

Serve it with potatoes cooked the way you like them – a dish of pommes de terre boulangère goes well – or boiled rice.

Note Unglazed absorbent cooking pots, which give the best results of all, should be cleaned only with very hot water, never, of course, with soap or washing-up liquid.

Bentley Pheasant Supreme

1 young pheasant
50 g (2 oz) butter
2 large onions
1 clove garlic
100 g (4 oz) streaky bacon
75 g (3 oz) breadcrumbs
2 teaspoons flour
1 egg, beaten
3 tablespoons cream

Put pheasant into a saucepan with half of the butter, half an onion, the garlic and 250 ml ($\frac{1}{2}$ pint) water. Cover and cook slowly for about $1\frac{1}{4}$ hours or until pheasant is cooked. While bird is cooking, chop the bacon very finely and fry until crisp. Add breadcrumbs and stir until brown. There should be enough fat from the bacon but if not add a little more butter. Put aside.

Take pheasant from pan. Discard bones and skin, roughly shred meat and place on a warm flat ovenproof dish. Keep warm. Chop the rest of the onions and cook them gently in the rest of the butter, then stir in flour. Strain the stock from the pheasant and stir 250 ml ($\frac{1}{2}$ pint) in with the onions. Let this cook slowly for 5 minutes and then strain, pressing the onion hard at the sides of the sieve. Mix beaten egg with cream, add a little of the hot sauce and then pour it back into the rest of the sauce; stir well. Pour over pheasant. Sprinkle with bacon and breadcrumb mixture. Place under the grill for a minute or two.

Wild Duck

Mallard, Widgeon and Teal are the species of wild duck most likely to end up in the game larder. The mallard is the ancestor of the ordinary farmyard duck but, being omnivorous, he is not considered quite as good to eat as the widgeon who feeds on grass. Yet it is the little teal who excites people most. Maybe it is their size that makes them more of a test to shoot, you will notice that anyone telling you the bag will always give the teal with a definite tone of pride. It is also a satisfactory duck to cook as it is exactly the right size for one person so that everyone may have it cooked as they wish – people being fussier over the degree of doneness of duck than with other birds. Any duck which has been shot on the foreshore is liable to have a fishy flavour, so if you suspect this, place an onion or potato inside its cavity with a teaspoon of salt. Place the bird in a pan with 5 mm ($\frac{1}{4}$ in) boiling water and bake in a moderate oven (180°C, 350°F, Mark 4), basting frequently, for 10 minutes. Drain bird; remove onion or potato.

Duck does not need prolonged hanging: 2–3 days is all that is necessary or it may become rancid. In the warmer weather, duck are better hung after they have been eviscerated. The guts can be 'fished' out carefully through the vent, using a headed nail like a button hook. As with other game, duck becomes tough if it is overcooked.

The webbing of the feet of a young duck can be torn quite easily; their feet are pinker in colour and their bills are brighter than the older birds.

All the recipes are for a mallard sized duck unless otherwise stated.

Roast Wild Mallard

Place whatever you wish in the cavity of the duck – apple, orange, onion, game stuffing, a knob of seasoned butter, or some butter with a bunch of herbs and juniper berries. Truss. Smear the breasts with softened butter, place in a very hot oven (230°C, 450°F, Mark 8), and baste frequently with butter, red wine, port, or orange juice. About 20 minutes will make them fairly rare so you may wish to leave them longer, up to 30 minutes. Do not overcook them.

If you have filled them with chopped apples or onions, try to remove this before serving as they look revolting if they burst out over the platter.

Add a little more wine or orange juice or redcurrant jelly to the juices, or serve with Sauce Bigarade and orange salad.

Roast Teal

1 teal
seasoned butter
flour

I have only eaten teal roasted or put a badly shot one in a pâté. As we seldom have enough for everyone I have never gone into the young and old question, but I don't remember any terrible complaints.

Roast teal as mallard: fill the cavity with seasoned butter – any other stuffing seems to overpower its flavour. Baste frequently with butter, dust slightly with flour just as it is ready and baste again. It will probably take from 12 to 20 minutes.

Serve with a thin gravy and an orange and watercress salad.

Roast Duck with Petit Suisse

1 wild duck
2–3 Petit Suisse or 2–3 tablespoons unsalted fresh cream cheese
parsley, thyme, basil or marjoram
1 tablespoon soft butter
2–3 strips streaky bacon

Many Europeans cook their duck and pheasant in this way.

Place inside the duck a couple of Petit Suisse or unsalted fresh cream cheese, with some herbs. Truss. Spread the bird with some softened butter and cover with several strips of streaky bacon. Roast in very hot oven (220°C, 425°F, Mark 7) until the bird is how you like it, about 25–30 minutes. The Petit Suisse should produce enough gravy.

Wild Duck in Rich Gravy

I am presuming that most households do not have a duck press and don't intend to go out and buy one; however, this recipe can be made to resemble Pressed Duck if you can manage to be in the kitchen up to the last moment.

Truss bird well, spread with butter and roast in very hot oven (220°C, 425°F, Mark 7) for 10–12 minutes. Stand the bird in a dish that will catch every drop of blood, for about 10 minutes, and then carve off the breasts, and the flesh from the legs if you think they will be tender enough. Place the meat where it will keep warm, but keep the juices. While the duck is cooking, combine the red wine, peppercorns, bayleaf, thyme and onion. Cook this until the liquid is reduced to just under half its volume. Thicken with a very little beurre manié. When the duck is cooked and the meat removed put the remaining carcass through a meat grinder. Strain this well, extracting all the juices which you add to the juices from the carving. Add them very gradually to the wine sauce, stirring hard until it thickens, but never let it even simmer. Slice breast and serve with sauce.

You may also add the duck's livers (previously cooked and worked through a fine sieve) just before the blood, and you may add 2 tablespoons brandy at the end.

1 duck
1 tablespoon butter
125 ml (¼ pint) red wine
5 peppercorns, crushed
1 small bayleaf
1 slice of onion
a little thyme
beurre manié (1 tablespoon butter, ½ teaspoon flour)

Tortière au Canard (Duck Pie)

In a pan melt the bacon fat, brown the minced onion and the duck which has been cut into pieces. Add the flour and brown. Moisten with the stock. Season with salt and pepper, clove, savory, nutmeg and cinnamon. Simmer for 1½ hours or 20 minutes in a pressure cooker.

During this time prepare the pastry with the flour, butter, a little salt and the milk. Line a pie dish with some of the pastry and when the duck is cooked pour it with the sauce, which should be quite thick, into the pie dish. Cover with the rest of the pastry. Seal the two ends by pinching them with your fingers. Put in the oven for 10 minutes at hot (200°C, 400°F, Mark 6) and then 10 minutes at a moderate temperature (180°C, 350°F, Mark 4).

100 g (4 oz) bacon fat (smoked or salted)
1 onion, minced
1 wild duck
250 ml (½ pint) chicken stock
salt and pepper
1 clove
savory
scraping of nutmeg
¼ teaspoon cinnamon

Pastry
500 g (1¼ lb) flour
200 g (8 oz) butter
salt
90 ml (3¾ oz) milk

Duck with Green Peppercorns

Place peppercorns and half of the butter inside the bird; use the rest of the butter to rub over the outside of the bird. Place on one side in casserole and pour over whisky or brandy. Cover well and place in a moderate oven (180°C, 350°F, Mark 4) for 1–1¼ hours. Turn bird at half time. 10 minutes before it is cooked, remove cover and put bird breast up in order to brown evenly. Add a few more peppercorns to the juices if you wish.

2 tablespoons green peppercorns
1 wild duck
25 g (1 oz) butter
2 tablespoons whisky or brandy

Mollie's Duck with Apples and Cider

1 medium sized duckling
salt
1 small bottle dry cider
1 small carton cream

Stuffing
75 g (3 oz) butter
100 g (4 oz) white fresh bread-
    crumbs
400 g (1 lb) cooking apples, pipped,
    cored, diced
salt and pepper
2 teaspoons sugar
ground cinnamon

This is another recipe from the Bolfracks' kitchen.

Rub salt into duckling skin. Melt butter in a frying pan. Add breadcrumbs and fry until golden brown. Add apples, cover, and cook until soft (15 minutes). Add salt and pepper, sugar and cinnamon. When cool, stuff duck and close tail end with skewer. Place in roasting tin with 2 tablespoons water. Place in a moderate oven (180°C, 350°F, Mark 4) and cook for 20 minutes per 400 g (1 lb). About 15 minutes before the end of cooking time, drain off fat, pour on cider and replace duck in oven. When cooked, lift duck from roasting tin, simmer until cider is reduced by half. Cut duck into four portions, arrange on serving dish. Put stuffing into a small basin. Add cream to duck gravy, strain over duck; serve with stuffing.

Swedish Roast Wild Duck with Fruit Stuffing

2 wild duck with their livers
½ teaspoon salt
¼ teaspoon pepper
375 ml (¾ pint) stock

meat extract
few drops of lemon juice

Stuffing
3–4 apples cut into sections
100 g (4 oz) prunes, partially cooked

Wipe ducks well, trim and clean livers, and rub inside and outside of ducks with the livers and the salt and pepper. Stuff birds with the prunes and apples. Truss. Sear and roast in oven or braise on top of cooker. Baste occasionally with stock. The total time of cooking depends on the age of the birds – old ones take as long as 2 hours and young ones as little as half an hour. To keep birds from browning too much, place buttered paper over the top during the last part of cooking. Do not overcook. Strain pan juices, add some meat extract for colour and flavour, and also a few drops of lemon juice. Reheat before serving but do not thicken.

Wild Duck Maison

2 wild duck
25 g (1 oz) butter
2 tablespoons oil
4 tablespoons Marsala
2 tablespoons tomato paste
2 tablespoons potato flour
375 ml (¾ pint) chicken stock
salt and pepper
1 bayleaf
5 mushrooms
1 red pimento, diced
½ green pepper, diced
small amount of orange rind, finely
    chopped
1 orange, segmented
3 tomatoes, skinned and sliced

This is from Dione Lucas who was a great friend of my mother's. They understood each other and much of what we both know I think was shown to Mother by her.

Cut ducks into serving pieces, brown all over in butter and oil, pour over Marsala, then remove ducks and add tomato paste and potato flour. Blend well and pour on chicken stock. Allow to come to the boil, put back birds, season with salt and pepper, add bayleaf and allow to simmer gently until tender, about 45 minutes. Meantime slice mushrooms, sauté them in butter, add pimento, green pepper, orange rind, orange segments and tomato slices; cook together very gently. Remove ducks from their gravy and add more potato flour if necessary. Add orange mixture and pour over ducks on a platter.

Salmis of Wild Duck

Fry bacon until crisp, put half of this aside. Add half of the butter, the onion and bouquet garni, and the ducks. Roast for 20 minutes in a moderately slow oven (170°C, 325°F, Mark 3), basting occasionally. Pour off fat and juices and skim off fat. In another saucepan melt rest of butter and fry flour till brown. Add stock and red wine, mixing until smooth, bring to the boil and simmer for 30 minutes or more. Add duck juices. Place duck meat in casserole with reserved bacon and a few olives if you like. Pour over sauce and simmer for 15 minutes.

150 g (6 oz) bacon, diced
75 g (3 oz) butter
1 onion, finely chopped
1 bouquet garni
2 wild duck
25 g (1 oz) flour
375 ml (¾ pint) good stock
250 ml (½ pint) red wine
olives (optional)

Marinated Wild Duck

Cut ducks in half and place them in a bowl with the marinade. Leave overnight or for about 6 hours, turning several times.

Dry the pieces of duck, sprinkle them with flour and brown in olive oil. Place all the pieces in a casserole and strain the marinade over them; add garlic. Bring to simmer and add mushrooms. Cover, and simmer slowly for 1½ hours or until duck meat is tender. Thicken the gravy with cornflour mixed with water. Season to taste.

2 wild duck

Marinade
100 ml (4 oz) brandy
125 ml (¼ pint) red wine
2 onions, sliced
1 tablespoon chopped parsley
½ teaspoon thyme
1 bayleaf
¼ teaspoon allspice

1 tablespoon flour
3 tablespoons olive oil
1 clove garlic, mashed
200 g (8 oz) mushrooms, sliced
1 teaspoon cornflour
salt and pepper

Easy Wild Duck with Tinned Cherries

When I was first married, food in Britain seemed so cheap after Canadian food that I thought everything was a bargain. Scottish smoked salmon was a delicacy that I had not met before, veal was good and cheap and I quickly discovered two recipes for duck which were within even my capabilities. It is now years since I have bought a domestic duck, but I still use my old faithful recipes, though now I have adapted them to the wild duck. The original ideas came from *Season to Taste*, by Peggy Harvey. Referring back to it after all these years, I'd forgotten what a good book it was.

2 wild duck
salt and pepper
50 g (2 oz) butter
1 tin stoned black cherries
250 ml (½ pint) port
1 teaspoon cornflour

Cut the ducks in half. Sprinkle with salt and pepper and brown in butter rather slowly so they get golden all over. Drain off butter. Add the juice from a tin of stoned cherries and the port. Cover and simmer for 1½ hours or until the birds are tender. Remove birds to a hot platter, cover, and keep warm.

Skim fat from juices, then add cornflour mixed with 50 ml (2 oz) juice from cherries or water. Bring to boil, stirring all the time, and simmer until thickened. Add the cherries and simmer until they are heated through.

Wild Duck with Turnips

3 tablespoons butter
1 tablespoon oil
2 duck
250 ml ($\frac{1}{2}$ pint) stock
125 ml ($\frac{1}{4}$ pint) white wine
bouquet of celery, parsley, bayleaf, thyme
salt and pepper
18 small onions
little sugar
400 g (1 lb) white turnips, or yellow as second choice, diced in 2.5 cm (1 in) cubes

Melt 1 tablespoon of the butter and the oil in a casserole. Brown ducks by turning them over in this and adding more fat if necessary – this should all be done quite slowly. Add stock, wine, bouquet, salt and pepper to casserole, and bring to simmer. Cook in moderate oven (180°C, 350°F, Mark 4) for 45 minutes.

Melt remaining butter in a pan, add onions, sprinkle with a little sugar and cook until golden. Remove. Add turnips and do the same. Add both of these to the casserole and cook for a further 45 minutes. Remove ducks, cut in half or in serving pieces, place on a platter and surround it with the vegetables. Skim fat from gravy and thicken slightly if necessary. Pour gravy over it all.

Wild Duck in Yoghurt

1 duck cut into serving pieces
1 onion, chopped
2 tablespoons oil
1 large tomato, chopped
$\frac{1}{8}$ teaspoon coriander seed
1 teaspoon cummin
1 teaspoon chilli powder
1 teaspoon tumeric
salt to taste
500 ml (1 pint) yoghurt
1 clove garlic, mashed together with 1 teaspoon ginger in 250 ml ($\frac{1}{2}$ pint) water

This sounds most strange but I was given it by an American and it is delicious and quite different from the ordinary. It's really a curry.

Brown duck and onion in oil. Add tomato, seasonings and yoghurt. Fry for a few minutes and then add water mixture. Cook uncovered for 5 minutes, then cover and simmer for 2 hours. Add more water if needed.

Lazy Duck with Orange

2 tablespoons butter
marjoram
parsley
$\frac{1}{2}$ orange
1 duck
thick cut marmalade
juice of 2 oranges
little stock or water
salt and pepper
squeeze of lemon

I remember the first time I saw a duck cooked with marmalade, it was at a dinner-party and as soon as we got into the car I announced with full horror: 'The duck was done with marmalade!' and my husband replied that he'd thought it was very good, and why not use marmalade instead of spending all that time making strips. I now use it often when I am in a hurry, and I once amazed my brother who said it was the best duck he had ever eaten and he has eaten one or two good meals.

Place a large lump of the butter, some marjoram and parsley if you wish and half an orange inside a duck. Truss. Spread the duck with butter and then enough marmalade (rather like toast for breakfast!). Squeeze the juice of 2 oranges into the bottom of the pan and add a little water or stock (during the holidays you can even use frozen orange juice). Cover loosely with foil and place in a moderate oven (180°C, 350°F, Mark 4). Baste frequently, adding more juice, water or stock if necessary, until the bird is how you like it – about $\frac{1}{2}$–$\frac{3}{4}$ hour. If it is an older bird you may do this in a casserole with a cover and cook it in a slower oven for longer. Ten minutes before the bird is ready remove foil, but keep basting. When the bird is ready, remove, keep warm, and scrape up all the juices with any brown bits. Taste to see what it needs – probably salt, pepper and a squeeze of lemon. You may wish to thicken it, but very slightly, or it will look even more like marmalade.

Wild Geese

Last Christmas holidays we had a young boy from Bermuda to stay with us who had never eaten any game. By the end he had tried everything except grouse, and with no hesitation he said that geese were his favourite. This caused great consternation amongst the family – what about partridge, woodcock, and that perfect roe deer? – but Chris remained firm. Luckily Ken, our keeper, is saintlike about plucking them because even knowing they are worthless and therefore completely free food, I don't think my thumb would be strong enough ever to manage one.

They need hanging for about three weeks – we've tried them for a shorter time but I don't think they were as good. Then there is the problem of marinade. I used to think it was absolutely necessary but as marinating brings out the gamey taste and my husband doesn't like very gamey things. I tried them without and cooked them longer, and most people seemed to like it better. I usually braise them with some liquid and cover them for most of the cooking, but really young ones can be roasted if you are prepared to stand around and baste them very frequently.

We are normally given Greylag or Pink-footed geese. The Greylag is rather larger weighing about 3.6 kg (9 lb), the Pink-footed weigh around 2.8 kg (7 lb), but this barely affects the cooking times. As all the geese we get are shot off fields, I have never encountered a fishy taste, but if you suspect it might be there, plunge the bird into boiling water with $\frac{1}{2}$ teaspoon bicarbonate of soda in it. Dry well before starting the recipe.

One of the most difficult parts of this book has been the problem of how to tell the age of a goose. I started by looking it up, to find it just was not there. Other cookery books were full of incorrect information and keepers can tell by the look and the feel but they can't really explain just what it is.

Information on ageing geese has been supplied by the Game Conservancy (see charts on pages 211 and 212). They say that it is unlikely that the bursa test would be any more accurate than the plumage, bill and legs except perhaps to the expert. In fact, in the end you are going to have to hope that someone you are with really knows his geese.

If you have more geese than you can get rid of or if you are unable to get them plucked, then you can very easily just pull the skin from the breast and with a sharp knife take the breast out and throw the rest away. This seems horribly extravagant unless you realize that there are farmers with literally thousands of wild geese grazing their grass and winter wheat and if you shoot a wild goose you are not allowed to sell it, so there are areas where to eat any part of a goose is being economical.

When you have several of these breasts you have enormous choice of what to do with them.

Roast Goose

1 goose

Stuffing
celery, chopped
apple, chopped
onion, chopped
orange
or
1 large onion, chopped
1 large apple, peeled, pipped and
　sliced
2 teaspoons dried sage, thyme or
　small handful of fresh herbs
grated rind and juice of ½ lemon
4–6 pickled walnuts, coarsely
　chopped (optional)
200 g (8 oz) breadcrumbs
1 egg, beaten lightly
salt and pepper
more melted butter if necessary

50 g (2 oz) softened butter

Either place any mixture of the first alternative for stuffing inside the goose, or stuff with the second alternative by melting the butter and lightly frying the onion and adding remaining ingredients except softened butter. As the goose has no fat of its own you wish the stuffing to be full of butter, though not saturated.

Truss goose well, getting legs and wings in as close as possible to the body. Rub bird generously with softened butter. Roast breast down, turning it from one side to the other occasionally or roast on a trivet. Place in a very hot oven (230°C, 450°F, Mark 8) for about 10 minutes, and then turn down the heat to (170°C, 325°F, Mark 3) and cook until done, about 1–1¼ hours. Baste frequently, adding orange juice, wine, or stock to the basting liquid. Place goose on a platter, skim fat off juices and thicken them very slightly, or make a sauce suitable for game.

Casseroled Wild Goose

1 onion
1 stick celery
1 wild goose
1 tablespoon oil
1 tablespoon butter
250 ml (½ pint) red wine or ½ red wine,
　½ stock
1 bayleaf
black pepper
1–2 sprigs thyme
1 tablespoon redcurrant jelly
cornflour

I find it best if you are cooking more than one goose to cook them in separate casseroles if you have them. You want a casserole that fits as neatly as possible and also have them as heavy as possible.

Place the onion and celery inside the bird and truss the legs together well.

Brown the bird well in a mixture of oil and butter in the casserole, leave the bird breast down, pour over the red wine or wine and stock, then put in the bayleaf, a good screw of pepper, and sprig of thyme. Bring to a simmer and place in a moderately slow oven (170°C, 325°F, Mark 3) for about 2 hours, basting occasionally. When the bird is cooked, strain off the juices. Melt the redcurrant jelly in the juices and thicken slightly with a little cornflour mixed with water.

This is just a very rough guide. You may add vegetables to the juices while it is cooking – sautéed onions or mushrooms – or you can add sour cream to the sauce. What is probably most important, as with all the really gamey game, is to have the serving dishes and plates really hot.

Breaded Wild Goose

1 wild goose

You need a very young fat goose to make this worth the trouble, but it is good and different.

Mix filling together and place in goose, sew up cavity and truss. Rub goose all over thickly with butter. Place breast-down on a trivet and roast for 1 hour in a moderately hot oven (190°C, 375°F, Mark 5), basting frequently. About 10 minutes before the bird is done, add the mustard to butter in pan. Stir. Take bird off trivet, place in pan on its back and sprinkle some breadcrumbs over it, baste it well again and sprinkle more crumbs until it is entirely covered. Finish roasting until the crumbs are golden brown. Serve with Brown Mustard Sauce (see page 188) and apple sauce if you wish.

Filling
liver of goose
1 slice of onion
½ clove garlic, mashed
little parsley
little thyme
5–6 juniper berries, crushed
25 g (1 oz) butter

50 g (2 oz) butter
1 teaspoon prepared mustard
100 g (4 oz) fine breadcrumbs (about)

Wild Goose with Green Peppercorns

Rosie Hanson made up this recipe for me, and though we have used it endlessly and therefore some of the geese must have been questionable, it has never been less than delicious. The birds are inclined to look very overcooked before you carve them, but have faith.

1 wild goose, about 2 kg (5 lb)
piece of fat
giblets
1 onion, sliced
1 carrot, sliced
salt and pepper
thyme
1 bayleaf
1 onion
1 carrot
little Cognac
1 small tin green peppercorns

Put a piece of fat on the breast of the goose and roast it in a hot oven (200°C, 400°F, Mark 6) for 20–30 minutes. Then make a stock from the giblets and the sliced onion and carrot.

Take the bird out of the oven and remove the fat. Salt and pepper it, put thyme, bayleaf, onion and carrot inside it, and put it back in the roasting tin, breast down. Pour the strained stock and a little Cognac over it, and cover with tinfoil.

Turn the oven right down to (150°C, 300°F, Mark 2) and braise it very slowly for 2¾ hours, basting with the juice and turning it several times. For the last 30 minutes I turn up the heat to (180°C, 350°F, Mark 4).

Then carve the meat. It should be quite tender, very dark brown meat all over. The juice should have become very rich and delicious during cooking. Strain it and add the green peppercorns into it in a small saucepan, let it reduce a bit and generally mingle flavours, then pour it over the meat which you have arranged on a flat dish. Put back in oven covered in foil for about 30 minutes until ready to eat.

Shepherd's Pie made with Breasts of Geese

Mince the breasts of geese fairly coarsely. Chop the onion and brown it slowly in the olive oil and add mince, stirring until it is brown also. Add liquid until the meat is just covered. Put in pot, cover, and simmer for an hour or two. You may also add the other vegetables if you wish, or you may cook them separately and add them as you make up the pie.

wild goose breasts
1 onion
100 ml (4 oz) olive oil
liquid to cover (stock, tinned tomatoes, or red wine)

optional
carrots, diced
celery, chopped
turnip, diced

mashed potatoes
1 tablespoon butter

Put the mince in a pie dish and add a little more liquid if it has cooked away. Cover with very creamy mashed potatoes, dot the top with butter.

This can take a thicker layer of potatoes than the usual shepherd's pie as the goose is richer and rather needs the stretching.

Breasts of Geese Done Anyhow

Having taken the breasts off the carcass, marinate them overnight or for a day. If they are thick, slice them on the bias into serving slices.

Take them from the marinade, dry them well, brown them in butter and then do as you wish. They probably will need to simmer for an hour or so in a liquid – strained marinade, stock, wine, tomatoes sautéed with onions and a green pepper, chopped. If to you they are free food, then don't be afraid to treat them as stewing steak or the cheaper cuts that you buy from your butcher.

Woodcock and Snipe

Woodcock is my favourite – even the thought of it in summer gives me a rather nostalgic yearning – yet many people genuinely dislike them. I once went to a dinner-party of eight, where we all had woodcock and I never remember being more impressed, but I would never have the nerve to do it – rather like steak tartare, you have to be sure everyone likes it as you do; and anyway, think of the sacrilege of wasting one on a non-believer! I like them hung for a short time – about three days – and then undercooked and ungutted. If my husband has to eat them, he likes them well cooked and never a gut to be seen, so it isn't very easy to commit yourself on how they ought to be done.

The Club National des Bécassiers have published a work on woodcock and I have used several of their recipes. They say that a woodcock must never be gutted, being the only game whose intestines become liquified when heated and blend with their contents. They say they should be hung from 5–15 days in a cool larder where the air circulates freely. Their methods of telling when woodcock are ready are as follows:

1. The bird must give off a hardly perceptible smell at very close range.
2. The stomach and flank feathers should give way at the slightest pull.
3. The skin on the stomach begins to take on a slight blue-greenish colouring.
4. The other approach is that the bird, having hung by the feet for so many number of days, will produce a droplet of blood on the end of its beak. This may however be misleading due to shot in the intestines. The bird may also be hung by the head and the droplet will fall to the ground.

Roast Woodcock I

This recipe and a few of the following ones are all kindly sent to us by Monsieur Guizard, President of the Club National des Bécassiers.

Melt a good lump of fresh butter in a thick-based saucepan so as to avoid the tongues of flame which could burn the juices. When bubbling, add the bird or trussed pieces of game, surrounded by a bard of fresh lard, thin like a sheet of paper. Brown over a gentle heat for 10–15 minutes. At this point, add salt, pepper and, according to taste, a lump of chopped shallot and a sprig of thyme, then sprinkle with a non-acid, medium quality white wine, a quality preferable to a vintage wine which lacks body when heated, or to a too ordinary wine which risks giving a coarse taste.

Leave to evaporate a short while. Cover the pan and leave to cook on a very low heat for an hour. Watch it and add a few drops of stock when necessary, but never, under any pretext, within the last 10 minutes. Finally, finish cooking without the lid, in the oven for a few moments to suitably brown. It seems surprising to roast the casserole covered, but that is the only way of getting a juicy bird which does not dry up, thanks to the steam condensing on the lid, for the water produced in this way falls back continuously on to the bird.

We emphasize woodcock *must* be cooked for a long time. Leave the game to simmer for a very long time so it will reveal its delicate treasures. We rebel vehemently against cookery books which give 25 minutes as the time necessary for the cooking of woodcock. The fashion of eating bleeding game is disastrous: an undercooked piece has no taste. This is a practice advocated by restaurants which, always in a hurry, cannot indefinitely overcrowd their ovens. Note that only white wine should be added, other than the seasoning; salt and pepper. Port, Madeira and Cognac should be taboo, for because of their strong, special flavour, they assert themselves too haughtily and standardize, to their profit, all the so subtle aromas of the different types of game.

We are not alone in our opinion, for here is what Jean Lurkin wrote: 'May those who like to drown the unfortunate animal (woodcock) in a full glass of Armagnac or flambed liqueur brandy, which turns it into a sort of game punch, never come and ask me for luncheon! Because they would be greatly disappointed, for, despite their chiding and threats, I would serve them woodcock *au naturel* so as to save the subtle juices of the roast.'

Preparation of the croûtons: After one hour to an hour and a quarter of cooking, the roast woodcock releases part of the contents of its abdomen, which must be collected in the bottom of the pan to be blended with that which remains attached to the bird inside, and which will be picked out with a small spoon. The scraps placed together, which will serve as a base for making a purée, should be placed in a bowl to be worked in with: 2 chicken livers or 3 blanched pigeon livers, crushed and sieved, or even with an equivalent quantity of 'mousse de foie gras'; a dessertspoon of full flavoured olive oil; 6 drops of old Dijon vinegar or lemon; a pinch of dry mustard or a knife-tip of Bordelaise mustard, according to preference; ground salt and pepper; a sprig of parsley finely chopped; a sprig of thyme and a lump (as big as a lentil) of shallot previously put in melted butter. For those liking very highly flavoured dishes, a few drops of old Cognac may be added.

From the English bread, cut out croûtons $5 \times 5 \times 1$ cm ($2 \times 2 \times \frac{3}{8}$ in) in size. Brown them in fresh butter, then soak them generously with purée. Again put them in the bubbling butter – half a minute is sufficient to cook the purée which is done when the red colour becomes whiteish. Place the whole or segmented birds on the croûtons and baste them all with the juices. It is important to serve very hot so that the juice does not solidify: like mutton, woodcocks and croûtons do not bear eating when lukewarm.

Portions: 2 croûtons per bird, one bird per two persons.

Roast Woodcock II

I like my woodcock very bloody and to eat every tiny morsel of it, including the brain. My husband says I'm revolting and it is unfortunate that some of my children take after me. I was lucky enough to be taught the more subtle nuances of this particular type of orgy by David Hely-Hutchinson. For this, as for so many other things, I will always be very grateful to him! Try to be as careful as possible when plucking the bird not to break the skin, and only remove the gizzard. The head should be left on, though skinned, and then tucked back close to the body.

Cover the bird generously with softened butter and place a slice of bacon over the breast. Place in a very hot oven (220°C, 425°F, Mark 7) for 10–15 minutes or longer or shorter depending on how you like them. Serve them on a croûton fried in butter. This can be plain or you can extract the entrails and mash them up with some salt, pepper, lemon juice and even a few drops of brandy, and spread this on the croûton, but I am usually so over-excited about my woodcock that I haven't the time. Serve them with a quarter of lemon.

1 woodcock
1 tablespoon butter
1 slice bacon
croûton
salt and pepper
squeeze of lemon juice
drop of brandy
¼ lemon

Cold Woodcock

Do you wish to offer your guests a perfect dish?
By M. Guizard.

Roast a pair of woodcocks three days before, in accordance with the method recommended above.

Do not allow to re-cool, but place immediately in a small sized pot and baste with their juices. Close, then, as for pâté, fit tightly the edges of the pot lid and keep the latter in a cool place. Your guests will be astounded to taste a succulent roast of such great delicacy: the game, after this interval of 62 hours, really gives the impression of having been conserved.

Salmis of Woodcock

Cut the woodcock and roast them in a hot oven (200°C, 400°F, Mark 6) for 20 minutes. Cut in half and keep warm. Mash intestines, livers and chicken livers into a paste and put through a fine sieve. Put paste into a pan and thin with the strong stock and red wine, then add a walnut sized lump of beurre manié, bouquet garni, garlic and peppercorns. Simmer this very gently for 15 minutes. Remove bouquet garni, stir in butter and add the lemon juice to taste. Pour sauce over woodcock and surround with croûtons fried in butter. You may also add a spoonful of cream or sour cream to the sauce if you wish.

2 woodcock (reserve liver and intestines)
4 chicken livers
50 ml (2 oz) strong stock or consommé
90 ml (3¾ oz) good red wine
beurre manié
bouquet garni of slice of onion, 3 sprigs parsley and 1 bayleaf
½ clove garlic
6 peppercorns
1 tablespoon butter
juice of ½ lemon
croûtons
1 tablespoon cream or sour cream (optional)

Woodcock en Cocotte

1 woodcock (reserve intestines)
1 tablespoon butter
1 slice streaky bacon
1 croûton
thyme or marjoram

If you are not a dedicated woodcock eater and prefer your birds gutted and therefore less strong, this is an alternative way of cooking them and decidedly less trouble. We always have croûtons 'with or without guts', thus pleasing the squeamish members of the family.

Clean the woodcock, reserving the intestines but discarding the gizzard. Rub the bird generously with softened butter and place a slice of streaky bacon over it. Put it in an earthenware casserole, as small as possible, cover with buttered paper and then the lid. Place in a hot oven (200°C, 400°F, Mark 6) and cook for about 20 minutes. Fry a croûton for each bird you have cooked, then, as you wish, spread these with a paste made of the mashed intestines, a little butter and a very little pinch of thyme or marjoram. Place these under the birds just before you serve them.

Woodcock Ragoût

By M. Guizard.

The following principle should be applied. It is logical to choose for a ragoût pieces more advanced than for a roast, because the process, consisting of preparing a bird drenched in a sauce, mellows to rather a large extent the overbearing flavour given by the hanging (*faisandage*).

Gut two woodcock and roast them. Take the livers and intestines as well as four pigeon livers and sauté them in melted fat for a few minutes only. Mash and sieve. Place the purée in a pan, thin with white wine and two spoonfuls of roast veal juice. Simmer for a few minutes, add salt, pepper, a drop of lemon, and pour this sauce on the woodcock, which has been cut beforehand into five portions: two legs, two wings, the fifth portion being the head and carcass.

Ragoût à la Crème et au Sang

Proceed as above. When removing the sauce from the heat, add a spoonful of cream and one of blood. After this addition, boiling should be ceased; that goes without saying.

Snipe

We are lucky enough to have a snipe drive. It is a long field with banks along either side, patches of dry and wet, with reeds in clumps and an overgrown hedge at the far end. As soon as you hear the words 'We are now going to do the snipe bog, will you all try to get into your places as quietly as possible,' you know that pandemonium is about to break out. Having negotiated a particularly treacherous barbed-wire fence where someone invariably lets loose a dog, there is a ditch normally fairly full of water. All the people wearing boots plunge over and look back to the forlorn souls standing sadly gazing at their shoes. Everyone then starts whispering advice and enormous 'Sh, sh, shss!' and after much splashing and cursing and apologetic glances at the host, they all move off to their places behind the hedge – only no one is ever in the right place so we shunt up and down pegging and unpegging dogs, banging shooting sticks and shaking cartridge bags so that by the time the drive is half over, everyone is in their right place and every snipe in the country must know exactly where we all are. Even after all that it is still one of the most exciting drives – it's just that maybe that is why I haven't cooked as many snipe as I might have!

There are three varieties of snipe – the Common Snipe, the Great Snipe, and the Jack Snipe. The Common Snipe is native, though the numbers are greatly increased by immigrants from North West Europe. He usually weighs about 100 g (4 oz) and has 14 tail feathers. The Great Snipe does not nest in this country so the occasional one that does appear has wandered in from migratory route. His average weight is 200 g (8 oz) and he has 16 tail feathers, the outer four on each side being mostly white. Then there is the dear little Jack Snipe. He does not nest in this country but comes down from the Arctic in September until March, never flying in very large numbers together. He flies very short distances and drops as though he had been shot, which can be amusing, for as he is being claimed by some proud gun he is inclined to flit off for another 50 yards and drops down again. This variety's weight is about 70 g ($2\frac{1}{2}$ oz), yet the egg weighs 40 g ($1\frac{1}{2}$ oz)!

As with woodcock, many people dislike snipe. Maybe it is because they have been told that they should be cooked without being cleaned and this subconsciously revolts them whether they are cleaned or not. Hang them for 3–4 days unless it is very cold, when they keep longer.

Grilled Snipe

Snipe are so small that they can be grilled very quickly instead of roasting them.

1 snipe
1 tablespoon melted butter
1 slice streaky bacon

Heat the grill. Brush the bird well with melted butter, place the streaky bacon over each breast and place under grill, only not too high as you don't want black bits.

Serve as Roast Snipe (see page 88).

Roast Snipe

1 snipe
1–2 tablespoons butter
1 slice streaky bacon
1 croûton of bread
lemon quarter

Try to be very careful when plucking the birds – handle them as gently as possible to avoid breaking the skin. Do not clean them but remove the gizzard. This is entirely up to you – if you clean them put a good knob of butter inside. The head should be left on but skinned, then turned back and the long beak used as a skewer.

Brush the bird well with melted butter and put the slice of streaky bacon over the breast. Roast in a very hot oven (220°C, 425°F, Mark 7) for 6–15 minutes, depending how you like them. When they are cooked, serve them on a croûton of bread fried in butter. Either you can take out the entrails, mash them and spread them on the croûton, or make a paste of sautéed chicken livers and a little butter and spread that on the croûton. Serve with a quarter of lemon and pan gravy.

Snipe cooked as Italians would cook Larks

5 tablespoons olive oil
12 small birds
1 small tin Italian tomato paste
6 rolled and pounded anchovies
salt and cayenne to taste
1½ cloves garlic, mashed
100 g (4 oz) black olives, chopped
6 tablespoons red wine, cider or vinegar
250 ml (½ pint) veal or chicken stock
Marsala or sherry to taste
fried croûtons, 2.5 cm (1 in) thick

Heat about 4 tablespoons of the oil and brown the birds lightly but quickly. Make a sauce by mixing tomato paste, anchovies, salt and cayenne, garlic, olives, red wine, cider or vinegar and stock. Simmer the sauce, put the birds in it, cover, and cook until tender, about 30 minutes. Stir in Marsala or sherry. Fry slices of brown bread in rest of olive oil. Place bird on bread and pour over sauce.

A Pilau of Small Game Birds (Snipe or Pigeon)

150 g (6 oz) rice
875 ml (1¾ pints) chicken stock
8 slices smoked bacon, minced
1 medium onion, minced
4 good stalks celery, finely chopped
6 eggs, beaten
8–10 small birds, cleaned
6 tablespoons wine vinegar
6 tablespoons mild French mustard
salt and pepper
olive oil

This is an old-fashioned recipe from Virginia, based on a recipe from *The Gentleman's Companion*.

Cook rice in chicken stock until not quite done. Drain and turn out in a shallow pan to dry in a warm oven. Fry bacon; reserve. In bacon fat, brown onion and celery lightly (you may need to add a little butter). Remove celery and onion from fat and mix with bacon. Mix these with rice and stir in beaten eggs. Stuff the birds with this and sew them up. Mix together vinegar and mustard. Season birds, brush with olive oil, and brown in a moderately hot oven (190°C, 375°F, Mark 5) for 30 minutes, basting frequently with the vinegar and mustard mixture. Place birds on serving dish, surround them with a ring of cooked rice, and pour the basting juices over everything.

You may substitute wild rice and raisins for the plain white rice and onions in the stuffing.

Snipe Loaf

From Mrs R. W. Lowe, Farmwood Cottage, Chelford, Cheshire.

150 g (6 oz) mushrooms
6 shallots
100 g (4 oz) streaky bacon
1 clove garlic
1 egg
1 800 g (2 lb) loaf bread
75 g (3 oz) butter, melted
8 snipe
1 tablespoon brandy, warmed
salt and pepper

Wipe and slice mushrooms. Peel and slice shallots, chop bacon and crush clove of garlic. Beat egg.

Cut off end of loaf and scrape out the crumbs. Reserve end. Brush inside and out of loaf first with half of the melted butter then with beaten egg. Bake for 7–10 minutes until brown and crisp.

Meanwhile place the garlic into remaining butter, carefully putting to one side of pan in order to discard garlic when butter is flavoured. Fry chopped shallots until tender and keep warm. Lightly fry snipe, turning carefully, and add to the shallots. Then fry bacon and add mushrooms to bacon fat. Moisten snipe with warm brandy and add freshly ground black pepper and salt.

Pack loaf first with bacon and mushrooms and then with snipe and shallots in layers. Secure end of loaf back into position. Parcel loosely in foil and bake in a moderate oven (180°C, 350°F, Mark 4) for 20 minutes. Remove foil and crisp for a further 5 minutes.

Serve cut into thick slices with green beans.

Pigeon

We never seem to have the right number of pigeons. It is either one or 26, and when you have one you are told that you can get 15p for them at the butcher, and when you have 26 the butcher says he doesn't want them. They are the easiest birds to pluck, the feathers almost float off, but then they go on floating and get into everything. Pigeons are definitely best plucked out of doors. If you are suffering from a glut, the quickest thing to do is to peel back the unplucked skin from the breasts and take out the breasts with a sharp knife. It sounds extravagant, but most of the meat is on the breast and often there isn't the time for a mammoth plucking session, and butchers are not always co-operative. It must be so much more inspiring to be one of those French housewives of whom we are always reading. They go to a market, buy a plucked squab all trussed and barbed and start from there. I normally start from a sack full of birds costing goodness knows how many cartridges, and I feel guilty because I should have done something about them yesterday.

There is no close season for pigeons, but as they are more plump and fat when they have been living off the farmers' fields, they are best between May and October. A young pigeon has softer, pinker legs than old ones, and a round plump breast. Wood pigeons make the best eating and may be distinguished by the white ring around their necks, except when immature. A pigeon does not need to be hung, though the crops should be emptied out as soon as possible.

Roast Pigeon

1 tablespoon chopped parsley or mixed
  herbs
100 g (4 oz) softened butter
salt and pepper
4 young pigeons
8 slices of pork fat or streaky bacon
  (pork fat is preferable as it stays on
  the bird better)
flour

Only very young plump pigeons are worth roasting.

Mix parsley or herbs with half of the butter, add some salt and pepper and put a lump in each bird. Truss and cover birds closely with pork or bacon. Place in a hot oven (200°C, 400°F, Mark 6) for 20–25 minutes, basting frequently with the remaining butter. Shortly before serving, remove fat, sprinkle with flour and allow to brown.

Pigeons in Cider or Beer

4 pigeons
2 onions, sliced
250 ml (½ pint) cider or beer
bouquet garni
pinch of mace
250 ml (½ pint) stock
beurre manié (flour and butter kneaded
  together)
juice of ½ lemon

Place pigeons closely together in a casserole and cover them with sliced onions. Pour over cider or beer, then add bouquet garni, mace and stock. Place in moderately slow oven (170°C, 325°F, Mark 3) for about 2 hours or until tender. Remove pigeons and keep warm. Remove bouquet garni and thicken gravy with beurre manié, add lemon juice to taste, pour over birds and serve.

Pigeon and Orange

From Mrs P. Coats.

4 pigeons
4 oranges or tangerines
4 rashers bacon
2 tablespoons lard
1 medium onion
2 shallots
200 g (8 oz) button mushrooms
1 tablespoon flour
salt and pepper
1 teaspoon mixed herbs
125 ml (¼ pint) Marsala or sherry

Stuff pigeons with oranges or tangerines and tie bacon over the breast. Brown in hot fat, then remove to a casserole. Chop onion and shallots finely and fry gently in fat until soft, but not coloured. Now add mushrooms and cook for a few minutes, shaking the pan. Sprinkle in the flour, salt, ground black pepper and mixed herbs, and finally stir in the Marsala or sherry gradually. Pour over pigeons, cover tightly, and put in a preheated moderately hot oven (190°C, 375°F, Mark 5) for 1–1½ hours.

Pigeons à la Duck

From Mrs G. Pilkington.

4 plucked and trussed pigeons
500 ml (1 pint) water
1 onion, quartered
pinch of mixed herbs
peppercorns
stock cube
1 bayleaf

Sauce
1 tablespoon brown sugar
grated peel and juice of 1 orange
200 g (8 oz) sliced mushrooms, fried
  in butter

It is important to boil the whole bird so that the breasts do not reduce in size as they do if struck off the bird and cooked separately.

Boil and simmer whole pigeons in water with onion, herbs, peppercorns, stock cube and bayleaf for 40 minutes, then let them cool in the juice.

Make a sauce by mixing the sauce ingredients together in a pan. Adjust seasoning. Remove breasts from pigeons, slice thinly, place in serving dish and cover with sauce. Warm and serve with appropriate vegetables.

375 ml (¾ pint) pigeon liquid (add more if necessary)
70 ml (2½ oz) sherry, brandy or port
1 tablespoon butter and flour melted and mixed (beurre manié) for thickening

Pigeon Pie

Cut the rump steak into small pieces, roll in seasoned flour and brown in hot dripping or oil in a frying pan. Place this on the bottom of a large pie dish. Place the pigeons or pigeon breasts on top and then the bacon or ham, thickly sliced eggs, salt, pepper and parsley. Pour in 2 tablespoons water. Cover with flaky pastry, leaving a hole in the centre.

Bake for about 2 hours in a moderate oven (180°C, 350°F, Mark 4). Just before serving fill up with boiling stock to which you have added the Worcestershire sauce.

400 g (1 lb) rump steak
seasoned flour
dripping or oil
3 pigeons or 8 pigeon breasts
100 g (4 oz) diced bacon or ham
2 hard-boiled eggs
salt and pepper
2 tablespoons chopped parsley
200 g (8 oz) flaky pastry
750 ml (1½ pints) good stock
1 teaspoon Worcestershire sauce, if you wish

Pigeon Breast Pie

This is a simple recipe from the *Women's Institute Cook Book*.

It is not necessary to pluck the pigeon for this recipe. Part the feathers and slit the skin over the breasts with a sharp knife; they can then be removed easily.

For every three breasts allow one hard-boiled egg and 50 g (2 oz) of fat bacon cut into strips. Simmer breasts in 250 ml (½ pint) stock or water plus stock cube with pepper and salt until tender. Remove meat from bones and put into a pie dish with alternate layers of bacon and sliced hard-boiled egg. Add pepper and salt and a little of the liquor the breasts were simmered in. Keep the rest as gravy for the pie. Cover with a flaky pastry and bake in a hot oven (200°C, 400°F, Mark 6) until the pastry is cooked, then continue at a lower heat for 30–40 minutes to allow the bacon to cook. Serve hot.

Button mushrooms may be added to the pie if available. Serve with green peas and mashed potatoes.

pigeon breasts
hard-boiled eggs
fat bacon
salt and pepper
flaky pastry
button mushrooms (optional)

Les Palombes à la Béarnaise

Elizabeth David.

The wild doves and the wood-pigeons of the Landes and the Béarn are particularly delicious little birds. The ordinary pigeons which one buys in England are rather dull and dry, but cooked à la Béarnaise they can be excellent.

93

First of all braise the pigeons in butter, in a covered pan, for 30–40 minutes, until they are tender. Take them out, cut them in halves and put into a bowl with the juice of a lemon, a glass of white wine or brandy, salt and pepper, and leave them in this marinade while you prepare a purée made from the hearts of cooked artichokes, at least three for each pigeon. Put this purée into an earthenware casserole with a lump of butter; sauté the livers of the pigeons in the butter in which the birds have originally cooked, adding the wine or brandy marinade, and press them through a sieve, with the liquid, into the artichoke purée, put the pigeons on top of the purée and heat it gently.

Failing artichokes, a purée of broad beans or of Jerusalem artichokes or of celery will serve quite well.

Casserole of Pigeon

3 or 4 young pigeons
100 g (4 oz) butter
100 g (4 oz) ham or streaky bacon, diced
150 ml (6 oz) red wine
250 ml (½ pint) white or game stock
bouquet garni of parsley, bayleaf, thyme
salt and pepper
100 g (4 oz) small mushrooms
12–18 small white onions
3 sticks celery cut into 2.5 cm (1 in) pieces
40 g (1½ oz) raisins
redcurrant jelly (optional)
beurre manié (optional)

Truss pigeons. Melt 50 g (2 oz) of the butter in a pan and brown bacon or ham first, then the pigeons. Add wine, stock, herbs and seasoning. Cover, and cook for 2 hours. During this time sauté mushrooms, onions and celery lightly in rest of butter. Add these and the raisins to the casserole. Cook for a further 45 minutes.

Remove from oven, cut pigeons in half and place on serving dish with the vegetables. Add redcurrant jelly to gravy if you wish, and thicken with beurre manié. Bring to boil, pour a little over the birds and serve the rest separately. Fried croûtons of bread are also good with this dish.

Casserole of Pigeon with Rice

By kind permission of James Beard.

4 young pigeons
250 ml (½ pint) olive oil
salt and pepper
2 cloves garlic, finely chopped
2 onions, finely chopped
1 green pepper, thinly sliced
100 ml (4 oz) broth or water
250 g (10 oz) rice
45 g (1¾ oz) pine or pignolia nuts (we substitute peanuts or almonds but if they are salted be careful not to add too much salt)
100 g (4 oz) mushrooms, sliced
3 pimentos, thinly sliced
2 teaspoons paprika
500 ml (1 pint) stock or water and 2 stock cubes

Singe, clean and draw the pigeons. Heat 200 ml (8 oz) of the olive oil in a casserole and brown the pigeons well on all sides. Add salt and pepper to taste, and garlic, onions, green pepper, and the broth. Cover casserole and place in a preheated moderate oven (180°C, 350°F, Mark 4) for 20 minutes. (If older pigeons are used make this 1 hour.)

Brown rice very lightly in the rest of the oil. Add this to casserole after the birds have had the first cooking, with the nuts, mushrooms, pimentos and paprika. Cover with either the stock or stock cubes mixed with the water. Do not cover the casserole. Replace it in the oven and cook until rice is cooked and flaky and the liquid is entirely cooked away. More liquid may be added if necessary. Pigeons may be split for this dish if you so desire.

Casserole of Pigeon with Tomatoes

This has an Italian flavour: in fact, if you were using only pigeon breasts you could cut them into cubes and use it as a sauce for spaghetti.

Brown pigeons in oil, remove. Lightly brown onion and garlic, celery and herbs. Add tomatoes and salt and pepper to taste, and stir around so they are all mixed. Replace pigeons, baste well with sauce, cover tightly and put in a moderate oven (180°C, 350°F, Mark 4) until the birds are tender, about 1½ hours.

4 pigeons
2 tablespoons olive oil
1 onion, chopped
1 clove garlic, mashed
2 sticks celery, chopped
1 bayleaf
a pinch of thyme and basil or a shake of Italian herbs
1 medium tin tomatoes
salt and pepper

Casserole of Pigeon with Rice and Bacon

This is another recipe from the *Women's Institute Cook Book*. It is simple and good.

Soak pigeons in salted water for 30 minutes, then put them whole in the casserole with the stock, rice and carrots cut in rings. Add bayleaf, wine and seasoning to taste. Cook, covered, in a slow oven (150°C, 300°F, Mark 2) for 3 hours. Add bacon fat after 2 hours and, if necessary, a little more boiling stock.

Serve with redcurrant or gooseberry jelly and sprouts, with a dash of nutmeg and a knob of butter added before serving.

2 pigeons
250 ml (½ pint) stock or water
100 g (4 oz) rice
3 carrots
1 bayleaf
1 tablespoon white wine
salt and pepper
2 rashers bacon fat

Pigeons en Cocotte

Heat butter and brown pigeons slowly, then remove pigeons and brown bacon and onions carefully; remove and brown mushrooms, cook quickly, remove. Shake in some flour, blend, and gradually add stock and wine. Season. Return pigeons, bacon, onions and mushrooms to pan, spoon over sauce, bring to boiling point, cover tightly, and cook in a moderately slow oven (170°C, 325°F, Mark 3) for about 2 hours.

Instead of wine and mushrooms you can substitute 2 cooking apples and cider.

25 g (1 oz) butter
4 pigeons
100 g (4 oz) bacon or ham, diced and blanched
1 onion, finely chopped, or 10–15 small white onions, or 1 packet frozen onions (remove white sauce before unfreezing)
100 g (4 oz) mushrooms, sliced
1 tablespoon flour
250 ml (½ pint) white stock
125 ml (¼ pint) white wine
seasoning

Pigeon Breasts with Cabbage

Cut cabbage into fine slices, removing the hard centre core, and parboil in boiling salted water for 7 minutes. Drain thoroughly and press out all the water. Wrap each breast in a slice of streaky bacon and secure bacon with a wooden toothpick. Brown breasts in butter or bacon fat, remove breasts, and very lightly brown the onion.

1 medium sized hard cabbage
10–12 pigeon breasts
10–12 slices streaky bacon
25 g (1 oz) butter or bacon fat
1 onion, sliced
2 carrots, sliced
several crushed juniper berries
salt and pepper
a scrape of nutmeg
375 ml (¾ pint) stock (about)

Put a layer of cabbage in a deep casserole, lay the breasts on top, then the onion, carrots, juniper berries, salt and pepper and nutmeg. Cover with the remaining cabbage, and pour in stock to about halfway up. Cover with greaseproof paper and then a tight-fitting lid. Cook in a cool oven (140°C, 275°F, Mark 1) for about 3 hours. The gravy may need to be reduced or thickened slightly.

Pigeons with Cabbage

Cook as for Sautéed Pheasant with Cabbage (see page 58). Use 2 or 3 fat pigeons cut in half instead of the one pheasant. The cooking times remain the same.

Spanish Pigeon in Chocolate Sauce

4 pigeons
1 large onion, sliced
4 tablespoons olive oil
125 ml (¼ pint) dry white wine
750 ml (1½ pints) chicken stock (about), lightly seasoned
16–24 pickling onions
90 g (3½ oz) butter
2 teaspoons sugar
1 tablespoon flour
1½–2 teaspoons grated Bourneville or bitter chocolate
1 lemon, cut into wedges

This is a recipe of Jane Grigson's which I cut out of *The Observer* several years ago, so I was very amused when she suggested that I use it from the new paperback edition of her book *Good Things*. She suggests that you lard the pigeon first, but as they are cooked slowly and then served with a sauce, I don't think it is entirely necessary – however, if you have the time, it could make that little difference.

Chocolate makes an excellent seasoning for game sauces. Italian dishes of hare with chocolate and pine kernel sauce are famous. Here's a Spanish recipe for a similar but lighter dish. Do not be nervous of the chocolate if you have not used it in this kind of recipe before; so little is used that it is unidentifiable, yet the difference it makes in richness of flavour is surprising. Another important point of the dish is the glazed onions. Their moist sweetness goes well with dark, close pigeon meat. In Spain plump squabs would be used, so I have had to adapt the recipe to our tougher wild birds.

Brown the pigeons and sliced onion in the oil, then fit them into a casserole, the pigeons breast down. Pour in the white wine and enough chicken stock to cover the birds. Bring to the boil and simmer for 1½–2 hours until the pigeons are cooked.

An hour before the pigeons are cooked, prepare the glazed onions: prepare enough to make a single layer in a large, heavy saucepan. Cover with water. Add 50 g (2 oz) of the butter and the sugar. Boil hard so that the liquid evaporates to a golden brown glaze. Keep a careful eye on the onions towards the end of the cooking, as they must not burn. Shake the pan gently so that they are coated in the caramel.

When the birds are almost done, i.e. when the legs move loosely, and the meat begins to part from the breast-bone, remove 500 ml (1 pint) of stock from the casserole. Reduce it by boiling to just over half (this concentrates the flavour, which is why you must start with lightly seasoned chicken stock). Skim off fat and foam as it rises. Mash the remaining butter with the flour (beurre manié) and add it in small knobs to the reduced stock, which should now be kept at simmer point. When the sauce has thickened, correct the seasoning and stir in the chocolate gradually, to taste.

Arrange the cooked pigeons on a warm serving dish, with the glazed onions round them. Pour a little of the sauce over the birds, and put the rest into a sauce-boat. Arrange the lemon wedges among the onions.

Rabbit

My husband does not like rabbit. He didn't like it before myxomatosis so it can't be that – it is probably because they cause him a great deal of trouble and he thinks of them as vermin. I have seen him being enthusiastic eating rabbit in the South of France, but then he had a very beautiful hostess. At home the reception would have been quite different. There is a very strong prejudice against eating rabbit except for the enlightened few, and even the fact that the French consider them a delicacy doesn't help. It is a great pity, as there are delicious ways of preparing rabbit, which still have a flavour and taste far better than broiler chicken.

Myxomatosis has also put many country people off eating rabbits, but your husband or gamekeeper will know if your ground is clean. If you suspect myxomatosis look around the rabbit's eyes, and if they are in anyway swollen or with any scars or bare patches above the eyes, throw them away.

A good young rabbit should have soft ears which are easily torn and sharp teeth and claws. They should be plump with smooth fur – a rabbit becomes grey with age. They should be cleaned before they are hung by the hind legs, though they are best eaten fresh.

As they have little natural fat, rabbits must be well barded or larded and cooked with plenty of butter or oil. If you wish to get rid of any strong taste, soak them in salted water for several hours, changing the water as frequently as possible. A slice of lemon added to the water will whiten the meat. A female is considered more tender than a male.

A rabbit improves with marinating, preferably overnight. Use white wine or lemon juice in the marinade, unless the rabbit is to be cooked in red wine.

At the end of this chapter there are three recipes for squirrel.

Roast Rabbit

Marinade
250 ml (½ pint) white or red wine
1 slice of onion
1 clove of garlic
1 bayleaf
3 tablespoons olive oil
a good squeeze of lemon juice or 2
   tablespoons wine vinegar

1 young rabbit
50 g (2 oz) softened butter
4 slices of pork fat or streaky bacon

If you wish to roast rabbit it is better marinated overnight to make it more tender and to increase the flavour.

Marinate rabbit for several hours or overnight. Remove and dry well. Strain marinade. Cover rabbit with butter, placing a knob inside. Place pork fat or bacon over it. Truss. Put in a hot oven (200°C, 400°F, Mark 6) for an hour, basting frequently with butter and marinade. Remove rabbit from oven and skim any excess fat from juices. Add more wine if you wish more gravy, and thicken with a little beurre manié.

Civet de Lapin

This is another of Aunt Jean's French-thinking recipes.

Cut up the rabbit and marinate in three-quarters of a bottle Burgundy, and the following: one or two carrots and one onion, cut up, 3–4 cloves garlic, a little oil, and a bouquet garni of parsley, thyme and a bayleaf. Marinate for 3–4 hours, turning rabbit from time to time. Remove and drain rabbit in a colander.

Put some chicken or pork fat or margarine or half oil and half butter in a large saucepan. When hot, add rabbit, and turn as it colours so all sides are coloured. Mix well. Add 2 tablespoons flour. Mix so rabbit is floured all over. Flambé with 2 glasses of Cognac. Add all the marinade contents and some stock, which may be made with stock cubes. Add 1 tablespoon tomato paste. Mix well and see that no flour sticks to the bottom. Add more stock to cover and, if necessary, some salt and pepper to taste. Cover and cook for about 30 minutes, slowly, almost an hour really. Look at it from time to time and shake the pan. When done, remove meat on to a dish and cover it.

Strain sauce into a small copper pot. Use a Chinoise strainer and twist a whisk to get all the sauce into the pot. If too clear, add beurre manié. If using the blood, add a little sauce to the blood – do this off the heat, then add this to the rest of the sauce on the heat. Put meat back into saucepan. Pour over the sauce and add the garnish and leave for 5–6 minutes on the heat to blend. Put on serving dish and spoon sauce and garnish over the rabbit. Sprinkle with chopped parsley and put large croûtons around the dish.

Garnish 300 g (¾ lb) smoked bacon, 300–400 g (¾–1 lb) mushrooms, about 20 small onions.

Cut bacon into lardons, blanch, refresh, drain. Sauté in frying pan till slightly coloured. Cut mushrooms into quarters after removing stems. Sauté in pan bacon was cooked in, add butter, salt and pepper if necessary. Cook onions in boiling water, refresh and drain. Sauté in a clean pan with butter, salt, pepper and a pinch of sugar, until golden.

Sweet and Sour Rabbit (or Hare)

The rabbit should first be marinated for several hours or overnight. It should then be jointed and the pieces lightly fried in olive oil with the onions, then put into a casserole with the onions and the oil, the tomatoes, carrots, celery and turnip, wine vinegar, olives, capers, raisins and sugar. The casserole should be cooked in a moderate oven (180°C, 350°F, Mark 4) for a good hour or until the rabbit is tender.

Marinade $\frac{1}{2}$ bottle red wine, 1 bayleaf, fresh thyme, rosemary, 2 tablespoons olive oil, 4 cloves, 4 peppercorns, 1 clove garlic, parsley.

1 rabbit
2 tablespoons olive oil
3 onions, sliced
6 peeled tomatoes, chopped
3 carrots, sliced
2–3 sticks celery, chopped
1 small turnip, chopped
250 ml ($\frac{1}{2}$ pint) wine vinegar
12 stoned olives
2 teaspoons capers
20 seedless raisins
6 tablespoons sugar

Optional Rabbit

This is a rough guide on how to cook a rabbit depending on what you have available and how you feel.

Dry rabbit well and roll in seasoned flour, then wrap each piece with slices of bacon. Secure with a wooden toothpick and brown with onions in butter. (Alternatively, brown rabbit pieces in the butter with coarsely diced bacon and onions.) Place in casserole with wine or cider, and stock, garlic and bouquet garni. Cover and simmer until tender, about $1\frac{1}{2}$ hours.

When the rabbit is tender, remove bouquet and strain off the sauce. Reduce if necessary, or thicken with flour mixed with a little stock. Pour back over rabbit and serve sprinkled with finely chopped parsley.

Variations Add some tomato purée or 3 sliced, cored and peeled green apples when you add the wine and stock. Or you may sauté some mushrooms and add them when you pour over the sauce at the end.

1 rabbit cut into pieces
200 g (8 oz) streaky bacon
2 tablespoons seasoned flour
2 large onions, thinly sliced
75 g (3 oz) butter
125 ml ($\frac{1}{4}$ pint) white wine or cider
250 ml ($\frac{1}{2}$ pint) stock
1 clove garlic, crushed
1 bouquet garni of bayleaf, parsley and thyme
1 tablespoon finely chopped parsley

Swedish Curried Rabbit

Cut rabbit into serving pieces. Rub pieces with salt and pepper and brown in butter all over, then remove from pan. Fry

1 medium sized rabbit
2 teaspoons salt

pepper
3 tablespoons butter
1 red onion, chopped
3 tablespoons flour
1 teaspoon curry powder
500 ml (1 pint) stock
2 teaspoons lemon juice
3 tablespoons cream

onion, flour and curry powder together, add stock and bring to boil. Replace meat, add lemon juice and simmer, covered, for about one hour or until tender.

Arrange on a hot platter, pour cream into gravy, bring to boil, season if necessary, and pour over meat. Serve with boiled rice.

Rabbit My Way

From Mrs Bo Thelander.

1 rabbit
8–10 potatoes
3 onions
2 tablespoons butter or margarine
salt and pepper
1 bottle light beer

Cut rabbit into serving pieces. Peel and slice potatoes and onions in not too thin slices. Melt butter and brown rabbit in a big stew pan. Season with salt and pepper to taste. Take out rabbit, then put sliced potatoes and onions in the pan and arrange rabbit on top. Add salt to flavour the potatoes, and pour the beer over the rabbit. Cover with a lid and let simmer slowly until rabbit is tender.

Fricassée of Rabbit

1 rabbit
1 onion, sliced
1 carrot, sliced
1 celery stick, sliced
4 tablespoons butter
salt and pepper
1 tablespoon flour
500 ml (1 pint) boiling white stock
150 ml (6 oz) white wine
1 bouquet garni
2 egg yolks
125 ml (¼ pint) double cream
squeeze of lemon juice
scrape of nutmeg
100 g (4 oz) mushrooms and/or 16 white onions

Cut up the rabbit into serving pieces and dry thoroughly. Sauté the onion, carrot and celery gently in the butter until they are soft. Add rabbit and turn in butter until golden. Cover and cook very slowly for 10 minutes. Sprinkle with salt, pepper and flour on all sides, and cook for a few minutes more. Pour in the boiling stock and white wine, add the bouquet garni and enough water so that the liquid covers the rabbit. Cover and simmer slowly for 45 minutes or until tender. Drain off liquid and reduce it to about 500 ml (1 pint). Whisk egg yolks with double cream, add some of the hot liquid to this and then whisk it back into the remaining sauce. Heat quickly, stirring all the time. Add salt and pepper if necessary, and lemon juice and nutmeg. Place rabbit in a serving dish, pour over sauce and surround with sautéed mushrooms or sautéed little white onions if you wish.

Rabbit in Red Wine

1 rabbit
100 g (4 oz) bacon
2 tablespoons olive oil
2 onions, sliced
salt and pepper
500 ml (1 pint) red wine
500 ml (1 pint) stock
1 tablespoon cornflour

Cut the rabbit into pieces and marinate for a day or more in the refrigerator.

Blanch bacon, cut into thin strips. Brown in olive oil and then add onions. Remove. Dry rabbit well and brown, adding more oil if necessary. Put onion, bacon and rabbit in casserole, and season with salt and pepper. Reduce strained marinade until it has nearly evaporated, then add red wine. Reduce this slightly and add stock. Pour all this into casserole and simmer slowly on cooker or in oven until tender, about 1½ hours. When ready, drain off sauce, skim off fat, then either reduce further or thicken with a little cornflour mixed with water. You may add mushrooms if you like. Sprinkle with parsley and surround with croûtons.

optional
400 g (1 lb) mushrooms, sautéed
1 tablespoon finely chopped parsley
croûtons

Marinade   125 ml (¼ pint) red wine vinegar, 3 tablespoons olive oil, 2 large cloves garlic, 1 large onion, sliced, a few crushed juniper berries, fresh ground black pepper, 1 bayleaf, marjoram, thyme.

Rabbit with Onions

This recipe was donated by Mrs Bo Thelander, who informed me that it was originally a Greek chicken recipe but she found it works wonders with rabbit.

1 rabbit
3 tablespoons butter or margarine
salt and pepper
125 ml (¼ pint) water
8–10 onions
2–3 tablespoons tomato paste
1 tablespoon vinegar

Cut rabbit into serving pieces. Melt half of the butter and brown the rabbit in it. Season with salt and pepper. Add water, cover with lid, and simmer over slow heat for about 15–20 minutes. Peel and slice onions. Melt the rest of the butter in a skillet and fry the onions until golden. Add tomato paste, vinegar, salt and pepper, and stir well. Put onions in a deep ovenproof dish. Put rabbit on top. Cover with lid or foil. Bake in moderate oven (180°C, 350°F, Mark 4) for 30–40 minutes or until rabbit is tender. Add a little more water if it seems to be dry.

Rabbit Covered in Onions

This is adapted straight from the hare recipe (see page 116).

Rabbit with Apples

Cut rabbit into pieces and marinate in the refrigerator overnight.
   Dry pieces and brown lightly in butter. Remove rabbit and add apples and onions. Put the rabbit back into this and add the cream. Cover, and cook this very slowly for about 1½ hours or until tender. Remove meat and keep warm, put the sauce through a liquidizer with the lemon juice. Reheat sauce and pour over rabbit.

1 rabbit
2 tablespoons butter
3 green apples, sliced, peeled and cored
3 onions, sliced
250 ml (½ pint) cream
juice of ½ lemon

Marinade   1 sliced onion, 1 sliced carrot, 2 sprigs parsley, 1 bayleaf, salt and pepper, thyme, 150 ml (6 oz) white wine, 1 tablespoon olive oil.

Rabbit with Mustard

1 rabbit
4–5 slices streaky bacon
2 tablespoons butter
2 tablespoons oil
3 medium onions, chopped
1 small clove garlic, mashed
3 carrots, sliced
2 tablespoons brandy
125 ml (¼ pint) dry white wine
125 ml (¼ pint) chicken stock
thyme
1 bayleaf
1 teaspoon English mustard
2 teaspoons Dijon mustard
125 ml (¼ pint) double cream
1 tablespoon finely chopped parsley

Cut a young tender rabbit into serving pieces and wrap each piece in streaky bacon, securing it with a wooden toothpick. Brown these until golden in butter and oil. Remove rabbit and brown onions, garlic and carrots in remaining fat. Replace rabbit and add brandy, dry white wine and chicken stock. Sprinkle with thyme and add bayleaf, then cover, and cook very gently until tender, about 2 hours. Remove rabbit from casserole and keep warm; discard bayleaf. Skim fat off sauce and whisk in mustards and double cream; stir well and heat carefully. Pour over rabbit and sprinkle with parsley.

Rabbit with Tarragon

1 rabbit and liver if you wish
1 tablespoon seasoned flour
75 g (3 oz) butter
125 ml (¼ pint) white wine
½ clove garlic (optional)
2 tablespoons fresh tarragon leaves or
    2 teaspoons dried tarragon

Cut rabbit into pieces and dust with seasoned flour. Melt butter in a casserole and brown rabbit quickly on all sides, taking care not to burn. Reduce heat and add the white wine – you may also put the garlic in with the wine as long as you remember to remove it before you serve the juices. Cover casserole and simmer gently for about 45 minutes or until tender. When ready, add tarragon leaves (if you must use dried ones, soak them first for 30 minutes in water and drain). Stir around so that all the leaves are moist and cook for about another 5 minutes. Take out garlic. The liver may be sautéed in butter, chopped and added before serving. If, to you, the juices seem rather insipid, you may add a little Bovril (½ teaspoon), but I like them as they are.

Rabbit with Black Grapes and Tomatoes

1 rabbit
3 tablespoons oil
2 onions, chopped
3 sticks celery, chopped
2 tablespoons flour
125 ml (¼ pint) red wine
250 ml (½ pint) stock
1 small tin tomatoes and juice
1 teaspoon tomato purée
salt and pepper
1 clove garlic, mashed
a splash of Worcestershire sauce
1 teaspoon mixed herbs
4 tablespoons blood
200 g (8 oz) black grapes
200 g (8 oz) tomatoes

Cut up rabbit into pieces, brown well in oil, remove and keep warm. Soften onions and celery in the pan, add the flour and brown lightly. Add wine, stock and tinned tomatoes and purée, seasoning, garlic, Worcestershire sauce and herbs. Bring to boil and add rabbit. Cook in a slow oven (150°C, 300°F, Mark 2) for about 1¼ hours. Mix 1 tablespoon of the gravy in with the blood then add this slowly back with the rest of the gravy. Add freshly cut tomatoes and pipped black grapes.

This freezes well, in which case add grapes and tomatoes when unfrozen.

Rabbit Rillettes

This is Jane Grigson's recipe. She suggests it as an hors d'œuvre or for children's teas. What it is very good for is spread on good thick slices of crusty bread and passed with drinks before a shooting lunch. As we always have our one-course lunches in a hut, this along with potted meats and pâtés is very popular while the guns stand around greeting each other as though they hadn't met for years instead of 15 minutes ago.

600 g (1½ lb) pork belly
100 g (4 oz) hard back fat
800 g (2 lb) rabbit joints
good sprig of thyme
nutmeg
cinnamon
salt and pepper
lard

Cut pork and pork fat into 3.5 cm (1½ in) cubes and place in a heavy-bottomed pan with rabbit, thyme and 5 tablespoons water. Cover, and cook over a low heat or in a cool oven (140°C, 275°F, Mark 1) for 4 hours or until all the meat falls off the bones. Pour into a large strainer over a bowl, remove bones, thyme and pork skin. Crush meat with a pestle, then tear it to shreds with a couple of forks. You may liquidize it, but do not pulverize it into sludge – it must remain thready. Season generously with nutmeg, cinnamon, salt and pepper, and add some of the strained juices – but not too much or they will congeal solidly as they set. Sterilize bottling jars or rillette mugs. Reheat rillettes to boiling point, add salt to taste, and pack into jars or mugs. Allow to cool, then cover with 1.5 cm (½ in) melted lard and jam-pot covers or plastic wrap. Keep in refrigerator if possible.

Squirrel

In this country we seldom eat squirrel, in America they consider it a great delicacy. Possibly we ought to try, as I have read that it is far superior to venison and a taste from which you do not tire. It would be a pity to shoot the pretty little red squirrel in order to test these recipes, but as the grey squirrel is a menace to every forester and occasionally eats eggs and is always unwelcome on the property, maybe he should not be discarded with the rest of the vermin but tried in the stew pot.

Brunswick Stew

Cut the two plump squirrels into serving pieces. Dredge the pieces in well-seasoned flour and brown them in the fat with the onions. Transfer the meat and onions to an earthenware casserole and add 3 cups boiling water, the tomatoes, red peppers and a generous pinch of thyme. Cover the casserole and simmer the stew for one hour. Add the lima beans and okra, the corn and chopped parsley and Worcestershire sauce. Cover the casserole, and simmer the mixture until the meat and vegetables are tender. Thicken the sauce slightly with equal amounts of the butter and flour kneaded together, and serve in casserole.

2 young squirrels
well seasoned flour (flour, salt, pepper and garlic, mixed)
2 tablespoons lard or oil
6 onions, thinly sliced
6 tomatoes, peeled and sliced
3 red peppers, chopped
pinch of thyme
800 g (2 lb) lima beans and okra
kernels from 6 ears of fresh corn or small tin of corn niblets
1 tablespoon parsley
1 tablespoon Worcestershire sauce
equal quantities butter and flour, mixed

Squirrels in Cider

3 squirrels
seasoned flour
100 g (4 oz) fat ham, diced
hard cider to barely cover
2 tablespoons butter
200 ml (8 oz) hot cream
½ tablespoon flour, 1 tablespoon butter
  mixed
salt and pepper

Skin, clean and disjoint the three plump squirrels. Soak the pieces in cold salted water for 20 minutes, wipe them dry and dust them with seasoned flour. In a heavy skillet, brown the diced fat ham. Add the squirrels and brown the pieces well on all sides in the ham fat. Add enough hard cider barely to cover the squirrel, cover the skillet, and simmer the liquid until most of it has evaporated and the meat is tender. Add the butter, increase the heat, and quickly brown the pieces of meat once more. Remove the squirrel to a warm serving platter, add the cream to the juices remaining in the skillet, then stir in all the brown bits from the bottom and sides of the pan. Stir in, bit by bit, the flour and butter paste, correct the seasoning with salt and pepper, and strain the sauce into a gravy-boat.

Belgian Squirrel — also good for Rabbit

3 squirrels
2-3 tablespoons butter
2 medium onions
3 tablespoons vinegar
large pinch of thyme
salt and pepper
18 prunes
1½ tablespoons flour

Clean the squirrels, wash and dry them thoroughly. Cut them up into serving pieces. Put the butter in a frying pan and melt. Put in the squirrel pieces and brown them on all sides. Do not cook them, just brown them. Remove the squirrel pieces and place them in a deep cooking pot. Slice the onions and brown them in the leftover butter in the frying pan. When they are done, put the onions and the melted butter on the squirrel pieces in the pot. Then add enough water to nearly cover the meat. Add vinegar, thyme, salt and pepper to taste. Cover the pot and place in a moderate oven (180°C, 350°F, Mark 4) for 1 hour. Now remove the pot and put the prunes in the water. Be sure to put them in the water so they sink. Then reduce the oven heat to moderately slow (170°C, 325°F, Mark 3) and bake for 45 minutes. Now remove the pot. Mix the flour in a cup of cold water and blend until it contains no lumps. Then add this to the sauce in the pot. Place the pot on top of your stove at medium heat. Stir until it thickens. This usually takes from 10 to 15 minutes. Timing in making a sauce or gravy is the important thing. Watch when the gravy begins to form bubbles. It is just right when a nape or a coating forms on your spoon or ladle when you dip it in to test the consistency of the gravy.

Serve the squirrel hot with lots of gravy, spooning the gravy onto potatoes or toast. It is just wonderful. A person who simply cannot stand wild game will learn to like it quickly after a taste of this dish.

Hare

When I started to cook game I hardly considered hare, but through the years I have come to respect it more and more. It used to be almost free food. Now we export huge numbers of them to Germany which has pushed the price up to nearly a pound for a fully mature hare. Still, 90p for a dinner for 6–8 people isn't bad, and young hares from your larder are still cheap as they must be 2.8 kg (7 lb) in weight to be suitable for export.

I don't like preparing a hare. I have to think of some beautiful thoughts to follow before I begin, and need quite a lot of fresh air. You tell a young hare by its soft thin ears which tear easily, by its small, white sharp teeth and by its smooth coat. An old hare will have large yellow teeth, a wavy coat and a more pronounced lip. They are at their best from harvest time to February. The hare who is eating your new roses during April will not be good – its flesh will be strong and tough.

The mountain hare, which in Scotland is called blue, is an inferior variety. It weighs between 2–2.4 kg (5–6 lb) and is really best kept for the stew or stock pot.

Hares should be hung head down, ungutted, for one to two weeks; as always, the time depends on the weather. Place a bowl underneath the hare to catch the blood. A teaspoon of vinegar in the bowl stops the blood from congealing. They lose about one-third of their weight when they are cleaned. A young hare (or leveret as they are called) does not need marinating, but it helps to give flavour. Much depends on its age and how long it has been hung as to how long you wish to marinate it. A marinade increases the flavour and lubricates the flesh, so if you are roasting it without this step make sure it is well larded or basted. Hare should be well cooked.

If you find that it is rather over-hung or musty inside, wash it in a solution of Milton.

Skinning a Rabbit or Hare

There are several ways of tackling this. Your rabbit will have been gutted before he was hung so won't be as messy as a hare. I gut my hare after it is skinned, particularly if I'm trying to catch the blood.

Sever all four legs at the first joint. Cut through the skin around the hind legs, just below the tail.

Peel skin down off hind legs as if you were taking off a stocking. Tie hind legs together and hang on a hook, then put a bowl underneath with 1 teaspoonful of vinegar in it to catch the blood. Pull skin down over body and forelegs. I dislike the head so I cut it off. Cut the hare up the middle, being careful not to cut into its gall bladder, and keep the liver. Much of the blood will have collected in the rib cage – try to catch this in the bowl. Rinse meat in cold water and dry with paper towels. Remove the blue membrane.

Marinade for Hare

1 bottle red wine
6 tablespoons olive oil
1 small sliced onion
5 juniper berries, crushed
1 clove garlic, crushed
1 bayleaf
a little thyme
black pepper

I can't commit myself on exactly what I put in a marinade – being capricious I will suddenly do something quite different to what I have done for years. Consider the meat that you are going to cook. The older it is the stronger (more acid) the marinade should be. This is a good one for hare, but you may substitute wine vinegar, lemon juice or brandy in a smaller quantity for the red wine, and of course you will need far less if you are only doing a saddle.

Roast Hare

1 hare
salt and pepper
French mustard
2 tablespoons melted butter
375 ml (¾ pint) beef stock (a cube will do)
2–3 juniper berries

Gravy
2 egg yolks
1 teaspoon cornflour
3 tablespoons cream
Worcestershire sauce
salt and pepper
2 tablespoons port (optional)

Kindly sent to us by Count Von Eggeling.

Prepare hare by cutting off the back legs, then cut the ribs lengthwise as close to the meat of the back as you can. Leave the back in one whole piece. The head, front legs and ribs can be used for stewing.

The roast back of a hare will serve four, but if there are more guests the back legs should be used as well. They are prepared in the same way but take about 10 minutes longer to cook than the back.

The fine skin covering the meat must be taken off as well as the whitish-blue skin, which has to be removed with a sharp knife. Salt and pepper the prepared meat, and brush well with French mustard. Baste with the melted butter and roast slowly in a moderate oven (180°C, 350°F, Mark 4), basting frequently with the remaining butter. When all the butter has been used up, continue to baste with beef stock. This should be done in small quantities in order to give the gravy time to mature. The juniper berries should be crushed and added as soon as roasting starts.

To make gravy, mix all ingredients together and add to the gravy from the hare. This should be done in a small saucepan, and the gravy from the hare brought to the boil before adding the egg mixture. The gravy should be strained before serving. The port can be added just before serving.

The hare is served with stewed apple, cranberry sauce, potatoes and red cabbage.

Roast Saddle of Hare

a marinade
1 saddle of hare
lard, bacon fat, dripping or butter
French mustard (optional)

Marinate the saddle for 24 hours. Either lard the saddle or cover well with bacon fat, dripping or butter, and French mustard if you wish. Place in a hot oven (200°C, 400°F, Mark

6), baste frequently and cook for about 35 minutes. Remove saddle and keep warm while you make a gravy in the pan by adding all gravy ingredients.

This should serve 3–4 people.

Gravy
strained marinade or red wine
cream
extra mustard or cream and chestnut
    purée

Jugged Hare I

Jugged hare is another of these dishes where you can let yourself go and put in roughly what suits you. You don't have to use little whole onions, you may use chopped or sliced onions or shallots. I have a huge list of ingredients that I have discovered are used in recipes for jugged hare, and every one has a different method. The first recipe is more classically British and it is jugged. Mollie's is just a variation done in a casserole and is more the German way of tackling the same problem.

You can buy large brown stoneware milk jugs which are perfect for the job as well as being ideal for cooking kippers in, or you may use a deep crock which is just as good and, so really is an ordinary casserole. The others just seem more fun.

Dust the pieces of hare with seasoned flour and brown them in butter or lard along with little onions and bacon. Pour off fat and add herbs and stock; bring to boil. Transfer all this into your jug or crock, cover well with foil and stand it in a deep pan of hot water. Put in a slow oven (150°C, 300°F, Mark 2) and cook until very tender, about 2 hours. Just before you wish to serve it, mash the liver in a little of the hot liquid, add the blood to this and then stir it back into the crock. Stir in port, redcurrant jelly and lemon juice to taste. Serve with forcemeat balls.

1 hare cut into pieces, keep liver and blood (marinate hare if wished)
2 tablespoons seasoned flour
25 g (1 oz) butter or lard
200 g (8 oz) small white onions or 2 packets frozen onions with white sauce (remove white sauce before unfreezing)
200 g (8 oz) streaky bacon cut into small pieces
thyme, bayleaf, parsley
250 ml (½ pint) good stock
70 ml (2½ oz) port
1 tablespoon redcurrant jelly
juice of ½ lemon
forcemeat balls

Mollie's Jugged Hare II

Clean and skin a joint of hare. Melt half of the butter in a frying pan. Sprinkle hare with salt and pepper and brown in butter. Place in casserole. Add onion, herbs, lemon juice, half of the port, the stock, salt and pepper to taste. Cover closely and bake in a moderate oven (180°C, 350°F, Mark 4) for about 3 hours or until tender. Half an hour before serving, thicken sauce with a paste made of flour and remaining butter. Add rest of the port and redcurrant jelly to taste. Serve with forcemeat balls.

1 hare
50 g (2 oz) butter
salt and pepper
1 onion with 6 cloves stuck into it
parsley, thyme, bayleaf
juice of 1 lemon
140 ml (5 oz) port
70 ml (2½ oz) stock
4 tablespoons flour
redcurrant jelly
forcemeat balls

Jugged Hare III

2 tablespoons butter
2 tablespoons flour
100 g (4 oz) pork fat or lard
1 young hare
1 bottle red wine or white wine
or
90 ml (3¾ oz) vinegar plus 250 ml (½
   pint) stock or water (about)
salt and pepper
2 bayleaves
parsley
200 g (8 oz) mushrooms
18–20 spring onions
25 g (1 oz) butter

This Dutch recipe and the following one were kindly given to Douglas Hutchison by Mrs Verschaffel as a donation to this book.

Make a roux using the butter and flour. When this is three-quarters fried, add pieces of lard to the sauce and keep it on a high flame for a couple of seconds. Then put in the hare, cut into pieces, and when it is browned, pour in the wine or vinegar. Then add either stock or water to the casserole. The stew must be soaked; in other words, the meat should be swimming in the sauce. Season with salt and pepper, taking note that the lard also gives salt to the stew. Add bayleaves, some parsley and mushrooms. Cook it on a moderate flame until the liquid is reduced by a quarter, about 45 minutes. Then take well cleaned spring onions all the same size and toss them in butter on a low flame. When they are golden and your casserole is almost ready, put them into it. After 15 minutes, take the casserole away from the heat. Taste to see if it is well seasoned and keep it on a low flame until you are ready to serve.

Braised Leg of Hare

hindquarters of a hare
salt and pepper
6 slices streaky bacon
200 g (8 oz) melted butter
1½ tablespoons flour
500 ml (1 pint) sour cream
250 ml (½ pint) hot water
2 tablespoons lemon juice

Split hindquarters lengthwise into two pieces, rub with salt and pepper. Arrange in an oiled casserole and cover with bacon. Cook in a very hot oven (220°C, 425°F, Mark 7) for 25 minutes, then lower to moderate (180°C, 350°F, Mark 4). Baste well with melted butter and cook for another 25 minutes. Sprinkle with flour, cover with sour cream, then add water and lemon juice. Cover, and cook for 20 minutes, stirring the sauce occasionally. When done reduce sauce if necessary.

Steamed and Roasted Hare

1 hare
50 g (2 oz) dripping
forcemeat balls

This is a good way of cooking a hare which may be a little tough. Serve with redcurrant jelly and a suitable sauce.

Prepare and truss a hare so that it will curl round to fit into a steamer. Steam until tender. Have ready a fairly hot oven (190°C, 375°F, Mark 5) and put the hare into a roasting tin with plenty of dripping and cook, basting well, until it is nicely browned. Serve with forcemeat balls which can be roasted with the hare for the last 15 minutes.

Creamed Saddle of Hare

Cover the saddle with pork fat (not butter). Spread with a paste made of dry mustard, vinegar and tarragon. Put in a hot oven (190°C, 375°F, Mark 5) for 40 minutes. When it is almost ready, add the cream and cover it with freshly ground pepper.

1 saddle of hare
4 strips pork fat
dry mustard
vinegar
tarragon
250 ml (½ pint) single cream
ground pepper

Salsa di Lepre

This is Elizabeth David's Hare Sauce for noodles.

Marinade the pieces of hare (legs will be sufficient, the back being used for another dish) in red wine, onions, garlic, bay-leaves, pepper, rosemary and sage, with a carrot cut into dice and some celery leaves. Leave for 2 days. Brown the meat in lard or oil, add some fresh herbs and vegetables, a few dice of ham or bacon, and pour over them 1 tumblerful of red wine. Stew the hare very slowly until the meat is falling off the bones; these must all be removed and the meat put through a sieve so that the thick purée is obtained. Reheat the sauce in a bain-Marie and pour over the cooked noodles.

Civet de Lièvre Alpenrose

Freddie von Siebenthal-Gobeli is the proprietor of the Alpenrose at Schonried, near Gstaad. He is the most wonderful host, cook and friend, always ready to tell us the secrets of his cooking. I wouldn't change a word of his recipe because it is Freddie's and brings back so many happy memories of fun and good food.

1 big hare (reserve blood)
1 tablespoon vinegar
1 big onion or 10 little white ones
2 carrots
salt and pepper
bouquet garni of parsley and bayleaf
1 bottle good red wine
100 g (4 oz) bacon
25 g (1 oz) butter
1 teaspoon flour

'So I shall do my possible to translate the recipe for "Civet de Lièvre" en anglais!' This dish is for about eight people.

Mix the blood of the hare with the vinegar and leave it in the refrigerator. Cut the hare into little pieces, put it in a pot with onions, carrots, salt, pepper and bouquet, cover with the red wine and turn it over once a day for three days.

Cut the bacon into cubes and roast it in a fireproof casserole with the butter until slightly brown. Add the flour and let it get brown as well. Slightly roast hare in another pan with fat then add it to fireproof casserole also. Add the marinade (wine) and let cook very slowly for 2–3 hours. Add blood and vinegar, finish seasoning and serve very hot.

My note – do not let it boil after adding the blood.

Rable de Lièvre à la Crème

This is one of my aunt's recipes and as she thinks in French when she cooks, she has had to translate it for me. As she is a real pro, do exactly as she says and it will be delicious.

Cut *une barbe du lard* (a large piece of pork fat) to fit the top of the hare, and cut pieces for legs. Wrap the top and tie with string. Wrap the legs separately and tie with string. Now tie legs together. Put in roasting pan, put margarine on it and salt and pepper. Put a cut onion in the pan. Put in a very hot oven (240°C, 460°F, Mark 8–9). After about 10 minutes reduce to 230°C, 445°F, Mark 8. Cook 40 minutes. Baste from time to time, turning the hare each time. When cooked, remove from pan. Remove grease from pan with spoon. Add a little stock or water to the pan, tasting it to make sure it is not too salty. Add 150 g (6 oz) thick or sour cream, stir with a whisk, let cool a minute and add a drop of potato flour mixed with water to thicken it.

While hare is cooking, prepare 300 g (12 oz) mushrooms. Slice them – they should be very white – and put in a small pot. Add half amount of water to amount of mushrooms, two nuts of butter, and juice of half a lemon. Salt and pepper. Cover. Bring to boil and boil for 2 minutes. Strain.

Cook a few small white onions in water with salt. Cook about 20 minutes – they should be *croquant* – just hard enough to hold their shape. Add mushrooms and onions to the sauce. Add salt and pepper if necessary.

To serve, cut strings off hare. Cut down centre of back and across top of rump – you have two *filets*. Cut flesh from legs and rump, each side in one piece. Put hare on serving dish. Cut flesh of legs and rump into escalopes, place on bones of legs. Cut *filets* on the bias in slices. Place on each side of body. Reheat in the oven.

Add a good glass of Cognac to the sauce and a little Madeira. Reheat, but don't boil. Put sauce over hare with spoon. Serve very hot with a *pilaff de riz* (250 g or 10 oz). Enough for 5 or 6.

Marinade
500 ml (1 pint) water
6 tablespoons wine or vinegar
parsley
bayleaf
thyme
sliced carrot
1 clove garlic

salt and pepper
50 g (2 oz) bacon fat or oil
150 g (6 oz) brandy
150 g (6 oz) single cream

Sauce
100 g (4 oz) single cream or buttermilk
1 teaspoon French mustard
handful of seedless grapes

Saddle of Hare with Grapes

Marinate hare for two days.

Dry saddle and season with salt and pepper. Rub saddle well with bacon fat or oil and cook in a very hot oven (230°C, 450°F, Mark 8). Add the brandy and cream to the strained marinade, and baste often, for 45 minutes. Remove and keep warm. Add the cream or buttermilk for the sauce to the pan, then add mustard and the grapes. Pour over the saddle and serve.

German Larded Saddle of Hare

Dry meat, leave whole or cut into four pieces, rub garlic all over meat and then rub meat in butter. Sprinkle with salt, paprika and cayenne, place in roasting pan, cover with bacon or salt pork and roast, uncovered, in a moderately slow oven (170°C, 325°F, Mark 3), allowing 20 minutes per 400 g (1 lb). When done, remove to a warm serving dish, pour over Sour Cream Sauce and decorate with slices of orange. Serve with redcurrant jelly.

(Make the Sour Cream Sauce in the pan after the hare has been removed in order to get all the juices – strain and reheat.)

1 saddle of hare (800 g–1 kg or 2–2½ lb)
1 clove garlic
3 tablespoons butter
2½ teaspoons salt
½ teaspoon paprika
¼ teaspoon cayenne
6 thin slices bacon or fat salt pork
Sour Cream Sauce (see page 190)
orange slices
redcurrant jelly

Hare Minute Steaks

If you think your hare is young you may cut the meat away from the saddle. Cut this into slices approximately 1 × 10 × 10 cm (½ × 4 × 4 in), beat them with a rolling pin or whatever else you may use for beating meat, and then fry them in butter like any other steak. Serve plain or with any of the game sauces you choose.

Hare Marinated and then Cooked in Beer

Put the pieces of hare in a bowl with the beer, garlic, bayleaf and onions, and leave in a cool place to marinate for a day or so.

Dry the pieces of hare, dredge them with flour and brown in the hot dripping – not too quickly. Place the pieces in a casserole, add the marinade, stock and vinegar, then bring to the boil. Cover, and cook in a moderate oven (180°C, 350°F, Mark 4) for about 2 hours or until tender. During the last 45 minutes you may cover the top of the casserole with thickly sliced boiled potatoes brushed with butter or dripping.

1 hare cut into serving pieces
375 ml (¾ pint) beer
1 clove garlic, crushed
1 bayleaf
400 g (1 lb) onions, finely sliced
2 tablespoons flour
50 g (2 oz) beef dripping
250 ml (½ pint) stock
1 teaspoon wine vinegar

Hare with Mustard

Cook as Rabbit with Mustard (see page 104). The saddle and hind legs of the hare are best for this dish.
Marinate the pieces first if you wish in either:
3 tablespoons olive oil and 3 tablespoons brandy
or
3 tablespoons olive oil, 3 tablespoons wine vinegar and herbs as you wish.

Hare Covered in Onions

1 young hare
2 tablespoons flour
3 tablespoons dripping or butter
3 large onions (about)
250 ml (½ pint) sour cream

This sounds too oniony but the long cooking makes it milder and it is a very good filling dish.

Cut the young hare into serving pieces. Dust with flour and brown in dripping or butter. Cover generously with sliced onions and then pour over the sour cream. Cover pan tightly and cook very gently for 1 hour or until the hare is tender.

Fillets of Hare

1 young hare
salt and pepper
2–3 tablespoons oil
100 ml (4 oz) wine

optional
a few sautéed mushrooms
2 tablespoons tomato purée
1 small clove garlic, mashed
or
fresh or sour cream
1 teaspoon tomato paste or red-currant jelly

Again if you have a young hare you may take the fillets off the saddle. This leaves you with the rest of the animal for soup, stew or pâté.

Cut the fillets in long thick slices down the back. If you have time soak them in oil for an hour or so. Season with salt and pepper and fry gently in the oil, turning several times and adding more oil if necessary. As they must be well cooked they will take 20–30 minutes. At about half time add the wine – this will give you the bases with which to make a sauce when they are cooked. At this stage you may also add a few sautéed mushrooms, or 2 tablespoons tomato purée with garlic; or at the end you may remove the fillets and add fresh or sour cream, 1 teaspoon tomato paste, some redcurrant jelly, or whatever else you happen to have. Heat up the sauce but don't let it boil if you have used cream. Pour over fillets. If you have used cream they are good with noodles.

Venison

Unfortunately, as all the family love it, we have never suffered from a game larder too full of venison. Ken, our keeper, manages to shoot us a couple of roe deer every year, and for red deer we have to rely on the charity of our friends. I have never cooked or eaten fallow deer but I believe it comes between the two for culinary purposes. I find the easiest way of telling the age of venison is to trust your friend, stalker or butcher – someone who knew the original beast. The fat of a young animal is whiter than that of an older one, and the flesh is dark red and finely grained – my butcher and daughter say that they can tell by the bone, but they have butchered more than I have. In normal circumstances someone ought to be able to tell you what it is – a young hind, the beast that was shot last week, or a first-class haunch from your butcher.

I usually intend to hang a beast from 2–3 weeks and less for a section of an animal. This depends so much on the weather – warm damp weather is by far the worst. It must be hung with plenty of ventilation. I had a haunch of red deer turn green almost overnight when suddenly the larder was filled with pheasants and it ceased to have room to breathe. Ken was about to throw it away when I swore him to secrecy, scrubbed it well in Milton, and no one knew what a narrow escape the housekeeper had had.

I don't necessarily lard the roe deer, though I do if I have the time or feel it needs it. Neither have I found it necessary to marinate it. If it is a good one it is so utterly delicious as it is that only overcooking makes it tough and tasteless. Anne, my daughter, is a most excellent butcher and keeps the choice scraps on one side for our first meal from the animal. These, sautéed quickly in butter and served with a sauce, are always considered the best of the beast. The saddle is the next favourite, seldom to be shared with guests. If it is good enough to roast or grill then don't overcook it. If it isn't then get out the stew pot.

Red deer may be hung even longer and need larding or barding as they have very little fat and almost no marbling effect in their flesh. If you have a cut of venison it is a good idea, having made sure it is thoroughly dry, to hang it in a piece of muslin filled with herbs. I like a young hind (female) better than a stag, but this is not traditional, the stag is reputed to have the better flavour.

Always, always make sure hot venison is served on very hot plates.

Roast Venison

Venison manages to go on cooking itself long after it comes out of the oven. If it is a good enough leg or haunch to be roasted then it should not be overcooked. I usually panic when I see the first slice, thinking it is far too bloody, but by the time I start to eat it, it appears rather grey.

Venison must be served on very hot plates as, of course, most dishes should, but with venison it is terribly important – capercaillie and blackgame are the same.

I have not been able to convince myself that a good leg needs marinating, but most people think it does, so if you are organized in time, this is probably a wise precaution.

It should be well larded. This is worth doing anyway as it gives you a great feeling of superiority and competence with very little effort. If, however, you have not got a needle, you can make little slits in the skin and push in the fat with the handle of a teaspoon or some similar object.

Having larded the roasting joint well with fat bacon or fat pork, rub it all over generously with butter and place it in a moderately hot oven (190°C, 375°F, Mark 5). Baste frequently – preferably every 10 minutes. It should take about 15 minutes per 400 g (1 lb) if it is large, and 20 minutes per 400 g (1 lb) if it is smaller (under 1.6 kg or 4 lb). This should make it slightly pink.

If you are going to eat the venison cold, cook it for a slightly shorter time as it will continue cooking as it cools and dries out.

Serve roast venison with one of the suggested sauces for venison or as follows:

Remove most of the fat from the pan and brown in the remaining fat with 2 tablespoons flour. Add either 250 ml ($\frac{1}{2}$ pint) marinade or red wine, 2 teaspoons tomato paste, salt and pepper, and 125 ml ($\frac{1}{4}$ pint) fresh or sour cream. Stir well and heat till just bubbling.

Alternatively, pour off the fat, add some flour and then some sour cream, a little redcurrant jelly, and a squeeze of lemon.

If you are drinking good wine with your venison, be careful not to dole out too much redcurrant jelly. It may be good with the venison but it doesn't help the wine at all.

For charts and information on venison, see page 215.

Roast Saddle of Venison

You may or may not marinate a saddle but lard it and rub it very well with butter. Roast it in a hot oven (200°C, 400°F, Mark 6), baste it frequently. You may add wine, port or strained marinade to the dripping in order to have more liquid to baste with. It should be served quite pink so 15 minutes per 400 g (1 lb) is long enough. If you wish to serve it cold, cook it for a shorter time.

Shoulder of Venison

10–12 medium sized potatoes
1 whole shoulder of venison
1 clove garlic
salt and pepper
2 tablespoons butter or margarine
4 tablespoons tomato paste

Sent to us from Mrs Bo Thelander.

Heat oven at very hot temperature (220°C, 425°F, Mark 7). Peel the potatoes. Rub the meat with garlic, salt and pepper. Brown the butter or margarine in a dripping pan. Put meat and potatoes in pan. Mix tomato paste and beef broth or water and pour over meat and potatoes. Bake in oven until meat is tender and potatoes are done. Baste now and then with tomato-gravy. Add more beef broth or water if needed.

Serve with fresh green peas and a salad.

Braised Saddle of Roe Deer

Mix olive oil, seasoning, juniper berries, thyme and garlic together and rub well into saddle. Allow to sit for an hour or so. Melt butter in casserole, cook the onions lightly and then add remaining vegetables. Stir around well to make sure they are all mixed. Place saddle on top of vegetables, cover with lid or foil, pouring half of the wine beforehand, and place in a moderately slow oven (170°C, 325°F, Mark 3) for an hour.

Remove saddle and put juices and vegetables through a mouli. Add flour to juices and stir over heat until it becomes thick, then add stock and the rest of the wine, lemon juice and vinegar. Stir well until smooth and boiling. Put saddle back in pan and pour over sauce. Cover, and return to oven until tender (this depends on the size of the saddle, about 20 minutes per 400 g (1 lb)). Remove saddle to serving dish. Stir sauce well to mix in new juices. Serve sauce separately.

2 tablespoons olive oil
salt and pepper
8–10 juniper berries, crushed
¼ teaspoon thyme
½ clove garlic, mashed
saddle of roe deer (1.6–2.4 kg or 4–6 lb)
50 g (2 oz) butter
800 g (2 lb) mixed vegetables (onions, carrots, cabbage, celery)
200 ml (8 oz) red wine
15 g (½ oz) flour
250 ml (½ pint) stock
1 tablespoon lemon juice
1 tablespoon wine vinegar

Danish Saddle of Young Venison with Waldorf Salad

Sent to us by Mrs Nina Fiske.

Lard or rub saddle with butter, as preferred, sprinkle with salt and pepper. Add stock so that it does not become dry when cooking. Place in a moderate oven (180°C, 350°F, Mark 4), basting occasionally. In Denmark the meat is enjoyed red so cooked for 45 minutes, but in England another 30 minutes' cooking time is advisable. Thicken gravy with beurre manié.

Serve with Waldorf Salad (see page 185) mixed with a dressing of 125 g (5 oz) mayonnaise and 5 tablespoons double cream.

saddle of young venison
40 g (1½ oz) butter or strips of salt pork fat or bacon for larding
salt and pepper
250 ml (½ pint) stock or beef cube and water
beurre manié

German Venison Stew with Potato Dumplings

Wipe meat and cut it into serving pieces. Heat butter, stir in flour and cook until browned. Add salt, stock, water; stir and mix well, then add onion, peppercorns, cloves and bayleaves and lemon juice, bring to boil and let boil for 5 minutes. Add meat, cover, and boil gently for 1½ hours. Add wine and mix, cook for another 15 minutes. Serve with potato dumplings: wash, peel and grate potatoes. Soak bread in a little cold water, and squeeze out as much water as possible. Mix bread, salt, pepper, onions and parsley together, add potatoes and eggs, mix well. Form into balls, roll in flour and drop into boiling water, cover pot tightly and boil for 15 minutes.

1.2 kg (3 lb) venison shoulder
50 g (2 oz) butter
100 g (4 oz) flour
1½ teaspoons salt
500 ml (1 pint) stock
1 litre (2 pints) hot water
1 onion
8 peppercorns
4 cloves
2 bayleaves
juice of ½ lemon
125 ml (¼ pint) red wine

Potato Dumplings
800 g (2 lb) potatoes
10 slices bread
1 teaspoon salt
¼ teaspoon pepper
1 onion, grated
1 teaspoon minced parsley
2 eggs, well beaten
50 g (2 oz) flour
1½ litres (3 pints) boiling salted water

Another Venison Stew

4 tablespoons oil
1.2 kg (3 lb) shoulder or neck of vension with skin and sinews removed, cut into cubes and marinated for a day or two
1 clove garlic, mashed
strained marinade
150 ml (6 oz) red wine
bouquet garni of celery, parsley, bayleaf and thyme
400 g (1 lb) fat salt pork, diced and parboiled in water to cover, then drained and dried
50 g (2 oz) butter
18–24 small white onions
4 medium carrots, diced and lightly sugared
200 g (8 oz) mushrooms, sliced, or 18–24 button mushrooms
salt and pepper
a little arrowroot
finely chopped parsley

Heat oil in a heavy casserole and brown venison a few pieces at a time. Place all the meat in casserole with garlic, strained marinade, wine and bouquet garni. Add enough water to barely cover the meat, bring to boil, cover tightly, and place in a moderately slow oven (170°C, 325°F, Mark 3) for 1½–2 hours.

Meanwhile brown salt pork in butter, remove; lightly brown the onions, remove; add the carrots and cook them for 5 minutes. Add more butter if necessary. Sauté mushrooms until they are nearly cooked. Add the vegetables to casserole and cook for another 30 minutes. Season with salt and pepper and thicken gravy if necessary with a little arrowroot mixed with 4 tablespoons water. Sprinkle with parsley.

James Beard's Venison Stew

One of the things I like best about James Beard's books is that he suggests the kind of food that you come in from out of doors to eat. They make perfect shooting lunch dishes and are often wonderfully easy to prepare.

This is made from the meat from the less desirable parts of the carcass. The meat should be cut into convenient pieces for stew. Allow the meat to marinate for two days, remove it and drain it well.

Place one cup of olive oil in a deep pan and heat. Sear the meat very quickly over a brisk flame. You will need about 1.2 kg (3 lb) for four people. Add a large slice of salt pork cut into cubes and let it dry out with the venison. Add, when the meat is nicely brown, enough of the marinade to completely cover the meat. Simmer. Add four or five ripe tomatoes, peeled and quartered, one half cup of red wine. Forty minutes should be sufficient for this if your venison is under two years old. Thicken the sauce if you wish with ball of butter and flour. Taste for seasoning and serve with mashed potatoes or purée of chestnut.

1.2 kg (3 lb) good quality venison
3 tablespoons oil
600 g (1½ lb) onions, sliced
salt and pepper
4 cloves garlic, crushed
250 ml (½ pint) beef stock or tinned consommé
500 ml (1 pint) light beer
2 tablespoons brown sugar
1 bouquet garni
1½ tablespoons arrowroot
2 tablespoons wine vinegar

Belgian Venison in Beer with Onions

The Belgians use beer frequently in their cooking. This casserole is a very good robust dish especially appreciated by people who have been outside all day.

Cut venison into 2.5 cm (1 in) cubes and brown in hot oil in a frying pan, a few pieces at a time. Remove meat, reduce heat and stir in onions, adding more oil if necessary. Brown lightly, stirring frequently for about 10 minutes. Add salt, pepper and garlic. Arrange venison and onions in layers in a casserole. Heat stock in frying pan, pour over the venison and onions. Add beer to cover. Stir in sugar and put in bouquet. Bring to simmer, cover, and place in a moderately slow oven (170°C, 325°F, Mark 3) for 2 hours, or longer, depending on how good the venison is. When cooked, drain off liquid, skim off the fat, beat in arrowroot and vinegar mixed, and simmer for a few minutes. Pour sauce over meat.

Swedish Braised Venison

Remove outer membranes from meat and lard with strips of fat pork or bacon which have first been rolled in salt and pepper, then salt and pepper the surface of the meat. Brown meat quickly over high heat in butter. Lower heat, add stock and cream, place uncovered in a moderately slow oven (170°C, 325°F, Mark 3) and baste fairly frequently for 2½ hours. When the meat is cooked and tender, remove to platter, skim fat from juices and strain them. Mix a paste of arrowroot and water, add this to the juices and heat, stirring, until smooth and thickened. Add jelly and season to taste. Carve meat and serve with black or redcurrant jelly or rowanberry jelly, tomatoes and cucumber in vinegar, and browned potatoes.

2.4 kg (6 lb) leg venison
strips fat pork or bacon
1 tablespoon salt
pepper
40 g (1½ oz) butter
250 ml (½ pint) stock
250 ml (½ pint) cream, fresh or sour
1 tablespoon arrowroot mixed to a paste with a little cold water
1 tablespoon black or redcurrant jelly

Braised Venison

Place venison in the marinade for 3–4 days, turning several times a day. Brown the diced salt pork in butter and oil until crisp, remove, brown venison in fats. Reduce marinade to about half and pour over meat, add pork, cover tightly, and cook in a moderately slow oven (170°C, 325°F, Mark 3) until tender, about 1½ hours. Remove meat and keep warm.

Reduce sauce slightly, thicken with butter and flour, add port and redcurrant jelly, season to taste, mix very well and strain sauce over venison. Garnish with mushrooms, onions and chestnuts.

2.4 kg (6 lb) saddle of venison
Marinade
wine
olive oil
onion
carrots
garlic
pepper
juniper berries
bayleaf
thyme

200 g (8 oz) salt pork, diced
4 tablespoons butter
4 tablespoons olive oil
beurre manié (1 tablespoon butter mixed with 1 tablespoon flour)
70 ml (2½ oz) port
1–2 tablespoons redcurrant jelly
salt and pepper

Fallow Venison, Braised in Wine and Vegetables

From Wendy Coles.

Cooked in this way fallow venison becomes extremely tender, the meat retaining a delicate flavour. The major part of the cooking can be done beforehand: the dish only requires heating before serving.

2.8–3.2 kg (7–8 lb) fallow venison, cut from the haunch
Marinade
2–4 carrots
1–2 onions
3–4 sticks celery
1 parsnip

7 tablespoons olive oil or butter
7 tablespoons wine vinegar
bouquet garni of (thyme, parsley,
   bayleaf)
6 juniper berries, crushed
1 sprig rosemary
1 large clove garlic, crushed
6 peppercorns, crushed
½ bottle red wine

hot oil
seasoned flour

Mirepoix of Vegetables
1 large parsnip
3–4 slices celery
1 leek
1 large onion
3 sprouts
2 carrots

1 tablespoon oil
3 slices bacon
250 ml (½ pint) stock
cornflour
1 tablespoon redcurrant jelly
salt and pepper

Chop and dice all vegetables for marinade, brown in a little oil or butter in a saucepan. Add remaining marinade ingredients, bring to the boil and simmer for 30 minutes. Cool. Pour over the joint to marinate in a deep dish, leave for one or two days, turning and basting each day. Remove venison from marinade and wipe dry. Seal meat in hot oil and cover with seasoned flour.

Prepare mirepoix of vegetables. Chop and dice all vegetables finely. Put oil in the bottom of a heavy casserole with bacon, add all the vegetables, the meat and stock, and some of the liquid from the marinade. Put into a moderately slow oven (170°C, 325°F, Mark 3) for 3¾ hours. Turn halfway through cooking, strain off stock and mirepoix of vegetables, which should be liquidized and strained through a sieve. Thicken with cornflour, add redcurrant jelly and salt and pepper to taste. Carve joint fairly thickly, place in deep dish, cover with sauce, and return to slow oven (150°C, 300°F, Mark 2) for 1¼ hours.

Serve with plain boiled rice, boiled or steamed courgettes, and a salad of melon cubes, white shredded cabbage and celery in French dressing, redcurrant or rowan jelly.

Haunch or Saddle of Venison in Beer

1.2 kg (3 lb) haunch or saddle, larded
   with pork fat or streaky bacon if you
   wish
1 tablespoon oil
1 very large onion, sliced thinly
250 ml (½ pint) ale
250 ml (½ pint) beef or venison stock
   or tinned consommé
1 clove garlic, crushed
2 teaspoons wine vinegar
2 teaspoons brown sugar
bouquet garni
black pepper
1 tablespoon flour

Brown venison in a heavy casserole in the oil, with the onion. Place meat on top of onions and add ale, stock, garlic, vinegar, sugar and bouquet garni, and lots of black pepper. Cover the pan tightly and cook in a moderate oven (180°C, 350°F, Mark 4) for 1–1½ hours, depending on the quality of the venison. Baste meat occasionally.

Just before serving you may coat the meat with a paste of mustard and cream (1 tablespoon thick cream to 2 teaspoons Dijon mustard). Return to oven while you skim the fat off the gravy, mix fat and flour together in a pan, add to gravy and reboil.

Civet of Venison

This is a beautiful venison stew from Jane Grigson's book *Good Things*. Depending on the age and what you call stewing venison, I would be prepared to allow for a slightly longer cooking period – 2 hours anyway.

Mix marinade ingredients together, season them well, and soak the venison in it overnight. Next day, melt the butter (sauce ingredients) in a heavy pan and brown the bacon in it, which you have first cut into strips about 2.5 cm (1 in) long and 5 mm (¼ in) thick. When the fat runs from the bacon, put onions and carrot and garlic into the pan to be browned slightly, then the well-drained venison. Stir the flour into the pan to take up the fat, and make a sauce by adding the strained marinade, plus enough stock to cover the ingredients and the bouquet garni. (Everything can be transferred to a deep casserole if this is more convenient.) Add the mushrooms and simmer until the venison is cooked, about 1½–2 hours. Skim off any surplus fat. (The cooking up to this point may be done the day before the venison is to be eaten.)

Half an hour before the meal, prepare the garnish and reheat the civet if necessary. Melt 25 g (1 oz) of butter with the sugar in a heavy pan. Turn the small onions in this until they are well coated. Add just enough stock to cover them and cook at a galloping boil. This will reduce the liquid to a spoonful or two of caramel. Be careful it doesn't burn, and keep shaking the onions about in it so that they are nicely glazed. Cook the mushrooms in 25 g (1 oz) of the butter, with salt and pepper. Cut the bread into triangles, and fry in the remaining butter.

Arrange the civet on a large hot serving dish, put the mushrooms and onions on top, pushing them down a little so that they look naturally part of the dish (but not too far so that they disappear). The croûtons go round the edge. Sprinkle with parsley and serve very hot. Serves 8.

1.2 kg (3 lb) stewing venison, diced and trimmed

Marinade
½ bottle red wine
1 medium onion, sliced
3 tablespoons brandy
3 tablespoons olive oil
salt and black pepper

Sauce
25 g (1 oz) butter
200 g (8 oz) streaky bacon in a piece
2 large onions, chopped
1 large carrot, diced
large clove garlic, crushed
2 tablespoons flour
beef or venison stock
bouquet garni
100 g (4 oz) mushrooms, sliced

Garnish
100 g (4 oz) butter
2 teaspoons sugar
24 small onions (pickling size)
beef or venison stock
24 small mushrooms
salt and pepper
8 slices bread
chopped parsley

Marinated Deer à la Cajsa Warg

Sent to us by Mrs Bo Thelander. Cajsa Warg was the first woman in Sweden who published a cook book, in 1755. This recipe is slightly modernized.

Bring all ingredients for the marinade to boil. Chill the marinade quickly. Put meat in a deep bowl, pour marinade over meat. Let stand at least 24 hours. Turn meat a few times.

Take out the meat and pat it dry on a clean towel. Mix flour and salt and turn meat in mixture until evenly covered. Melt butter in a pan. Fry meat until brown all round. Add anchovies, beef broth or water, and some of the marinade. When meat is half ready take it out and cut it into serving pieces. Put it back in pan, add mushrooms, lemon stuffed with cloves. Cover and let simmer until meat is tender. Add more beef broth or water if necessary. Take out lemon with cloves. Put the meat on a serving dish and serve the gravy as a sauce, or serve it directly out of the pan.

Marinade
500 ml (1 pint) vinegar
500 ml (1 pint) water
1 bayleaf
2 celery stems
2 cloves
2 cloves garlic, crushed
2 onions, sliced
2 carrots, sliced
4 juniper berries, crushed

1.2 kg (3 lb) roasting meat of fallow or red deer
2 tablespoons flour
2 teaspoons salt
75 g (3 oz) butter
2 anchovies
125 ml (¼ pint) beef broth or water
¼ lemon
100 g (4 oz) mushrooms
2 cloves

Venison Steaks

4 thick venison steaks
3 tablespoons butter
salt and pepper
crushed juniper berries
grated onion
125 ml (¼ pint) beef stock or consommé
125 ml (¼ pint) red wine
125 ml (¼ pint) sour cream
redcurrant jelly

Melt butter in a thick frying pan, sprinkle steaks with salt and pepper and crushed juniper berries, and brown in butter until done, about 4 minutes each side. Remove and keep warm. Turn down heat and add some grated onion, mix well with all the bits left in the pan and add stock and wine, cook gently until sauce has thickened. Add sour cream and a little redcurrant jelly, simmer and strain over steaks. A few sautéed mushrooms sprinkled over the top is good.

Venison Steaks in Salt

Mix a bowl of coarse salt and water so it is thick enough to hold its shape and spread it on one side of the steak, 1 cm (½ in) thick. Put under a hot grill, salt side up. Grill until salt is a bit brown. Turn, cover other side with salt, grill again. When cooked, chip off salt, add butter and pepper to taste, and serve with any sauce for venison. Cooking a steak this way seals any gravy into the meat and seems to make venison less dry.

venison steaks

Marinade
125 ml (5 oz) red wine
2 tablespoons French mustard
1 tablespoon soft brown sugar
2 tablespoons puréed tomatoes
1 tablespoon Mexican chilli powder
2 small onions, sliced
2 cloves garlic, crushed, lightly fried in oil

flour

Mollie's Thick Venison Steak per Person

Thoroughly mix all ingredients for the marinade in an electric mixer. Pour over meat and leave covered for 24 hours, turning occasionally. Drain meat from marinade, dust with flour. Barbecue over faintly glowing embers of dying charcoal fire, basting from time to time with the marinade.

Serve with salad, baked potatoes and vegetable marrow.

'Lots of wine needed at this meal,' says Mollie.

1.2 kg (3 lb) venison steaks, cut about 2 cm (¾ in) thick from loin or leg
1 teaspoon salt
4 peppercorns
1 medium onion, sliced
1 carrot, sliced
4 sprigs parsley
½ teaspoon thyme
1 bayleaf
125 ml (¼ pint) white wine
125 ml (¼ pint) olive oil

Sour Cream Sauce
2 tablespoons butter
2 tablespoons flour
2 shallots, chopped
4 tablespoons white wine
2 peppercorns, crushed fine
250 ml (½ pint) sour cream
salt and pepper
juice of ½ lemon

German Venison Steaks with Sour Cream Sauce

Season steaks with salt, place in bowl, mix in peppercorns, onion, carrot, parsley, thyme, bayleaf, wine, and 5 tablespoons of the olive oil. Pour over steaks, cover, and let stand in the refrigerator for 24 hours, turning occasionally.

Remove meat from marinade and pat dry. Heat 3 tablespoons olive oil and cook venison for 3 minutes on each side – longer if you like it well done. Remove and keep warm while you make the following sauce. Pour off excess fat from pan, melt butter in it, stir in flour and shallots, mix well, scraping the bottom of the pan. Add wine and peppercorns gradually. Mix well. Add cream and salt and pepper if needed. Cook, stirring, until thickened, and add lemon juice before serving. Serve with puréed lentils and red cabbage.

Grilled Fillets of Venison

If the venison is young and perfect, it is quite unnecessary to treat it in any way other than you would treat the finest beef. It is usually a good idea to let it soak up a little olive oil and pepper before grilling it, and you can also sprinkle it with fresh herbs.

Cut fillets 1.5 cm ($\frac{1}{2}$–$\frac{3}{4}$ in) thick, pour over olive oil, sprinkle with pepper and herbs and leave for an hour or two. Grill 3–5 minutes on each side and serve with a suitable sauce.

Boned Loin of Venison in Sauce Poivrade

Slice about 600 g ($1\frac{1}{2}$ lb) venison and cut into 2 cm ($\frac{3}{4}$ in) thick strips. Place them on a platter, pour some wine and a little olive oil over them, sprinkle well with pepper and leave them for an hour or two.

Meanwhile make the Sauce Poivrade (see page 189), and if you like you may add a few soaked raisins and a few peanuts to the sauce.

Dry meat well and fry in hot oil until it is how you like it, but remember that it will continue to cook on its way to the serving table. Place the meat on a hot platter, spoon a little of the sauce over it and serve the rest separately. Croûtons of fried bread may be placed around the serving dish.

600 g ($1\frac{1}{2}$ lb) boned loin or slices from the haunch
2 tablespoons olive oil
75 ml (3 oz) red wine
pepper
750 ml ($1\frac{1}{2}$ pints) Sauce Poivrade
50 g (2 oz) stoned raisins
2 tablespoons peanuts or cashew nuts
croûtons

Fillets of Venison in Sauce Poivrade

Cut venison into strips about 2 cm ($\frac{3}{4}$ in) thick and marinate them for an hour or more in olive oil, red wine and pepper.

Make Sauce Poivrade (see page 189) and add the raisins and nuts to it. Fry croûtons. Dry venison and cook in hot olive oil until just done but still slightly pink, about 4 minutes each side. Place the meat on a hot serving dish, put croûtons around the edge, pour a little sauce over the meat and serve the rest separately.

Breaded Venison Cutlets

Soak cutlets in oil for about an hour. Drain them well, dredge them with seasoned flour, dip in beaten egg and then cover with breadcrumbs, patting them on well. Sauté in 40 g ($1\frac{1}{2}$ oz) of the butter for 10–12 minutes, adding more butter or a little oil if necessary. Turn the cutlets frequently. Place them on a warm platter, sauté the mushroom tops in remaining butter and place on each cutlet. Sprinkle if you wish with finely chopped parsley. Mix jelly with the pan juices, bring to boil, and serve with cutlets.

8 cutlets taken from leg or loin
5 tablespoons olive oil or cooking oil
seasoned flour
1 egg, well beaten
fine dry breadcrumbs – the quickest way to do these is in the liquidizer
8 large mushroom tops
100 g (4 oz) redcurrant jelly

Venison Cutlets with Mushrooms and Sauce

4 slices of venison cut 2 cm (¾ in) thick from leg or loin

Marinade for Venison
oil
50 ml (2 oz) red wine
250 ml (½ pint) Sauce Poivrade (see page 189)
100 g (4 oz) mushrooms, sliced
50 ml (2 oz) whipped cream
1 hard-boiled egg, chopped

Marinate the slices of venison for a day or two, turning occasionally. Dry well. Brown them in plenty of hot oil for 3 minutes on each side. Remove meat to a warm platter. Discard remaining oil and add red wine and Sauce Poivrade to pan; cook for 2 minutes. Add mushrooms, stir in whipped cream and hard-boiled egg. Pour sauce over cutlets.

Grilled Venison Chops

In order to keep the chops from drying out, wrap each chop in belly of pork fat. You may soften this in warm water first to make it easier to fold, and secure with a toothpick. Salt and pepper the chops first, wrap in the fat and grill under a high heat for 5 minutes and then under a medium heat until done, about 20 minutes in all. Pour over some melted butter in which you could have stewed some mushrooms or crushed juniper berries.

Venison Cutlets in the Ardennes Style

8 cutlets or 4 thick loin chops
12 crushed juniper berries
dried marjoram or thyme
salt, freshly ground black pepper
lemon juice
50 g (2 oz) butter
1 small onion, chopped
2 carrots, diced
small glass white wine or vermouth
small glass water
about 3 tablespoons chopped cooked ham
75 g (3 oz) breadcrumbs
half a bunch of parsley, chopped
extra butter
2 teaspoons redcurrant jelly
juice of half a bitter orange

This is Elizabeth David's great recipe, of which I would never change a word.

Mix juniper berries with some dried marjoram or thyme, salt and pepper. Pour lemon juice over the meat and rub with the juniper mixture. It's a good idea to do this an hour or two before you start the cooking. Melt 50 g (2 oz) butter in a shallow pan, add onion and carrot. When they are golden brown, put in the meat and brown it on both sides too. Pour in wine or vermouth, and boil steadily to reduce it a little. Add the water. Put some chopped ham on top of each cutlet or chop (transfer them, if more convenient, to a shallow ovenproof serving dish), then some breadcrumbs mixed with the chopped parsley. Dab a little butter on top of the breadcrumbs. Bake in a slow oven (150°C, 300°F, Mark 2) uncovered.

The time required will depend on the condition of the venison, varying from 1 to 2 hours. After about ¾ hour, pierce one of the chops gently with a larding needle or skewer to see if it's nearly ready.

When the meat is tender, pour off the juices into a wide pan (keep the meat warm in the oven, at a reduced temperature) and boil them down until the flavour is well concentrated. Stir in the redcurrant jelly and bitter orange juice (one could use a little dark marmalade when Seville oranges are not in season). Pour over the cutlets. Serve very hot, with a few boiled potatoes.

Capitaine à la Campagne

See pheasant recipe, page 64.

Venisonburgers

As venison lacks the fat of the usual beef which goes into a hamburger, it is better to add either minced streaky bacon or pork sausagemeat.

Mix all the ingredients together and form into flat round cakes. Wrap each burger in streaky bacon secured with a toothpick if you wish. Fry in hot fat until well browned on both sides. Remove from pan. They will probably need some gravy which you can make in the pan by adding a little stock, redcurrant jelly and a squeeze of lemon, or else serve with a hot tomato sauce.

400 g (1 lb) venison minced together with 200 g (8 oz) streaky bacon or pork sausagemeat
2 tablespoons breadcrumbs
1 egg, well beaten
salt and pepper
as much finely chopped onion as you wish
1 slice streaky bacon per burger (optional)

Venison Meat Loaf

Caroline Stroyan ought to be writing this section on venison as she really knows what it is all about. Everyone who stays with them at Monar must marvel at the way she runs the lodge at Pait by radio communication with her deep freeze at the other end of the loch. She makes the property almost self-sufficient with its venison and trout, and with the salmon and birds: the rest of the year even in Edinburgh she seldom needs a butcher. She has been so generous with any secrets I have asked of her and with advice.

venison, minced
bacon
onion
1 tablespoon flour
stock cube
browning
Worcestershire sauce
tomato ketchup
salt and pepper or curry powder
2 eggs
hard-boiled eggs

Mince up any leftovers of venison to which you can add minced bacon or other scraps if available. Prepare loaf tin, grease well and line with bacon both sides and base. Sauté onion in dripping using as much sediment as possible, and when cooked stir in flour, stock cube and browning, and make enough gravy to bind the minced venison. To the mixture of gravy and venison add Worcestershire sauce, tomato ketchup, salt and pepper, and, as an alternative, curry powder. Then finally beat in two raw eggs. You can then put the whole mixture into the loaf tin or just half and line the centre with hard-boiled eggs, finishing off with meat mixture on the top. Stand in a tin of water and bake in a moderate oven (180°C, 375°F, Mark 4) till the bacon looks cooked.

Serve either hot with fresh tomato sauce or cold for picnic lunches.

You can vary the ingredients according to what you have available.

Venison Shepherd's Pie

800 g (2 lb) minced venison
1 large onion, chopped
4 carrots, diced
2 sticks celery, diced
1 small clove garlic, mashed (optional)
125 ml (¼ pint) olive oil or other fat –
 bacon fat, butter, oil, or a mixture if
 you think olive oil is too strong
enough liquid to come high enough
 to where you can see it. This can be
 stock, tinned tomatoes, tomato juice,
 red wine, or water with a stock cube,
 or a mixture to taste
salt and pepper
a few crushed juniper berries
a pinch of thyme

I suppose it ought to be called 'Stalker's Pie'. This is very good as long as you use twice as much fat as you normally would to sauté the vegetables in as in a shepherd's pie, and you need a lot of vegetables as well or you end up with a dry, dull slab of meat covered with potato. Mince the meat through the big holes on the mincer to try to stop it packing down. You may use either cooked or uncooked meat – if it's the latter it will need to be browned with the onions and cooked in a saucepan, like mince, for an hour or so before you put it in the oven with the potato on top. For six people you will need about 800 g (2 lb) meat.

All this may be changed to suit what you have at hand.

Brown the onion in the olive oil then the other vegetables. Add meat and stir in the oil and vegetables until thoroughly mixed. If it is uncooked let it brown well. Pour over liquid and add seasonings. Put in deep pie dish and cover with creamy mashed potatoes.

Venison Steak Stroganoff

1.6 kg (4 lb) best venison
4 tablespoons butter
200 g (8 oz) mushrooms, thickly sliced
1 tablespoon flour
200 ml (8 oz) sour cream
salt and pepper

Another dish for the best part of the animal, but it is always delicious and even better when reheated the next day.

Cut meat into strips 2.5 cm by 5 mm (1 in by ¼ in). If possible, cut it across the grain. Melt 3 tablespoons of the butter in a heavy pan and when bubbling add meat. Cover, and cook slowly, stirring occasionally. After 15 minutes add mushrooms, cover, and cook for another 10 minutes. Put this in the top of a double boiler over a low heat.

Melt the rest of the butter in a separate pan, add the flour, stir until smooth, add sour cream and stir over a very low heat for about 3 minutes. Do not let it boil.

Pour the sauce over the meat and mushrooms in the double boiler and simmer for 10–15 minutes. Make sure the water is well below the level of the top pan. Season with salt and pepper. Serve with noodles or rice.

Venison Liver

3 tablespoons butter
1 small onion, minced
1 venison liver, sliced fairly thin –
 about 5 mm (¼ in) thick
1 tablespoon flour
4 tablespoons red wine

It's there and some people love it – yes, for breakfast! I can eat it but find it strong. It must be very fresh. If I had to cook it for breakfast I would slice it very thin and sauté it quickly in butter, hoping that it wouldn't become tough. If I were to cook it for supper, this is what I'd do.

Melt butter in pan and sauté onion until golden. Put in slices of liver and cook each side for about 1½ minutes. Remove liver and keep warm. Sprinkle pan with flour, stir, add wine and finely chopped mushrooms, then simmer and stir until thick. Add lemon juice, salt and pepper. Put back slices of liver and warm briefly in gravy.

a few mushrooms, finely chopped
1 teaspoon lemon juice
salt and pepper

Roe Venison Kidneys in Cream Sauce

Sent to us by Mrs S. Prior.

Peel kidneys and put them whole into pan containing the stock, and bring to the boil. Remove from the heat and allow to cool in the stock for approximately 5–10 minutes. This is to remove any bitterness from the kidneys.

Meanwhile melt the butter and oil together in a roomy frying pan. Prepare the onion, dicing it fairly small, and fry it gently in the oil and butter until it is transparent. When the kidneys are ready and slightly cooled, remove from stock and cut them into thin slices and add to the mushrooms which you have previously prepared and sliced. Toss them into pan and stir briefly to seal juices. Turn up the heat to high and put in the brandy. Hold the pan over heat and ignite. When the flame is nearly finished, douse it with 250 ml (½ pint) of the stock, mixed with the sherry, lower heat and cook very gently for 5 minutes. Remove kidneys and mushroom mixture from stock and keep warm if it is to be used immediately, if not put on one side in a dish.

Pour on cream and let it bubble together with the stock until it is thick and reduced in quantity, about 10 minutes. When it has reached the desired consistency, turn down heat and add kidney mixture. Reheat very gently and briefly and taste for seasoning. If needed, add salt and pepper.

Serve with plain boiled rice. Serves 4–6.

15–20 kidneys
500 ml (1 pint) stock
1 tablespoon butter
1 tablespoon oil
1 medium onion
200 g (8 oz) mushrooms
2 tablespoons cooking brandy
70 ml (2½ oz) cooking sherry
125 ml (¼ pint) thick cream
salt and pepper to taste

And finally a recipe for wild boar.

Boar in Sweet and Sour Sauce

Bianca Muratori sent this recipe from Italy. We haven't any wild boar in this country but possibly people coming home from Europe might bring back a cut and wish to know how to cook it. I think it might be very good tried with venison.

Into an enamel pan pour the white wine, wine vinegar, onion, carrots, celery, bouquet garni, clove, thyme, salt, pepper and juniper berries. Allow this mixture to boil for 15 minutes and let it cool down. Remove the hairy rind from the

Marinade
1 bottle dry white wine
¼ litre (½ pint) wine vinegar
1 onion, sliced
2 carrots, sliced
1 stick celery
bouquet garni of parsley, bayleaf
1 clove
thyme
salt and pepper
10 juniper berries
2 tablespoons olive oil

piece of boar
2 tablespoons lard
salt and pepper
100 g (4 oz) streaky bacon, diced
bouquet garni of parsley, bayleaf,
thyme
1 carrot, sliced
1 onion, sliced
200 ml (8 oz) white wine
1 tablespoon caramelized sugar dissolved in stock
2 tablespoons drinking chocolate dissolved in a little stock
3 teaspoons wine vinegar
50 g (2 oz) sultanas soaked in tepid
water
10 dried prunes
small quantity of candied peel
handful of pine seeds (optional)

piece of boar, wash it thoroughly in water and vinegar, dry it and place it in a china salad bowl. Pour the above mixture over the meat, add the olive oil and allow the meat to marinate for 24 or 48 hours, according to quality.

Remove the meat from the liquid, dry thoroughly, and after having rolled and tied it, place it in a saucepan with the lard. Let it brown quickly then add salt and pepper together with the diced bacon, bouquet garni, carrot and onion. When the vegetables become brown too, add the white wine; and when this has evaporated cover the meat with water. Continue to cook very slowly until the meat is tender and can be pierced with a fork. Remove the meat from the saucepan and keep it warm. Skim the fat from the gravy which must be sieved after removing the bouquet garni. Replace it in a saucepan and add caramelized sugar dissolved in stock, drinking chocolate dissolved in stock, wine vinegar, sultanas, and prunes cut in small pieces. If available add candied peel and pine seeds. Heat this sauce till it thickens and then pour over the meat already sliced.

Game Fish

Originally when we planned this book we were going to ignore fish completely. The Game Conservancy does not involve itself with fishing, and as a family we do not fish very much ourselves. When I handed in the manuscript I was aware that it ought to include a brief note on fish, and as Collins also felt this, I have added this chapter, mainly for the girl who is trying to run a shooting lodge by a river and is not used to a dozen or so trout arriving in the kitchen day after day when the fishing is good. She can also find herself landed with a pile of mackerel if the children have been out trolling with a line in the sea, a bucket or two of mussels, or lobsters and crabs if they have been skilful at setting their pots. It can be hard to keep your cool when, after planning dinner around a haunch of venison, you are told that 'they' would prefer the fresh sea trout instead.

This is not a comprehensive chapter on fish cookery. It is more a few suggestions with what you could do with what you might find dumped on your kitchen table during a sporting holiday.

A Guide to coping with Game Fish

How to Tell the Freshness of Fish

I rely on the brightness of its eyes and whether or not they have sunk in, and also the smell should be fresh. The scales, too, of an old fish may be rough and dull, and if it has been kept in the damp it sometimes develops a scum, especially inside, if it has been cleaned.

So look for:

1. Bright eyes.
2. Shiny, healthy scales.
3. Clean, fresh smell.
4. Flesh that feels resilient and in no way flabby.

How to Clean a Fish

The only really important thing you need when cleaning a fish is a beautifully sharp, longish, thin knife. Hacking your way up its belly doesn't improve its looks and takes far more time. Catch the tip of the knife in the fish's vent and slit it up to the head. Remove all the intestines and cut away the fins. With the large dorsal fin on the back, it is better to make a gash down each side of it and then give it a hard jerk towards the head: that way you get the root bones as well. If you wish, cut off the head above the collar bone and the tail. I use my thumb-nail for removing the vein of blood which runs along the backbone. Wash fish quickly under running cold water, making sure you remove any leftover blood or membranes.

How to Fillet a Fish

With a sharp, thin knife, cut along the back of the fish and down to the backbone. Then, starting at the head, with your knife lying flat, cut into the backbone and slice the flesh away from the ribs, working down the backbone until the one side comes away whole. Turn the fish over and do exactly the same on the other side.

How to Smoke Salmon

Instructions for smoking salmon can be found at the end of the fish section, on page 144.

Salmon

Salmon is King among fish. There are people, and I am one of them, who say that they prefer to eat sea trout or turbot, but the salmon has a certain fascination: its extraordinary life cycle, the magical way it leaps, the tenuous reasons as to when it will or will not be caught. Thus he earns his superiority, and whatever one's whims, it is excellent to eat hot or cold.

'Uncle Robert always said the tail piece was the best,' is a family saying, and unless I can have the whole fish, I am convinced Uncle Robert was right. Also you can get some great bargains in tail pieces – fishmongers will often give you a big reduction.

Steaks are usually cut too thin. They need to be at least 20 mm ($\frac{3}{4}$ in) thick or they dry out and become woolly.

Instructions for home-smoked salmon can be found on page 144.

Poached Salmon

The normal way of cooking a whole salmon or a large piece is to poach it gently in a court bouillon. I am lucky enough to have a fish kettle fitted with a trivet with handles. If you haven't a trivet in your kettle or pot, wrap the fish in muslin or cheesecloth, leaving a generous amount at either end to use as handles.

Bring all ingredients except the salmon to the boil and then simmer for about an hour. Place fish in the pot, increase the heat until it returns to simmer, cover, and cook, making sure it doesn't boil, for about 8 minutes per 400 g (1 lb). Remove fish, and if you wish to skin it, do so gently while it is still warm.

If you wish to use the court bouillon in a sauce or in aspic, reduce it by boiling and then strain. If you are making aspic, clarify the liquid by beating an egg white and shell together with some of the liquid, and then returning this to the rest of the liquid. Cook slowly and stir for a few moments, then allow the egg to rise to the surface. Leave the pot over a very low heat for about 10 minutes, turning the pot around gently every few minutes, so that the egg goes across the top of the liquid, catching the particles.

Line a sieve or colander with muslin or cheesecloth and very gently strain the liquid through this.

Court bouillon for a large fish
3 litres (almost 6 pints) water
1 litre (almost 2 pints) white wine
250 ml ($\frac{1}{2}$ pint) wine vinegar
3 onions, stuck with 3 cloves in each
3 carrots
2 large stalks of celery or the tops and leaves from a bunch of celery
2 bay leaves
5–6 large sprigs of parsley
1 tablespoon salt

1 large salmon

Serve poached salmon with:

1. Velouté Sauce
2. Hollandaise Sauce
3. Mousseline Sauce
4. Béchamel Sauce
5. Sauce Verte

This is also the most satisfactory way of preparing a cold salmon.

Salmon Baked in Foil

salmon steaks
butter

During the autumn months when we are in the North, my cooker is totally inadequate for cooking anything much more exotic than boiled eggs, and the oven makes the maximum fuss over just managing to heat up a medium sized chicken. I can't describe the excitement when a friend flew over from Canada with a huge barbecue plus a hood – it has changed my Highland scene. It removes a certain amount of chaos from an overcrowded kitchen, and many of the things we have cooked have surprised me at how delicious they are. The first time I was persuaded to try a whole salmon on it I was reluctant as I felt I could ill afford a failure, but now I wouldn't use any other method.

Follow the instructions for the preparation of the foil given in the recipe for Sea Trout Baked in Foil. Before wrapping the fish in the foil you may place a couple of bayleaves, peppercorns, a stick of celery, or a branch of fresh fennel on it. Then just before you fold up the last end of the foil, pour in 50–100 g (2–4 oz) of white wine. This helps to give you lovely juices after it is cooked.

Oven If you wish to bake it in the oven, place in moderately slow oven (170°C, 325°F, Mark 3) for about 20 minutes per 400 g (1 lb). It makes a great deal of difference as to whether your fish is at room temperature or out of a cold refrigerator. You are trying to get it so that it just flakes away from the bone and no more.

Barbecue Light the barbecue in plenty of time so the charcoal has settled and is hot and glowing all over. If you are lucky enough to have a hood, place the fish on the middle rack – you don't want it too close to the fire. Cook it for about 15 minutes per 400 g (1 lb). If you haven't a hood you should place the fish closer to the fire and you will have to roll it over gently from time to time. This may make the skin stick a bit, but only upsets the look of the final dish, not the taste. If it looks too bad you can skin it.

Salmon Steaks Baked in Foil

Have steaks cut fairly thick, about 20 mm (¾ in), and weighing about 150 g (6 oz). Wrap each steak in very well buttered or oiled foil. Be generous with the foil in order to have plenty around the edges to tuck together to prevent the juices from escaping. Bake in a moderate oven (180°C, 350°F, Mark 4) for about 15 minutes. If the steaks are to be served cold, allow them to cool before opening the foil.

Grilled Salmon Steaks with Savoury Butters

Season the steaks with salt and pepper. Brush them with oil or melted butter. Allow them to stand for 15 minutes if possible, then grill them under a medium heat (about 7 cm (3 in) from the flame) for 3–4 minutes each side. Baste frequently. Transfer them to a hot platter and place a teaspoon of one of the following butters on top of each steak.

Lemon and Parsley Butter for 4 steaks. Either pound all the ingredients in a mortar or work them together in a bowl, mashing them with a fork. Chill.

Mustard Butter for 4 steaks. Either pound all the ingredients together in a mortar or mash them in a bowl with a fork. Chill.

Brown Butter for 4 steaks. Melt and cook butter until it is light brown, then add lemon juice.

Watercress Butter for 4 steaks. Carefully pick over the watercress, retaining only the perfect green leaves. Dry and chop these finely. Either pound the ingredients in a mortar or mash in a bowl with a fork. Chill.

salmon steaks, each weighing 125–150 g (5–6 oz)
salt and pepper
plenty of oil or melted butter for basting

100 g (4 oz) butter, softened
2 tablespoons very finely chopped parsley
juice of ½ lemon
salt and pepper to taste

100 g (4 oz) butter, softened
1 teaspoon Dijon mustard
juice of ½ lemon
salt and pepper to taste
a little finely chopped parsley

100 g (4 oz) butter
juice of ½ lemon

100 g (4 oz) butter
3–4 tablespoons watercress
squeeze of lemon juice
salt and pepper to taste

Sautéed Salmon Steaks with White Wine

Dust steaks lightly with seasoned flour. Melt butter in a heavy frying pan, and when bubbling, cook steaks quickly on each side. Pour in wine, cook, and simmer, basting frequently, for about 20 minutes.

4 salmon steaks, each about 2 cm (¾ in) thick
seasoned flour
40 g (1½ oz) butter
125 ml (¼ pint) dry white wine

Baked Salmon Steaks in Cream

2 salmon steaks, each 5 cm (2 in) thick,
or 4 steaks 2.5 cm (1 in) thick
salt
250 ml (½ pint) fresh or sour cream
(sour cream is better but not as
easily available)
1 tablespoon lemon juice
1 tablespoon finely chopped dill leaves
1–2 tablespoons Dijon mustard (optional)
finely chopped parsley

The thicker the steaks, the better they bake. I find it better to use one large one between two people, but it is easier to serve if there is one each. Vary the cooking time accordingly.

Sprinkle steaks with salt and place in a baking dish. Mix other ingredients together, except for parsley, and pour over the steaks. Place in a moderate oven (180°C, 350°F, Mark 4). A 5 cm (2 in) steak will take about 30 minutes. When cooked, sprinkle with parsley.

Note: Sautéed sliced mushrooms or some shrimps may be added to this before cooking.

Salmon Steaks with Mushrooms and Little Onions

4 salmon steaks, each about 2.5 cm
(1 in) thick
salt
a little melted butter
70 ml (1 gill) red wine
water
slice of onion
sliver of garlic
sprig of parsley
4 peppercorns
2 egg yolks
4 tablespoons cream
50 g (2 oz) butter
salt and pepper
squeeze of lemon juice

Garnish
100 g (4 oz) small white onions,
skinned and cooked in boiling water
until just soft – not mushy
100 g (4 oz) small mushrooms
50 g (2 oz) butter
finely chopped parsley

Place steaks in an ovenproof dish, sprinkle with salt, brush with melted butter and place under grill until they have a golden touch. Add wine and enough water to come just to the top of the steaks, then add onion, garlic, parsley and peppercorns. Cover with buttered paper and bake in a moderate oven (180°C, 350°F, Mark 4) for 15 minutes.

While this is cooking, sauté onions and mushrooms in butter until the onions are lightly golden. Keep warm.

When salmon is cooked, strain off liquid and discard onion, garlic, parsley and peppercorns. Keep salmon warm. Reduce liquid until it is about 70 ml (½ gill). Beat egg yolks with cream and slowly add liquid. Continue beating over hot water until sauce has thickened. Beat in the 50 g (2 oz) butter, in little lumps, then season with salt and pepper and stir in lemon juice.

Place mushrooms and onions around salmon and pour over sauce. Sprinkle with parsley.

Salmon Pie

800 g (2 lb) salmon, cut into cubes
with all bones and skin removed
3 or 4 hard-boiled eggs (optional)
200 g (8 oz) shrimps (optional)
1–2 tablespoons grated onion
3 tablespoons chopped parsley
salt, pepper, paprika
500 ml (1 pint) Velouté or Béchamel
Sauce
100 ml (2 oz) white wine, vermouth,
sherry or Madeira
creamy mashed potatoes or rich pastry

You may change this as you would any other fish pie, adding tomatoes, a little curry powder, or some finely chopped celery.

Place salmon, eggs and shrimps if used, onion, parsley, salt, pepper and paprika in a casserole and mix together. Make a Velouté or Béchamel sauce, add wine to it and pour over mixture. Cover with either mashed potatoes or rich pie crust (if pastry brush with beaten egg) and place in a very hot oven (220°C, 475°F, Mark 7) for 15 minutes, then lower heat to moderate (180°C, 375°F, Mark 5) and cook for a further 15 minutes or until the top is nicely browned.

Salmon Kedgeree

This is a classic way of using up fish, and is especially popular as a breakfast dish. Everyone has their own idea as to how it should be made, and it can also be made with many other fish – smoked haddock is one of the nicest.

Place all ingredients in a double boiler and cook over hot water until heated through. Stir occasionally.

400 g (1 lb) salmon, flaked with bones and skin removed
4 hard-boiled eggs, sliced
2 teacups cooked rice
50 g (2 oz) butter
3–4 tablespoons cream
salt and pepper

optional
2–3 tablespoons chopped parsley
a little grated onion (but not for breakfast)
1–2 tablespoons curry powder

Salmon Fishcakes

Quick, easy and good. If the fishing has been bad and the children are hungry, tinned salmon will do and so will other kinds of fish. You may vary the proportions of fish and potato.

Mash salmon in a bowl. Mash the potatoes which have been well drained and dried over a gentle heat. Add potatoes, seasoning and butter to the salmon, and mix well with a wooden spatula. If the mixture is too dry, add a little milk or thin cream until it will hold together without being sticky. Shape into cakes of even size and dust them with flour. Fry in hot fat until golden brown, making sure they have enough time to get hot right through.

200 g (8 oz) salmon, with all bones and skin removed
300 g (12 oz) potatoes, peeled and boiled
salt and pepper
25 g (1 oz) butter
about 1 tablespoon top of the milk or thin cream if the mixture is dry
2 tablespoons minced parsley (optional)
flour
fat for frying

Salmon Quiche

This isn't taken from *Mastering the Art of French Cooking* by Simone Beck, Louisette Bertholde and Julia Child, but it is through this book that I have learnt how to make quiches and so many other things besides. I don't understand how any amateur cook can live without it, and their Pâté Brisée makes, we find, the best pastry - especially if it is being asked to travel.

In this recipe the proportions of salmon and mushrooms may be changed as you like. You may even use all salmon.

Cook the onions gently in the butter but do not allow them to get brown. Add mushrooms and let them cook for a minute or two, then add salmon, salt, pepper and Madeira or wine. Cook for a few minutes, then cool slightly.

Beat eggs with cream, tomato paste, seasoning and herbs if used, and add gradually to the salmon mixture. Place pastry shell on a baking dish and gradually add the filling. Sprinkle the top with cheese and bake in a moderately hot oven (190°C, 375°F, Mark 5) for 25–30 minutes, until it is puffed and browned.

2 tablespoons minced shallots or green onions
40 g (1½ oz) butter
100 g (4 oz) mushrooms, sliced
100 g (4 oz) flaked salmon
salt and pepper
2 tablespoons Madeira or white vermouth
3 eggs
200 ml (8 oz) thick cream
1 tablespoon tomato paste
a little parsley or dill (optional)
1 20 cm (8 in) pastry shell, partially cooked
50 g (2 oz) Swiss cheese, grated

Salmon Soup

1 salmon head and bones
400 g (1 lb) raw fish bones and trimmings from your fishmonger
1 leek, chopped
1 stalk celery, chopped
1 large onion, chopped
1 clove garlic
2 teaspoons salt
12 peppercorns
1 bayleaf
bunch of parsley with stalks
1½ litres (almost 3 pints) water
2 tablespoons olive oil
1 onion, chopped
3 white parts of leeks, chopped
3 large tomatoes, skinned and chopped
250 ml (½ pint) white wine

This is a wonderful way of using up the carcass of a salmon.
If possible, reserve some of the flesh to put in the soup.

Place the first 11 ingredients in a large saucepan and boil for
about 30 minutes. Strain.
  Heat olive oil in saucepan and lightly fry onion and leeks.
Add tomatoes, fish stock and wine. Cook for 20 minutes. Test
for salt and pepper. Just before serving, add any leftover flakes
of salmon.

Optional You may also add 1 large tablespoon of grated
parmesan cheese, 4 tablespoons thick cream, and 1 small tin
of salmon to the soup.

Gravad Lax — Salmon or Sea Trout

To every 800 g (2 lb) filleted fish add:
3 tablespoons salt
3 tablespoons sugar
2 tablespoons crushed white peppercorns
plenty of dill

I know at least four people who will buy this book just to
have this recipe of Betty Campbell's. Anyone who has been
to Scandinavia will probably be familiar with Gravad Lax. It
is vaguely similar to smoked salmon but more moist and tender.

Clean and fillet the fish, but do not wash. Take a dish
with sides which as nearly as possible fits the piece of fish.
On the bottom spread a layer of the salt, sugar and pepper
mixture, and a layer of dill stalks. Spread a layer of salt mixture
on the cut side of each fillet. Knead well into the flesh. Put one
fillet skin side down in the dish and cover with dill. Place the
other fillet on top, cut sides together. Cover with the rest of
the salt and some dill, then cover with foil. Make a few holes
in the foil. Place a light weight on top and leave in a cool
place (not a refrigerator) for 48 hours, turning the fish once.
It is then ready to eat. Scrape away the dill and pepper. Cut
into slices as you would smoked salmon and serve with Dill
Sauce, brown bread and butter. It freezes well.
  I have also been sent almost the identical recipe from my
great friend in Canada. The only difference is that she weights
hers more heavily, keeps it an extra day, and if no cool place
exists puts it in the refrigerator. She serves it with a Sour
Cream and Cucumber Sauce.

Dill Sauce

Mix together mustard, sugar and vinegar. Add oil, drop by
drop, stirring continually as you would for mayonnaise, until
you have a thick sauce. Add dill leaves, finely cut with scissors.

Note: Swedish mustard is not available in England. It is a sweet mustard, and its nearest equivalent is Idun Sennep (Mild Type) which can be obtained from the Norway Centre, Knightsbridge.

Dill grows quickly and easily. Cut it when the fronds are feathery. It freezes well.

1 tablespoon Swedish mustard
1 tablespoon sugar
2 tablespoons vinegar
125 ml ($\frac{1}{4}$ pint) oil, approximately
2 tablespoons dill leaves

Ruthie's Sour Cream and Cucumber Sauce for Gravad Lax

Mix together the cream, sugar, vinegar, pepper and dill. Pour over the sliced cucumbers.

150 ml (6 oz) sour cream
75–100 g (3–4 oz) white sugar
4 tablespoons cider vinegar
freshly ground black pepper
lots of chopped dill
2 cucumbers, thinly sliced

Rimmed Lax — for Salmon or Sea Trout

This is another recipe from Betty Campbell.

Clean and fillet the fish. Do not wash them. Prepare in exactly the same way as for Gravad Lax, leaving out the dill. It will be ready after 2 days. Serve with slices of lemon or with Dill Sauce, brown bread and butter.

Note: I had a little trouble buying saltpêtre and found that smaller chemists were more inclined to stock it than the larger ones.

To each 800 g (2 lb) fish add:
3 tablespoons salt
1 tablespoon sugar
1 teaspoon saltpêtre
2 tablespoons crushed white pepper-corns

Salmon Mousse I

There are many variations of mousses: the first of Elizabeth David's from *Summer Cooking* is lighter than the following one. Mrs David says she wishes to wage a war against the mousse as too many meals in private houses start or end with a gelatinous mess, but on hearing my plea she admitted that it was a comfort for the overworked housewife to have one safely behind her in the refrigerator.

1 large cupful of cooked salmon
1 tablespoon grated parmesan
salt
a little cayenne pepper
a squeeze of lemon
150 ml (6 oz) aspic
60 ml (2$\frac{1}{2}$ oz) thick cream
2 egg whites, stiffly beaten

Pound salmon and parmesan in a mortar and season with salt, cayenne and lemon juice. (My note: you may do this in the liquidizer but it does not give you the same consistency.) Stir in the melted aspic and cream. Put in refrigerator until it is all but set and then fold in stiffly beaten egg whites. Turn into a soufflé dish just large enough to hold the mousse.

If you are using fish stock for aspic (see Poached Salmon) allow 5–10 g ($\frac{1}{4}$ oz) or 1 scant tablespoon per 375 ml ($\frac{3}{4}$ pint) liquid.

Salmon Mousse II

300 g (12 oz) cooked, skinned and
  boned salmon
75 g (3 oz) creamed butter
6 tablespoons cool Béchamel Sauce
2 tablespoons sherry, Madeira or
  white wine
2 tablespoons cream
salt and pepper

Garnish
250 ml (½ pint) fish aspic
a few thin cucumber slices
a few peeled slices of tomato
a few sprigs of parsley or tarragon

Place salmon in a mortar with butter and Béchamel Sauce.
Pound well. (This may be done in a liquidizer but it is not so
good.) Add sherry, Madeira or wine, then cream, and test for
seasoning. Turn into a soufflé dish and allow to cool.

Cover with a thin layer of aspic which is cool but not quite
set. Dip the cucumber, tomato, parsley or whatever else you
wish to decorate the mousse with into the remaining aspic
and place on top of the mousse. Allow to cool. Finally, fill up
the rest of the dish with the remaining aspic which is cool but
not yet set.

Potted Salmon

Use equal quantities of:
cooked, boned and skinned salmon
soft butter
a little white pepper
a little white wine or lemon juice
a pinch of nutmeg
melted clarified butter

This does not keep as well as potted meat. It needs to be kept
in a refrigerator and eaten fairly quickly.

Pound all these well together until the consistency is soft and
even. Add only enough wine or lemon juice to make it so.
Test for seasoning. Put in small pots. Cool. When cool, cover
with a layer of clarified butter, which although liquid, is not hot.

HOW TO SMOKE SALMON

Alan Carrick Smith is a member of the Glen Lyon Players.
Besides his enormous musical talent, he also produces the best
home-smoked salmon I have tasted outside Norway. This is an
abbreviated version of an article written by him and published
in *Country Life* in February 1966. Smoking salmon is far easier
the second time when you have everything collected and have
seen exactly how it works. It takes about 40 hours, so take
courage and have a go.

Equipment

1. A container or bath large enough to hold the fish immersed in brine.
2. A large flat platter, marble slab or stone larder shelf.
3. A rectangular box, open on one long side, that when standing on end
   will be broad and long enough to hang the two sides of the salmon
   from two hooks which you have placed in the inside top. Bore a small
   hole in the top to aid the draught, or raise one of the boards with a
   chisel.
4. A sack, and maybe a couple extra to help cover gaps in the trench.
5. A trench 30 cm (1 ft) deep, 30 cm (1 ft) across, and about 3 m (10 ft)
   long, pointing along the line of the prevailing wind.
6. Old corrugated iron or fairly heat-proof boards which will cover the
   trench.

Ingredients

1 salmon, probably over 4 kg (10 lb), as it will lose half its weight during the smoking process. It does not need to be a prime fish.

400–600 g (1–1½ lb) soft brown (best) or demerara sugar.

1½–3 kg (4–7 lb) cheapest cooking salt.

1 potato.

A small barrow-load or 70 cm (28 in) sack of oak chips (best) or sawdust from any hard wood (not conifer), usually obtainable from the local joiner or woodworker.

Method

Clean fish, making sure you remove as much of the blood from the backbone as possible. (If you wish to make salmon caviar, retain the egg sacks of a hen fish.)

Make brine by putting the potato in enough tepid water to cover the fish (but do not put in the fish at this stage), and then add salt until the potato floats. Immerse the fish for 15–20 hours – the exact time is relatively unimportant, though a longer time is better than too short a time. Remove fish and wash well under cold tap. With a very sharp-pointed knife, remove the tail and head, leaving the firm bone by the gills; then split the fish, remove backbone, fins and any stray bones.

Smother the two sides in sugar and plenty of salt. If the fish is large, make a few small nicks along the deep part of the back and press a little more salt in with your thumb. Lay the two sides on a platter, shelf or slab for 12–15 hours. Turn them occasionally and be prepared to collect or mop up all the surplus liquid which will be produced.

Smoking

Place the box upright in the far end (down the wind) of the trench with its open side facing up the trench. Light a small fire with any wood at the near end of the trench. When this has died down to glowing embers, place your chips along the trench so that the near end will catch from the fire and start to smoke. If there is a breeze it should go well. Make sure the chips are really smouldering and then place the corrugated iron or boards over the trench, covering any gaps from which the smoke might escape. Then check that the smoke is moving along the channel and up and through the box.

Take the two sides, wash them under a cold tap, dry them, put a small loop of strong string through the shoulder-bones, and hang them by these loops on the hooks in the box. Cover the front of the box with the sack and check again that the smoke is flowing freely through the box. Leave for 12–15 hours.

Watch the chips from time to time – if there is too much draught they will turn red and give too much smoke, in which case you must seal off the end of the trench for a time with sacking or boards. If the draught is too little you must use a board or dig a small trench to convey air through the tunnel more quickly. You will soon learn how to get it right. A steady gentle smoke is better than a hot cloud, even if it takes a little longer, as the fish will taste and keep better.

If the chips are still smouldering after 12–15 hours, leave the sides until the fire has gone out. This will do no harm and will help the fish to keep a little longer. Take the sides from the box and hang them in the larder. Do not put them in a refrigerator or deep freeze unless you absolutely have to. If you think there may be flies, hang them in cheese-cloth or greaseproof paper.

When you wish to carve it, remove any stray bones with tweezers or pliers, and you may wish to cut away any surface flesh which has caught the smoke. To carve, use a long, thin very sharp knife – a ham knife is ideal. Carve from the centre towards the tail, keeping the knife flat to get the slices as thin as possible.

Salmon Caviar

This is also from Alan's article in *Country Life* and really is worth trying. Whenever I have had it at Innerwick there has never been enough. He recommends eating it on its own, with a little chopped hard-boiled egg, toast, butter, lemon juice, pepper, and a glass of vodka – or as a topping to cold consommé with a poached egg in it.

Holding the egg sack on a plate with one fork, tear the eggs from the sack with another fork, separating them as you go. Place the eggs, which you have released, in a basin, adding small handfuls of salt. Continue until the sack is a stringy mess, then hold it up with one fork and continue to tear gently with the other until it is empty. Put the eggs into a sieve and wash well under a cold tap, tossing gently until they glisten and shine. All loose bits of sack and membrane will settle on top. Pick these off and with a silver spoon ease the eggs into very small clean screw-top jars, sprinkling liberally with salt as you go. Close jars and place in the refrigerator. They should keep for a fortnight or more.

Trout

This is about trout which are caught in rivers, burns, lakes and lochs, that are fresh and full of their own flavour. They do not need elaborate treatment: it is an insult to them. However, if large quantities are being caught they do become rather a problem. An Abu Smoker is a great help, or even two of them if you are going to feed hungry hoards. Fresh, warm, smoked trout is always a great treat, and being able to smoke your own fish for pâtés and mousses gives them a unique flavour.

It is always easier to make rules than to keep them, especially with your children, but if every child was brought up to think that cleaning a trout was part and parcel of catching it, life in the kitchen might be a great deal easier, and dinner or breakfast more likely to be on time.

Sautéed Trout

This very easy way of cooking trout is the classic way; every other method seems to be a rather desperate attempt to find something different. If your trout is fresh, there is nothing better you can do, but it does need care. If the butter is too hot the skin of the fish will burn and ruin the taste, but if the butter is not hot enough the fish will lose its firmness.

trout
seasoned flour
butter
parsley
lemon juice

Clean the trout and wipe it, then dust lightly in seasoned flour. Fry until golden in plenty of butter (preferably clarified). Place on a serving dish, pour over any butter from the pan, and sprinkle with parsley. You may also sprinkle with a little lemon juice, or melt some more butter in the pan, sprinkle lemon juice into it and then pour it over the fish. Or you could brown extra butter until it starts to smell nutty to serve with it.

Trout with Bacon

This is another super breakfast dish.

For each trout you will require:
3 strips thinly cut streaky bacon
butter
flour
maybe a little salt

For each trout fry about three strips of thinly cut (No. 4) streaky bacon until it is crispy, and has supplied you with the fat in which to cook the fish. You may have to add a little bit of butter. Dust the trout with flour and fry in the fat. Don't add salt until you are sure that the bacon hasn't given you enough.

Trout Fried in Oatmeal

This is a normal way of frying herrings, but it is also good with trout, especially for breakfast.

Whole Fish Clean trout, cut off head and fins, and dry. Pat seasoned oatmeal on to it and fry in hot dripping or a mixture of butter and oil until it is brown on both sides. This should take about 8 minutes for a 250 g (10 oz) fish.

Split and Boned Fish   Clean fish and remove head. Open it and force it apart, flesh side down. Turn it over and, starting at the tail, pull backbone away with the side bones. With a little practice and firmness you will find none of the bones will break off. Dry fish, pat in seasoned oatmeal and fry in hot dripping or a mixture of butter and oil for 3–4 minutes on each side.

Norwegian Recipe for Small Trout

trout
butter
thick cream
salt and pepper

Again from Betty Campbell.

Clean trout, wipe, but do not wash. Fry quickly in a little butter until brown on the outside. Pour in a little thick fresh cream. Season with salt and pepper and leave to simmer until fish is cooked and the sauce is thick and golden.

Baked Small Trout with Cream and Yoghurt

trout
butter
natural yoghurt
thick cream
salt and pepper

This is not unlike the preceding recipe but the yoghurt makes a change of taste.

Clean trout, wipe, but do not wash. Fry quickly in an oven-proof casserole in a little butter until just golden on the outside.

For six small trout, mix together 1 small carton of natural yoghurt, an equal amount of thick cream, and a little salt and pepper. Pour mixture over fish and bake in a moderately slow oven (170°C, 325°F, Mark 3) for about 20 minutes.

Truite au Bleu

trout
salted water
vinegar
melted butter

This is a classic dish. The main snag is that the fish is supposed to be alive when it goes into the water. Because of this, it is normally done with trout from a tank near the kitchen. You stun the fish and plunge it into a boiling mixture of salted water and vinegar – three parts water to one part vinegar – and poach it until it is just cooked through, about 5 minutes. Serve with melted butter separately and boiled potatoes. It is the vinegar which turns the skin the dark blue colour, giving the dish its name.

Poached Trout

Truite au Bleu may be the classic, but this is a good deal more realistic and also an excellent way of cooking trout if you wish them cold.

Mix all the ingredients together. Court bouillon is best if simmered for about an hour before adding fish. If you are going to turn it into aspic later it will be richer and more tasty if you boil some fish heads and bones in the water for about 45 minutes. Strain and use that stock in the bouillon.

Poach trout gently in just enough court bouillon to cover. They won't need more than about 4–6 minutes. The more shallow the pot, the easier they will be to get out. Serve with any suitable sauce or with just browned butter.

Court bouillon
1 litre (almost 2 pints) water
375 ml (¾ pint) white wine
70 ml (1 gill) wine vinegar
1 onion, stuck with 3 cloves
1 carrot, sliced
1 stalk celery
1 bayleaf
1 sprig thyme
2 sprigs parsley
salt and pepper

Smoked Trout

You can now buy Abu Smokers almost anywhere. Most large department stores, hardware shops and sporting equipment shops have them, as well as the large bags of extra wood dust which you will need. Make sure you take plenty, though one 400 g (1 lb) bag will supply about fifty smokings. Follow the instructions and don't overload it with too much fish. It is better to split the fish into two or three lots than to have an indifferently uncooked batch. Smoked trout should be served with horseradish sauce. Try to avoid the horrid bottled variety. If you haven't any fresh horseradish of your own, then buy horseradish powder. French's make a good one.

Horseradish Sauce with Fresh Horseradish

Fold horseradish into the cream and add lemon juice and seasoning. Allow to sit for about 10 minutes to mellow.

If you must use the bottled variety, then add about 5 tablespoons whipped cream to 2 tablespoons sauce.

1 tablespoon or more grated horseradish
125 ml (¼ pint) lightly whipped cream
1 teaspoon lemon juice
salt, pepper and a little sugar (if you like)

Smoked Trout Paste

Pound the flesh in a mortar, then work in the butter and finally the lemon juice and seasoning. Watch out for any little hair-like bones as you pound, and pick them out. Pack the paste into small pots and cover the top with melted, but not hot, clarified butter.

This may be made in the liquidizer with melted, but not hot, butter, but the consistency is not quite so good. When you go to scrape it from the liquidizer you will find that any left-over small bones will have collected around the blades, so be careful to pick them out.

about 150 g (6 oz) smoked trout flesh with all the skin and bones removed
75 g (3 oz) soft butter
juice of ½ lemon
salt, pepper and a little mace

Having said that I don't approve of freshly caught trout being 'mucked about' with, my daughter says that when she ran a fishing lodge she couldn't have coped without Trout Mousse. Her employers fished all day, the trout poured in, and no one really liked eating them – so finally in desperation she flung them all in a mousse for a Sunday lunch-party. Everyone was thrilled. Both recipes are based roughly on her Winkfield Place cookery notes and adapted to a different environment.

Trout Mousse I

800 g (2 lb) trout, preferably half of it smoked
50 g (2 oz) butter, well creamed
210 ml (3 gills) cold Béchamel Sauce
125 ml (¼ pint) mayonnaise
2 teaspoons gelatine, dissolved in half a small glass of white wine or water
125 ml (¼ pint) lightly whipped cream
salt and pepper

This calls for 600 g (1½ lb) of trout fillet. The taste is best if you smoke two of the trout and poach the rest. This also gives you some fish stock for the Béchamel Sauce.

Smoke and poach the trout. Discard all skin and bones. Mix fish well together and pound until smooth. Add butter, Béchamel Sauce, mayonnaise and finally the dissolved gelatine. Fold in cream. Season to taste. Turn into a soufflé dish or mould. Garnish with sliced cucumber and serve with Horseradish Sauce.

Trout Mousse II

4 smoked or poached trout
6–8 stalks celery, finely chopped
25 g (1 oz) gelatine
250 ml (½ pint) white wine or wine and fish stock
1 green pepper, blanched and diced
1 tablespoon horseradish cream
salt and pepper
250 ml (½ pint) lightly whipped cream

This may also be made with half-smoked trout and half-poached, or completely with smoked trout.

Discard all skin and bones from trout. Flake trout carefully and mix with celery. Dissolve gelatine in half of the white wine (or wine and fish stock) over a gentle heat, then add the rest of the liquid. Stir gently into the trout and celery (you don't want to mush the fish). Add pepper and horseradish cream. Season well. Fold in cream and turn into mould. Serve with cucumber salad.

Sea Trout

Sea trout is the migratory species. The best known brown trout is non-migratory. Fishmongers and the French are inclined to call them salmon trout, but whichever you call them they make the most superb eating. I can never understand why people pay more for salmon if they can get sea trout more cheaply. To me there is the same difference between sea trout and salmon that there is between partridge and pheasant. Sea trout being a smaller fish than salmon is more often than not served whole. Most of the salmon recipes may be used with sea trout as well, but keep it simple – don't lose the delicate flavour in a strong sauce.

Sea Trout Baked in Foil

I don't think there is any point in cooking sea trout any other way. With this method you retain every bit of its flavour and the remaining juices with maybe a little more melted butter, are all the sauce that you need, though you may make Hollandaise if you wish. Be careful when you pull out the foil that there are no crumbs underneath as this will tear the foil when you spread on the butter. When you measure the foil with the fish, make sure you have dried the fish first as if it drips on to the foil the butter will not spread on the wet and the fish will stick at that place. Be generous with the foil and the butter. The more butter that you use, the more buttery juices you will get. Dry the fish thoroughly. Measure a piece of aluminium foil with the fish, making sure that you have about 7 cm (3 in) left over at each end and that it is wide enough to go round the fish, leaving enough to fold and pinch together well. Butter the foil generously as if you were buttering bread, and make sure that you go out far enough to ensure that the fish will not touch any part of the foil which is unbuttered. Place the fish in a cool oven (140°C, 275°F, Mark 1). Allow about 30 minutes per 400 g (1 lb). When it is ready, unwrap, and be careful to catch the juices. If you wish to serve it cold, skin it gently while it is still warm.

Sauces for Fish

Hollandaise

My family are hooked on Hollandaise; if you give them Hollandaise on something you can fool them that they have had a good meal. Because of this I have developed all grades of Hollandaise – the well made, hand-beaten genuine one because I feel like it; the middling one made with a hand-beater when they are going to eat at least three artichokes each, and the liquidizer kind when I've forgotten to make it and everyone looks sad.

Having just read several books on the subject, I find I tend to use a greater proportion of butter to egg yolks, so I will say 3 egg yolks to 150–175 g (6–7 oz) butter, but I don't think it is really necessary, though it is probably safer. When Hollandaise is used with fish you may boil down about a cupful of fish stock until it is reduced to 3 tablespoons and use it instead of water and lemon juice.

Proper Hollandaise

3 egg yolks
2 tablespoons cold water
150–175 g (6–7 oz) unsalted butter
salt and pepper
about 1 tablespoon lemon juice

Have egg yolks at room temperature and the butter even a little warmer so that it is soft. You will also need a double boiler or a bowl which will fit over a saucepan, but make sure that the bowl is above the hot water, not in it.

Place yolks and water in the top of the double boiler or bowl and place over hot, but never boiling, water. Start whisking. Add a lump of butter (about one-sixth of the total) and continue whisking until it is taken up and the sauce starts to thicken. Continue adding lumps of butter in this way until it has all been used up. Watch that the water doesn't get too hot. Season with salt, pepper and lemon juice to taste. You can keep the sauce over warm water for about 30 minutes, stirring occasionally. My daughter thinks nothing of keeping it for an hour or more, but I haven't the nerves!

Quick Hollandaise

3 egg yolks
2 tablespoons cold water
150–175 g (6–7 oz) melted butter, but not boiling hot
salt and pepper
about 1 tablespoon lemon juice

This is made the same way only with an electric handbeater and melted butter. If you are using salted butter, avoid using the milky residue as it ruins the delicate taste.

Follow the previous instructions but start by adding the butter very slowly. As the sauce thickens, you may pour in the butter in a fine stream. You have to be a little more careful if you wish to keep this warm as it is already slightly warmer and therefore rather more inclined to curdle.

Liquidizer Hollandaise

3 egg yolks
1 tablespoon lemon juice
1 teaspoon cold water
½ teaspoon salt
pepper
150–175 g (6–7 oz) hot (almost boiling) butter

Place yolks, lemon juice, water, salt and pepper in liquidizer. Blend very quickly and then pour in the butter in a fine stream. Do not overblend. Test for seasoning. You may wish to add more lemon juice, salt or pepper. This all happens very quickly so don't keep blending any longer than is necessary. Don't use the milk residue from the hot butter.

Sauce Mousseline

3 parts Hollandaise Sauce
to
1 part whipped cream

Fold the whipped cream into the Hollandaise Sauce just before serving. You may need a little extra seasoning.

Béchamel Sauce

Basic Béchamel Sauce is made with milk, butter, flour, salt and pepper, and maybe a scrape of nutmeg. When using it as a sauce with fish, it is a great deal better if you can substitute fish stock for some of the milk.

250 ml (½ pint) milk
40 g (1½ oz) butter
2 level tablespoons flour
salt and pepper
scraping of nutmeg (optional)

Heat the milk. In a separate saucepan melt the butter until it bubbles, but do not let it brown. Stir flour well into the butter. Over a low heat, gradually add warm milk, stirring occasionally, so there is never a lump. I use a whisk. Once all the milk has been added, season to taste and simmer very gently for about 10 minutes, stirring most of the time. If you wish to keep it warm or reheat it, do so over hot water. If you wish to keep it and to prevent a skin forming, dot the top with butter while it is still hot.

Variations

Velouté Sauce. If all the milk in a Béchamel Sauce is substituted for stock it becomes velouté. A little cream may be added.

To Béchamel Sauce you may also add any of the following:
1. 3 tablespoons tomato juice.
2. 2 tablespoons anchovy paste, a little more butter and a squeeze of lemon.
3. Chopped hard-boiled egg and finely chopped parsley.
4. Dijon mustard.
5. Dill.

Sauce Bretonne

This is one of my favourite cold sauces. I love it on almost everything, but especially mackerel. It is easier to make than mayonnaise and the taste depends a great deal on the quality and quantity of the mustard and the vinegar that you use. You may use considerably less of both. Choose whichever herbs you wish.

2 egg yolks
salt and pepper
1 tablespoon Dijon mustard
1 teaspoon tarragon or wine vinegar
fresh herbs – parsley, fennel, chives, tarragon, chevril, dill – whatever you wish
75 g (3 oz) very soft butter

Stir egg yolks with salt, pepper, mustard, vinegar and finely chopped herbs. Then little by little stir in the butter until the sauce is as thick as mayonnaise. This is best made just before serving, but if it loses its consistency, it can be brought back again by stirring over warm water.

Mayonnaise

3 egg yolks
250 ml (½ pint) olive oil
large pinch of salt
a little tarragon or wine vinegar or lemon juice – too much can ruin the whole thing

If you don't know how to make mayonnaise then I don't think this is probably the book to start from, but you certainly need it if you have a lot of cold salmon. The only rule I can think of is don't be frightened of it and it won't fall apart over you. As with Hollandaise, I don't find three egg yolks essential, two will do, but three are safer.

Whisk the yolks until they start to go pale and thick, and then begin whisking in the oil drop by drop. Keep adding the oil very slowly until the sauce starts to really thicken, then add an occasional drop of vinegar or lemon juice, and finish by whisking in the oil in a fine stream. This should work. If you wish to keep it for a day or two, stir in 2 tablespoons of boiling water.

Liquidizer Mayonnaise

1 egg
½ teaspoon dry mustard
1 teaspoon salt
pinch of cayenne
250 ml (½ pint) olive oil
2 tablespoons tarragon or wine vinegar or lemon juice (I find this a little much but it helps if you are mixing it with bought mayonnaise)

You may make mayonnaise in a liquidizer. I find it rather heavy, but it is better than nothing, and quite adequate if you wish to stretch the bought variety for a large party. Liquidizer mayonnaise is usually made with a whole egg and slightly more vinegar or lemon juice.

Place egg, mustard, salt, cayenne and about a quarter of the oil in the liquidizer. Cover, and blend well. Take off cover and slowly add half of the remaining oil, then the vinegar or lemon juice. Blend well again and then slowly add remaining oil. If you wish to keep it, blend in 2 tablespoons boiling water.

Sauce Verte

10 leaves of fresh spinach (or more if you are unable to get watercress)
10 sprigs of watercress
3–4 sprigs of parsley and tarragon (not huge branches)
a few chives (optional)
250 ml (½ pint) mayonnaise

This, if you can collect the fresh greens, is the perfect sauce for cold salmon or sea trout. I think it's still worth making even if you are unable to get the watercress – it won't be quite the real thing but it will still look pretty.

Pick the leaves off the watercress, tarragon and parsley, and discard the stalks. Blanch all the leaves in boiling water for 2 minutes, then drain, and squeeze until completely dry. Pound them with the chives until they are almost a dry dust. Just before serving, stir them into the mayonnaise.

Mackerel, Mussels, Lobsters, Crabs

None of the above have much to do with game fish except that they are inclined to appear on a game-fishing holiday. They are also full of memories from childhood, and how thrilled one was as a child when your catch too was appreciated and eaten with relish at dinner.

Many experienced cooks may not have had to cope with these live or special things before. This may just help.

Mackerel

Mackerel is a most underrated fish, probably because it is only at its best when very fresh so that people in towns seldom have a chance to taste it in its prime. Mackerel and mustard go very well together.

Grilled Mackerel

Score each side of a whole mackerel two or three times and brush well with oil or melted butter. You may put some Dijon mustard in the slits if you wish. A whole fish takes from 10–15 minutes to cook. Fillets are better grilled for 8 minutes on the flesh side and 3 minutes on the skin side.

mackerel
oil or melted butter
Dijon mustard (optional)

Baked Mackerel in Foil

Bake as you would Trout in Foil. A whole fish will take 35–40 minutes.

Smoked Mackerel

Fillet the mackerel and smoke the fillets as you would trout in your Abu Smoker.

Cold Mackerel

Either bake it in foil or poach it for about 20 minutes in a court bouillon. Allow to cool, then skin and fillet if you wish. Serve with Sauce Bretonne.

As well as the above, most recipes for trout will do.

Mussels

If you happen to be having your sporting holiday by the coast, then you may find yourself with an unlimited quantity of mussels, and quite often people don't know how lucky they are or how to cope with them. It is probably wise if you are near a village to gather them away from any sewage outlet, but once you have established where that is, you may gather at will, and children are willing helpers. Mussels must be well cleaned and kept in cold water until they are cooked. A famous old seadog told me that the easiest way to get rid of grit is to put the mussels in a bucket under a very slightly running tap and to throw in a handful of oatmeal. The mussels digest the oatmeal which removes the grit. Discard any broken or open shells, or ones that rub loosely together. Scrape away the beard and bits of seaweed or barnacles that might be sticking to them. Change the water several times. Then all you have to do is to decide how simple or grand you want them to be.

3 litres (almost 6 pints) of mussels would be sufficient for 4 people.

The easiest way, and certainly the least trouble, is to steam them open in white wine or cider and sprinkle with chopped parsley. Place mussels in a wide pan, pour over approximately 125 ml ($\frac{1}{4}$ pint) white wine or cider for each litre (2 pints) of mussels. Cover, and cook over a fairly hot heat, shaking the pan every minute or so, until they open, which should be in about 5 minutes, depending on how many you are cooking. Place mussels in a warm dish. Strain the stock through muslin over the mussels.

That is the very easiest form and I think a few extras make a worthwhile difference. To the mussels and the wine add a chopped onion, 2 or 3 sprigs of parsley, a sprig of thyme, some freshly ground pepper. Cook as above. After straining the stock, taste it and reduce it if necessary; then reheat it with 50 g (2 oz) of butter. Or you may add less butter and some thick cream. Sprinkle with parsley and serve quickly. You need plenty of bread to mop up the juices.

Lobsters

The best lobsters are small or middle-sized. Big ones are inclined to be tough. Unfortunately they must be cooked alive. It is nicer for you if someone has trussed them first so they don't wriggle as much, but they say lobsters are fairly insensitive and that boiling water kills them almost instantly.

After all, since it's been caught someone is going to kill it, you want to eat it – so it's fairly hypocritical not to be able to do it yourself. Just think of something else.

For up to an 800 g (2 lb) lobster boil 3 litres (almost 6 pints) of well salted water. Pick up the lobster by the back of its neck and plunge it in. Cover, and let it simmer for about 4 minutes per 400 g (1 lb) – a little more if it is small, a little less if it is large. When it is cooked, take it out of the water and, with a strong knife, slit it from head to tail down its front. Remove the long intestine and the stomach. All the other green and coral coloured parts are good to eat.

Cook as you wish. When it is this fresh I just like it grilled with lots of butter. Nutcrackers are useful for the claws.

Crabs

I used to be terrified of cleaning crabs as I'd heard there was part of them that was deadly poisonous and I had visions of wiping out the whole family just for a cheap meal. I don't think the gills are deadly poisonous, they just aren't very nice to eat. When you pull off the back they are the white spongy fingers that are lying there. You just pull them off and throw them away.

Like lobsters, the big ones tend to be tough. Boil crabs in salted water for about 8 minutes per 400 g (1 lb). When they are cool, pull off the backs – you may need to insert a knife to help you – remove the gills, split the body so you can get at the meat, and crack the claws.

Soup

Game Stock

1 tablespoon fat, pork or bacon dripping or butter
1 onion, sliced
1 leek, cut in 2.5 cm (1 in) pieces
3 carrots, sliced
1 stalk celery, sliced
400 g (1 lb) stewing venison
some old bones, an old pheasant, 2
   old partridges or pigeons
1 pig's trotter
1 knuckle of veal (optional)
6 parsley stalks
6 peppercorns
4 juniper berries
1 bayleaf
a pinch of thyme

This may vary enormously depending on what meat, bones or carcass of game you have available.

Melt fat in soup pot, stir in vegetables and cook lightly. Cut up game and add meat and bones and brown a little, then add herbs and 1½ litres (3 pints) cold water. Bring to boil and simmer for about 3 hours. Skim and strain.

Game Soup

Having made game stock, reserve a few pieces of meat, throw away the bones and any skin and liquidize the remaining meat and vegetables. Return to stock and thicken with a little beurre manié (1 tablespoon butter mixed with 1 tablespoon flour) added in little bits, whisking as you do it. Season with salt and pepper and add some port or lemon juice, or redcurrant jelly if you wish, though this is better with venison soup than feathered game. Add the pieces of meat, and heat soup until it is very hot.

Cream of Game Soup

Depending on how extravagant you wish to be, you may use all egg yolks and cream, or a little rice, or butter, flour, egg yolks and cream. I'm inclined to be extravagant as the stock has hardly cost you anything.

3 or 4 egg yolks
250 ml (½ pint) cream
1 litre (2 pints) hot game stock

Beat yolks well and add cream. Beat into this mixture a cup of hot game stock and then beat this back into the remaining stock. Continue to beat over a low heat until the soup has thickened, but do not let boil – a double boiler reduces the worry of this.

If you wish to use fewer egg yolks and cream then start by making a roux or add a little cooked rice.

Clear Game Soup

Make game stock and when it is cold remove fat – it should be clear and strong enough to be served as consommé.

You may add sherry, port or Madeira, a little rice or pasta, very finely chopped green pepper, a few finely sliced mushrooms sautéed in butter, or small cubes of bread sautéed until golden in butter.

any mixture of legs and carcasses of birds, or heads, forelegs or bones of rabbits or hares, any scraps of venison
200 g (8 oz) shin of beef
1 pig's trotter and 1 litre (2 pints) water or 1 litre (2 pints) beef stock
1 carrot, sliced
1 onion, sliced
1 stalk celery, sliced
bouquet garni of parsley, bayleaf, thyme
several juniper berries, crushed
salt and pepper
port and/or lemon juice

Game Soup for small amounts of Game

Simmer all ingredients together except for port and lemon juice, until the meat is off the bone. Strain. Pick out bones and skin and liquidize the rest, or if you wish a clear soup, cool and skim off fat. Test seasoning and add port and/or lemon juice. Serve with forcemeat balls or croûtons.

Stracciatella made with Game Stock

This is always incredibly popular. The better the stock and parmesan, the better the soup.

625 ml (1¼ pints) good clear game stock
2 eggs
2 tablespoons grated parmesan cheese
1 tablespoon semolina

Heat stock. Beat eggs well with parmesan and semolina. Continue beating while you add a cup of hot stock to the egg mixture and then add this slowly to the rest of the hot stock, beating all the time for several minutes. Allow the soup to sit over a moderate heat until the mixture just begins to break. Serve quickly.

Portuguese Hare Soup

This was sent to us by Senhor Martins, and it is delicious. As the translation left much to the imagination we have had quite a few versions of this soup. Sometimes we have had it as a clear soup just thickened with blood, sometimes I have added pieces of meat to this, and other times I have added liquidized meat. This is roughly what it says and you can use your imagination – it's worth it.

Collect the blood while skinning and cleaning the hare. Fry onion, garlic and 3 bayleaves in oil. Cut the hare into small pieces and fry in this sauce until it is nicely toasted. Add 2 glasses of red wine and fill pan with water. Add 20 cloves and 30 peppercorns. Cook for 7 hours at low fire. When it is almost ready, join the blood mixed with half a glass of whisky in the electric mixer.

My notes – I use 2 large onions, sliced, 2 cloves garlic, 250 ml ($\frac{1}{2}$ pint) red wine, and after much dithering, half a whisky glass of whisky! Having 'joined' the blood and whisky add some of the hot soup to this mixture and then add it back to the rest, slowly. Do not let it boil after this. Serves 8–10.

Merganser Soup

1 merganser
2 carrots
1 leek
4–5 medium sized potatoes
1 parsnip
1$\frac{1}{2}$ litres (3 pints) water
salt and pepper
1 teaspoon crushed allspice
parsley

From Mrs Bo Thelander.

Bring water to boil. Put the bird into the water and let boil a few minutes without lid. Skim off the scum. Cover, and let bird simmer while you prepare the vegetables. Peel and cut the carrots, leek, potatoes and parsnip into slices. Add vegetables and spices to the soup. Boil until bird feels tender. Take out bird, cut the meat from the bones. Cut into suitable pieces (not too big). Put meat back into soup. Chop and add parsley. Serve the soup piping hot. Hot toasted cheese sandwiches taste good with this soup.

Partridge and Cabbage Soup

2 old partridges (you may skin them instead of plucking). Cut them into pieces
100 g (4 oz) lean smoked bacon or ham or a smoked pig's trotter

This is a one-course meal. Served with toasted French bread, it is a very good shooting lunch dish. If you wish to be more refined you may liquidize it with the meat and thin it down with stock or thin cream.

Put partridges, bacon and water in a large pot, bring to the boil. Add all the other ingredients. Bring back to boil, cover, and simmer for 2–3 hours or until the partridges are tender. Strain. Discard bones and skin. Discard parsley and bayleaf. Remove bacon and partridges. Cut meat into small pieces and return to the soup.

3 litres (6 pints) water
800 g (2 lb) cabbage, sliced thickly – cut away most of hard core
8–10 peppercorns, crushed
2 cloves garlic, mashed
2 medium onions, sliced
2 carrots, sliced
1 bouquet garni of 6 sprigs parsley, bayleaf

Mollie's Hare Soup

Collect blood from hare. Split head in two and pour over blood. Leave for 1 hour. Add stock and bring hare very slowly to boiling point. Add vegetables which have been sliced and fried in dripping, herbs, bayleaf, salt and peppercorns. Simmer slowly for 2½–3 hours. Remove hare from soup. Cut some flesh from back and legs of hare. Keep on one side. Remove bayleaf and peppercorns from soup. Liquidize vegetables. Return soup. Fry flour until golden brown in dripping. Whisk into soup until boiling. Add cut up hare and port, and season to taste.

1 hare
1½ litres (3 pints) stock
40 g (1½ oz) dripping
4 carrots
2 onions
½ turnip
1 stick celery
bunch herbs
1 bayleaf
6 peppercorns
1½ teaspoons salt
40 g (1½ oz) flour
70 ml (2½ oz) port

The custom at Bolfracks is to serve boiled potatoes with hare soup instead of toast. Very good after a long day's shooting.

G.C.—L

Pâtés, Baking and Cheese

Game Terrines and Pâtés

It is difficult to commit yourself on how the perfect pâté should taste and look, personal opinions differ widely. I find my taste hard to rely on as I know I am inclined to use too much garlic with game and too little salt. Then when I am finally satisfied with the result someone usually remarks that they liked the last one better.

A good pâté, like good wine, must be given time to ripen and mellow. If you have time leave the mixture for several hours or overnight before you put it in the terrine to bake. Then after it is weighted and cold, it likes several days in a cool place before you eat it. Perhaps you have noticed that if you eat a pâté over a period of several days it is usually much the best just as it is finished.

If you are using hare or venison allow rather more fat as their flesh is drier than that of game birds. Don't panic if you find, as I often do, that you cannot buy veal. Pork fillet does very well as a substitute, but try for veal. I sometimes can find it frozen, but if it is frozen dry it well after it is thawed before you mince it.

Try to get your butcher to mince the pork and veal for you as it is a strain on your domestic mincer and also a bore. Unfortunately an unknown butcher can produce endless reasons why he doesn't want your fat pork in his mincer. My Mr Keith and I are both now resigned to him having a little pork left in his mince and me with a little mince in my pork – a good perk for our peke!

Before you begin, decide whether or not you wish strips of game as a layer through the middle of the pâté. I don't think it matters much but if you do, cut them out of the breast and marinate them for an hour or so. If you find it difficult to remove the flesh

162

from the bones of a bird, it is easier if you half roast it in a moderate oven (180°C, 350°F, Mark 4) for 20 minutes, but be sure you catch all the juices and add them to the pâté.

Which spirits you use also is a matter of taste. I like wine and brandy, but port and Madeira are very popular. I spent a year trying to get a good result with gin because I thought it made sense that it should go with juniper berries, but it was never as successful as brandy. I feel I've failed and am rather annoyed at this.

After the terrine has cooled, it helps if you weight it: this gets rid of any pockets of air and makes it firmer and more easily sliced. First cover the top of the pâté with several layers of greaseproof paper. Then find something like a board which fits inside the terrine and then put weights on this. It's the 'something like a board' part that can waste ages while you search for it. I have compromised with two wooden spatulas placed end to end, or a large tin of cassoulet which I bought years ago and have never been able to eat as it is far too useful being a board and weight in one. Some day it will probably blow up. Keep your eyes open for old-fashioned weights in junk shops. They are so much easier than four or five tins of soup balanced on top of each other.

Norwegian Duck Terrine

Ever since Mary Jakhelln sent me this it has been my standby and everyone who has tasted it has gone home with the recipe.

Remove 4–5 slices of breast from the duck, then less carefully remove all the other flesh and place in marinade overnight in the refrigerator. Cut rind from bacon and flatten slices with a knife until they become translucent. Place these around the sides and bottom of a 500 ml (1 pint) terrine dish. Remove duck from marinade, mince all the ingredients, except the strips of breast, together. Mix into a soft moist paste with the strained marinade. Place half of the mixture in the terrine, add the strips of breast and cover with the rest of the mixture. Cover, and sit the dish in a moderate oven (180°C, 350°F, Mark 4) for $2\frac{1}{4}$ hours or until a skewer comes out clean. Allow to cool for a few moments and then pour off as many juices as possible. Retain juices. Leave to cool for an hour and then weight the pâté until it is cold. Remove all the fat from the juices. When cold, decorate with orange segments and bayleaves. Cover with aspic made of the ingredients plus the remaining juices. Strain over pâté and allow to become cold.

1 mallard

Marinade
juice of 1 large orange
2 tablespoons brandy
1 stock cube, crumbled
1 small onion, finely chopped
pinch of rosemary

200 g (8 oz) streaky bacon
200 g (8 oz) chicken livers
1 Spanish onion, coarsely chopped
1 clove garlic, mashed
50 g (2 oz) breadcrumbs

Garnish
3 or 4 orange segments
2–3 bayleaves

Aspic
1 stock cube
15 g ($\frac{1}{2}$ oz) gelatine
250 ml ($\frac{1}{2}$ pint) less 2 tablespoons water
2 tablespoons orange juice

Mary says that this pâté freezes extremely well if you don't bother with the garnish or aspic. I personally would suggest that if you intended to freeze it for any length of time you should omit the garlic.

Eggleston Grouse Terrine

1 brace grouse
150 g (6 oz) tongue in 2 slices, shredded
2 shallots, finely chopped
200 g (8 oz) sausagemeat
2 teaspoons mixed herbs, chopped
100 g (4 oz) fat bacon, preferably in the piece
1 bayleaf
luting paste
strong jellied stock

This is another recipe kindly sent by Eggleston Hall Finishing School.

Cut all the meat from the birds, shred and add to the shredded tongue, set aside.

Place the shallots, minced pork, sausagemeat and herbs in a bowl and mix well together. Line the terrine with fat bacon and press a third of the minced farce into the terrine, then lay half the shredded meat, half remaining farce, remaining meat, and finally the remaining farce. Smooth the top over, press bayleaf on top, cover, and seal the lid with luting paste, or tightly cover with foil.

Cook in a bain Marie in a moderately slow oven (170°C, 325°F, Mark 3) for 2 hours. Remove lid or foil, press overnight using a 1.6 kg (4 lb) weight, and then fill up the dish with stock.

Jean's Terrine de Lapin

1 rabbit
200 g (8 oz) lard cut into 5 mm ($\frac{1}{4}$ in) strips and 5 mm ($\frac{1}{4}$ in) deep
250 g (10 oz) ham, cut same way as lard
1 tablespoon chopped shallots
mixed spice
100 ml (4 oz) white wine
100 ml (4 oz) Cognac
50 ml (2 oz) Madeira
seasoning
600 g (1$\frac{1}{2}$ lb) sausagemeat (cher de porc)
liver of rabbit
1–2 chicken livers (optional)
bard of pork
thyme
1 bayleaf
2 or 3 tablespoons flour mixed with water

The terrine should have a hole in the lid.

Place flesh of rabbit in flat dish. Add strips of lard and ham. Sprinkle with chopped shallots. Add mixed spice, wine, Cognac and Madeira, and seasoning. Mix well so the liquid moistens the meat. Marinate for at least 1 hour. If all the liquid has not been absorbed add it to the sausagemeat, which is in a bowl. Also add the livers to the sausagemeat, and a little more seasoning. Stir well with wooden spatula.

To line the terrine, place bard (sheet of lard) on a chopping board. Put lid of terrine on bard and cut round it with a knife. Place in bottom of terrine – it should fit exactly. Cut another one and put aside to be used later to cover the terrine. Cut two bands about 7 cm (3 in) wide and line sides of terrine: it should be entirely lined with the fat.

Divide sausagemeat into four equal parts. Wet fingers in cold water, put a quarter of the sausagemeat in the bottom of the terrine. Wet fingers again, put the sausagemeat in place with knuckles. Make a layer of flesh and lard strips, side by side (the flesh is not in strips, just in pieces). Press down with damp knuckles. Keep it neat and tidy, patting sides to keep it firm. Now put a layer of sausagemeat. Repeat process above, then add a layer of ham and fat strips and a layer of sausagemeat. Then a layer of rabbit and lard strips, and finally a layer of sausagemeat, always keeping terrine firm and tidy.

Place the piece of bard, already cut, on top. Put small piece of thyme and a bayleaf on the bard. Place lid on. Make a paste with the flour and water. Mix with fingers: it will be sticky. Place along border of lid to seal it. Cook over a bain Marie, on top of stove for about 5 minutes, until the water boils, then put in a very hot oven (230°C, 450°F, Mark 8). Cook for a good 1½ hours. Be sure water is always boiling in bain Marie, and when you add more water it must be boiling too.

If you want to eat this terrine cold it will take a day or a night to cool.

This recipe may be used for Terrine of Chicken – cook it for 1¼ hours, or for Terrine of Pheasant – cook it for 1½ hours.

Game Pâté

This pâté resembles the usual pâté maison which you find in most charcuteries in France. Change the ingredients as you like, especially the seasoning, and add more or less game the next time if you wish.

300 g (12 oz) game meat (liver optional)
2 tablespoons brandy
1 small onion, minced (optional)
25 g (1 oz) butter (optional)
200 g (8 oz) fresh pork fat
8 tablespoons wine, port or Madeira
300 g (12 oz) lean pork, minced
300 g (12 oz) lean veal, minced
1 egg, slightly beaten
½ teaspoon salt
generous amount pepper
6–8 juniper berries, chopped
1 clove garlic, mashed (optional)
3 mm (⅛ in) thick sheet pork back fat, blanched salt pork or blanched fat bacon, if you wish to line the terrine

Cut some strips 5 mm (¼ in) thick from the breast of the bird and marinate them in the brandy for an hour or so. Mince the rest of the game with the liver. If you are using the onion, sauté it slowly in the butter for 8 minutes but do not let it brown. Chop the pork fat into little cubes but retain enough to make strips with, for decorating the top of the pâté. Mix all the ingredients together, including the brandy from the game strips, but not the strips or strips of pork fat. Beat well. Allow to sit for an hour or more if you have time.

Line a terrine dish with pork fat or bacon. This is not necessary but it helps to keep it together if you are going to take the pâté out of the dish or if you freeze it. Place half of the mixture in the terrine, then the strips of game, and cover with remaining mixture. Make a criss-cross pattern on the top with the remaining strips of fat. Cover the terrine with foil and then the lid. Set in a pan of hot water in a moderate oven (180°C, 350°F, Mark 4) for about 1½ hours. If the water evaporates add more. The pâté is cooked when it has shrunk from the sides of the dish. Do not overcook it. Cool, then weight it until it is cold.

Knappach Pigeon Pâté

This was sent to us by Anne Pelham Burn who informed us that it is a very good pâté to freeze, but to cover it with foil before doing so.

5 or 6 pigeons
2 onions, sliced
2 carrots, sliced

dripping
flour
375 ml (¾ pint) stock or stock cube and water
herbs
3–5 tablespoons red wine, port or brandy
1 clove garlic
salt and pepper
400 g (1 lb) butter
melted butter

Do not bother to pluck the pigeons, skin them, feathers and all, and cut off the breasts.

Brown them, the onions and carrots in the dripping, add a little flour, then the stock, herbs and 2–3 tablespoons of the wine, port or brandy. Stew slowly till tender and leave overnight.

Next day put the pigeon through the mincer then pound with a pestle, adding a clove of garlic crushed in a level teaspoon of salt. Work in about 400 g (1 lb) softened butter. Taste and add more seasoning if necessary. If it appears dry add a little of the liquid in which the pigeons were stewed. Add remaining red wine, port or brandy.

Press into ramekin dishes or a small soufflé dish and cover with melted butter. Allow to set. Serve with hot brown toast and butter.

Pheasant Liver Pâté

200 g (8 oz) pheasant livers
1 teaspoon salt
grating of nutmeg
1 teaspoon dry mustard powder
⅛ teaspoon ground cloves
small slice onion
slice of garlic
1–2 tablespoons brandy
100 g (4 oz) butter, melted

If you are eating a lot of pheasants then it doesn't take long to accumulate 200 g (8 oz) livers. They are stronger than chicken livers but if you are used to eating game, then you shouldn't find this offensive. If I'm doubtful about my friends, then I just dilute it with more butter or half pheasant livers and half chicken livers. It is better if it sits a day or two in a refrigerator before serving.

Put pheasant livers in a pan with water barely to cover, cover pan with lid and simmer for 20 minutes. Place them in a liquidizer with all the other ingredients, liquidize until they have formed a smooth paste, pour into dish, cover, and chill.

If you haven't a liquidizer you may mince the cooked livers and then mash them with the rest of the ingredients. Have the butter softened instead of melted, chop the onion and mash the garlic.

Uncomplicated Pâté

about 100 g (4 oz) streaky bacon
about 600 g (1½ lb) uncooked or partly cooked game flesh, minced
about 600 g (1½ lb) fat pork, minced
2 tablespoons brandy
8 tablespoons wine
1 small clove garlic, crushed
1 teaspoon salt
plenty pepper
6–8 juniper berries, chopped

Chop half of the bacon into small cubes, reserving the other half, and mix together with the other ingredients. Allow to stand for an hour or so if you have time. Turn into a terrine and decorate with remaining bacon cut into thin slices and place diagonally across the terrine. Place uncovered in baking tin of hot water and cook in a slow oven (155°C, 310°F, Mark 2) for 1¼–1½ hours. It is done when it starts to come away from the side of the dish. Allow to cool and then weight it.

Potted Game

This is a much quicker and easier way of using up odds and ends than making pâté, and delicious in a shooter's sandwich.

Chop the meat coarsely, add clarified butter. This is better pounded with a pestle and mortar, but if you are short of time it may go in the liquidizer. Whatever you do, don't mince it. Season generously and add cayenne and lemon juice. Pack it into small china or glass pots, and when these are cold, cover with melted but not hot clarified butter.

If you are using older game which has been stewed first, make sure it is absolutely dry or else the moisture will collect at the bottom of the pots.

Well stewed venison in red wine and seasoning is usually more successful than roast venison.

200 g (4 oz) cooked game meat, without skin or sinews
50 g (2 oz) fattish cooked ham
60 g (2½ oz) clarified butter
salt and pepper to taste
few grains of cayenne
few drops of lemon juice
melted butter for sealing (preferably clarified)

Farmhouse Loaf filled with Game and Mushrooms

This is really a chicken dish. Remember that overcooked dried game is not going to improve greatly with a few minutes' cooking in stock. The game must be in reasonable condition.

Cut the top off the loaf and scoop out the bread inside. Brush the remaining crust and lid with half of the melted butter and beaten egg and place in a moderate oven (180°C, 350°F, Mark 4) until golden brown. Sauté onion in remaining butter. Stir in flour and then the stock, bring to a boil, simmer for 5 minutes, test for seasoning. Add game cut into thin strips. Sauté mushrooms in a little butter and add to sauce with Worcestershire sauce and sherry or Madeira if used. Place all this in the loaf, cover with the top of the loaf, and return to oven for about 10 minutes. Half a chopped green pepper may be added to the mushrooms if wished.

Another similar way of preparing this dish is to cut 6–7 cm (2½–3 in) cubes out of a loaf of bread. Cut out the centre of the cubes only don't go right through, leave about 1 cm (½ in) at the bottom. You may use a biscuit cutter to do this. Then fry the cubes in deep fat until they are golden. Fill them with the sauce but retain one whole mushroom cap per cube to put on the top.

1 farmhouse or milk loaf
50 g (2 oz) butter, melted
1 egg, beaten
1 onion, finely chopped
1 tablespoon flour
200 ml (8 oz) stock
salt and pepper
300 g (12 oz) cooked game (about)
300 g (12 oz) mushrooms, sliced
dash of Worcestershire sauce (optional)
1 tablespoon sherry or Madeira (optional)

Cold Game Pie

1 thick gammon rasher, about 200 g (8 oz)
2 pheasants or grouse (old birds)
1 medium onion, chopped
parsley
salt and pepper
pinch mace
lemon rind
3 hard-boiled eggs
100 g (4 oz) mushrooms, sliced and sautéed
forcemeat balls
100 ml (4 oz) good Burgundy
25 g (1 oz) gelatine soaked in 50 ml (2 oz) water
500 ml (1 pint) stock (about)
200 g (8 oz) shortcrust pastry

From Miss June Gray.

Soak the gammon in water for an hour. Then place in stew-pan or casserole with the birds (which may be jointed), onion, parsley, pepper, salt (a teaspoon at this stage because of the gammon), mace, and the rind of the lemon cut thinly with a potato peeler. Stew gently on the stove or in the oven until tender. Leave to cool. Now cut the flesh from the birds and the gammon into neat pieces, slice hard-boiled eggs, mushrooms, forcemeat balls, previously fried, and fill pie dish. Put bones and carcass of birds back into the stock and boil until reduced to one-third of its previous quantity. Add Burgundy, and season to taste. Add gelatine soaked in water to a saucepan and dissolve over heat. Pour stock over meat in pie dish until two-thirds full. Cover with a good shortcrust and cook at the top of a hot oven (200°C, 400°F, Mark 6) until brown. Then lower heat and put pie on bottom shelf for a further 30 minutes. Cool and fill up with remaining stock through pie funnel.

This recipe may also be cooked in a game pie mould using a suitable pastry such as pâté moulée. Serves 6–8.

Hot Game Pie

600 g (1½ lb) game meat – retain the bones and carcasses
1 onion, sliced
1 carrot, sliced
1 stick celery, sliced
750 ml (1½ pints) stock or bouillon cube and water

Marinade
125 ml (¼ pint) red wine
2 tablespoons olive oil
slice of onion
1 bayleaf
parsley

40 g (1½ oz) butter
200 g (8 oz) raw tongue, chopped
beurre manié (2 tablespoons flour, 2 tablespoons butter)
salt and pepper
6 slices bacon
125 g (4 oz) sausagemeat
200 g (8 oz) pastry
1 egg, beaten

There are any number of changes you can make in this recipe. This is just a vague guide. You may like to add mushrooms, little white onions, forcemeat balls, or use stock and red wine.

Place bones and carcasses, onion, carrot and celery in a pot with stock. Cover, and simmer for 2 hours or more. Strain, cool, and skim off fat.

Cut meat into pieces and marinate for a few hours or overnight, turning occasionally. Drain meat and dry well. Brown quickly in 40 g (1½ oz) of the butter. Place in casserole, with tongue and hot stock, slightly thickened with beurre manié. Season with salt and pepper. Cover, and cook in slow oven for 2 hours. Cool slightly and skim off any extra fat. Line pie dish with bacon and then sprinkle with sausagemeat. Add game and enough stock to cover. Cover with pastry, brush pastry with beaten egg, and bake in a moderate oven (180°C, 350°F, Mark 4) until brown and cooked through, about 20 minutes.

Cakes and Baking

Baking is not really my scene but I have learnt that the few classic breads and cakes are all you need. They have become the classics because they are the right thing for shooting meals. They are mainly thanks to Caroline Stroyan.

Flapjacks

There was a particularly horrible day out stalking when I had spent most of the morning on the verge of tears, and when we finally had our 'piece' it appeared to be totally inedible except for a remarkably good piece of flapjack. Since then I have considered them a form of life preserver.

75 g (3 oz) butter
75 g (3 oz) softened brown sugar or castor sugar
2 tablespoons golden syrup
125 g (5 oz) rolled oats

Melt butter in a pan large enough to hold all the ingredients. Add sugar and syrup, blend, add rolled oats and mix thoroughly. Press mixture into shallow baking tin (20 cm (8 in) square) and bake in a moderate oven (180°C, 350°F, Mark 4) for 25 minutes. Cut while warm.

Shortbread

Cream butter well and add the castor sugar slowly. Sift the flours together and add them quickly, making a paste. Press into a baking sheet – it should be about 2 cm ($\frac{3}{4}$ in) thick. Mark the slices with a palette knife. They are normally oblong, but for picnics they are less inclined to break if they are square. Sprinkle with a little extra castor sugar and bake in a moderately hot oven (190°C, 375°F, Mark 5) for 15–20 minutes. Cool before removing from tin.

150 g (6 oz) butter (preferably unsalted)
75 g (3 oz) castor sugar
150 g (6 oz) plain flour
75 g (3 oz) rice flour
extra castor sugar

Monar Gingerbread

Neither Caroline or I have managed to establish the exact temperature or timing for this. You are better to cook it slower and longer than to let it burn and get hard. I put it in a moderately hot oven (190°C, 375°F, Mark 5) and turn it down at once to 180°C, 350°F, Mark 4 so that the heat won't come on again. Put the saucepan on the scales and then weigh in the treacle and syrup to the 400 g (1 lb) – that saves a lot of mess.

200 g (8 oz) treacle
200 g (8 oz) syrup
200 g (8 oz) margarine
300 g (12 oz) castor sugar
300 g (12 oz) plain flour
1 teaspoon baking soda
1 teaspoon ground ginger
1 teaspoon mixed spice
2 eggs, beaten
150 ml (6 oz) boiling water

Bring treacle, syrup, margarine and castor sugar to the boil. Sieve the dry ingredients, add boiling mixture, add beaten eggs and then boiling water. Beat well. Pour into greased papered tin. Bake in a moderate oven (180°C, 350°F, Mark 4) for about 50 minutes.

Pait Brown Bread

25 g (1 oz) butter
200 g (8 oz) self-raising flour
200 g (8 oz) brown wheaten flour
1 teaspoon salt
½ teaspoon bicarbonate soda
1 teaspoon cream of tartar
2 teaspoons syrup
approximately 175 ml (7 oz) milk and water mixed

Quote from Caroline:
'This is so easy it's not true, and so good, especially with smoked salmon. We all eat it hot or still warm as it's most impressive at a dinner-party to feel you've just made it!'

Rub butter into sieved flours, salt, bicarbonate soda and cream of tartar. Add syrup and milk mixture. Put into buttered and floured loaf tin and cover tightly with foil. Bake in a moderate oven (180°C, 350°F, Mark 4) for 1¼ hours.

Monar Cake

200 g (8 oz) glacé cherries
200 g (8 oz) plain flour
1 tablespoon mixed spice (level)
shake of salt
900 g (2 lb 4 oz) mixed fruit
150 g (6 oz) almonds
250 g (10 oz) margarine
250 g (10 oz) sugar
6 or 7 eggs
juice of ½ lemon
whisky

From Caroline.

Halve the glacé cherries and put into a large basin. Sieve the flour, spice and salt over the cherries to separate them, then add the mixed fruit and almonds split in half. In the Kenwood bowl, cream the margarine and sugar together until floppy, then add eggs one by one, beating all the time. Gradually spoon in dry ingredients to egg mixture, stir with beater, mixing lastly the lemon juice.

Grease and paper large cake tin, put in mixture and place in a moderately slow oven (170°C, 325°F, Mark 3) for 1 hour. Then cover if necessary and turn oven down to very cool (130°C, 250°F, Mark ½) and leave for 3 hours. When cake comes out of oven pour a generous dram of whisky over the top of it and let it sizzle through the cake. This makes it stay moist and keep well.

Cici's Biscuit Cake

125 g (5 oz) margarine
150 g (6 oz) mixed chocolate
75 g (3 oz) soft brown sugar
4–5 tablespoons syrup
400 g (1 lb) digestive biscuits

None of us love Cici for introducing us to this invidious stuff, it must put on inches everywhere, but goodness it's good instead of the usual chocolate biscuit.

Melt the margarine, chocolate, sugar and syrup together in a pot. Add the well-broken digestive biscuits. Mix well. Press the mixture into a greased tin and allow to set.

Special Fruit Cake

This recipe was kindly sent to us by Wendy Coles, wife of Charles Coles, the Director of the Game Conservancy.

Cream butter and sugar. Add eggs and beat well, then add treacle and continue beating. Add the flour, salt and mixed spice, continue to work well. Add rum and lastly the fruit. The mixture should be of dropping consistency, if not, add an extra egg or rum. The baking time depends on the oven – from 2½ hours if in a moderate oven (180°C, 350°F, Mark 4), or 3 hours if in a slow oven (150°C, 300°F, Mark 2). Line a tin well with about three well-buttered layers of greaseproof paper. Round the outside of the tin place a double layer of brown paper tied well and a piece to cover the top of the tin. This is a very moist cake.

200 g (8 oz) butter
200 g (8 oz) Scotch mist sugar
5 large eggs
1 tablespoon black treacle
225 g (9 oz) self-raising flour
pinch of salt
1 teaspoon mixed spice
2 tablespoons rum
100 g (4 oz) ground almonds
100 g (4 oz) glacé cherries
100 g (4 oz) glacé pineapple
100 g (4 oz) citron peel
700 g (1¾ lb) mixed fruit (raisins, currants, sultanas)

Mr Guinness's Cake

Cream butter and sugar together until light and creamy. Gradually beat in the eggs. Sieve flour and mixed spice together and fold into mixture. Add the raisins, sultanas, mixed peel and walnuts. Mix well together.

Stir 4 tablespoons of the Guinness into the mixture and mix to a soft dropping consistency. Turn into a prepared 17 cm (7 in) round cake tin and bake in a moderately slow oven (170°C, 325°F, Mark 3) for 1 hour. Then reduce heat to a slow oven (150°C, 300°F, Mark 2) and cook for another 1½ hours. Allow to become cold.

Remove from cake tin. Prick the base of the cake with a skewer, and spoon over the remaining 4–8 tablespoons Guinness. It is *very important* that this cake is kept for one week before eating.

200 g (8 oz) butter
200 g (8 oz) soft brown sugar
4 eggs, lightly beaten
250 g (10 oz) plain flour
2 level teaspoons mixed spice
200 g (8 oz) seedless raisins
200 g (8 oz) sultanas
100 g (4 oz) mixed peel
100 g (4 oz) walnuts, chopped
8–12 tablespoons Guinness

Anne's Dark Fruit Loaf

Put the fruit, sugar, water, margarine and baking soda into a pan and boil for 5 minutes. Allow to cool slightly and then add the flour and eggs, mix well and put into a loaf tin. Bake in a hot oven (200°C, 400°F, Mark 6) for ¾–1 hour.

300 g (12 oz) fruit (sultanas, raisins or currants mixed)
150 g (6 oz) castor sugar
150 ml (6 oz) water
50 g (2 oz) margarine
1 heaped teaspoon baking soda
300 g (12 oz) self-raising flour
2 eggs

Anne's Light Fruit Loaf

Put the fruit, milk, sugar and margarine into a pan and boil for 5 minutes. Allow to cool slightly and then add the flour and egg. Bake in a hot oven (200°C, 400°F, Mark 6) for ¾–1 hour.

150–175 g (6–7 oz) fruit (dates and walnuts are a good mixture)
150 ml (6 oz) milk
150 g (6 oz) castor sugar
100 g (4 oz) margarine
300 g (12 oz) self-raising flour
1 egg

How to Find Yeast

Writing on how to make bread is far more difficult than the actual making of it, but to buy yeast you have to become a Sherlock Holmes. If you breeze into a bakery and ask for yeast they feel trapped. Everyone is busy and no one knows the price or has the authority to give it away and they don't want to encourage you to come back. Try a small butcher. Ask him who is the kindest person most likely to let you have some and he will probably recommend the small baker who puts the pastry on his steak and kidney pies, so you can mention his name, and you all become friends. They will think you are rather eccentric but that appears to be an endearing quality.

If you haven't a book which tells you how to make bread then buy a little pamphlet called *The Baking of an English Loaf*, by Elizabeth David. You can obtain it at the shop which bears her name at 46 Bourne Street, London, S.W.1, or at any branch of Habitat. Your first loaf of bread is one of the great satisfactions of cooking.

Cheese — or How to Live with a Stilton

Much of the shooting season seems to revolve around keeping 'The Stilton'. If it is a good one, then it is a joy and lasts no time at all, if it is poor, it hangs around for months, seldom improving and usually making you feel guilty in case the cause is your neglect. One year I decided that had we a butler it would be his responsibility, so therefore as we hadn't it should be my husband's. This didn't turn out to be the solution. I have tried every area of the house to find the place where the cheese likes to live best. Finally it has chosen the cupboard between the two front doors, where it is away from the central heating and not liable to frost. The larder is quite reliable until December, but after that it is hardly worth running the risk of waking up on a gloriously crisp winter morning and then remembering with a sickening thud that you've probably frozen the Stilton again. If you cannot get a really good Stilton then there is no point in having one. By the end of the season people have become great connoisseurs – so no amount of time, trouble and money is wasted in making sure you have the best.

There are other wonderful blue cheeses, especially Blue Wensleydale and Blue Cheshire, and if you can find them they are often more appreciated than the Stilton as they are a change. They need the same loving care. It always used to be correct to wrap a white napkin around the outside of the Stilton and then occasionally sprinkle this lightly with water and vinegar to help keep it moist. Now far more people slice the cheese rather than dig into the middle so the napkin has more or less disappeared as it gets in the way. It is not a bad idea to ascertain the house rules before you attack the cheese. I've had some horrible blasts. Hosts can be just as shirty over their Stilton as they can be about how your dog behaves!

For years we have had a Taleggio as an alternative to the blue cheese. It is a large cheese, about 30 cm (1 foot) square, made in Lombardy of whole cow's milk. As it doesn't keep for more than a week or two you may not need more than a half or a quarter, but try to avoid the small pieces left over in the shops.

For school holidays there is no more comforting thing to have than a small Cheddar or Cheshire, they serve every purpose. It is a pity that one is inclined to be put off them as they remind you of the rows of plastic wrapped slabs in supermarkets.

Reblochon is a good shooting and picnic cheese. It is a semi-hard cheese, made in Savoy, and packs well. My ideal picnic cheese is one that is finished so that there are no grubby bits to use up when you get home. They are in two sizes so you can choose the quantity, and is good in your fingers or on biscuits or bread.

If you intend to give your hostess cheese as a present, it is wise to warn her in advance. A whole Brie could make her whole weekend far easier or she might find it difficult to look thrilled if she already has three cheeses in the larder and no idea how to get through it all.

Winter Vegetables and Salads

If you live near a large town you will usually be able to buy whatever vegetables you wish or even to be able to count on the classic watercress salad. Unfortunately many shooting people are not so lucky, as the smaller villages are notoriously unreliable; one week there seems to be everything you could wish for and the next time you go to the shop you can't even find some celery for the soup let alone a piece presentable enough to serve with the Stilton. These are a few suggestions for some vegetables that might be available either from shops or the garden or can be stored easily in the larder.

Braised Brussels Sprouts with Chestnuts

600 g (1½ lb) Brussels sprouts
400 g (1 lb) chestnuts
60 g (2½ oz) butter
375 ml (¾ pint) brown stock or 250 ml (½ pint) tinned consommé and 125 ml (¼ pint) water, or 1 beef stock cube and 375 ml (¾ pint) water
salt and pepper

Blanch Brussels sprouts in large pot of boiling water and simmer, uncovered, for 6 minutes. Drain.

Place chestnuts in a casserole with 25 g (1 oz) of the butter and cover with stock; add more water if necessary. Bring to simmer, cover, and place in a moderately slow oven (170°C, 325°F, Mark 3) for ¾–1 hour or until tender. The liquid should be reduced to a syrup, but if not, boil it down and pour it back over the chestnuts. Roll them around to coat them.

Place sprouts and chestnuts in layers in a buttered casserole, add salt and pepper, and pour over remaining butter, melted. Cover tightly, bring to sizzle on top of the cooker, and place in a moderate oven (180°C, 350°F, Mark 4) for 20 minutes.

Purée of Brussels Sprouts

Drop Brussels sprouts into rapidly boiling salted water, bring to boil again quickly and then boil gently, uncovered, for 10 minutes. Put them in the liquidizer. Reheat in double boiler with butter and cream. Season well and add a little nutmeg.

600 g (1½ lb) Brussels sprouts
25 g (1 oz) butter
2 tablespoons cream
salt and pepper
a little grated nutmeg

How to Peel Chestnuts

Frying Pan Slit each chestnut with a sharp knife. Put them in the frying pan with enough oil to coat them. Stir and cook over a moderate heat for about 10 minutes, then allow to cool. When cool enough to handle remove shells and skins with a sharp knife.

Oven Slit chestnuts with a sharp knife and coat them with oil. Bake in a very hot oven (230°C, 450°F, Mark 8) for 20 minutes; allow to cool. Remove shells and skin with a sharp knife.

Deep Fat Cut chestnuts all around with a sharp knife. Place a few of them in a wire basket, put in moderately hot fat (190°C, 375°F, Mark 5) until the shells open. Drain on paper towels. When cool enough to handle, remove shells and skins.

Boiling Slit each chestnut and put in boiling water to cover. Boil for 20 minutes. Drain and cool. Peel off shells and skins.

Chestnut Purée

A wonderful accompaniment for game.

Pour milk and stock or water over chestnuts to cover, bring to boil and simmer until tender, about 20 minutes. Melt 25 g (1 oz) of the butter, add onion and cook gently, not letting it brown, until it is tender. When chestnuts are cooked, drain them, add onion, mash them and then put the mixture through a mouli. Add plenty of salt and pepper and whisk in remaining butter and the cream. Reheat gently or in a double boiler.

400 g (1 lb) peeled chestnuts
½ milk and ½ stock or water to cover the chestnuts
40 g (1½ oz) butter
1 onion, finely chopped
salt and pepper
6 tablespoons cream

Chestnut Croquettes

Melt butter and fry shallots lightly, do not let them brown. Mix them with purée, salt and pepper, 1 beaten egg. Shape into small balls, dust with seasoned flour, dip in other beaten egg, roll in breadcrumbs and fry until golden in deep fat.

15 g (½ oz) butter
2 shallots, chopped
200 g (8 oz) chestnut purée – this may be tinned
salt and pepper
2 eggs
seasoned flour
dried white breadcrumbs
deep fat

Steamed Cabbage with Celery Salt

1 medium sized cabbage
50 g (2 oz) butter
1 tablespoon celery salt

This is my favourite way of cooking cabbage. My mother always cooks it this way and I can eat it by the soup-plateful.

Remove the outer leaves from the cabbage. Cut it in quarters and remove the hard white centre. Slice the quarters fairly thinly and put them in a steamer. Steam for about 20 minutes – you want it just cooked and no more. Remove to a hot dish and stir in butter and celery salt.

Red Cabbage with Apples and Onions

1 red cabbage, about 800 g (2 lb)
2 onions, sliced
3 large cooking apples, peeled, cored and sliced
1 clove garlic, crushed
50 g (2 oz) brown sugar
salt and pepper
$\frac{1}{4}$ teaspoon each of powdered nutmeg, allspice, cinnamon and thyme
250 ml ($\frac{1}{2}$ pint) red wine or 3 tablespoons port
2 tablespoons wine vinegar

Red cabbage is a classic accompaniment to game, especially to venison and goose. It is usually fairly easily obtainable yet very seldom served in this country. Because it is cheap and delicious, I am including several recipes for it. It is also a great help in adding colour to winter salads.

Remove outer leaves of cabbage, cut into quarters and remove the hard white stalk. Slice cabbage thinly. Place in casserole in layers with onion, apple, garlic, sugar, salt, pepper and spices. Add wine or port and vinegar. Place in a slow oven (150°C, 300°F, Mark 2) for at least 3 hours.

This may be prepared the previous day. It improves with reheating.

Red Cabbage with Orange

1 red cabbage
1 onion
finely grated rind of 2 oranges
juice of 3 oranges
1 clove garlic, crushed
50 g (2 oz) castor sugar
3 tablespoons wine vinegar
salt and pepper

Follow the preceding recipe, using these ingredients instead.

Dutch Red Cabbage

1 medium sized red cabbage
60 g (2$\frac{1}{2}$ oz) rice
juice of 1 lemon
200 g (8 oz) Bramley apples
cloves
salt and pepper
25 g (1 oz) butter

This is very good with venison, goose or caper. It was given to Charles Coles by John Swinnock, a famous chef.

Finely shred the red cabbage and wash in salt water. Take a saucepan with a tight-fitting lid and pour in water to a depth of 1 cm ($\frac{1}{2}$ in). Bring to the boil and add the drained, shredded cabbage, and rice and lemon juice.

Peel and grate the apples and add to the cabbage when half cooked. At the same time add cloves, salt and pepper to taste. Cook with lid on for approximately 15 minutes, then remove lid and continue cooking until water has vapourized. Finish by tossing in the butter and correct the seasoning.

Red Cabbage with Red Wine and Chestnuts

Remove rind from bacon, cut into strips and blanch for 10 minutes. Drain. Sauté bacon, carrots and onion in fat without browning.

Remove outer leaves from cabbage, cut into quarters and remove hard white stalk, then cut into 1 cm (½ in) slices. Stir cabbage well into onion and carrot mixture, cover, and cook slowly for 10 minutes. Stir in all the other ingredients except chestnuts. Bring to a simmer, cover, and place in a moderately slow oven (170°C, 325°F, Mark 3) for 3 hours.

Add chestnuts, cover, and cook for a further 1½ hours. The chestnuts should be tender and all the liquid evaporated. Test for seasoning.

100 g (4 oz) bacon
3 carrots, thinly sliced
2 onions, sliced
40 g (1½ oz) pork fat or butter
800 g (2 lb) red cabbage
3 cooking apples, peeled, cored and sliced
1 clove garlic, mashed
¼ teaspoon ground bayleaf
a pinch of ground cloves, nutmeg and pepper
½ teaspoon salt
375 ml (¾ pint) red wine
375 ml (¾ pint) brown stock or tinned consommé
24 peeled chestnuts

Curried Cauliflower

Fry a little chopped onion in ghee or butter until soft; add about 2 teaspoons ground curry spices. Fry for 2–3 minutes and add coarsely chopped raw cauliflower. Turn gently until tender. Season to taste.

onion, chopped
ghee or butter
2 teaspoons ground curry spices
1 cauliflower
salt and pepper

Braised Celery

Unless you have grown these vegetables in the garden, you will find that they are astronomically expensive but so much better than the frozen vegetables which you have eaten fresh all summer. They are an ideal accompaniment to game *en cocotte*. Take out a generous spoonful of the juices from the bird and add it to the vegetables for the last 5–10 minutes of cooking. You may serve the birds on top of the vegetable or separately.

30 stalks celery (about)
6 slices bacon
50 g (2 oz) butter
1 onion, chopped
1 carrot, chopped
375 ml (¾ pint) beef or game stock or tinned consommé
4 tablespoons white wine (optional)
bouquet garni of parsley, thyme, bay-leaf
salt and pepper
parsley, finely chopped

Cut the roots and tops off the celery (saving the tops for soup), and wash each stalk thoroughly. Drop into a large pot of boiling salted water and simmer for 15 minutes. Drain and cover with cold water. When cold, drain thoroughly and press in a towel. Simmer bacon in plenty of water for 10 minutes.

In a fireproof casserole, melt 40 g (1½ oz) of the butter and cook onion and carrot until tender – do not let them brown. Remove. Arrange celery in casserole, close together but in one layer. Cover with carrot and onion and bacon strips, add stock and wine to cover, and the bouquet garni and seasoning. Cover tightly, bring to simmer on cooker and then place in a moderate oven (180°C, 350°F, Mark 4) for 1½ hours. Remove cover, increase heat to hot oven (200°C, 400°F, Mark 6) and let brown, basting several times for about 20 minutes. Reduce cooking liquid until it thickens and becomes syrupy – just under 250 ml ($\frac{1}{2}$ pint). Thicken with cornflour mixture if you wish; if so simmer for another few minutes. Sprinkle with parsley.

Braised Chicory (Belgian Endive)

12 tightly closed chicory
75 g (3 oz) butter
salt
juice of $\frac{1}{2}$ lemon
100 ml (4 oz) water
2 tablespoons parsley, finely chopped

My favourite.

Trim the chicory, cutting off the hard base and taking off any soft outside leaves. Wash well in cold water. Drain.

Spread 25 g (1 oz) butter around a casserole. Place chicory in it in two layers. Sprinkle with salt and lemon juice, and dot with 40 g (1$\frac{1}{2}$ oz) of the butter. Pour in water, cover, and boil gently for about 10 minutes. Uncover, and boil until the liquid is reduced to a couple of tablespoons, about 10 minutes. Cover with buttered paper and then the lid of the casserole and bake in a moderately slow oven (170°C, 325°F, Mark 3) for an hour. Remove lid, not paper, and continue to bake for further 30 minutes until the chicory are golden. If you like them more brown, baste them with remaining butter, melted, and place under the grill. Sprinkle with parsley.

Braised Leeks

12 fat leeks
75 g (3 oz) butter
salt
2 tablespoons chopped parsley

Trim the bottoms of the leeks, remove soft outer leaves and cut off the top, leaving the leeks about 15–18 cm (6–7 in) long. Wash very well under running water. Place leeks in casserole in layers, and pour in water so that it comes to about three-quarters of the way up the leeks. Add butter and salt, bring to boil quickly, cover, but leave room for steam to escape. Cook briskly for about 30 minutes, when the leeks should be tender and most of the water evaporated. Cover loosely with foil and bake in a moderately slow oven (170°C, 325°F, Mark 3) for 30 minutes or until the leeks are golden. Sprinkle with parsley.

Purée of Lentils

400 g (1 lb) dried lentils
1 litre (2 pints) stock
100 g (4 oz) smoked sausage or salt pork
2 sprigs parsley
2 small onions, sliced
1 clove garlic
1 bayleaf
2 cloves
25 g (1 oz) butter
125 g (5 oz) heavy cream
salt and pepper

Wash lentils and drain. Cover with cold water and soak overnight. Drain, cover with stock, add sausage or pork, place parsley, onions, garlic, bayleaf and cloves in loose muslin bag and add. Bring slowly to boil, simmer for about 1$\frac{1}{2}$ hours. Remove bag after an hour. Add boiling water if it becomes too thick. When done, put through sieve, set over heat and whip in butter, cream, and season to taste.

Brown Braised Onions

Melt butter with oil; when bubbling add onions and cook over a medium heat, rolling them around until they are brown – about 10 minutes. Add the liquid, salt, pepper and bouquet garni. Then either cover and simmer on top of the cooker until they are tender – about 45 minutes – or place them with fat in a baking dish large enough so that they only need to be in one layer. Put this in a moderate oven (180°C, 350°F, Mark 4) for about 45 minutes, turning them occasionally.

Either way they should be tender but retain their shape.

20 g (¾ oz) butter
1½ tablespoons oil
18–24 white onions, peeled
250 ml (½ pint) liquid – brown stock, tinned consommé, red or white wine or water
salt and pepper
bouquet garni of parsley, thyme, bay-leaf

White Braised Onions

Place all ingredients in a pan. Cover, and simmer slowly, shaking the pan occasionally for about 45 minutes. The onions should remain white, be tender and yet hold their shape. You may need to add a little more liquid. Remove bouquet garni.

12–18 white onions, peeled
125 ml (¼ pint) stock, white wine or water
25 g (1 oz) butter
small bouquet garni of parsley, thyme, bayleaf

Game Chips

I don't seem to have any trouble with game chips – provided they are given half a chance they always seem to turn out well. I try to let them sit in cold water for an hour after they are sliced, and usually dry them well because if I don't they spit at me. The only two important rules I have discovered is not to have the fat too hot when you put them in, and to keep them moving until they lose their sogginess. If you cook them in small batches the latter isn't necessary. I don't bother with a basket, just using a large pot and chip draining ladle. This is how they should be made, but once you get your nerve you can be far more casual. Allow 600 g (1½ lb) potatoes for about six people.

Peel potatoes and slice as thinly as possible. Soak in a large bowl of cold water for an hour, stirring them around so they don't stick together. Drain and dry in a towel, separating the pieces so that they don't stick together.

Heat oil to 180°C, 350°F, and fry slices a few at a time until they come to the top; remove. When they are all cooked, turn up heat to 200°C, 400°F, and fry in larger batches until they are golden brown. Keep pushing them around so they don't stick together. Drain on paper towels. They will stay quite crisp in a warm oven on the paper towel as long as you don't cover them.

Italian Potatoes suitable for Game, especially Wild Duck

600 g (1½ lb) mashed potatoes
juice of 2 oranges
grated rind of 2 oranges
40 g (1½ oz) butter

Mrs Nina Fiske sent us this from Denmark but she says it is Italian. It is simple and very good.

To the mashed potatoes add the orange juice, the rind of 1 orange and 25 g (1 oz) butter. Place in an ovenproof dish, dot with the rest of the butter and sprinkle with remaining rind. Place in a moderate oven (180°C, 350°F, Mark 4) until brown, about 15 minutes.

Orange Potatoes

6 large potatoes
2 teaspoons salt
2 cloves
60 g (2½ oz) butter
2 eggs
4 egg yolks
grated rind of 4 oranges

This recipe of Dione Lucas is rather more complicated than the previous recipe, but well worth it for a dinner-party.

Peel the potatoes and cut them in half. Put in saucepan, cover with cold water and bring to the boil. Add salt and cloves. Simmer briskly until potatoes are soft. Drain, remove cloves, and shake pan over fire until the potatoes are thoroughly dry. Put them in a mixing bowl and beat in butter, eggs, egg yolks and orange rind. Beat well. Spoon in mounds on oiled baking tin, sprinkle with melted butter and brown under grill.

Alternatively, spread the mixture on a flat platter, cover with transparent wrap, and chill well. When cold, take mixture by a tablespoon, roll each spoonful lightly in flour, and roll with your hands to form a large cork-shaped cake. Brush these with a whole beaten egg, roll in fine breadcrumbs, and fry in deep fat at 180°C, 350°F, a few at a time until they are golden. Drain on paper towels.

Oven Brown Potatoes

800 g (2 lb) potatoes
salt
40 g (1½ oz) butter
2 tablespoons olive oil

Wonderful for most dishes whether roasted or stewed.

Peel potatoes and cut them into 2 cm (¾ in) cubes. They really should be cut into small rounds with a potato scoop. Put them in a pan, cover with cold water, add salt and bring to the boil. Drain. Melt butter with oil in casserole or small roasting pan large enough for potatoes not to crowd each other. Put potatoes in pan, roll around in fat so they are coated all over, and place in a moderate oven (180°C, 350°F, Mark 4) for about 1¼ hours. Turn them occasionally. They should be golden brown and quite crispy.

Plain Scalloped Potatoes

Good with cold venison or other cold game.

800 g (2 lb) potatoes
50 g (2 oz) butter
2 tablespoons flour
1 teaspoon salt
pepper
250 ml (½ pint) hot milk

Peel potatoes and slice them as thinly as possible. Leave them in a bowl of cold water until you wish to use them.

Spread a large baking dish (25 cm or 10 in) with 15 g (½ oz) of the butter. Drain and dry potatoes and spread them in three layers, dusting each layer with flour and dotting them with butter. Put salt and pepper in hot milk and pour over potatoes. Place in a moderate oven (180°C, 350°F, Mark 4) for 1½ hours. You may cover the dish for the first 30 minutes.

Variations
1. Slice a large onion, divide into rings and place the rings between the layers of potatoes.
2. Grate 100 g (4 oz) Swiss cheese. Spread potatoes in two layers only, putting half of the cheese between the two and the other half over the top.
3. Substitute brown stock for milk, but increase the butter to 75 g (3 oz).
4. Mince 100 g (4 oz) bacon and fry until crisp. Spread between the layers of potatoes but reduce the salt quantity.

Kilrie Potatoes

Peel and then cut the potatoes into 2.5 cm (1 in) pieces. Place in cold salted water and bring to the boil. Boil for 5 minutes. Drain them well.

Heat a large pot of fat, but it doesn't want to be too hot, and put the potatoes in it. Stir them occasionally and keep an eye on them until they are the colour you like. It depends on the size of the pot as to how long this will take – an average of 15 minutes. Drain the potatoes well on paper towelling and keep warm, uncovered, in the oven. These seem to be the ideal potato for a remarkable number of dishes.

Sautéed Potatoes

800 g (2 lb) potatoes
60 g (2½ oz) butter
salt and pepper
sprinkling of fresh herbs or parsley

Peel potatoes, place in pot, cover with water, bring to the boil, drain, and dry well. Cut into thick slices. Melt butter in a frying pan, add potatoes and some salt and pepper. Shake pan until they begin to brown, fry gently, shifting them around until they are cooked – about 15 minutes. Pile on dish and sprinkle with chopped herbs.

Purée of Celeriac and Potatoes

1 large celeriac
100 g (4 oz) butter
the weight of the celeriac in potatoes
salt and pepper
2 tablespoons cream

Peel and cut celeriac into 2.5 cm (1 in) cubes, blanch in boiling water for 10 minutes, drain off water, add 75 g (3 oz) of the butter, then cover and cook gently for 20 minutes. Sieve or put through a mouli.

Peel and boil potatoes, sieve or mash them well and add to celeriac. Season with salt and pepper and whisk in remaining butter and the cream.

Purée of Turnips

I find turnips the hardest winter vegetable to organize as I forget to pick them up on the dog walk and refuse to buy them in a shop. Canadians can't believe it when they see fields of them lying around in winter instead of being neatly stacked in supermarkets. The best ones for cooking are what we call Swedes. They have a purple skin and a rather orange flesh. Middle sized ones are the best – take two rather than one big one. I like them mashed with lots of butter, pepper and a little cream but find that a purée is far more popular.

Peel the turnip and cut into 2.5 cm (1 in) pieces. Cover with salted water and boil until tender. Drain. Then either put through a food mill or liquidizer. Beat in 75 g (3 oz) butter and lots of pepper to taste, and 100 g (4 oz) of thick cream. Beat well to make it light and add more cream if you like. You can keep it hot in a double boiler. Very good for shooting lunches.

To vary, use half purée of turnip and half mashed potatoes, and add a little more butter.

Casserole of Celery and Potatoes

1 medium head of celery
3 medium potatoes
25 g (1 oz) butter
1 teaspoon finely chopped onion or shallot
salt and pepper

This goes well with pheasant.

Trim the bottom of the celery and remove damaged stalks. Separate stalks, cut celery and potatoes into strips about 3 mm ($\frac{1}{8}$ in) thick and 5 cm (2 in) long. Put the potatoes in water.

Heat butter in casserole, add celery and onion, cover, and cook for 5 minutes, shaking the casserole frequently. Drain potatoes, dry them well, put them into a casserole with salt and pepper. Stir all the ingredients to make sure they are well mixed, cover with greaseproof paper and lid, and cook either on top of the cooker or in a moderate oven (180°C, 350°F, Mark 4) until potatoes are tender, about 10 minutes.

Wild Rice

1 cup uncooked rice makes 3 cups cooked rice or 4–5 servings.

Wash rice thoroughly in cold water and if possible soak for an hour or more.

To boil Bring 2 litres (4 pints) water to the boil, add 2 teaspoons salt and 150 g (6 oz) washed rice, and cook slowly for 40 minutes. Drain.

To Steam Stir 150 g (6 oz) washed rice slowly into 500 ml (1 pint) boiling water. Add 1 teaspoon salt, cover, and steam over a low heat for 35–45 minutes until the rice is tender and the water absorbed.

To Steep Pour 1 litre (2 pints) boiling water over 150 g (6 oz) washed rice and let stand for 30 minutes. Drain, add another 1 litre (2 pints) and let stand for 30 minutes. Repeat twice more, adding 2 tablespoons salt to the last water. Drain. Keep hot in double boiler. This last method is considered the best.

Pilaf de Riz

Chop the onion very finely. Melt the butter in sauté pan. When it bubbles (it should not colour at all) add the onions. They should not colour either but should be soft. Cook for 2–3 minutes. Add rice, mix with wooden spatula. Use a measure for the rice that can be put in boiling water. Add twice the amount of boiling water as rice. Add salt and pepper. Cover with tight lid. Put in a moderate oven (180°C, 350°F, Mark 4) for exactly 20 minutes. If you have to cook the rice on top of the stove, cook it for 5 or 6 minutes longer, but it will not be as dry. Serves 5 or 6.

1 medium onion, finely chopped
40–50 g (1½–2 oz) butter
250 g (10 oz) rice
boiling water
salt and pepper

Winter Ratatouille

Very probably ratatouille does not go with game and I am just biased as it is one of my favourite things. But I think it goes with venison and especially with cold venison, and I'd feel guilty if I left it out. Alas, as aubergines and peppers are now the same price as beef, ratatouille has become very expensive. We can seldom buy red peppers so I substitute fewer green ones; tomatoes in the winter are not worth buying so I use tinned ones. They are not nearly the same but good enough, and I don't bother with wizened courgettes. This is based on Elizabeth David's recipe but I don't expect she'd like to claim it.

3 large aubergines
3 red peppers or 2 green ones
200 g (8 oz) tin peeled tomatoes,
    drained
150 ml (6 oz) olive oil
3 medium onions, thinly sliced
1–2 cloves garlic, crushed
1 teaspoon coriander seeds
dried basil or parsley

Slice the unpeeled aubergines into 1 cm ($\frac{1}{2}$ in) slices and then into cubes. Place them in a colander, sprinkle with salt, and weight so that the excess juice will drain away. This takes about an hour. Cut the tops off the peppers, scoop out all the seeds and any white pith, slice them in thin strips. Drain tomatoes and cut off any hard ends and chop them.

Heat olive oil in a wide, heavy, shallow pan. Put in onions, and when they are soft add aubergines, peppers and garlic. Cover pan and cook gently for 40 minutes. Add tomatoes and coriander seeds. Test for seasoning. Cook for another 30 minutes until vegetables are soft but not mushy. Stir in basil or parsley. This may be served hot or cold. It improves if it is kept for a day, and may be reheated.

Winter Salads

There are so many different permutations of winter salads that I have only included a few that are the classical accompaniments for game.

Here is a list of other ideas which might help to inspire:
Tomato and Orange Salad
Beetroot and Chicory Salad
Beetroot, Orange and Chicory Salad
Celeriac and Raisin Salad
Coleslaw
Carrot and Raisin Salad
Red Cabbage and Apple Salad

French Dressing

Do not economize on the quality of your olive oil and wine vinegar. The dressing should taste of oil rather than vinegar, which means that the classic three parts oil to one part vinegar or lemon juice is rather too much vinegar – rather 4:1 or even 5:1. Salt and pepper are the only additions, though some people add mustard and sugar. It is important to turn a salad over very thoroughly so that each piece is coated in dressing.

Celery Salad

Eliza Actow in her book published in 1845 says: 'Young celery alone, sliced and dressed with a rich salad mixture, is excellent, it is still in some families served thus always with roast pheasant.'

Orange Salad

Remove the rind as thinly as possible off the half orange. Shred and blanch in boiling water for 5 minutes; drain and dry. Peel the rest of the oranges, removing every trace of the white pith. Slice oranges thinly, spoon over French dressing and scatter with peel.

If you prefer you may cut the oranges into their natural sections, discarding the white skin between the sections.

Brandy instead of vinegar may be used in the dressing, especially if you are serving the salad with wild duck.

rind of ½ orange
3 oranges
French dressing (1 tablespoon vinegar to 4 tablespoons olive oil)

Orange and Chicory Salad

Trim the base of the chicory and remove any bruised leaves. Wash well and dry. You may either cut it across or lengthwise.

Remove the rind as thinly as possible from half of the orange and blanch in boiling water for 5 minutes. Drain and dry. Peel the rest of the orange and remove pith. Cut orange into segments, leaving the white skin between the sections behind. Mix chicory, orange sections, peel and French dressing.

3 heads of chicory
rind of ½ orange
1 large orange
French dressing (2 teaspoons vinegar to 3 tablespoons oil)

Orange and Watercress Salad

Wash and pick over watercress. Dry in a towel and leave in refrigerator until ready to use. Peel oranges and remove pith. Cut into thin segments. Chill. When ready to serve, place watercress in a salad bowl, then oranges, pour over dressing and toss well.

4 bunches watercress
2 oranges
French dressing (2 tablespoons vinegar or 1 tablespoon each of vinegar and lemon juice, and 8 tablespoons olive oil)

Watercress and Beetroot Salad

Scrub beetroot, cut away stems and roots. Bake in a moderate oven (180°C, 350°F, Mark 4) until tender. Cool. Peel and slice thinly. Mix with equal quantity of watercress and serve with French dressing.

beetroot
watercress
French dressing

Variation
¼ beetroot, cooked and sliced into strips.
¼ celery, coarsely chopped.
½ watercress.

Waldorf Salad

An American classic and good with game. Mix all ingredients together.

1 cup diced celery
1 cup diced apple (peeled or unpeeled as you wish)
1 cup grapes, halved and pipped (optional)
½ cup walnuts or pecan nuts
French dressing with 1 tablespoon mayonnaise added

Sauces

Bread Sauce

50 g (2 oz) fresh white breadcrumbs –
the better the bread, the better the
sauce. You may use wholemeal if
you wish, but it will not be as light –
better for caper or goose
250 ml (½ pint) milk
1 onion stuck with 2 cloves
salt and pepper
pinch of mace
good grating of nutmeg
25–50 g (1–2 oz) unsalted butter
1–2 tablespoons thick fresh cream
1 heaped teaspoon Gruyère (not essential)
a squeeze of lemon juice (optional)

Bread Sauce is a personal taste and some people go into
raptures over it. Pamela Vandyke Price almost convinced me
that I liked it in one of her articles for *The Spectator*. Her recipe
is almost identical to mine only she adds Gruyère cheese and
lemon juice. You can't taste the cheese but it enriches the sauce.

As early as possible place in the top of a double boiler breadcrumbs, milk, onion stuck with cloves, salt, pepper, mace and
nutmeg. Let this stand until you are ready to cook it. Place
over hot water and whisk in butter, cut into small pieces.
Cook for about 30 minutes. Remove onion, taste for seasoning,
stir in cream and then, if you like, the Gruyère and lemon;
whisk for another few minutes. You may need to add more
cream and butter if you reheat it.

Buster's Breadcrumbs

50 g (2 oz) butter or bacon fat
50 g (2 oz) bacon or ham, finely
chopped

The proud creator of this dish complains that when you serve
the crumbs to your friends they never mention any of the other
food, just what wonderful breadcrumbs they had.

Melt butter or fat, fry bacon or ham until it starts to brown (you will need less fat if you use streaky bacon), then stir in the mushrooms. Cook for a minute or two, then add the bread-crumbs. Continue stirring over a moderate heat until the breadcrumbs are golden.

50 g (2 oz) mushrooms or mushroom stalks, finely chopped
40 g (1½ oz) breadcrumbs

Fried Breadcrumbs

Melt butter – if it is not clarified skim well. Add breadcrumbs and stir over a moderate heat until they are pale brown.

50 g (2 oz) clarified butter
40 g (1½ oz) fresh breadcrumbs

Gravy for Game

Most recipes for Roast Game say that it should be served with strong clear gravy, but there is seldom any brown glaze at the bottom of the pan, particularly if you have had a croûton under a bird. It is as well not to count on the bird for help, but to be prepared. It is easily frozen so make plenty when you do.

Wash giblets and dry them. Cut them into pieces with the beef and fry them gently with the onion in the dripping until they are pale brown. Add about 75 ml (3 oz) of the stock or water and cook slowly, stirring occasionally, until it is reduced to a brown glaze. Add remaining stock or water, herbs, salt, peppercorns and juniper berries if wished. Bring to the boil and then simmer, with the lid slightly off, for about an hour – it should be reduced to 500 ml (1 pint). Strain, cool, and skim off fat.

400 g (1 lb) giblets – if you have not enough game giblets, you may use chicken. If you use the feet make sure to blanch and scrape them first. Any leftover game carcasses will do, too
200 g (8 oz) shin of beef
1 tablespoon dripping or bacon fat
1 onion, chopped
750 ml (1½ pints) stock or water
bouquet garni of parsley, thyme, bay-leaf
salt
8 peppercorns
8 juniper berries if you wish

Celery Sauce

A classic English sauce for birds which have been boiled.

Wash and shred the celery, put into a saucepan and cover with cold water. Bring to the boil, then pour away the water and pour the stock or milk over the celery and cook until it is quite tender. Rub through a fine sieve. Melt the butter in a saucepan, stir in flour and add, by degrees, the celery purée. Stir till it boils and thickens. When removed from heat add the cream or milk, pepper and salt to taste, and a little more butter. Stir well.

1 small head of celery
375 ml (¾ pint) white stock or milk
15 g (½ oz) butter
25 g (1 oz) flour
2 tablespoons cream or milk
salt and pepper

Brown Sauce

This sauce is as good as the stock that goes into it – beef cubes will not do.

1 carrot, chopped
2 onions, chopped

100 g (4 oz) fat (beef, veal or pork dripping)
50 g (2 oz) flour
1½ litres (3 pints) brown stock
1 stalk celery, chopped
1 clove garlic
1 bayleaf
3 sprigs parsley
little thyme
3 tablespoons tomato purée

Brown carrot and onion lightly in fat, add flour and stir until it becomes well brown. Add 500 ml (1 pint) stock, celery, garlic and herbs, and cook, stirring, until the mixture is thick, then add 625 ml (1¼ pints) stock.

Simmer slowly for 1½ hours, stirring occasionally and skimming off fat until the sauce is reduced by half. Add tomato purée, stir in well and then sieve. Add the rest of the stock and simmer for another hour, skimming the surface when necessary.

Panic Brown Sauce

1½ tablespoons clarified butter
1½ tablespoons flour
375 ml (¾ pint) good brown stock or beef consommé

This is not nearly as good as the real thing, but if you are pushed it will just help as a substitute.

Melt butter and stir in flour, then cook over a low heat until the mixture is pale brown. Slowly add stock or consommé, stirring continually, bring to the boil, and cook for about 5 minutes. Simmer for 30 minutes, stirring occasionally, skim off fat and strain the sauce.

Brown Mustard Sauce

50 g (2 oz) minced onion (about)
15 g (½ oz) butter and 1 tablespoon oil melted in a saucepan, or degreased roasting pan juices
200 ml (8 oz) white wine, or 125 ml (¼ pint) dry vermouth
375 ml (¾ pint) brown sauce
3 tablespoons Dijon mustard mixed in with 2 tablespoons soft butter and a pinch of sugar
2 tablespoons finely chopped parsley

This is good with venison, hare or any heated up leftovers.

Cook onion slowly in butter and oil or in the juices in roasting pan for about 10 minutes until golden. Add wine and boil rapidly until it is reduced to a quarter. Add brown sauce and simmer for 10 minutes. Check seasoning. Remove from heat and before serving beat in mustard and butter mixture and the parsley.

Brown Sauce with Tomatoes and Mushrooms — Sauce Chasseur

50 g (2 oz) minced onion
25 g (1 oz) butter
1 tablespoon olive oil
250 ml (½ pint) tomato pulp – either fresh tomatoes, skinned, seeded and chopped, or tinned tomatoes, drained, seeded and chopped
½ clove garlic, mashed
salt and pepper
½ teaspoon basil
125 ml (¼ pint) white wine
125 ml (¼ pint) brown sauce
200 g (8 oz) mushrooms, sliced and sautéed in butter
finely chopped parsley or basil

Being a tomato lover I like this sauce on almost everything. You may vary the ingredients as you wish. Fresh tomatoes are best but tinned will do.

Sauté onion for a minute in butter and oil, add tomatoes, garlic, salt, pepper and basil. Cover, and simmer for 5 minutes; check seasoning. Add wine and brown sauce, then add mushrooms and simmer for a minute. Having poured the sauce over whatever you wish, sprinkle with parsley or basil.

Madeira or Port Brown Sauce

Reduce wine until it is at about a quarter of its original volume, add brown sauce and simmer for a few moments; add a little more wine if it is needed. Before serving beat in butter.

You may add 200 g (8 oz) mushrooms, thickly sliced, sautéed in 25 g (1 oz) butter, to the sauce with the brown sauce.

250 ml (½ pint) Madeira or port
500 ml (1 pint) brown sauce
40 g (1½ oz) butter

Sauce Poivrade

This is a very popular sauce to serve with venison, particularly when it has been marinated. It is also used in making other sauces. When making it, it is sensible to make enough to have some to freeze.

Brown carrot and onion in the oil. Sprinkle over flour, and when it is brown add stock and tomato purée. Stir well to avoid lumps and then add bouquet garni and bones. Cover, and simmer for 2 hours. Skim off fat. Mix vinegar and marinade with peppercorns and reduce until it is nearly half its original volume. Add it to strained sauce, simmer about 30 minutes longer; add salt if necessary. Just before serving stir in butter.

1 carrot, chopped
1 onion, chopped
3 tablespoons olive oil
50 g (2 oz) flour
750 ml (1½ pints) strong beef stock (a cube will not do)
1 tablespoon tomato purée
bouquet garni of bayleaf and parsley
bones of game
125 ml (¼ pint) wine vinegar
125 ml (¼ pint) strained marinade
8 peppercorns, crushed
2 tablespoons butter

Variations

1. To 375 ml (¾ pint) of boiling Poivrade add 125 ml (¼ pint) red wine and 125 ml (¼ pint) from the marinade. Cook for 30 minutes, skimming when required. Add 1 teaspoon sugar and cook until reduced to about half its original quantity. Before serving stir in 2 tablespoons butter.

2. Bring 500 ml (1 pint) Sauce Poivrade to the boil and cook for 10 minutes. Remove from heat and add 125 ml (¼ pint) Madeira wine and 3 tablespoons of blanched, roasted, slivered almonds and 2 tablespoons small raisins, warmed in a little boiling water.

3. 500 ml (1 pint) hot Sauce Poivrade with 100 g (4 oz) red-currant jelly and 100 g (4 oz) thick cream beaten into it just before serving. Good with venison.

4. Heat 250 ml (½ pint) Sauce Poivrade and 250 ml (½ pint) redcurrant jelly together. Stir with a whisk until there are no lumps left from the jelly. Stir in 100 g (4 oz) drained tinned black cherries. Good with venison, duck and goose.

Francatelli's Venison Sauce

Francatelli was Queen Victoria's chef.

Simmer together for 5 minutes. Strain into hot sauce-boat.

2 tablespoons port wine
200 g (8 oz) redcurrant jelly
small stick of cinnamon, bruised
thinly pared rind of lemon

Jelly Sauce for Game

250 ml (½ pint) redcurrant jelly
250 ml (½ pint) red wine
pinch of ginger
pinch of cloves
squeeze of lemon juice
1 teaspoon cornflour mixed with a
  little water
2 tablespoons brandy

This is not unlike Francatelli's sauce: it is not as simple, nor as sweet.

Melt jelly slowly and add wine, mixing well with a whisk. Simmer for a few minutes until smooth, add spices and lemon juice, thicken with cornflour mixture, simmer for a few more minutes, then add brandy.

Variation Omit brandy and add 1 tablespoon grated horseradish.

Apricot and Brandy Sauce for Duck

125 g (5 oz) apricot pulp
100 g (4 oz) sugar
cornflour
1 tablespoon brandy or apricot brandy
juice of ½ lemon

Put the apricot pulp through a sieve. Add 250 ml (½ pint) water and the sugar; simmer. Thicken with a little cornflour. Add brandy or apricot brandy and lemon juice.

Quick Chestnut Sauce for Roast Saddle of Hare or Venison

125 g (5 oz) chestnut purée
500 ml (1 pint) cream

Remove saddle from roasting pan, pour off excess fat and add chestnut purée and cream. Scrape around the pan to get any of the good crispy bits, bring to the boil and serve.

German Sour Cream Sauce

2 shallots, chopped
4 tablespoons butter
2 tablespoons flour
375 ml (¾ pint) stock
125 ml (¼ pint) white wine
2 tablespoons sour cream
lemon juice

Good with hare or venison.

Sauté shallots in butter for 5 minutes. Stir in flour and blend well. Add stock and wine, stir and cook over low heat until thickened, about 15 minutes. Add sour cream, and lemon juice to taste.

If you prefer you may leave out the stock and add more sour cream.

Sauce Bigarade (Bitter Orange Sauce)

2 bitter oranges (Seville)
50 g (2 oz) butter
1 tablespoon flour
150 ml (6 oz) hot beef, veal, or game
  stock
salt and pepper

A beautiful sauce with duck.

Peel the rind off the oranges as thinly as possible and cut into thin shreds. Boil for 5 minutes, then drain.

Melt butter, stir in flour and cook slowly until it is pale brown, add hot stock and whisk until smooth; simmer for 5 minutes. Add the strained juice from 1 or 2 oranges – depending on how juicy they are. Season with salt, pepper and sugar and add any meat juices and some port or Madeira if you wish.

1 tablespoon sugar
meat juices from roasting pan if you have any
a little port or Madeira

Grape Sauce for Duck or any other Game

Scald grapes and simmer until nicely plumped, then drain and put in saucepan with butter, Madeira and cloves. Cover tightly and simmer for 6 minutes. Stir in dried mushrooms (or a truffle) and lemon juice. Simmer for another minute.

400 g (1 lb) Malaga or Muscat grapes
50 g (2 oz) butter
100 ml (4 oz) Madeira
pinch of ground cloves
3 teaspoons dried mushrooms, finely chopped
1 tablespoon lemon juice

Orange Gravy

Pour off any extra fat from roasting pan and add the orange juice and a little grated orange rind. Cook for about 10 minutes, scraping around the pan occasionally. Strain the sauce – it should be about half its original volume.

Peel the rinds off the half lemon and half orange as finely as possible. Cut into thin shreds and boil them for 5 minutes. Strain. Add these to the sauce.

Bring the thick cream to boiling point and stir in the port and redcurrant jelly. Mix this into sauce and heat, but do not let boil. Taste for seasoning. If you wish you may parboil the liver of the bird or a couple of chicken livers, sieve them and add them to the gravy.

125 ml (¼ pint) orange juice
rind of ½ orange
rind of ½ lemon
150 g (6 oz) thick cream
3 tablespoons port
2 tablespoons redcurrant jelly

Bitter Orange Sauce for Duck

Remove any excess fat from the pan in which the ducks have been roasted and to the juices add all the ingredients. Simmer sauce until evenly mixed.

4 teaspoons grated bitter orange or grapefruit peel
3 tablespoons lemon or lime juice
1 dash Worcestershire sauce
1 tablespoon Curaçao
6 large tablespoons bitter orange marmalade
salt and cayenne
2 tablespoons brandy

Cold Orange Sauce

Heat jelly and sugar until melted and smooth. Add all the other ingredients. Serve cold with any game.

6 tablespoons redcurrant jelly
3 tablespoons sugar
2 tablespoons lemon juice
3 tablespoons port
rind of 2 oranges, grated
2 tablespoons orange juice
salt and pepper

Mustard Sauce to go with Wild Goose

Melt butter, stir in flour, then mustard, vinegar, and very slowly add the stock. Continue stirring until the sauce is thick and smooth. Add salt and pepper to taste.

2 tablespoons butter
1 tablespoon flour
1 teaspoon prepared mustard
1 small teaspoon wine vinegar
200 ml (8 oz) good game stock
salt and pepper

Green Peppercorn Sauce

trimmings of game
oil
carrot
onion
celery
bacon
thyme
70 ml (2½ oz) wine vinegar
1 tablespoon Bovril
250 ml (½ pint) brown sauce
mushroom peelings
2 tablespoons marinade
1 teaspoon green peppercorns
salt and pepper
1 teaspoon redcurrant jelly

This is made with tinned green peppercorns and not the large vegetables which you put into salads. It is a very good sauce to make if you have some leftover game carcass and marinade.

Fry some trimmings of game in oil and add a little finely diced carrot, onion, celery and bacon and a sprinkling of thyme. When brown add wine vinegar and reduce until liquid has all but gone. Add the Bovril and brown sauce, mushroom peelings and marinade. Add green peppercorns and cook for 1 hour. Remove any grease, sieve, season, and add 1 teaspoon redcurrant jelly. Dilute if necessary with game stock or consommé.

Cumberland Sauce

I have tried different Cumberland Sauces for years until I met this one of Elizabeth David's. Unfortunately it doesn't matter how much I make there is never enough left to see if it keeps for several weeks in the refrigerator.

This best of all sauces for cold meat – ham, pressed beef, tongue, venison, boar's head, or pork brawn – can be made in small quantities and in a quick and economical way as follows:
   With a potato parer cut the rind, very thinly, from two large oranges. Slice this into matchstick strips. Plunge them into boiling water and let them boil 5 minutes. Strain them.
   Put them in a bowl with 4 tablespoons of redcurrant jelly, a heaped teaspoon of yellow Dijon mustard, a little freshly milled pepper, a pinch of salt and (optional) a sprinkling of ground ginger.
   Place this bowl over a saucepan of water and heat, stirring all the time, until the jelly is melted and the mustard smooth. It may be necessary at this stage to sieve the jelly in order to smooth out the globules which will not dissolve. Return the sieved jelly to the bowl standing over its pan of hot water.
   Now add 7–8 tablespoons (70 ml or 2½ oz) of medium tawny port. Stir and cook for another 5 minutes. Serve cold. There will be enough for four people. Made in double or triple quantities, this sauce can be stored in covered jars and will keep for several weeks.

N.B.—On no account should cornflour, gelatine or any other stiffening be added to Cumberland sauce. The mixture thickens as it cools, and the sauce is invariably served cold, even with a hot ham or tongue.

Marieka Sauce for Cold Game

Place the redcurrant jelly into a saucepan with rind and juice of oranges. Heat gently until jelly has completely dissolved. Allow to cool slightly and then stir in Pernod. Allow to become completely cold, stirring occasionally to prevent a skin forming.

400 g (1 lb) redcurrant jelly
juice and finely grated rind of 2 oranges
1–2 tablespoons Pernod

Game Stuffing

Peel, core and dice the apples. Chop the onions and celery. Mix these ingredients together with the marjoram or thyme and the nutmeg.

2 medium apples
2 medium onions
4 sticks celery
½ teaspoon marjoram or thyme
a grate of nutmeg

Walnut Stuffing

For duck or goose.

Fry onion, garlic, apples and pork in the butter gently for about 15 minutes. Mix with the other ingredients. The chopped liver of the bird may also be added.

100 g (4 oz) chopped onion
1 large clove garlic, crushed
2 large eating apples, peeled, cored and diced
300 g (12 oz) belly of pork, minced
50 g (2 oz) butter
100 g (4 oz) breadcrumbs
50 g (2 oz) walnuts, chopped
2 teaspoons honey
1 large egg
1 tablespoon chopped parsley
salt and pepper

Cranberry Stuffing

For goose or a boned roast of venison.

Fry suet until it is crisp. Add cranberries and sprinkle with the sugar. Stir until the berries are transparent. Add breadcrumbs, orange rind, salt and pepper. Mix well.

25 g (1 oz) suet, finely chopped
400 g (1 lb) cranberries, chopped
300 g (12 oz) sugar
150 g (6 oz) breadcrumbs
1 tablespoon grated orange rind
salt and pepper

Forcemeat Balls

Mix ingredients together and roll into small balls. You may use them as they are or fry them in lard until they are golden.

100 g (4 oz) white breadcrumbs
40 g (1½ oz) suet – if you haven't any suet you may substitute melted butter
1 tablespoon chopped parsley
1 tablespoon chopped mixed herbs or ½ tablespoon thyme
salt and pepper
1 egg, beaten

A General Marinade for Game

½ bottle red wine
4–6 tablespoons olive oil
1 onion, sliced
3 sprigs parsley
1 bayleaf
8 peppercorns, crushed
¼ teaspoon thyme

optional
3 tablespoons wine vinegar or 3 tablespoons brandy
2 carrots, sliced
3 cloves
6 juniper berries, crushed
1 clove garlic, mashed

The purpose of marinating game is to increase the flavour and to make it more tender. This means that you must decide for yourself how much extra flavour or tenderizing is necessary. The acid ingredients are what help to break down the flesh, so if you feel the meat might be tough, reduce the wine and add stronger wine vinegar or lemon juice. You cannot get away with using bad wine in a marinade or for cooking. You may use cheap wine or the dregs which have been opened but then corked again and kept in the dark, but once the wine is bad and been kept too long not only does it make a disgusting smell but it ruins the meat. It took me a remarkably long time to discover this.

Rowanberry Jelly

400 g (1 lb) sugar
to
500 ml (1 pint) juice

The Rowan trees seem to be covered with berries up to the day you decide to pick them and then you find that you have left it one day later than the birds. You want them just ripe, firm and dry, and so do the birds. I personally prefer them mixed with a couple of cooking apples or crab-apples for jelly, and it also seems to help them jell. However, this is a matter of taste and experiment. It is by far the best jelly to serve with grouse and venison.

Pick the berries from the stalks, place them in a large pan, cover them with water and boil them until they are soft, about 10–15 minutes. Mash them lightly with a potato masher and strain them through a jelly bag. Mix juice with appropriate amount of sugar, bring slowly to the boil, stirring until the sugar has melted, then increase heat and boil rapidly until it becomes jell. It is impossible to say how long, and each batch is different – probably from 20–40 minutes. Put it in pots and try to get into a routine so you are eating this year's next year as it improves with the keeping.

Horseradish Cream Sauce

2–4 tablespoons grated horseradish
4 teaspoons wine vinegar
½ teaspoon salt
1 teaspoon or more sugar
2 tablespoons chopped chives (optional)
250 ml (½ pint) heavy whipped cream or thick sour cream

Mix all ingredients together and allow to sit for about 15 minutes.

Variation Omit vinegar and add ½ teaspoon prepared mustard and 3 tablespoons mayonnaise.

Shooting Picnics and Lunches

Shooting Stews

What a sorry thing a shooting stew can be – too thinly sliced stewing steak with some carrots covered in a synthetic gravy. Do some wives punish their husbands for having a pleasant day's shooting by providing them with this uninspiring dish? Making stews is so satisfying and rewarding, especially if you have eight hungry men ready to appreciate your efforts.

I was in Paris one October and there decided that the ideal shooting dish in Scotland must be the classic French Cassoulet. The day before I flew home I staggered out of Fauchon on the Place de la Madeleine carrying bags of precious ingredients. I taxied them to Orly, changed planes at Heathrow, put them in a car at Turnhouse and finally got them home. I shopped carefully for the other items I needed and then spent three days putting all this together. I was so excited and couldn't wait for the morning to end. Finally the moment arrived, I dished out my cassoulet. 'Goodness, did the meat have maggots?' asked our neighbour. Nonchalantly I took my place and watched as everyone else pushed their food around their plates very unenthusiastically while glowering at a rather effeminate garden architect who went into raptures over the unlikelihood of finding such a magnificent and civilized dish in a place like Scotland. No one had a second helping, not even the garden architect, and I was left with a gallon of cassoulet and a husband who claimed he had indigestion.

It was a lesson, and since then I have watched very carefully. Any good stew – beef, mutton, game, chicken – as long as it is the best, is always appreciated. Curry is a winner and they devour more chutney than you would believe possible. Lasagne and moussaka are considered very clever, which surprised me as I thought they might be too foreign! Spaghetti isn't as popular, possibly because it demands a certain concentration and everyone wishes to keep talking about how they have been getting on. Steak and kidney pie is fun to serve because everyone looks so surprised if it's a really good one! Remember that you can be generous with seasoning – everyone will have been outside all morning, then probably will have had a strong drink, though this does not mean that they wish to taste garlic all afternoon.

Some Tips for Helping Make the Picnic Season Easier

Keep a list of all the basics which every picnic includes and check them off each time – salt, pepper, mustard, mayonnaise, sugar for coffee, knives, corkscrew, bottle opener or punch for tins, paper table napkins, container for garbage, cups, and plates. During the summer we usually return them straight to the picnic hamper as soon as it has been cleaned out.

If you are running a lodge where people are following various pursuits, it is an idea to lay out the selection for lunch at breakfast-time with a supply of polythene bags and let them make up their own. It doesn't take them a minute and you will be surprised at the different requirements and tastes.

Lettuce keeps better if the outer leaves are removed and then it is cut in quarters rather than separating each leaf. Wash all salad ingredients, dry them well, put them in a plastic box with a snap-on lid, and if you have time chill them for an hour or so – you can do this the evening before and they will be cool and crisp for an early departure. Then, depending on how much room you have, you can put the box in an insulated bag. As well as tomatoes, lettuce, celery and cucumber (the young adore cucumber) my family like carrots, cabbage, chicory and cauliflower.

Slice cold meat at home as you can get it thinner and it saves it from being hacked at by the masses. Salamis and pâtés I take whole (remember a knife) as they are not as likely to be demolished. If it is very hot you will need to keep the pâté insulated or it will melt. If you haven't an insulation bag, wrap the pâté well in foil, make sure it is well chilled, and then wrap it in cold, very damp newspaper. This is Elizabeth David's hint on how to keep wine cool for a picnic, but with the help of foil it works with all kinds of other things within reason.

Remember how all the picnics you have had on the Continent have centred around the loaf of bread. If you have good bread your problems are almost solved, even the most stoic of slimmers will relent this once. If you cannot buy good bread and you have a freezer, then buy it when you can and freeze it. It is even worth flying it up in your suit-case from London. My daughter has sat on the aeroplane with 25 sticks of French bread from Walton Street on her knee, feeling an absolute idiot. Bread is not difficult to make but you do have to be around at moments when you'd rather be out with the others. If you have a holiday cook you will find that she can manage it easily, and once she has established a routine it will be no trouble at all. Good bread is no worse for you than the pudding she might make instead. If your bread is very fresh, it slices easier if it has been in the refrigerator for an hour. If you butter it right out to the edge it helps to stop sandwiches from going soggy. French bread cut into 8–10 cm (3–4 in) chunks, slit sideways and with some of the crumbs pulled out makes a sound basis for a substantial sandwich. It sounds recklessly extravagant to suggest buying a roast of beef to cook and serve cold for picnics, but it is what most people like best and you may console yourself that it will go farther cold and thinly sliced than it would as the Sunday joint. The meat should be red and juicy though not shiny, and a lean, boned roast, tied tightly, will prevent any waste. It is certainly worth doing with venison if you have plenty. A meat slicer makes all this very quick and simple. If you are packing the slices for a picnic, place a piece of greaseproof paper between each slice and then wrap it well in foil.

Thermoses

Thermoses are no problem when they are used for soups, stews, anything that is partly liquid – but they are more difficult when you wish to keep something hot without it becoming soggy. This is caused by steam so you have to do everything that is possible to eliminate it. Having warmed the thermos, make sure that it is absolutely dry. If you are filling a thermos with a liquid you should fill it as full as possible, but if it is to be filled with sausages, angels on horseback, baked potatoes or whatever, allow enough room at the top for a 7 cm (3 in) layer of crumpled paper towel. This catches the steam as it rises and prevents it from falling back on the food. Drain the food first on paper towels as thoroughly as possible, as spending a few hours in warm fat doesn't improve it either.

We have broken several thermoses, trying to get ice cubes out of them by letting a warm hand touch the sides. Thermoses with plastic type liners are therefore better for ice.

Rice in a Thermos

Cook the rice until it is still a little underdone, drain it in a sieve and pour hot water through it to wash away any remaining starch. Place the sieve over a pot of gently boiling water, place a doubled clean tea-cloth over the rice and steam like this for about 20 minutes. Occasionally fluff up the rice with a fork. Heat as much butter as you think you will need until it is bubbling. Warm the thermos, dry thoroughly. Put the rice in the thermos with a good screw of pepper, pour over the hot butter, stir with some implement long enough to reach the bottom (a wooden fork), put a good layer of crumpled paper towelling on the top and put on the lid. Stir again before serving.

I have done the same with spaghetti and noodles, they aren't as reliable but I have never been mortified by the results.

Shooting Stews

Hundred-of-Fordingbridge Pea Soup

A contribution from Stuart Wilson.

This good shooting lunch is served as two courses and is made of packet 'marrowfat' peas, hock of bacon, onions, pepper, and nothing else. If the fore-hock is used, allow one per person: if the hind or ham-hock, one per two people, and one 300 g (12 oz) packet of marrowfat peas per four people. Un-smoked or 'green' hocks are best as they seem to come out more tender, but whichever are used they must be well soaked, with changes of water, for three days. The peas must be soaked according to directions on the packet. Indeed, the various and absolutely essential soakings are almost the only work that has to be done. For the rest, put the hocks, the peas and one large onion per packet of peas, with quite a lot of mill pepper, in a large saucepan with plenty of cold water and boil with lid on merrily for $3\frac{1}{2}$ hours. The peas should 'break down' early on and water quantities should be adjusted to give a nice thick soup. First serve the soup, and then the hocks with some of the peas, and potatoes in their jackets with butter. If you wish to spoil your guests, do not forget the freshly mixed English mustard. The same soup plates can be used for the second course as the hocks will be left very hot in the big pan.

Note: 'Hocks' of bacon are often called 'knuckles'. If they are not soaked as instructed the dish will be too salty. On no account add salt. If the peas have been too long in the packet they will not 'break down' and the dish will fail. Peas grown specifically to be inserted into railway guards' whistles should be avoided. Do not allow your guests to quail at the size of the meat helping: it is a good half bone and the best of it is the 'near-fat' scraped from inside the skin.

Lancashire Hot Pot

From Stuart Wilson.

A Lancashire Hot Pot is the best shooting lunch dish there is, as it is easy both to cook and serve, and everybody likes it: you can only go wrong if you try to be clever. The secret of its excellence lies in simplicity, long cooking, and the right pot.

Use three ingredients only, best-end-of-neck of lamb, rather lean, and cut into chops, potatoes and onions – and a pot rather deep and giving as big a surface as possible, which is to say that it must have curved or sloping sides, as the golden-brown crust on top is the glory of the dish.

Half-fill – or nearly fill – the pot with potatoes cut up small and mixed with chopped onion at the rate of about one onion to seven potatoes of the same size. Then pack in tightly one complete layer of the neck chops, filling the entire area of the pot. On this sprinkle chopped onions, pepper and salt, and cover with more cut-up potatoes and onion to within about 2 cm ($\frac{3}{4}$ in) of the top, then change over to big potatoes sliced thinly on the mandolin and fill nearly to the top, using no more onion. Fill with hot water – not boiling – till the thinly sliced top layer is nicely awash, and cook with the lid on in a moderate oven for 3 hours. From time to time look at the dish and press down the crust which forms into the water below, at the same time adding boiling water so that the surface is just awash, not more. If much fat comes to the top remove it with kitchen paper. After 3 hours, and pressing down the ever-forming crust several times into the moisture below, take off the lid and continue just the same, occasionally going round the edge with a small sharp knife for another 2 hours, which makes 5 hours' cooking in all. A Lancashire Hot Pot cannot be created in less time than that, though more is all to the good, and from which it would perhaps follow that for a shooting lunch the dish should be started the day before, leaving the last 2 hours with the lid off for the day it is needed, a treatment which indeed seems to improve the dish.

If you get it just right, with the entire surface a crisp but not dry golden-brown crust, it will be a joy to show it round to your guests before you serve it – so make sure the pot is a fine one – and the smell of it will be a greater joy still!

Boys' Shoots

'What will we have for your shoot?'

'Why not Shepherd's Pie?'

'Because we had Shepherd's Pie the last boys' shoot and I think one last year. They'll think we eat nothing else.'

'Well, they liked it, didn't they, they didn't leave any, did they?'

'No, they ate half a pound of mince per head.'

'Why not fish pie, then, or spaghetti with masses of sauce and cheese?'

He is right – what else can you dish up to 25 people in record time when stew is unpopular? Stew is stew until you are about 18 – it seems to mean school and that holidays end. Devilled chicken is popular and most of them like curry – well, the side dishes anyway. A tomatoey garlic sauce is far more popular than gravy – you can almost get away with stew if it is covered in tomatoes and not brown looking.

Afterwards you have brandy butter with apple crumble and celery with cheese. I have not placed them the wrong way round – they reverse with age, or do they?

A Very Quick Shepherd's Pie

3 packets frozen casserole vegetables
50 g (2 oz) butter
1.6 kg (4 lb) mince
2 handfuls dehydrated onions
2 beef cubes
125 ml ($\frac{1}{4}$ pint) water
1 large tin tomatoes
2 cloves garlic, mashed
mashed potatoes

Defrost vegetables on paper towels if you have time, if not cut down the water; sauté vegetables in butter.

Brown meat in a large saucepan and add all ingredients. Simmer for $1\frac{1}{2}$ hours. This is much better done the day before it is eaten. Then cover with stiffly mashed potatoes and place in oven until really hot. Serves 12.

Picnic Lunches

The Field ran a competition to find the best ideas for a haversack lunch for shooters. Out of the letters they printed, we listed all the items suggested and then counted what was mentioned most. The result of this intense research was to discover that most of their readers thought their ideal picnic lunch should consist of:

> Fresh and crispy white or brown bread, cold ham, a wedge of bacon and ham pie, tomato, lettuce and celery, apple, fruitcake, biscuits and cheese (unspecified), a chocolate biscuit or plain biscuit, thermos of clear soup well laced with sherry, and a thermos of coffee.

Every shooting man I have shown this to has considered it very reasonable and completely agrees.

My family made up their list and after a certain amount of compromise produced: brown rolls, potted shrimps or shrimp and celery buns, salami, devilled chicken, tomato, lettuce, celery, cucumber with a tube of mayonnaise, gingerbread and coffee. The need for cheese and soup was never really settled – just that a cube of Cheshire was preferable to Brie on a soggy biscuit.

This is very general because as shooting picnics in Scotland begin in August, walking up a grouse moor, and continue until the last old cock pheasant is slayed on the first of February, the requirements change. What you wish to carry in your pocket out stalking in August bears no resemblance to what you hope you might find in the back of the Land-Rover in January. Avoid supplying too many choices: several alternatives are all you require, ensuring that no one need eat something they dislike in order to refrain from being hungry all afternoon. There is little point taking 15 minutes to lay out a lunch and as long to collect it again when at the most you will be allowed 45 minutes for the whole performance. I have become rather anti the picnic quiche – it demands so much attention in case some dreadful accident befalls it, and it's not particularly easy to serve or to eat away from a table. Pastry rolls with many of the same fillings are much easier to control.

Drink is decided by the host, and hosts have definite feelings. This spring I asked a child if her family would mind her drinking lager at a point-to-point. She replied: 'Oh, I'm not drinking it because I like it, I don't at all, but I'm trying to get to like it because it's all they ever take up on the hill next holidays and I'm always so thirsty out shooting.' She had a very sympathetic audience! Drink is extremely cumbersome and no one is going to the effort of supplying a dozen people an unlimited choice of drink 10 miles away from a main road, especially when the non-beer drinkers are usually merely camp followers. But if the host has a moment to spare he might put in a tin or two of bitter lemon, some-one might be very grateful. Gin was never acceptable on the hill and today many people still disapprove, but I have never had a look as thankful for a good lunch as I have for an ice-cold gin and tonic on a hot day.

Sandwiches

Of the many things I've learned since starting this book, the one I still find most puzzling is that the popular sandwich is a fried egg in a bun. I had always presumed when I saw one that the wife was in bed with 'flu and the husband, faced with the test of cooking his breakfast and making his lunch, just combined both jobs. This appears not to be the case – it is the great favourite, particularly stalking. You are given instructions how the egg must not be overcooked or undercooked, and occasionally a little bacon sprinkled on it would be nice though relatively unimportant. Of course they add that if you happened to have some fillet of beef or smoked salmon that would be very nice, though possibly rather a waste on them in the circumstances. The other first choice is cold beef, and usually with homemade horseradish sauce and a little lettuce. Lettuce is inclined to make sandwiches slip, especially if they have to go into a pocket, so wrap them as securely as possible in tinfoil. Rolls are really better for pockets.

These are some other suggestions which I've found are popular:
(mayonnaise, mustard, chutney and pickles I leave to you)

Chicken and Cucumber
Tomatoes and Blue Cheese
Prawns (frozen or tinned) with mayonnaise, a little ketchup and a dash of brandy
Chopped Hard-boiled Egg with mayonnaise, chives and curry powder
Italian Salami, Lettuce and/or Tomato
Tuna Fish, Lettuce, Tomato and Hard-boiled Egg, sliced
Game Hash – a mixture of chopped game, hard-boiled eggs, tomato, lettuce and celery salt

If your bread isn't inspiring and you don't feel that it is worth taking all that exercise and then eating stodge, these are a few suggestions:

Cold Meat rolled around Lettuce or Shredded Cabbage and secured with a toothpick
Celery Stalks filled with Cottage Cheese or Cream Cheese and some herbs or chives, or Blue Cheese spread
Potted Shrimps
Black Olives – these seem in the wrong environment but disappear almost instantly
Chicory – the firm inside filled as for celery
Pâtés – these really need bread but seem to lose their appeal when turned into sandwiches for you. If you haven't the right bread or rolls, then use the Scandinavian-type bread
Charcuterie and salad – all kinds of salads individually packed in small plastic screw-top jars or yoghurt tubs with snap-on tops which you have saved. If you need French dressing on them, take it separately
Anything left over from the barbecue
Dried Figs and Apricots to finish

Bacon and Marmalade Sandwiches

Lt.-Col. C. G. Austin writes: 'This is a useful haversack ration to take out hunting, fishing or shooting. It does not fall to pieces and is easy to eat. Very filling and sustaining.'

bread, thick slices
fried or grilled bacon slices
marmalade

Toast the bread. Split in half. Lay grilled or fried bacon on the inside (crumb side) and cover one slice with marmalade. Put the other piece on the marmalade, thus making a sandwich with toasted outsides.

Devilled Chicken

8 portions of cut up chicken
4 tablespoons tomato ketchup
4 tablespoons olive oil
3 teaspoons Worcestershire sauce
1 tablespoon French mustard
salt and pepper

Score the skin on the chicken pieces with a sharp knife. Mix all other ingredients together and dip the chicken in it. Place on a rack and either grill, barbecue or roast them in a hot oven (200°C, 400°F, Mark 6), basting frequently until the chicken is tender and the skin is slightly burnt. Drain on paper towelling and leave to cool.

Nigel Gray's Spanish Omelette for a Pocket Lunch

1 medium potato, diced and fried
2 rashers of bacon, chopped and fried
1 small tomato, chopped
pieces of mushroom and onion, fried (optional)
green pepper, chopped
3–4 eggs
salt and pepper
garlic

Mix the potato, bacon, tomato, mushroom, onion and green pepper with three eggs – since my appetite is small – some would prefer four, salt, pepper and garlic if desired, then cook in the normal way as an omelette.

It can be done the night before, wrapping tightly in polythene to exclude all air and stored in a refrigerator.

In fact, although nourishing, it is not very filling and therefore I have two or three Ryvita biscuits and cheese to top up with. All of this can be easily put in the pocket.

A Sausage for Shooting Lunches

neck and liver of a goose
100 g (4 oz) lean pork (fillet)
1 clove garlic
1 teaspoon chopped parsley
1 bayleaf
375 ml (¾ pint) water and stock cube or stock
salt and pepper
1 egg, well beaten
goose fat to cover

This unusual idea was sent to us. It is one which could produce endless variations.

Take the neck of the goose, cut the skin close to head and body and roll off entire. Take the neck, lean pork, garlic, parsley, bayleaf, stock, pepper and salt. Simmer together in the stock until the meat can be picked off the neck. Chop the goose meat and pork finely, add the uncooked liver of the goose, chopped finely, moisten with a well beaten egg.

Tie up one end of the neck skin, stuff with the prepared mixture and tie off the sausage into a ring. Cook, fully covered in goose fat for 1½ hours (if the goose fat will not cover, put a small bowl in the centre of the pan to deepen the level of fat).

Serve cold in slices in crusty rolls, or as an hors d'œuvre with a salad of orange slices and watercress.

Cornish Pasties

Cornish pasties were originally produced in about 1800 by miners' wives in the tin-mining region of Cornwall around Bodmin, as an 'all-in-one' lunch for their husbands to take to work. This particular recipe was supplied by a Mrs P. Pope, age 87, whose family lived and mined at Marazion. The recipe has been handed down from generation to generation.

Make pastry by rubbing fat into flour and salt, then add water a little at a time, mixing to a firm dough. Divide into three or four pieces. Shape each piece into a round on a floured board, then roll out into a long oval. It is easier to make smaller pasties than large ones. Slice potato very thinly and put a layer over the bottom half of the pastry, leaving a 'margin' round the edge.

Slice on a little turnip. Cut the meat into very thin strips, about 3 mm ($\frac{1}{8}$ in) thick, and lay on top, then thinly sliced onion. Sprinkle with parsley, season with salt and pepper. Moisten the 'margin' with water, fold down the top flap, then turn the margin all round and pinch with fingers to seal.

Put on to a baking sheet. Have a very hot oven ready (230°C, 450°F, Mark 8), but turn down immediately to 200°C, 400°F, Mark 6. Bake at this heat for about 30 minutes, then turn down heat to 180°C, 350°F, Mark 4, and bake for a further 20 minutes (50 minutes in all). If the crust is too hard, cover with a tea towel for a few minutes after removing from oven.

Pastry
75 g (3 oz) lard or margarine
200 g (8 oz) plain flour
$\frac{1}{2}$ teaspoon salt
small amount cold water

Filling
potatoes
turnip
200 g (8 oz) lean steak – skirt or hough is very good
onion
chopped parsley
salt and pepper

Partridge Shooter's Picnic

A contribution from Stuart McHugh.

In the *Pickwick Papers* by my great-grandfather, Charles Dickens, the wild shooting of Mr Winkle greatly disturbs the long, tall Gamekeeper who says: 'We shall very likely be up with another covey in five minutes. If the gentleman begins to fire now, perhaps he'll just get a shot out of the barrel by the time they rise. Something will be killed before long. I've no family myself, Sir, and this boy's mother will get something handsome from Sir Geoffrey if he's killed on his land. Load again, Sir, load again.'

Because of a lame leg Mr Pickwick joins the party for lunch, pushed in a wheelbarrow by Sam Weller.

'Here's the place,' cries Mr Wardle, 'and here's the boy with the basket, punctual as usual.' Sam proceeds to unpack the basket with the utmost dispatch.

'Weal Pie,' says Sam. 'Wery good thing is a weal pie when you know the lady as made it, and is quite sure it ain't kittens which is so like weal that the wery Pie-men don't know the difference. Tongue; well that's a good thing when it ain't a woman's. Bread – knuckle o' ham re'lar picter – cold beef in slices, wery good. What's in them stone jars?'

'Beer in one. Cold punch in t'other,' says the boy.

It needed no second invitation to induce the party to do full justice to the meal; and as little pressing did it require to induce Mr Weller, the long Gamekeeper and the boys to station themselves on the grass at a little distance and do good execution upon a decent proportion of the viands.

Preparation of the Picnic Food

The 'weal' pie is best made by stewing several hefty veal bones and not much veal. Lightly boil a dozen sausages and hard-boil half a dozen eggs. Line a loose-bottomed tin with cold water pastry. Fill with alternate layers of veal, sausage and sliced eggs, sprinkle each layer with dried herbs. Spoon veal-bone jelly in and around, adding a little melted gelatine to make certain of a good set. Clap on a pastry top with ventilation holes and bake slowly (150°C, 300°F, Mark 2) for about 50 minutes.

Tongue to be boiled for a long time covered with water, cloves and strips of orange peel. When the skin splits easily and small bones can be nipped out, it is ready. Peel with all speed; force into close-fitting vessel and cover with a flat plate weighed down by something heavy.

Knuckle of ham should be boiled quickly in cider until the skin is easily pulled off. Allow to stand in the liquor till cold.

Beef (if you can afford it) should be severely scorched on both sides for 20 minutes, then reduced in heat until done, which depends on the size of the joint. While hot carve a thick slice from the top, disclosing the 'rare' part which can be thinly sliced when the joint has cooled. Then re-seal by putting back the top slice and turning the joint upside down.

Here are a few suggestions from *The Field* which we thought interesting.

F. Dudley Rose
Lyndrettes
Upper Wanborough
Near Swindon

Two or three rounds of well-buttered wholemeal bread in the form of sandwiches composed of a layer of ham, a layer of Cheddar or Cheshire cheese, a layer of chutney topped with a layer of tongue sprinkled with chopped chives (seasoning to taste).

Mrs G. E. Ruggles-Brise
Housham Tye
Harlow
Essex

Loaf sliced longways in three or four and filled with layers of flaked salmon in a buttery sauce; minced egg mixture and sliced cold sausage or rough pâté wrapped in tinfoil and cut when wanted: cold, boned wild duck (easy to cut), stuffed with minced bacon, mushrooms and sausagemeat or cold, boned, fried sea trout (small ones).

Shooting lunch for two: Take one long French twisted loaf, split lengthwise, remove and discard most of crumb from both pieces; butter remainder liberally and fill both sides with a filling made from bacon, chicken, mushrooms, seasoned to taste and bound with a parsley sauce; replace both pieces together and wrap in tinfoil. Slice and eat as and when required. This can be followed by a fresh fruit salad, well sugared and made in screw-topped honey jars. One jar per person. And do not forget the teaspoons.

Mrs C. F. H. Churchill
Ffynnon-Cadno
Ponterwyd
Near Aberystwyth
Cardiganshire

Send your husband off with a Cornish pasty, either hot in an insulated box or cold.

Rosanna Gurowska
Normanton House
Amesbury
Wiltshire

Pastry: 400 g (1 lb) flour, 100 g (4 oz) suet, 100 g (4 oz) margarine, 1 teaspoon salt, water to mix, and butter.

Filling: 75 g (3 oz) diced raw steak or corned beef, 75 g (3 oz) diced raw potatoes, 75 g (3 oz) diced raw onion. Gently soften potatoes and onion with a little butter, do not burn, mix and roll out pastry thickly so as to support ingredients; cut pastry round a 25 cm (10 in) plate; put meat, vegetables and their juice on one half of circle, leaving a wide margin; season and add a knob of butter; fold pastry over and seal strongly with water; wrap in silver foil and cook at 185°C, 370°F or Mark 4–5 for 30 minutes (if raw steak is used, up to 50 minutes). This recipe can be cooked days in advance.

Grouse shooting: Chicken Waldorf (pieces of chicken, chopped raw celery, and apple and walnuts with mayonnaise on lettuce) in small plastic containers. Fruit mousses in small screwtop jars. Potted shrimps with slices of cucumber and squeeze of lemon in new brown bread buns. *Partridge shooting*: Scotch eggs and radishes, apple tarts, slices of salmon loaf with salad in plastic container. *Pheasant shooting*: Egg and bacon pie, bonfire potatoes with cream cheese (in insulated container), scrambled egg and anchovy baps. Mulligatawny soup, mince tarts, hot dogs – for children in Christmas holidays (in insulated container).

Mrs T. W. R. Davies
Wood House
Foston
York

Useful Information and Game Charts

Deep Freezing

Once February arrives I don't wish to cook game until it reappears in August as something new and exciting. This means that I try not to freeze much game but somehow still end up with a certain amount in the freezer. Venison is different. I am quite happy to produce a haunch in the Easter holidays, but the birds usually end up in a kind of panic pâté for the Point-to-Point, trying to clear the freezer out before the summer.

There are many good books on freezing telling you what to do and what not to do, and really all I have learnt is that you ought to obey them blindly. I find cooking for an unknown emergency uninspiring, but as we shoot on Saturdays and Mondays I freeze most of the Monday stews knowing that there will not be time to make one. The rest of my freezer is filled with things to make my life easier and cheaper. Large quantities of bread and rolls, the butcher' 'specials' which I cannot resist (and he knows it), half cases of butter, margarine and lard, catering sized packages of vegetables and shrimps and scampi, and a certain amount of fresh fruit sorbet. I do not love my family or friends enough to spend my summer working in the garden and kitchen in order to make their dreary old winter taste like summer. Organizing summer to taste like summer is quite enough work.

Game Only freeze the best and don't overhang it. If of course the keeper suddenly arrives in the kitchen with a dozen skinned badly shot pheasants which were impossible to sell, I consider it quite permissible to throw them all in a bag and freeze them for a couple of days while I catch my breath. I am lucky as I have a big walk-in deep freeze which makes this kind of holding process very easy. Freezer burn is the first menace which I find very hard to avoid, the second is broken bones piercing the wrapping. First pad anything that might be sharp with paper or foil, then put the meat in cotton stockinette and finally in a special heavy freezer bag. Ordinary polythene plastic bags are not thick enough, but if you are really pushed use three of these. I then suck out the air, the opposite way to blowing up a balloon, twist the end and fold it over and tie down. Freeze on the coldest shelf, not touching anything else, and stack the packages once they are frozen. Label everything with quantity and date no matter how obvious it seems. Meat is supposed to be best defrosted as slowly as possible. 400 g (1 lb) takes about $3\frac{1}{2}$ hours in a refrigerator and 1 hour at room temperature. As the weight increases it takes slightly less time per pound. In an emergency you may defrost it quicker in cold, warm or running water. As it is presumably in an airtight package, do not unwrap it until you have completely defrosted it and taken it from the water. Game keeps for about nine months: they say it keeps longer but I don't find it as good.

If a bird appears to be slightly dried by freezer burn after it has thawed, soak it in milk or thin cream for 2–3 hours. This process should make the bird more tender and bring back the original flavour.

Bread This must be airtight but don't suck out so much air that the rolls or loaves lose their shape – they don't seem to bounce back. French bread is the worst to wrap. Freezer paper and tape is the only solution unless you can find the right size bag to put on each end and to meet and be taped in the middle. It takes two people for the performance as you still have to try to get the air out. Bread defrosts very quickly so it is seldom necessary to put it in the oven. Though you may if you wish. You may also slice it when it is still quite frozen, and the frozen slices toast almost as quickly as unfrozen bread. Bread keeps for about three months.

Stews I am convinced that a frozen stew is better if you add the lightly sautéed vegetables after it has been defrosted and cook them as you re-heat the stew. A certain amount of vegetable flavour will be in the stock, and the vegetables seem to lose their texture with the comparatively slow cooling and freezing which they get in a stew. Garlic goes off after about a week, celery becomes too strong after two weeks, and mushrooms go soggy. I find the result better if you cook the stew for about three-quarters of its time, maybe with a few sliced onions but not little white ones, nor should you thicken the gravy. Cool it overnight in the refrigerator and freeze it. Then once it is thawed and put back to boil, add the vegetables and simmer another three-quarters of an hour and then thicken the gravy if necessary. If you are putting a casserole in the freezer make sure that it is unbreakable and rustproof. Stews like being frozen, it is just the vegetables that don't like being frozen in that manner. They should only be kept in the freezer for about three months.

Pâtés It is very difficult thinking of a way to ask your hostess if her pâté was frozen. I don't think they freeze terribly well. Highly seasoned food doesn't freeze well anyway, and many pâtés tend to separate. The liquid forms crystals, which break away from the fat and you lose the right consistency. It doesn't happen as much with potted meats or liver pastes but more with pâtés cooked in terrines. If you are going to freeze a terrine, try undercooking it slightly, and once it is cold turn it out of its terrine and wrap it well in foil and a freezer bag. Then when you have thawed it put it back into its terrine, put the terrine in a pan of hot water, place it in the oven again and cook it for another 45 minutes. This will help to bring it back together again. I still don't know why you need to freeze pâtés when they keep quite well in a cool place for a week or more. If you are going to freeze a pâté for more than two weeks, don't put any garlic in it.

Shooting Food

Before you have to worry about how to cook the game in your larder it has to be shot, so the people who shoot it have to be fed. They have not come to partake of a gastronomical orgy. They have come to shoot, and what you give them to eat will be an accompaniment to the day and not the focal point. What happened to the birds in the drive before lunch or what is whose number after lunch is, I'm afraid, rather more important than the pâté. Of course if the pâté is good you will pick up an appreciative grunt, and if all the food is good you may hear the greatest compliment, 'Like coming here, always get a decent lunch.' In an odd way they aren't terribly hungry, thirsty maybe, but if you have an afternoon's shooting ahead of you, you don't want to set off feeling like a stuffed Strasbourg goose.

Cooking Away From Home

Whether you are renting a house or being employed as a holiday cook, it is always unnerving when you have your first moment to sum up the kitchen. You will presumably be feeding a fair number of people who at times will be very hungry and cold and at other times will require a vast variety of picnics suitable for every kind of excursion. As our house is usually full of young freelance cooks, I have asked them to make a list of what they would hope to find and what they would take of their own when they go to a seasonal job. I have had to edit it slightly as they do not realize that because you are in residence in a shooting lodge you have not the unlimited resources of a Merchant Bank.

If you have electricity they would be thrilled
to see:
electric hand beater
liquidizer
toaster

They would expect to find:
bread knife
some other knives
spatula
wooden spoons
scissors
good efficient tin opener
good scales
flan rings and cake tins
bread tins
pâté terrines
gratin dish
casseroles of adequate size
adequate pots and pans
kettle
5-hour timer
sieve
colander
lemon squeezer
bowls
measuring cup

rolling pin
chopping board
potato peeler
grater
metal whisk
good firm mincer
chip pan and draining ladle
roasting pan
corkscrew
good pepper grinder
string
sharpening steel
adequate washing-up equipment

They would be pleased to find as well:
garlic press
tongs
mouli
game shears
mandoline

They think it would be nice for everyone if you were going fishing to have an Abu smoker with plenty of sawdust.

They would intend to bring their own:
chopping knife
butcher's knife
cook's knife
paring knife
filleting knife
wooden spatula
plastic spatula
game scissors
piping bag
metal whisk
flan ring
swivel peeler
palette knife
apron
cookery books

They would look at the store cupboard
and hope to find:
salt
black peppercorns
sugar – granulated, brown, icing, castor,
   and coffee if you like it
tea
coffee – Nescafé or ground, as you like
jams, marmalade, honey, etc.
cooking oil
olive oil
wine vinegar
mustard – dried English and Dijon
bayleaves
flour – white or wholemeal if you wish
   them to make bread
baking powder
baking soda
cornflour
cream of Tartar or arrowroot
cooking chocolate
stock cubes
meat extract
herbs – if not in the garden, then dried
   parsley, thyme, tarragon, marjoram, basil
paprika
cayenne
cooking wine, white and red
cooking brandy and port
gelatine
curry powder
juniper berries

rice
vanilla essence
powdered milk, if milk is difficult to get
ground ginger
mixed spice
allspice
mace
nutmeg
cinnamon
tomato purée
Worcestershire sauce

In the refrigerator or larder:
milk
butter
margarine
lard
eggs
bread
onions
potatoes
garlic

They think they would make out a shopping list which might include:
breakfast cereal
bacon
matches
redcurrant jelly
cranberry sauce
tomato juice
celery salt
celery
carrots
dehydrated onions
tinned tomatoes
cheese
cream
sour cream
yeast
muslin
lemons and PLJ juice
parmesan cheese
rolls
dried horseradish powder
tomato purée
spaghetti and noodles
biscuits for cheese
digestive biscuits

ingredients for a fruitcake	tinfoil
paper towels	foil
greaseproof paper	golden syrup
polythene bags	treacle

They would know that after all this sooner or later someone would be furious because they couldn't produce every ingredient for a specialist's Bloody Mary at an instant. It happens to them all!

Cooking Terms

Bard   Any lean meat, especially that of game, benefits from barding. This is simply covering the meat with slices of salt fat pork or streaky bacon, making sure that the breast bone and thigh bones are particularly covered. Tie these on with string. You may wish to remove the fat several minutes before the bird is cooked in order to allow it to become brown.

Beurre Manié   A paste of kneaded butter and flour (approximately 25 g (1 oz) flour to 20 g ($\frac{3}{4}$ oz) butter), used for thickening gravies, soups and sauces. Add little pieces of the paste to the boiling liquid and stir until it has thickened.

Bouquet Garni   This is a small bunch of herbs tied together or put in a small muslin bag so that they may easily be removed before serving. It is used for flavouring liquids and food cooked in liquids and is normally composed of a bayleaf, parsley and thyme, though other herbs may be included when necessary.

Braise   Cook food which you have normally browned first, then add a layer of boiling liquid and simmer in a tightly covered pot.

Brown   Quickly fry meat so that the outside is brown without the inside being cooked. The meat must be completely dry or sprinkled with flour, and it will not brown if there are too many pieces in the pan. The pieces should not be touching each other.

Civet   A stew: game in it is normally furred.

Clarified Butter   This keeps for ages in the refrigerator so as its always being needed it is as well to make more than you need at the time and store it. To make it, melt butter over a low heat and just let it bubble but never start to brown. Cool it until the sediment sets, and then filter it. The correct way is through a fine cloth wrung out in hot water. I usually use a Melita coffee filter in the bottom of the port strainer – you just have to be careful that you don't burst it and that you wash the port strainer well or you'll get the sack!

Croûtons   Slices of bread with their crusts trimmed, cut into various shapes and fried in oil or butter.

Dice   Cut into small cubes.

Dredge   Cover lightly by sprinkling or rolling the food in flour or whatever else the recipe suggests.

Green Peppercorns   Tinned peppercorns in their soft undried state.

Juniper Berries   Purple-blue berries which are an important flavour in gin. They are wonderful with game but should be used in small quantities and always crushed or chopped to release their flavour.

Lard   1. Cooking fat.
      2. Inserting strips of pork fat or bacon into very lean meat to give it moisture while cooking. This is done usually with a larding needle but one is not absolutely necessary. You may make a slit in the meat and push the strips in with any implement. They should be placed about 2.5 cm (1 in) apart.

Marinade   A highly seasoned mixture usually comprising wine, lemon juice or vinegar; olive oil, vegetables, herbs and seasoning. Meat is left to stand in this to increase its flavour and to make it more tender.

Marinate   To put meat in a marinade.

Mouli   A food mill for making purées, especially useful when a liquidizer will destroy the required texture.

Pepper   Every recipe that calls for pepper means freshly ground black peppercorns from a pepper grinder.

Petit Suisse   A French, paper-wrapped, cylindrical, unsalted, fresh cream cheese. The woman who first marketed it in Paris had a Swiss farm manager. It is sometimes called Petit Gervais – he was her partner.

Reduce   Evaporate a liquid by boiling it uncovered over a high heat until you have the quantity you wish. This increases the flavour.

Roux   A blend of butter and flour, mixed together over a low heat. It is capable of absorbing six times its own weight when cooked.

Salmis   A bird which has been partially roasted, carved and served in a rich sauce.

Sauté   To fry gently in a little butter or oil.

Simmer   To cook just under boiling point with bubbles just at the sides of the pan.

Trivet   A rack which will support game, breast down, for roasting. They are usually adjustable.

Wild Rice   A seed of a grass which grows wild in the Northern United States and Canada. As it is difficult to harvest, it is expensive.

The Ageing of Geese

The species in probable order of number of birds shot are:

Pink-footed goose	Many
Greylag goose	
White-fronted goose	
Canada goose	
Barnacle goose	
Bean goose	Very few

The first two would account for most of the birds shot.

In general, birds of the year tend to lack the strong clear-cut markings of the adult; but where the adult is plain on the breast and belly, there is often a fine soft-edged speckling in the juvenile. However, by the end of the shooting season many of the adult characteristics will be well developed.

One feature which is distinctive for part of the winter is the notch in the tail feather of the juvenile where the downy feather was once attached. The notch is a V, about 3 mm ($\frac{1}{8}$ in) deep and wide. It must not be confused with a *broken* tail feather: since moulting occurs progressively during the winter there may be only one juvenile feather to be seen. After the loss of this one, other characteristics have to be assessed. As the season progresses, ageing becomes less certain.

Juvenile characteristics	Adult characteristics

Pink-footed goose

Bill: blotchy flesh colour	banded pink on black
Head: pale and brownish	dark blackish tint
Breast and belly: speckled	plain
Legs: pale pink	pink

Greylag goose

Bill: pale orange	orange
Body: markings soft	markings distinct
Breast and belly: few speckles	distinct spots if present
Legs: greyish pink	pink

White-fronted goose

Bill: white forehead absent but developing later	white forehead
Belly: no black bands but developing later	variable black bands present
Legs: paler and pinker than adult	orange

Canada goose

Cheek patch: greyer than adult	white
Body: markings similar to adult. Nearly indistinguishable late in season	less softer brown feathers

Barnacle goose

Much as for the Canada goose – no brown feathers, only black and white

Bean goose

Much as for the Pink-footed goose but in adult bill yellow and black and head less dark

Up to about mid-November the tail feathers of geese are definitive for ageing – as with ducks:

old

young

After that it is not always possible to tell positively, except for late young, which are undersized and underweight.

Geese for Eating

The best eating are Greylag and Pink-footed, which are indistinguishable as a dish, flavour-wise, and Canada, which have a different flavour but are very good. European White-fronted geese are also very tasty, but the Greenland White-fronts are inferior, particularly when they have been feeding on the roots of common cotton grass (*Erio-phorum augustifolium*).

If *properly* cooked, an old goose is as delicious as a young one. This applies more to geese than game.

GAME CHARTS (as supplied by The Game Conservancy)

Game	Number of Servings	Shooting Seasons all dates incl.	Av. Weights	Approximate Roasting Times and Oven Temperatures
Duck	2–3 servings	below high tide mark September 1st to February 20th	**Mallard** 1.1–1.3 kg (2½–2¾ lb)	very hot oven 230°C, 450°F, Mark 8, 20–30 minutes
	1 serving	elsewhere September 1st to January 31st	**Teal** 300–370 g (11–13 oz)	very hot oven 220°C, 425°F, Mark 7, 10–15 minutes
	2 servings		**Widgeon** 700–900 g (1½–2 lb)	very hot oven 220°C, 425°F, Mark 7, 15–25 minutes
Geese	6 servings	as for duck	**Pink-footed** 2.7–3.2 kg (6–7 lb) **Greylag** 3.7–5 kg (8–10 lb)	old goose – braise or stew young goose – very hot oven 220°C, 425°F, Mark 7 for 10 minutes, then moderately slow oven 170°C, 325°F Mark 3, for 1 hour
Wood Pigeon	1 serving	no close season	500–600 g (1–1¼ lb)	very hot oven 220°C, 425°F, Mark 7, for 20 minutes
Hares	6–10 servings	no close season but they may not be offered for sale during March to July, inclusive	3–3.2 kg (6½–7 lb)	young hare – hot oven 200°C, 400°F, Mark 6, for 20 minutes per 400 g (1 lb); slow oven 150°C, 300°F, Mark 2, for 1½–2 hours

Rabbits	3 servings	no close season	1.1–1.6 kg (2½–3½ lb)	hot oven 200°C, 400°F, Mark 6, for 1 hour
Grouse	1–2 servings	August 12th to December 10th	600–700 g (1¼–1½ lb)	moderately hot oven 190°C, 375°F, Mark 5, for 35 minutes
Blackgame	3 servings	August 20th to December 10th	1.4–1.8 kg (3–4 lb)	preferably braise or stew, very young birds – moderately hot oven 190°C, 375°F, Mark 5, for 40–50 minutes
Ptarmigan	1 serving	Scotland only, August 12th to December 10th	400–600 g (1–1¼ lb)	braise or stew
Capercaillie	1 serving	October 1st to January 31st	2.7–5.5 kg (6–12 lb)	braise or stew
Partridge cock hen	1–2 servings	September 1st to February 1st	350–450 g (13–15 oz) about 400 g (12½–14½ oz)	very hot oven 220°C, 425°F, Mark 7, for 30 minutes
Pheasant cock hen	4 servings	October 1st to February 1st	1.4–1.6 kg (3–3½ lb) 900 g–1.1 kg (2–2½ lb)	moderately hot oven 190°C, 375°F, Mark 5, for ¾–1 hour
Common Snipe	1–2 per person	August 12th to January 31st	100–130 g (3½–4½ oz)	very hot oven 230°C, 450°F, Mark 8, for 6–15 minutes
Woodcock	1 serving	*England and Wales* October 1st to January 31st *Scotland* September 1st to January 31st	230–400 g (8–14 oz)	very hot oven 220°C, 450°F, Mark 7, for 15–20 minutes

A rough guide to what's what, based on the British Deer Society's pamphlet of Venison Recipes.

Notes on the Venison Chart
Clean means without stomach, entrails, etc.

The information on the weights of the deer has been very kindly compiled for us by F. J. Taylor Page of the British Deer Society.

The following weights for Red Deer are given by Whitehead in his book *Deer and Their Management*.

	lb	oz
head and antlers	25	1
head and neck skin	13	2
tongue	1	9
hooves and shins (forelegs) with skin	3	12
hind legs with skin on	4	0
body skin	17	4
neck	25	14
windpipe	11	10
testicles, etc.	1	7
heart	2	9
liver	5	14
skirt	1	14
lungs	6	0
spleen	0	14
kidneys	0	15
suet round kidney and back	8	3
carcass less all of the above	266	0
Total	396	0

This may not be of great interest to most people but I personally find it fascinating. The measurements are for an unusually large stag.

Roe Deer

Sex	Shooting Season England	Scotland	Weight
Buck	No Statutory Season	May 1st to October 20th	17–22 kg (38–50 lb)
Doe	November 1st to February 28–29th	October 21st to February 28–29th	15–20 kg (33–45 lb) (but there is considerable variation in locality)

Fallow Deer

Sex	Shooting Season England	Scotland	Weight
Wild Buck	August 1st to	August 1st to	57–65 kg (9–10 stone)
Park Buck	April 30th	April 30th	65–95 kg (10–15 stone), cleaned, and in good condition
Wild Doe	November 1st to	October 21st to	38 kg (6 stone)
Park Doe	February 28–29th	February 15th	40–44 kg (7–8 stone), in good condition

Red Deer

Sex	Shooting Season England	Scotland	Weight
Wild Stag	August 1st to	July 1st to	89–101 kg (14–16 stone), cleaned
Park Stag	April 30th	October 20th	152–172 kg (24–27 stone), as killed / 101–152 kg (16–24 stone), depending on amount of available food
Wild Hind	November 1st to	October 21st to	42–70 kg ($7\frac{1}{2}$–11 stone), cleaned / 89–95 kg (14–15 stone), as killed
Park Hind	February 28–29th	February 15th	65–95 kg (10–15 stone), depending on amount of available food

Index

FAMOUS
FRENCH
COOKERY

By
Hyla O'Connor

Fawcett Publications, Inc.
67 West 44th Street
New York, N.Y. 10019

CONTENTS

LARRY EISINGER: *Editor-in-Chief*

GEORGE TILTON: *Executive Editor*

SILVIO LEMBO: *Creative Director* • HAROLD E. PRICE: *Associate Director*

ELLENE SAUNDERS: *Editor*

PAMELA RIDDLE: *Editorial Assistant*

HERBERT JONAS: *Layout*   ALLEN WILSON: *Layout*

ELAINE E. SAPOFF: *Production Editor*   ALAINE TROW: *Production Assistant*

Editorial Staff: JOE PIAZZA, RAY GILL,
DAN BLUE, FRANK BOWERS, AMY MORRIS

Art Staff: MIKE GAYNOR, ALEX SANTIAGO, JOHN SELVAGGIO,
JOHN CERVASIO, JACK LA CERRA, JOSEPH MAYA

Ralph Owen, Decorative Art

Printed in U.S.A. by
FAWCETT-HAYNES PRINTING CORPORATION
Rockville, Maryland

INTRODUCTION

Mention French food and French cooking and everyone immediately thinks of the Grande Cuisine. But what of French home cooking? Like her American counterpart, the French housewife has three meals to cook each day, and pressed duck or flaming crêpes are not a part of her family's daily fare. She cooks with ingredients that are at hand, stewing, simmering and flavoring much the same as any busy American wife and mother.

When she yearns for fancy food, the French woman dines out, just as we are wont to do here in America. Food served in a top flight French or American restaurant is much more elegant because all the cooking is not done by just one person. There are many chefs, each handling a specific job—meats, sauces, vegetables, etc.—as well as the grand master chef, who oversees the whole operation and is the soul of a really good restaurant. For at-home parties, the French hostess orders pâté en croûte or a fancy main dish from a store in the neighborhood that specializes in select cooked meat dishes. Then she completes her meal with a selection of wondrous desserts from the local bakery.

Americans tend to think of French food as being invariably covered with rich cream sauces or simmered in wine and blazing in cognac. But again, just as a cook in Georgia prepares Southern Fried Chicken or a Maine housewife makes New England Chowder, the French woman turns out the various regional specialties which her country offers. These dishes evolve, as they do in America, because of the food and produce raised in the area. Dairying, for example, is a major industry in Normandy and the dishes of the region tend to be rich with butter and cream. Since apples are abundant, many of the dishes are cooked with cider or applejack. Fish dishes are popular all over France because the country is surrounded on three sides by water and many rivers flow through it. Wine is as common for a French woman to cook with as water is for us, because wine is produced in almost every part of the country. It is used as a flavoring to add to the taste of a dish, much as we use onions or other spices.

Thanks to the gourmet corner in most supermarkets, you will be able to find the items you need to prepare the recipes in this book. Expensive truffles and pâtés are used here for flavoring and are fun to use for special occasions regardless of cost.

Shallots, those tangy members of the onion family, are being carried by many supermarkets. If you see them, buy a few, for they keep well and you can use them on your next French cooking spree.

You probably will not need any special equipment for French cooking. A set of good knives is, of course, a must, and learning the art of using a French knife can make cutting chores easier. A set of heavy pots and pans will fill the bill for the long, slow cooking of stews and sauces. The only thing to remember is to use either an enamel or stainless steel pot when cooking with white wine, to prevent the sauce from turning dark. You may want an omelet or crêpe pan, and if you're planning on soufflés, a straight-sided soufflé dish is necessary.

Other basics include wooden spoons for stirring, rubber scrapers for getting out the last drop, and wire whisks for beating and making smooth, creamy sauces. Beating egg whites can be done with a whisk if you have a good right arm, but a rotary beater works just as well.

Now that you have a little background and knowledge of the tools you'll need, it's time to start exploring the delectable world of French cooking.

Bread, Cheese, & Wine

Served with all meals and a must with cheese and wine, bread is truly the staff of life for the French people. It is not uncommon for them to make as many as three daily trips to the baker. The first purchase is made early in the morning. French breakfasts or "petits dejeuners" are much lighter than ours, consisting of an assortment of rolls (croissants and brioches) and French bread served with café au lait, a delicious blend of half hot coffee and half hot milk. The bread is always freshly baked and warm—a delightful breakfast. If lunch is eaten at home, bread is bought again, and another trip to the "boulangerie" is a must before dinner.

French housewives rarely do their own bread baking, preferring the baker's inimitable crusty loaves. Even rural areas are supplied by bakery trucks from the town, ensuring each French family of its "petit pain". A common sight in French towns is French children improvising walking sticks and bats from loaves of bread intended for the family table. The long loaves are seen peeping out of housewives' shopping bags or dangling from their bicycle baskets.

Unfortunately, the bread produced in France could never really be duplicated here, for they use a different type of flour, different ovens, and different baking techniques. However, we are including recipes for bread, croissants, and for brioches which will be great fun to try. Serve them at a leisurely Sunday brunch along with a hearty platter of bacon and eggs, or try them the French way with butter and café au lait.

In France, the favorite part of a meal, or in many cases the whole meal, is an assortment of cheeses served with crusty French bread and a glass of wine. This is a custom which can well be adapted to American dining, if not for every day, certainly for special occasions or light meals.

You are undoubtedly familiar with the kinds of domestic cheese made in America. We have American cheddar, liederkranz, Swiss, cream, cottage, Monterey Jack and a few specialty cheeses. Many of these are used for sandwiches, salads and dips, but they also take kindly to the French treatment with bread and wine.

The marriage of cheese and wine is one of the world's most enduring. Dry red wine is best with most cheeses. The tangier the cheese, the more full-bodied the wine should be. Dry white wine is excellent with goat cheeses and champagne is wonderful with all cheeses.

French cheeses should be removed from the refrigerator one to two hours before serving because they are best enjoyed at room temperature. Round cheeses, such as Brie, Camembert or Port Salut should always be cut from the center out so that everyone can enjoy the tasty center.

If you are not familiar with French cheeses, here is an introductory assortment. After you have tried these, branch out and try other kinds, not only from France, but from many other parts of the world as well—there are as many as 2000 different varieties!

Wine is a traditional part of the French diet, and any French meal is considered incomplete without a good wine to complement the food. This does not mean that a great vintage wine is served with every meal, but there is always at least an inexpensive vin ordinaire. Even in France, the great wines are reserved for the great occasions.

There are several schools of thought concerning the selection of wines. Dyed-in-the-wool purists insist that there is no wine like the native French product, while others will defend the domestic varieties from California and New York. The finest vineyards in California are located in the San Francisco Bay region and produce many good wines, both red and white. As with French wines, there are many great California wines. A label with the name of the grape or the name of the vintner is a good guide to choosing a good wine. There are also excellent inexpensive wines produced in California. New York State has several outstanding wine companies. The grapes, which are strictly American, produce an entirely different kind of wine. Taste and experiment, to find the ones that agree with your palate.

Any wine expert will tell you that the average person should drink the wine that tastes the best to him, without regard for things like vintage years and labels. Start your wine education by trying wines that appeal to your pocketbook and taste. Judge wine, as a professional does, by appearance, aroma or bouquet, and taste. First, hold the glass by the stem, raise it to the light and check the color and clarity. All wines should be crystal clear. Any cloudiness means that the wine is sick and may not be good. Swirl the wine gently in the glass to release the bouquet, and then take a hearty sniff. You can judge the wine

◄ Golden brown and buttery, flaky Brioche can be a real treat when served piping hot for breakfast with a steaming cup of strong coffee with hot milk.

Fleischman's Yeast

by the pleasant aroma. Eventually, you will be able to distinguish many wines by the aroma alone. Finally, you are ready to sip the wine. For full enjoyment, hold the wine in your mouth for a moment and roll it around the tongue before swallowing it.

The wines of the world are divided into two general categories, table wines and dessert or appetizer wines. The differences between the two are the alcoholic content and the relative dryness. The table wines generally have an alcoholic content of about 12 per cent. As a rule, they are dry wines and are served with the main part of the meal. Appetizer wines, such as sherry and Dubonnet, are of higher alcoholic content and served before or between meals. Dessert wines are generally served after the main part of the meal, with dessert. Here the alcoholic content is about 20 per cent. Falling in between are the rosés and champagne which can be served before, during and after meals.

Wine is a living thing and should be treated as such. French wines have a life cycle of youth, maturity, old age and death. This means that wines keep on working and growing right up to the time they are consumed. Some wines taste best when they are young and others have to mature for several years before they reach a peak of perfection. Good wines should be stored on their sides, to keep the cork moist, and kept in a dark, well-ventilated place at a temperature of around 50°F. They should never be shaken.

There is much discussion about wine glasses. If you do not have a different glass for each kind of wine, do not despair. An all-purpose wine glass made from clear glass with a stem and a capacity of eight to nine ounces, will serve every need. When serving wine, fill the glass half full (less if serving sweet wine) to allow room in the top for the aroma to gather, so that it can be inhaled as well as drunk. Champagne is no longer served in flat champagne glasses, for this is a quick way to lose all the bubbles; use your all-purpose tulip-shaped glass for champagne also.

Red wines are served at room temperature. This does not mean that they should be warmed, but should always be brought out of storage about four hours before being served. The cork should be removed about one-half hour to an hour before serving to allow the wine time to breathe. White wines, rosés and champagnes are always served chilled. They can be refrigerated two to four hours before serving. They should never be placed in the freezer, for if they are too cold, they lose much of their taste.

Appetizer or apéritif wines are sweetened, fortified and flavored before-dinner wines. Some of the most popular in the United States are Dubonnet, either red or white, Byrrh, vermouth, and sherry. In France, the before-dinner drinking is limited to one, because the dinner is going to have wine with it and they do not like to linger and ruin their appetites before beginning the feast. An apéritif is served to stimulate the palate for the food to come. The prolonged American cocktail hour is no time to serve your best wine. Reserve it for true wine lovers.

As a rule of thumb, red wines are used for red meats and game. Light-bodied red wines from the Bordeaux area complement turkey, veal and lamb. They also go well with beef and lamb stews, bouillabaisse, hamburgers, steaks and patés. Rich, full-bodied red wines from Burgundy go with richer meats such as duck, goose, kidneys, games and meats marinated in red wine. Red wines are also excellent with cheeses, although some mild flavored cheeses may call for a white wine.

White wines can be either dry or sweet, depending upon personal preference. Sweet white wines, such as sauternes, make excellent dessert wines and go well with a very rich foie gras or paté, but some people like them with the entire dinner. Serve dry white wines with fish and shellfish, egg dishes, poultry and very light veal dishes. Although white wines are generally used with white meats, if the fish or poultry has been prepared with a red wine, one should drink a red wine with it to complement the taste of the dish.

Rosé wines can be served with anything and can go right through a whole dinner as the basic wine.

Champagnes can be served and enjoyed with any kind of food at any time. Start with a Brut (dry) champagne with the appetizer, continue with dry champagne with the main course, and finish off with a sweet champagne with dessert and coffee. However, even in France, champagne is something special and reserved for festive occasions.

Dessert wines are sweet wines to complement the ending of a meal. They can be Madeira, sauterne, cream sherry or not-too-dry champagne. Port becomes an after-dessert drink because it is very rich and heavy, pleasant to sip with nuts or candies.

PETITS BRIOCHES

½ cup milk
½ cup butter or margarine
⅓ cup sugar
1 teaspoon salt
¼ cup warm water (105-115°F.)
1 package or cake yeast, active dry or compressed
3 whole eggs
1 egg yolk
3½ cups unsifted flour
1 egg white
1 tablespoon sugar

1. Scald milk and cool to lukewarm.
2. Cream butter or margarine in large mixing bowl. Gradually add sugar and salt and cream until light and fluffy.
3. Measure water into a small warm bowl. Sprinkle or crumble in yeast and stir until dissolved.
4. Add lukewarm milk, dissolved yeast, eggs, egg yolk and flour to creamed butter mixture. With a wooden spoon beat vigorously for 2 minutes.
5. Cover bowl and let rise in a warm place, free from draft, until more than doubled in bulk (about 2 hours).
6. Stir down and beat vigorously for 2 minutes. Cover tightly with aluminum foil and refrigerate overnight.
7. In the morning beat down the dough. Turn soft dough out on a lightly floured board. Divide into 2 pieces, one about ¾ of the dough and the other about ¼ of the dough.
8. Cut large piece into 24 equal small pieces. Form into smooth balls. Place balls in well greased medium-sized muffin pans. Cut smaller piece into 24 equal pieces. Form into smooth balls.
9. Make a deep indentation in center of each large ball. Dampen slightly with cold water. Press a small ball into each indentation.
10. Let rise in a warm place, free from draft, until doubled in bulk, about 50 minutes.
11. Heat oven to 375°F.
12. Beat together 1 egg white and 1 tablespoon sugar.
13. Brush top of each brioche lightly with beaten egg.
14. Bake 15 to 20 minutes, or until lightly browned and baked.
15. Turn out of pans immediately to cool.
16. Makes 2 dozen brioches.

RAPID MIX FRENCH BREAD

3 to 3½ cups unsifted flour, divided
4 teaspoons sugar
1½ teaspoons salt
1 package active dry yeast
2 tablespoons soft margarine
1¼ cups very hot tap water
Corn meal
1 egg white, slightly beaten
1 tablespoon water

1. In a large bowl throughly mix 1 cup flour, sugar, salt and active dry yeast. Add soft margarine.
2. Gradually add very hot tap water to dry ingredients and beat 2 minutes at medium speed of electric mixer, scraping bowl occasionally. Add 1 cup flour, or enough to make a thick batter. Beat at high speed for 2 minutes, scraping bowl occasionally. Stir in enough additional flour to make a soft dough.
3. Cover bowl tightly with plastic wrap or aluminum foil and let stand 45 minutes.
4. Stir down dough and turn out onto a heavily floured board. With floured hands mold into an oblong, 15 inches long. Taper ends. Sprinkle a baking sheet with corn meal. Carefully place dough on baking sheet. Cover and let rise in a warm place, free from draft, until doubled in bulk, about 40 minutes.
5. Heat oven to 400°F.
6. With a sharp knife, make 5 diagonal cuts on top of leaf. Bake 25 minutes. Brush loaf with combined beaten egg white and cold water. Return to oven and bake 15 minutes longer, or until done.
7. Remove from baking sheet and cool on wire rack.
8. Makes 1 large loaf.

¾ cup butter or margarine
3 cups unsifted flour, divided
¾ cup milk
¼ cup warm water (105-115°F.)
1 package or cake yeast, active dry or compressed
3 tablespoons sugar
1 teaspoon salt
1 egg, beaten
1 egg
1 tablespoon milk
Sugar

1. Work butter or margarine into ¼ cup unsifted flour until mixture is smooth paste. Place between two sheets of waxed paper and roll into a 10- by 4-inch rectangle. Chill for 1 hour.
2. When margarine mixture is chilled, prepare dough. Scald milk and cool to lukewarm.
3. Measure warm water into a large warm bowl. Sprinkle or crumble in yeast and stir until dissolved. Stir in 3 tablespoons sugar, salt, beaten egg and 1 cup flour. Beat until smooth. Stir in remaining flour until completely blended.
4. Turn dough out onto a well floured board. Roll out into a 12-inch square. Carefully peel waxed paper away from chilled butter or margarine slab. Place slab over center third of dough. Fold an outside third of dough over the center third then cover with remaining third of dough. Give dough a quarter turn. Roll out into a 12-inch square. Fold in thirds as before. Turn dough, roll and fold 3 more times. Wrap in waxed paper and chill for 2 hours.
5. Divide chilled dough in thirds. Shape one third at a time, refrigerating the remainder. Roll one third out on a lightly floured board into a circle 12 inches in diameter. Cut into 8 pie-shaped wedges or pieces. Beat together 1 egg and 1 tablespoon milk, Brush point of each piece with egg mixture. Roll each piece up tightly, beginning at wide end. Seal points. Place on a greased baking sheet with points underneath. Curve to form crescents. Brush with egg mixture and sprinkle with sugar. Repeat with remaining dough.
6. Let rise in a warm place, free from draft, until light, about 30 minutes.
7. Heat oven to 375°F.
8. Bake about 12 minutes or until lightly browned and done.
9. Makes 24 croissants.

Note: To freeze croissants, wrap tightly in aluminum foil and place in freezer. To thaw, heat in unopened foil wrapping in hot oven (400°F.) 15 to 20 minutes, or until warm.

PICTURED FRENCH CHEESES

1. **Valençay** (vah-lahn-say) A pyramid shaped goat cheese. The crust is usually scraped before it is eaten. Goat cheese comes in many varieties, sizes and shapes. All have a special flavor and are highly appreciated by cheese fanciers.

2. **Caprice des Dieux** (kah-prees-day-dyoo) A mild, soft, buttery cheese shaped in an oval. The edge of the crust is usually cut away. The rest of the crust may or may not be eaten as desired.

3. **Roquefort** (rowk-for) A genuine Roquefort is aged in the famous natural caves in the town for which it is named. It is made exclusively from ewes' milk and is marked with green streaks which help impart the cheese's tangy flavor.

4. **Grape or Tomme au Marc** (tum-oh-mark) An interesting and tasty cheese the crust of which is made with grape pulp (marc) that remains after grapes are pressed for wine. It has a delicate distinctive flavor and creamy texture. The crust is generally not eaten.

5. **Pont L'Eveque** (Pohn-l'eh-vek) A soft, yellow, paste cheese with thousands of tiny holes. It has a rich hearty flavor. The crust may or may not be eaten. Usually the buttery crust is scraped and the edges cut before eating.

6. **Port de Salut** (pohr-duh-saloo) This yellow, smooth, buttery cheese with its mellow flavor was originated by Trappist monks in Brittany over 150 years ago. It is a pasteurized cheese sold in wedges and small and large wheels. Similar cheeses are St. Paulin and Bonbel.

7. **Brie** (bree) A soft, creamy, pale yellow cheese with a buttery crust which may be eaten. It is often referred to as the "prince of cheeses".

8. **Roblochon** (roh-bluh-shun) This buttery cheese is produced high in the Alps and seems to retain a good deal of the aroma of the mountain air. The crust is not eaten.

9. **Carré de l'Este** (kah-reh-duh l'est) This is a soft buttery cheese with a delicately sharp flavor. The crust may or may not be eaten. The unusual flavor of this cheese is attributed to the qualities of the chalky soils where the cows graze.

10. **Camembert** (kah-mem-behr) A soft cheese, creamy in texture, with a delicately pungent flavor. The buttery crust is edible. Camembert ripens slowly and is at its best when yellow in color and has the same consistency throughout.

11. **Bonbel** (bone-bell) Similar in taste to the Port de Salut.

12. **Camembert** An individual portion is shown.

Appetizers and Soups

In France most meals begin with a variety of appetizers or a soup, just as they end with a variety of cheeses and fresh fruit. Country restaurants serve a first course consisting of an astonishing array of cold vegetables marinated to perfection, a whole board loaded with sausages and smoked meats, and always the pâté of the restaurant or the area, called a Pâté Maison.

For a grand feast at home, there is an overwhelming variety of appetizers. If the main part of the meal is light, the housewife rounds out the meal with several appetizers. However, most days she has only one or two very simple dishes to start a meal.

In this country, our food and eating habits are different. We usually serve a variety of these foods only when we are entertaining. Many would make wonderful hors d'oeuvres for your next party, or you may like to try one or two of them as a first course, served in the French manner with French bread and a bottle of wine.

CHICKEN LIVER PÂTÉ

½ envelope (1½ teaspoons) unflavored gelatine
½ cup bouillon or consommé
    Pimiento
    Capers
    Truffles or ripe olives
1 pound chicken livers
½ teaspoon Ac'cent
6 tablespoons butter or margarine, divided
2 tablespoons minced onion
½ teaspoon salt
1 teaspoon dry mustard
¼ teaspoon cloves
⅛ teaspoon nutmeg
2 tablespoons brandy

1. Sprinkle gelatine over bouillon in a small saucepan to soften. Place over low heat, stirring constantly, until gelatine is dissolved. Pour a thin layer of the bouillon mixture in bottom of an 8- by 4- by 2½-inch loaf pan. Let thicken slightly. Press a design of pimiento, capers and truffles into thickened bouillon. Pour remaining bouillon mixture carefully over design and chill while preparing pâté mixture.
2. Sprinkle chicken livers with Ac'cent. Melt 2 tablespoons of the butter in a skillet. Sauté chicken livers and onion in the butter for 6 or 7 minutes. Remove from heat.
3. Scrape chicken and onions into blender container. Add salt, dry mustard, cloves and nutmeg. Turn on blender and blend until smooth. Add remaining 4 tablespoons butter and brandy. Blend until smooth.
4. Turn mixture into prepared loaf pan. Chill.
5. To unmold, quickly dip pan in hot water up to top. Loosen with a sharp knife. Invert on a serving platter.
6. Makes 24 servings.

Shown: Chicken Liver Pâté, Lobster Barquettes, Almond Mushrooms, Stuffed Tomatoes, Deviled Eggs, Crabmeat Quiche, Vegetables Vinaigrette.

Ac'cent

LOBSTER BARQUETTES

1 package (10 ounces) pie crust mix
1 tablespoon butter
1 can (5 ounces) lobster, finely chopped
1 tablespoon chopped onion
1 tablespoon snipped parsley
2 tablespoons brandy
½ teaspoon Ac'cent
2 teaspoons lemon juice
⅓ cup warm light cream
1 egg yolk
    Grated Parmesan cheese
    Buttered bread crumbs

1. Heat oven to 375°F.
2. Prepare pie crust mix according to package directions. Roll dough out on a lightly floured board to ⅛-inch thickness. Invert 3-inch barquette molds on dough. With a sharp knife cut ⅓ inch out from edge of each mold. Fit piece of cut out pastry into each mold; press down to bottom and sides with finger tips. Trim excess pastry around rim of mold. Prick bottom all over with a fork. Fit a small piece of foil in each barquette. Fill shells with rice or beans. Bake 10 minutes. Remove from oven and remove foil with rice or beans. Return to oven and bake until bottom is lightly browned. Cool shells and remove carefully from molds.
3. Melt butter in a skillet. Add lobster, onion and parsley. Cook gently until onion is tender but not browned.
4. Remove from heat and stir in brandy. Sprinkle with Ac'cent and lemon juice. Combine warm cream and egg yolk. Stir into skillet. Spoon mixture into baked barquettes. Sprinkle with Parmesan cheese and bread crumbs.
5. Heat broiling compartment of range. Put barquettes on broiler pan and broil, about 5 inches from source of heat, until lightly browned.
6. Makes about 16 barquettes.

ALMOND MUSHROOMS

1 pound large mushrooms, about 1½ dozen
  Ac'cent
⅓ cup dry bread crumbs
2 teaspoons lemon juice
⅛ teaspoon rosemary
⅛ teaspoon marjoram
¼ teaspoon salt
¼ cup finely chopped almonds
1 tablespoon capers, optional
3 tablespoons butter
3 tablespoons finely snipped parsley

1. Heat oven to 350°F.
2. Wash mushrooms. Remove stems and reserve. Pat mushroom caps dry with paper toweling. Sprinkle inside of mushroom caps with Ac'cent.
3. Chop mushroom stems very fine. Combine with bread crumbs, lemon juice, rosemary, marjoram, salt, almonds and capers. Spoon mixture into mushroom caps. Place in a greased shallow baking pan. Dot each mushroom with butter.
4. Bake 20 to 25 minutes.
5. Sprinkle with chopped parsley and serve immediately.
6. Makes 1½ dozen mushrooms.

STUFFED TOMATOES

1 pint cherry tomatoes
1 can (7 ounces) tuna fish
¼ teaspoon salt
½ teaspoon curry powder
2½ tablespoons mayonnaise
2 teaspoons lemon juice
2 teaspoons onion powder
  Parsley

1. Rinse tomatoes with cold water and pat dry with paper toweling. With a sharp knife, cut a circle in top of each tomato and remove about half the pulp. Invert tomatoes and allow to drain.
2. Drain tuna and break in small pieces. Add remaining ingredients and toss until well blended.
3. Stuff tomatoes with tuna mixture. Refrigerate until serving time.
4. Garnish with parsley.
5. Makes enough stuffing for 20 to 25 tomatoes.

DEVILED EGGS

6 hard-cooked eggs
¼ cup mayonnaise
1 teaspoon vinegar
½ teaspoon Worcestershire sauce
¼ teaspoon dry mustard
  Rolled anchovies
  Pimiento

1. Peel eggs and carefully cut in halves lengthwise. Remove egg yolks, being careful not to break egg whites.
2. Mash egg yolks with a fork. Mix with mayonnaise, vinegar, Worcestershire sauce and dry mustard.
3. Spoon mixture into egg white halves. Refrigerate until ready to serve.
4. Garnish tops of eggs with rolled anchovies or pimiento.
5. Makes 12 halves.

CRABMEAT QUICHE

1 8-inch unbaked pie shell
2 eggs
1 cup light cream
1 teaspoon Ac'cent
¾ teaspoon salt
¹⁄₁₆ teaspoon cayenne pepper
3 ounces Swiss cheese, grated
3 ounces Gruyere cheese, grated
1 tablespoon flour
1 can (6½ ounces) crabmeat, flaked

1. Heat oven to 450°F.
2. Prick bottom and sides of pie shell with a fork. Bake until delicately brown, about 10 minutes.
3. Beat together eggs, cream, Ac'cent, salt and cayenne. Combine grated cheese, flour and crabmeat. Sprinkle evenly over bottom of pie shell. Pour cream mixture over top.
4. Lower oven heat to 325°F. Bake quiche 45 minutes to 1 hour, or until tip of knife inserted in center comes out clean.
5. Cut in small wedges for appetizers or large pieces for a luncheon dish.
6. Makes 16 small servings.

A Veal and Ham Mousse is easy to prepare and can be made well in advance. Served with crackers or bread it can accompany cocktails with elegance.

National Biscuit Co.

ONION QUICHE

1 9-inch unbaked pie shell
3 eggs
½ cup milk
½ cup light cream
¾ teaspoon salt
½ teaspoon Tabasco
⅛ teaspoon nutmeg
¼ pound Swiss cheese, grated
¼ pound Gruyére cheese, grated
1 tablespoon flour
1 large onion, cut into quarters and thinly sliced

1. Heat oven to 450°F.
2. Prick pie shell all over with a fork. Bake 5 to 10 minutes or until delicately brown. Remove pie shell and reduce oven heat to 325°F.
3. Beat together eggs, milk, cream, salt, Tabasco and nutmeg. Combine grated cheese and flour. Sprinkle evenly in pie shell. Pour in cream mixture. Top with onion slices.
4. Bake 45 minutes or until point of knife inserted in center of pie comes out clean.
5. Makes 16 appetizers or 6 luncheon servings.

VEGETABLES VINAIGRETTE

Cooked vegetables, marinated in some kind of French dressing are always a part of hors d'oeuvres or appetizer service in France. Here are a few that you may like to try.

White Beans: Sprinkle ½ teaspoon Ac'cent over 3 cups cooked white beans. Add 1 chopped onion and 2 tablespoons snipped parsely to beans. Add 1 cut clove of garlic and ½ cup French dressing. Toss lightly and chill thoroughly. Remove garlic before serving.

Cucumbers: Peel and cut 3 cucumbers into very thin slices. Use a vegetable peeler for paper-thin slices. Combine ½ cup vinegar with 2 tablespoons sugar and 2 tablespoons water. Pour over cucumbers. Add 1 cut clove garlic and sprinkle with chopped dill. Chill thoroughly. Remove garlic before serving.

Artichoke Hearts: Drain 2 cans (1 pound each) artichoke hearts. Sprinkle with 1 teaspoon Ac'-cent. Add ½ cup French dressing and 2 tablespoons lemon juice. Sprinkle with diced pimiento and capers. Toss lightly and marinate in refrigerator.

French Onion Soup is almost as popular as the Eiffel Tower. Hearty beef stock, rich with onions, makes a whole meal served with French bread.

Salton Inc.

MUSHROOMS À LA GRÈCQUE

½ pound small mushrooms
Juice of ½ lemon
½ teaspoon salt
¼ teaspoon freshly ground black pepper
1 tablespoon olive oil
1 teaspoon prepared mustard
1 tablespoon chopped parsley

1. Wash and trim mushrooms. Leave whole. Place in a small saucepan with lemon juice, salt, pepper and oil. Cover. Cook for 10 minutes. Let stand in juice until cool.
2. Chill in refrigerator in liquid until cold.
3. Place mushrooms in a serving dish. Blend mustard and marinade well and pour over mushrooms. Sprinkle with parsley.
4. Makes 4 servings.

VEAL AND HAM MOUSSE

1 envelope unflavored gelatine
¼ cup cold water
½ cup boiling water
1 can (10½ ounces) condensed beef consomme
½ cup mayonnaise
¾ teaspoon salt
¼ teaspoon nutmeg
1 tablespoon grated lemon peel
1 tablespoon minced onion
½ cup finely minced celery
2½ cups ground cooked veal
1 cup ground cooked ham
½ cup onion cracker crumbs, (approximately 10 crackers, finely rolled)
1 cup heavy cream, whipped

1. Soften gelatine in cold water. Add the boiling water and stir until the gelatine is dissolved. Add consomme.
2. Measure out ¾ cup of the consomme mixture. Pour into a lightly oiled 9-inch loaf pan. Chill until just set.
3. In a large bowl combine mayonnaise, salt, nutmeg, lemon peel, onion and celery. Stir in remaining consomme mixture. Fold in veal, ham and crumbs. Fold in whipped cream.
4. Pour mixture over set aspic in bottom of loaf pan. Chill 5 to 6 hours or overnight in the refrigerator.
5. Unmold on a large serving platter. Garnish top with pasteurized processed cheese spread from a pressure can, if desired.
6. Makes 10 to 12 first course servings.

ESCARGOTS BOURGUIGNONNE

1 can (4 ounces) escargots (French snails)
Red wine
Bay leaf
1 clove garlic, crushed
6 peppercorns
1 package snail seasoning
4 tablespoons sweet butter, softened

1. Heat oven to 425°F.
2. Drain escargots and discard liquid. Place in a bowl. Cover with red wine. Add bay leaf, garlic and peppercorns. Place in refrigerator and let stand at least 24 hours. Toss occasionally.
3. Prepare snail seasoning according to package directions using 4 tablespoons of butter instead of 6 tablespoons called for on package. Drain escargots.
4. Put a dollop of seasoned butter on one end of each escargot; insert in shell, butter side down. Place an additional small dollop of seasoned butter on top of each escargot.
5. Place shells in escargots dish. If you do not have a dish, half fill a baking pan with heavy coarse salt. Stand shells in salt so that they will not tip over during baking.
6. Bake 10 to 15 minutes, or until butter is bubbly.
7. Makes 18 to 24 escargots.

MOUSSE AU ROQUEFORT

6 egg yolks
6 tablespoons cream
1½ envelopes unflavored gelatine
¼ cup cold water
¾ pound Roquefort cheese
1½ cups heavy cream, whipped
3 egg whites, stiffly beaten
Watercress

1. In the top part of a double boiler beat the egg yolks with 6 tablespoons cream. Set over hot water and beat the mixture until it has thickened slightly and is creamy.
2. Soften gelatine in cold water. Add to egg yolk mixture and stir until gelatine is completely dissolved. Remove from heat.
3. Force Roquefort cheese through a sieve, add to egg yolk mixture, stirring until well blended.
4. Cool mixture. Fold in whipped cream. Fold in stiffly beaten egg whites.
5. Pour the mousse into an oiled mold. Chill for 2 hours or until mixture is firm.
6. Unmold mousse on a chilled serving plate and garnish with watercress. Serve with rounds of toast.

BEEF STOCK

2½ pounds soup meat
3 tablespoons butter or margarine
1½ pounds marrow bones, sawed in small pieces
3 quarts cold water
1 tablespoon salt
2 onions, each stuck with 2 cloves
3 or 4 carrots
2 stalks celery
3 sprigs parsley
1 bay leaf
2 leeks, cleaned thoroughly
Sprig of thyme or pinch of dried thyme
2 egg whites, optional

1. Cut soup meat in chunks. Melt butter in heavy, deep kettle. Add meat and bones and brown quickly, stirring occasionally.
2. Add cold water. Bring to a boil and boil briskly a few minutes, then skim the top off the liquid. Reduce heat to low, cover and simmer about 3 hours.
3. Skim off the foam that forms on top of the soup from time to time during cooking process.
4. After 1 hour of cooking add salt, onions, carrots, celery, parsley, bay leaf, leeks, and thyme. Continue simmering.
5. Strain the hot soup through cheese cloth into a bowl. Let stand 5 minutes and skim fat off surface with a spoon. Wrap paper towel around an ice cube and use to collect the small particles of fat that float on the surface.
6. If you are not going to use the stock immediately, chill in the refrigerator and skim off fat easily when it has all risen to the top and solidified.
7. If you wish to clarify the broth, combine it with 2 egg whites, lightly beaten. Allow to come to a boil and boil for 2 minutes. Strain through 2 layers of cheese cloth.
8. The beef stock may be frozen and used in recipes calling for stock or bouillon.
9. It may be served as soup with the addition of vegetables, tiny pastas etc.
10. Makes 2½ to 3 quarts stock.

ONION SOUP

1½ pounds dry onions
4 tablespoons butter
2 tablespoons salad oil
1 teaspoon salt
Pinch of sugar
2 tablespoons flour
2 quarts canned beef bouillon
½ cup dry white wine or dry white vermouth
Bread
Swiss or Parmesan cheese, grated

1. Peel and cut onions in very thin slices. Melt butter and oil in a large saucepan or a heavy Dutch oven. Add onions and simmer over low heat about 15 minutes.
2. Sprinkle salt and sugar over onions. Raise heat to moderate and cook about 30 minutes, stirring occasionally, until onions are tender and have turned an even golden brown.
3. Sprinkle flour over top of onions and stir and cook for 2 minutes.
4. Stir in beef bouillon and wine. Taste and add salt and pepper if necessary. Simmer for 30 to 40 minutes.
5. Serve piping hot with slices of plain or toasted French bread and grated Swiss or Parmesan cheese.
6. Makes 6 to 8 servings.

CONSOMMÉ

2½ pounds lean stew beef
2 tablespoons butter
1½ pounds marrow bone
1½ pounds veal knuckle
3½ quarts water
1 pound chicken wings and backs
2 onions stuck with 4 cloves
4 carrots, sliced
3 whole stalks celery, with leaves
3 to 4 leeks, cleaned and sliced
1½ tablespoons salt
3 sprigs parsley
2 sprigs thyme or a pinch of dried thyme
1 clove garlic
1 bay leaf
6 peppercorns
2 egg whites

1. Cut 1½ pounds of the beef in 1-inch cubes. Leave remainder in 1 piece.
2. Melt butter in a large heavy soup kettle. Add beef cubes and brown quickly on all sides.
3. Add whole piece of meat, marrow bone, veal knuckle and water. Bring to a boil and allow to boil a few minutes. Skim off foam from top.
4. Lower heat, cover and simmer about 1 hour.
5. Add chicken wings and backs, onions, carrots, celery, leeks, salt, parsley, thyme, garlic, bay leaf and peppercorns. Cover and simmer about 4 hours. Skim occasionally.
6. Strain the hot soup through cheese cloth into a bowl. Let stand 5 minutes and skim fat off surface with a spoon. Wrap paper towel around an ice cube and use to collect the small particles of fat that float around on the surface.
7. You may chill the consommé quickly, then skim off all the fat that has risen to the surface and solidified.
8. Combine the stock with 2 beaten egg whites. Bring to a boil and boil for 2 minutes. Strain through 2 layers of cheese cloth.
9. Serve hot or cold. Taste for seasonings.
10. Makes about 3 quarts.

Variations

Add a small amount of cooked rice or cooked pastas in fancy shapes. . . . Serve with Parmesan cheese. . . . Cut vegetables in julienne strips and cook in soup. . . . Add cooked peas or green beans just before serving. . . . Add thin slices of avocado just before serving. . . . Add thinly sliced raw mushrooms to soup just before serving. . . . Flavor consomme with a small amount of sherry. . . . Serve clear, well seasoned consomme with a poached egg in the soup dish.

WATERCRESS SOUP

2 bunches watercress, washed and cut up
4 potatoes, peeled and cut up
1 tablespoon salt
6 cups water
1 cup milk
1 tablespoon butter
6 slices French bread, dried in a slow oven

1. In a large saucepan combine watercress, potatoes, salt and water. Bring to a boil. Cover and simmer 30 minutes or until vegetables are well cooked.
2. Strain vegetables, reserving liquid. Put vegetables through a strainer. Return puree to saucepan. Add liquid and bring to a boil.
3. Add milk and bring to the boiling point but do not allow to boil.
4. Butter slices of bread and place it in bottom of soup bowls. Pour soup over bread and serve.
5. Makes 4 servings.

VICHYSSOISE

6 or 7 leeks
2 small onions
3 tablespoons sweet butter
7 medium potatoes
6 cups water or chicken broth
1½ tablespoons salt
3 cups milk
3 cups medium cream
1½ cups heavy cream
Chives

1. Wash leeks and remove roots. Thinly slice just the white part of the leeks. Discard green tops.
2. Slice onions.
3. Melt butter in a large kettle. Add leeks and onions and cook until limp, but not browned.
4. Peel and slice potatoes. Add to leeks with water and salt. Bring to a boil and cook gently 35 to 40 minutes, or until potatoes are tender.
5. Rub leek and potato mixture through a fine strainer or whirl in a blender.
6. Return to heat and add milk and the medium cream. Add additional seasoning if necessary. Bring mixture just to the boiling point, but do not boil.
7. Cool. Rub through a very fine strainer. When soup is cold, stir in the heavy cream.
8. Chill thoroughly, several hours if necessary, before serving. Serve topped with finely chopped chives.
9. Makes about 12 servings.

Note: This will keep nicely in the refrigerator for several days.

COUNTRY SOUP

3 tablespoons butter
2 medium carrots, cleaned and sliced
3 leeks, white part only, cleaned and cut into small pieces
2 cups chopped cabbage
2 stalks celery, cut into 1-inch pieces
1 teaspoon salt
½ teaspoon sugar
1 quart water
3 cups beef bouillon
1 cup cooked white beans
2 medium potatoes, cubed
6 slices French bread fried in butter
Grated Swiss cheese

1. Melt butter in a large, heavy saucepan. Add carrots, leeks, cabbage and celery. Simmer over low heat, stirring occasionally, about 20 minutes.

2. Add salt, sugar, water and bouillon. Bring to a boil. Add beans and potatoes. Cover and simmer 45 minutes or until vegetables are tender.
3. Strain vegetables. Reserve liquid. Put vegetables through a strainer to make a puree. Put the puree back in the saucepan and stir in liquid. Season to taste and heat.
4. Serve over slices of fried bread in large soup bowls. Sprinkle with grated cheese.
5. Makes 4 to 6 servings.

BEAN SOUP

2 cups dried beans
Water
1 teaspoon salt
1 tablespoon butter or margarine
1 carrot, diced
2 leeks, minced
1 onion, chopped
¼ pound salt pork or 1 ham bone
2 sprigs parsley
1 stalk celery
½ bay leaf
Pinch of thyme
Grind of fresh pepper

1. Wash and pick over beans, discarding hulls and imperfect beans. Cover with water and let soak over night.
2. Drain beans. Cover with fresh water, about 1½ quarts, add salt and bring to a boil. Skim top of soup as beans boil.
3. Melt butter in a saucepan. Add carrots, leeks and onion and cook until golden brown. Add to beans. Add salt pork, parsley, celery, bay leaf, thyme and pepper. Reduce heat and simmer, covered, 1 to 2 hours or until beans are tender.
4. Remove salt pork and reserve. Remove parsley, celery and bay leaf and discard. Drain beans in a sieve, reserving liquid. Rub the beans through the sieve to make a puree. Return puree to soup pot. Add enough of the cooking liquid to make the soup the desired thickness. Season to taste. If soup is too thick, thin with a little milk.
5. Cut salt pork into tiny cubes. Serve soup hot topped with cubes of salt pork.
6. Makes 6 servings.

OXTAIL SOUP

¼ **cup butter or margarine**
2 **pounds oxtails, cut in pieces**
2 **large carrots, peeled and sliced**
1 **medium turnip, peeled and diced**
1 **large onion, diced**
2 **stalks celery, sliced**
1 **large leek, sliced**
2 **veal knuckles**
3 **quarts beef consommé**
¼ **cup catsup**
¼ **cup dry sherry**
Salt and pepper

1. Melt butter in a large soup kettle. Add oxtails and cook until lightly browned on all sides. Remove oxtails and reserve.
2. Add carrots, turnip, onion, celery and leeks to melted butter in soup kettle. Cook, stirring, until vegetables are golden brown.
3. Return oxtails to soup pot. Add veal knuckles and beef consommé. Bring mixture to a boil and skim off top foam. Lower heat, cover tightly, and simmer about 3 hours.
4. Remove veal knuckles. Stir in catsup and dry sherry. Season to taste with salt and pepper. Simmer about 15 minutes to blend flavors.
5. Makes 12 servings.

CLASSIC FRENCH PÂTÉ

½ **pound lean veal cut into ¼-inch strips**
1 **can (⅞ ounces) diced truffles**
3 **tablespoons Cognac**
Pinch of salt
Grind of fresh pepper
Pinch ot thyme
Pinch of allspice
1 **tablespoon minced shallots or green onions**
½ **cup finely minced onion**
2 **tablespoons butter**
½ **cup Madeira or Cognac**
¾ **pound (1½ cups) finely ground lean pork**
¾ **pound (1½ cups) finely ground lean veal**
½ **pound finely ground pork fat**
2 **eggs**
1½ **teaspoons salt**
⅛ **teaspoon pepper**
Pinch allspice
½ **teaspoon thyme**
1 **clove garlic, mashed**
Fresh pork fat or fat salt pork cut into very thin sheets
½ **pound lean boiled ham cut into ¼-inch strips**
1 **bay leaf**

1. Combine in a bowl the veal strips, truffles and their juice, cognac, pinch of salt, pepper, thyme and allspice, and minced shallots. Let stand while preparing the ground meat mixture.
2. Cook onions slowly in butter until they are tender but not browned. When onions are tender, scrape into a large mixing bowl. Add Madeira or cognac to skillet in which onions were cooked and boil it down until it is reduced by half. Scrape into bowl.
3. Add ground pork, veal, pork fat, eggs, 1½ teaspoons salt, ⅛ teaspoon pepper, pinch allspice, ½ teaspoon thyme and garlic. Beat vigorously with a wooden spoon until mixture is thoroughly blended. At this point take a small spoonful of the mixture and fry in a small skillet. Taste and add additional seasoning if desired.
4. Place sheets of fresh pork fat between sheets of waxed paper and pound until it is ⅛-inch thick. If you can't get fresh pork fat, slice salt pork in ⅛-inch thick slices. Place pork slices in a saucepan. Cover with cold water. Bring to a boil and simmer 10 minutes. Rinse well in cold water and dry with paper towels. Line the bottom and sides of an 8-cup terrine, baking dish, casserole or loaf pan with pork fat.
5. Heat oven to 350°F.
6. Drain veal strips and reserve marinade. Beat marinade into ground meat mixture.
7. Put ⅓ of the ground meat mixture in bottom of mold. Cover with half the strips of veal and half the strips of ham. Place diced truffles down center of strips. Cover strips with second third of the ground meat mixture and the remaining veal and ham strips. Top with remaining ground meat mixture. Place bay leaf on top of mixture. Cover top of meat with a layer of pork fat.
8. Cover top of mold tightly with aluminum foil. Set mold in pan of hot water. The water should come halfway up the mold.
9. Bake 1½ to 2 hours. The pâté is done when it has shrunk slightly from the sides of the mold or when the fat runs clear when it is pierced with a sharp knife.
10. Remove pate from water pan. Place a heavy weight on top of the pâté to press it down while it is cooling. (Place a couple of bricks on top of foil, or place a smaller loaf pan on top and weight down with canned goods or other heavy objects.)
11. Allow to cool thoroughly then chill in the refrigerator before serving.
12. Pâté may be served right from the mold or turned out onto a platter. Cut into slices.
13. Makes about 18 slices.

PÂTÉ DE PÂQUES

(shown opposite)

2 packages pie crust mix
1 cup grated Bonbel or Port Salut cheese
5 eggs
¼ cup water
2 tablespoons butter
1 large onion, minced
1 garlic clove, mashed
1½ pounds ground lean veal
1½ pounds ground lean pork
1 pound bulk sausage meat
1 tablespoon salt
½ teaspoon pepper
½ teaspoon marjoram
6 hard cooked eggs, halved

1. Mix together pie crust mix with ½ cup of the grated cheese. Beat 2 eggs well with ¼ cup water. Stir into pie crust mix and stir until dough makes a ball in the middle of the bowl. Turn out on a lightly floured board and knead until smooth and elastic.
2. Line a greased 13- by 4- by 2½-inch loaf pan with heavy duty aluminum foil, allowing foil to extend over edges of pan.
3. Roll out ⅔ of the pastry on a lightly floured board to a 20- by 11- inch oblong. Use pastry to line the bottom and sides of the pan, allowing excess pastry to extend over the edges of the pan. Let chill in refrigerator with remaining pastry while making filling.
4. Heat oven to 350°F.
5. Melt butter in a small skillet. Add onions and garlic and cook until tender, but not browned. Scrape mixture into a large mixing bowl.
6. Add veal, pork, sausage meat, salt, pepper and marjoram.
7. Beat 3 eggs and set aside ¼ cup of the eggs to use later. Add eggs to meat mixture and mix until smooth and well blended.
8. Spoon half of the mixture into the pastry lined pan. Top mixture with halved eggs. Sprinkle with remaining ½ cup grated cheese. Spread evenly with remaining meat mixture.
9. Turn pastry extending over sides of pan over the meat. Brush pastry with beaten egg.
10. Roll out remaining pastry on a lightly floured board and cut into a 13- by 4- inch oblong to fit top of pan. Put pastry on top and seal edges firmly. Brush top with beaten egg and decorate top with cutouts from scraps of pastry. Brush again with beaten egg.
11. Bake 2 hours or until pastry is richly browned.
12. Cool for 20 minutes. Remove from pan by pulling up foil overhang. Place on a serving platter and remove foil.
13. Serve hot, cut in slices, as a luncheon dish.
14. To serve cold, as a first course for dinner, leave pate in pan and chill for several hours. Remove from pan and cut in thin slices.
15. Makes 10 to 12 luncheon servings.

COUNTRY STYLE PÂTÉ

1 pound ground lean pork
1 pound ground veal
½ cup finely chopped onion
½ cup finely snipped parsley
1½ teaspoons salt
½ teaspoon ground black pepper
1 tablespoon Worcestershire sauce
1 teaspoon basil leaves
2 tablespoons dry sherry
4 eggs, lightly beaten
Small sour pickles

1. Heat oven to 375°F.
2. Place all ingredients in a large mixing bowl. Blend thoroughly with hands or a large wooden spoon.
3. Turn mixture into an ungreased 9- by 5- by 3-inch loaf pan.
4. Bake about 1 hour or until loaf is set.
5. Cool meat in baking pan. Turn out of pan, wrap in aluminum foil and refrigerate.
6. Cut in thin slices and serve with small sour pickles as a first course.
7. Makes 12 to 16 slices.

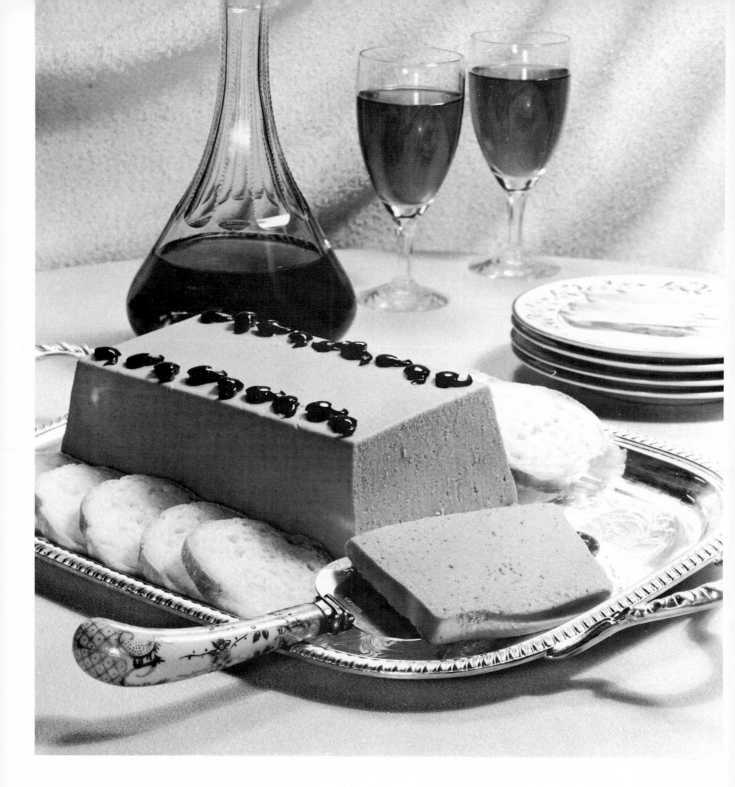

QUICK PÂTÉ

2 envelopes unflavored gelatine
½ cup cold water
2 cans condensed bouillon
6 tablespoons brandy
4 cans (4¾ ounces each) liver pâté
Ripe olives

1. Sprinkle gelatine over cold water in a saucepan. Place over moderate heat and stir until gelatine dissolves. Add bouillon and brandy.
2. Chill mixture in refrigerator until it is the consistency of unbeaten egg white. Add liver pâté and beat with a rotary beater until mixture is well blended and smooth.
3. Turn mixture into a 5-cup mold or loaf pan.
4. Chill until firm.
5. Unmold and garnish with ripe olives cut in fancy shapes with canapé cutters.
6. Makes 24 servings when served as an appetizer.

PÂTÉ EN CROÛTE

4 cups unsifted flour
Salt
Butter or margarine
Water
4 eggs
1 pound lean veal, cut into ¼-inch strips
½ cup chopped shallots
⅔ cup brandy
1 pound ground lean veal
¼ pound pork fat, finely chopped
1 teaspoon thyme
1 can (⅞ ounces) truffles, chopped
1 pound ground pork
⅛ teaspoon allspice
⅛ teaspoon pepper
½ pound cooked ham, cut into ½-inch strips
3 bay leaves
1 egg yolk
1 envelope unflavored gelatine
2 cans (10½ ounces each) condensed beef consommé, undiluted

1. In a large bowl combine flour and 1 teaspoon salt. With a pastry blender or 2 knives cut in ⅔ cup butter, until mixture resembles coarse crumbs.

2. In a bowl combine ⅔ cup water and 2 eggs. Beat with a fork until well blended. Pour into flour mixture and stir with a fork until combined. When mixture gets stiff, knead with the hands until well blended. Shape into a ball and wrap in waxed paper. Chill in the refrigerator for several hours.

3. In a small bowl combine veal strips, 1 tablespoon shallots and 2 tablespoons brandy. Mix well. Cover and refrigerate.

4. Melt 2 tablespoons butter in a small skillet. Add remaining shallots and cook until tender, about 3 minutes. Add remaining brandy and simmer over medium heat until mixture is reduced to ½ cup.

5. In a bowl combine ground veal, pork fat, the shallot-brandy mixture, 1½ teaspoons salt, and thyme. Blend well. In a small bowl, blend truffles into 1 cup of this mixture. Set aside.

6. To veal mixture in large bowl add ground pork, 2 eggs, allspice and pepper. Blend well and set aside.

7. Line the sides and bottom of a 9- by 5- by 3-inch loaf pan with a double thickness of heavy-duty aluminum foil, allowing a 1-inch overhang.

8. Roll out two-thirds of the chilled pastry on a lightly floured board into a 12- by 15-inch rectangle. Fit pastry into foil-lined pan. Trim pastry, leaving a ½ inch overhang.

9. Remove 1 cup of the ground veal-pork mixture and set aside. Turn remaining mixture into pastry-lined pan. Pat down to make a 1 inch layer over bottom and up two sides of pan.

10. Line sides and bottom of mixture with almost all of the veal strips, then with almost all of the ham strips. Fill center with the reserved veal-truffle mixture. Top with remaining ham strips, then remaining veal strips. If there is any brandy left from veal strips, pour over the top.

11. Spread the reserved veal-pork mixture over top, patting it into an even layer. Arrange bay leaves on top.

12. Heat oven to 350°F.

13. Roll out remaining pastry into a 12- by 8-inch rectangle. Beat egg yolks with 1 teaspoon water. With a pastry brush, brush egg mixture around pastry overhang on pan. Place rectangle of pastry on top of pan. Pinch pastry together at edges to seal. Trim off excess pastry.

14. Roll out pastry trimmings and cut into desired shapes. Brush top crust with egg mixture then place cutouts on top. Brush decorations with egg mixture. Cut two holes, ½ inch in diameter, in top crust for steam vents. Insert a meat thermometer through one steam vent into center of meat.

15. Bake about 2½ hours or until meat thermometer registers 180°F. If fat begins to boil out of meat, place a piece of foil on rack below pâté. Remove pâté to wire rack.

16. Combine gelatine and 1 can consommé in a small saucepan. Stir. Place over low heat, stirring constantly, until gelatine is dissolved. Remove from heat and stir in remaining can of consommé.

17. With a funnel or bulb baster, add some consommé mixture to pâté through steam vents. Keep adding more every 10 or 15 minutes as pâté cools at room temperature. When pâté is cool, place in refrigerator. Add consommé at intervals until it is all used. Refrigerate pâté overnight before serving.

18. To serve, loosen pastry and foil around sides and ends. Carefully lift out pate and peel off foil. Place on a serving platter. Cut in thin slices for serving.

19. Makes 12 servings.

Egg Entrees

A typical American breakfast consists of fruit, bacon and eggs, toast and coffee, while in France breakfast is generally limited to rolls and coffee. Eggs are saved for lunch or dinner. Because they use eggs as the feature of main meals, the French have created numberless ways of serving them.

Every French housewife has a repertoire of her family's favorite omelets. Soft cooked and poached eggs are used in a variety of dishes, often served cold as well as hot. And the famous soufflés appear both as main courses and as desserts.

CHEESE SOUFFLÉ

(shown opposite)

2 tablespoons butter
2 tablespoons flour
¾ cup milk
½ teaspoon salt
¼ teaspoon freshly ground black pepper
Pinch of nutmeg
1 cup grated Swiss cheese
4 egg yolks
5 egg whites

1. Heat oven to 375°F.
2. Butter a 1½-quart soufflé dish.
3. Melt butter in a heavy saucepan over low heat. Stir in flour and cook 1 minute. Remove from heat.
4. Slowly stir in milk and seasonings. Cook, stirring constantly, until mixture boils and is smooth and thickened. Add Swiss cheese and stir over very low heat until cheese is melted.
5. Remove from heat and stir slowly into beaten egg yolks, blending well.
6. Beat egg whites until mixture stands in stiff peaks and is glossy but not dry. Fold half of the egg white mixture into cheese mixture, folding in until it is thoroughly blended. Fold in second half until it is incorporated but still may be a little rough and lumpy.
7. Turn mixture into prepared soufflé dish. Run the back of a knife around top of soufflé, about 1 inch from the edge, to make a "top hat" when soufflé is baked.
8. Bake 25 to 30 minutes or until lightly browned and puffed.
9. Serve immediately.
10. Makes 4 servings.

SOUFFLÉ PANCAKES

6 eggs, separated
⅓ cup buttermilk pancake mix
⅓ cup dairy sour cream
½ teaspoon salt

1. Beat egg yolks until thick and lemon colored. Fold in pancake mix, sour cream and salt.
2. Beat egg whites until stiff, but not dry. Carefully fold egg whites into yolk mixture.
3. Heat a griddle until hot. Grease the griddle well. Drop mixture by tablespoonfuls onto hot griddle. Bake until golden brown on both sides.
4. Serve piping hot with fresh fruit or honey.
5. Makes 6 servings.

Omelets

A good French omelet is a smooth, golden oval of perfectly cooked eggs. The omelet is cooked quickly so that the eggs are set on the outside and remain moist and creamy on the inside.

Every French household has a skillet used only for omelets. It is a heavy pan, from 7 to 8 inches across the bottom and with sloping sides. Because it is handled carefully and used only for omelets, it is never washed, merely wiped out after each use.

If you are buying an omelet pan, don't buy one larger than 7 or 8 inches as this is the perfect size for a 2 or 3 egg omelet. An aluminum or iron pan should be treated before using. Scrub the pan with steel wool and scouring powder. Rinse and dry. Heat for a minute or two until the bottom gets hot. Rub the bottom with cooking oil on a paper towel and let stand overnight. Before using it the first time, sprinkle the bottom with salt and rub vigorously; discard salt. After using, merely wipe out until the next use. Some of the new omelet pans are coated with Teflon and of course will present no problem of sticking.

For good omelets, the eggs should be out of the refrigerator for about 1 hour before cooking. The eggs should be beaten with a fork, only enough to blend the whites and yolks. Do not beat eggs with a whisk or beater. The pan should be preheated and is ready to use when the butter stops bubbling and is just beginning to turn slightly brown. Then the eggs are turned into the pan and very quickly made into an omelet. It takes practice and a little patience but it is well worth the effort.

OMELET

2 to 3 eggs
Pinch of salt
Small grind of pepper
1 tablespoon butter

1. Combine eggs, salt and pepper. Beat lightly with a fork, just until yolks and whites are combined.
2. Heat butter in omelet skillet over high heat just until it begins to turn brown.
3. Add eggs and immediately stir them briskly with a fork. When eggs have thickened, stop stirring. With left hand, shake the pan gently back and forth to loosen eggs and brown slightly.
4. Remove skillet from heat and tip it gently. With a fork, fold one third of omelet over center. Then fold other third over first. Slide omelet out of pan onto a heated serving dish.
5. Makes 1 to 2 servings.

Cheese Omelet: When eggs have just set, sprinkle 1 to 2 tablespoons grated Swiss cheese or Cheddar cheese over top and finish omelet as above.

Ham Omelet: Before cooking, fold 2 tablespoons minced cooked ham and a pinch of prepared mustard into beaten eggs.

Herb Omelet: Add ¼ teaspoon basil, thyme, oregano, or parsley flakes to egg before beating.

COUNTRY STYLE OMELET

2 tablespoons butter or margarine, divided
½ cup diced salt pork, bacon or ham
2 potatoes, partially cooked and finely diced
6 eggs
Chopped parsley
Chopped chives
Salt

1. Melt 1 tablespoon butter in omelet pan. Add salt pork and cook until salt pork is lightly browned. Remove salt pork.
2. Add potates to fat in pan and cook until potatoes are soft and lightly browned.
3. Beat eggs with a fork, just until yolks and whites are blended. Add a pinch of parsley, pinch of chives and a large pinch of salt.
4. Return salt pork to skillet with eggs. Stir quickly and thoroughly with a fork. When eggs start to set around edges, lift edges and put remaining butter around edges. Shake omelet pan gently to keep omelet from sticking. When lightly browned on the

bottom, flip over with a spatula, and brown second side lightly.
5. Serve piping hot.
6. Makes 3 to 4 servings.

OPEN FACED OMELET

6 slices bacon, cut into pieces
1 onion, thinly sliced
½ green pepper, thinly sliced
1 clove garlic, minced
1 teaspoon salt
Pinch of freshly ground black pepper
2 tomatoes, peeled and cut in pieces
10 eggs
2 tablespoons butter

1. Cook bacon in a large heavy skillet, until pieces are crispy and the fat has fried out. Remove bacon. Add onion, green pepper and garlic. Cook until tender but not browned.
2. Add salt, pepper and tomatoes. Simmer about 15 minutes or until tomatoes are tender.
3. Beat eggs with a fork, just until yolks and whites are mixed.
4. In a large skillet heat butter over high heat just until it begins to turn brown. Add eggs and stir briskly with a fork, just until eggs are set. When mixture is set and eggs are still moist let stand a few seconds to brown bottom Spread tomato mixture over surface. Sprinkle bacon over top.
5. Cut in pie-shaped wedges and serve immediately.
6. Makes 6 servings.

PUFFY CHEESE OMELET

6 eggs
½ teaspoon salt
Dash of pepper
½ cup grated Cheddar cheese, divided
1 tablespoon butter

1. Separate eggs into 2 large bowls.
2. Beat egg whites with a rotary beater until stiff but not dry.
3. Using same beater, without washing, beat egg yolks about 2 minutes. Fold in salt, pepper and ¼ cup cheese.
4. Pour yolk mixture over egg whites and fold into egg whites with a rubber scraper, until almost all the white is dispersed.
5. Heat butter in a large skillet over low heat.

6. Turn egg mixture into skillet and cook about 5 minutes. As eggs cook, lift outer edges up with a fork or spatula, so that the uncooked mixture can flow to bottom of pan. Cook until eggs are set and lightly browned on bottom and top has puffed a little, but is not dry. Top should still be moist.
7. Sprinkle remaining cheese over top. Place on broiler rack about 4 inches from source of heat and broil until top is puffy and lightly browned.
8. Cut into pie-shaped wedges for serving.
9. Makes 4 to 6 servings.

POACHED EGGS

1. Fill skillet about two-thirds full of water. Add 1 tablespoon salt and bring water to a boil. Reduce heat to simmering point.
2. Break each egg into a cup or saucer. Slip egg into water. Repeat, placing eggs side by side.
3. Cook 3 to 5 minutes or until whites are solid and yolks are done to desired degree of firmness.
4. Remove eggs with a slotted spoon or pancake turner.

EGGS BENEDICT

4 slices cooked ham, about ¼-inch thick, or Canadian bacon
2 English muffins
4 poached eggs
Quick Hollandaise Sauce

1. Brown ham slices or Canadian bacon in skillet over medium heat.
2. Split English muffins in half. Toast and butter lightly.
3. Poach eggs to desired degree of doneness.
4. Arrange ham on top of muffins. Top each with a poached egg. Cover with Hollandaise Sauce. Serve immediately.
5. Makes 2 dinner or luncheon servings.

Note: In France, Eggs Benedict are often served in flaky pastry shells rather than over muffins.

QUICK HOLLANDAISE SAUCE

½ cup butter or margarine
1 egg
2 tablespoons lemon juice
¼ teaspoon salt
Pinch of cayenne pepper

1. Melt butter in top of double boiler over hot, *not boiling*, water.
2. Add egg, lemon juice, salt and cayenne. Beat with a wire whisk until mixture is thick.
3. Remove at once from hot water. Serve over eggs.
4. Makes ¾ cup sauce.

EGGS BOURGUIGNONNE

2 cups dry light red wine
2 shallots, minced
1 bay leaf
Pinch of thyme
1 teaspoon salt
Pinch of pepper
1 sprig parsley
4 tablespoons butter, divided
Clove of garlic
8 slices French bread
8 eggs
1 tablespoon flour

1. Combine wine, shallots, bay leaf, thyme, salt, pepper and parsley in a skillet. Bring to a boil. Lower heat and simmer 15 minutes.
2. Melt 3 tablespoons butter in another large skillet. Rub cut piece of garlic over slices of French bread. Fry bread in butter until golden brown on both sides.
3. Break eggs, one by one, into a saucer and slide into wine sauce. Simmer to the desired degree of doneness, or until whites are firm and yolk is still soft. Spoon liquid over top of eggs as they poach.
4. Place fried bread on serving dishes. Place one poached egg on top of each slice of bread. Keep warm.
5. Bring wine mixture to a boil. Blend together remaining tablespoon of butter with flour. Mix to a paste. Stir into boiling wine. Cook and stir until slightly thickened. Taste for seasoning. When cooked down a little and slightly thickened, pour over eggs.
6. Makes 4 servings.

EGGS MORNAY

2 tablespoons butter or margarine
2 tablespoons flour
½ teaspoon salt
Grind of fresh pepper
½ teaspoon paprika
Dash of Tabasco
Dash of Worcestershire sauce
1½ teaspoons prepared mustard
2 cups milk
½ cup grated Swiss cheese
6 eggs

1. Heat oven to 400°F.
2. Melt butter in a small saucepan over medium heat. Stir in flour, salt, pepper, paprika, Tabasco and Worcestershire sauce. Cook 1 minute. Remove from heat and stir in mustard and milk. Return to heat and cook, stirring constantly, until sauce is smooth and thickened. Stir in cheese and mix until smooth.
3. Pour a thin layer of sauce into 3 well-greased individual baking dishes. Slip 2 eggs into each dish. Pour remaining sauce over tops of eggs, leaving yolks partially uncovered.
4. Bake 15 to 20 minutes or until eggs are of desired doneness.
5. Makes 3 servings.

EGGS COCOTTE

3 tablespoons butter
½ cup coarsely chopped mushrooms
Pinch of cayenne pepper
1 teaspoon flour
¼ cup chicken bouillon
½ teaspoon salt, divided
4 eggs

1. Heat oven to 400°F.
2. In a small skillet heat 1 tablespoon butter. Add mushrooms and cook over high heat, stirring constantly, for 2 minutes. Add cayenne and flour and cook until lightly browned. Stir in chicken bouillon and ¼ teaspoon salt. Lower heat and simmer 5 minutes.
3. Butter 4 small baking dishes or custard cups with remaining butter. Place 1 tablespoon of the mushroom mixture in bottom of each dish. Break 1 egg in each cup over mushrooms. Sprinkle with remaining salt.
4. Place cups in a pan of hot water. Bake about 10 minutes or until whites are well set. Serve immediately.
5. Makes 4 servings.

FLUFFY SHIRRED EGGS

4 eggs
¾ teaspoon salt
4 slices toast

1. Heat oven to 350°F.
2. Separate eggs, keeping each yolk separate in a custard cup.
3. Add salt to egg whites. Beat until stiff but not dry.
4. Trim crusts from toast slices and place on a baking sheet. Pile egg whites on top of toast slices. With a spoon make a well in center of whites. Slip an egg yolk into each well.
5. Bake 10 to 12 minutes or until yolks are baked to desired degree of consistency.
6. Makes 2 to 4 servings.

SHIRRED EGGS WITH BACON

4 slices Canadian bacon
2 thin slices Swiss cheese, cut into 2 pieces
4 eggs
½ teaspoon salt
¼ teaspoon white pepper
¼ cup dairy sour cream

1. Heat oven to 400°F.
2. Place bacon in bottom of an 8-inch pie plate. Place slices of cheese over bacon. Break eggs on top of cheese.
3. Combine salt, pepper and sour cream. Spoon over tops of eggs.
4. Bake 15 to 20 minutes or until whites of eggs are set. Serve from dish.
5. Makes 4 servings.

SCRAMBLED EGGS

8 eggs
¾ teaspoon salt
⅛ teaspoon pepper
½ cup milk or light cream
2 tablespoons butter or margarine

1. Combine eggs, salt, pepper and milk in a mixing bowl. Beat with a fork, just until yolks and whites are blended.
2. Melt butter in a large skillet, tilting skillet so that bottom and sides are covered.
3. Pour in eggs and reduce heat to moderately low. Cook slowly, stirring gently with a wooden spoon. Cook just until eggs are set and still moist.
4. Serve immediately on heated plates.
5. Makes 4 servings.

EGGS BEURRE NOIR

2 tablespoons butter
4 eggs
1 teaspoon wine vinegar

1. Heat butter in a medium skillet. Let butter brown without burning.
2. When it is dark in color, break eggs into the pan and fry until whites are thoroughly cooked.
3. Remove the eggs to a heated platter. Add vinegar to heated butter in pan, stir 1 minute and then pour over eggs.
4. Makes 2 servings.

EGGS COOKED IN THE SHELL

1. Have unshelled eggs at room temperature. Place in a saucepan and add enough cold water to cover eggs by at least 1 inch.
2. Cover saucepan and bring to a rapid boil.
3. Remove from heat; if cooking more than 4 eggs, let stand over very low heat. Let stand covered:
   Very soft cooked eggs, 2 minutes
   Medium soft cooked eggs, 3½ minutes
   Firm soft cooked eggs, about 4 minutes
   Hard cooked eggs, 15 minutes.
4. Run cold water over eggs as soon as cooking time is up to stop further cooking and make them easier to handle.

EGGS EN GELÉE

6 eggs
Boiling water
2 envelopes unflavored gelatine
2 cans (12½ ounces each) chicken consommé
½ cup dry white wine
1 tablespoon tarragon vinegar
¾ teaspoon salt
12 fresh tarragon leaves
4 tablespoons liver pâté
1 teaspoon heavy cream

1. Gently lower eggs into boiling water in a medium saucepan. Remove from heat. Cover and let stand 5 minutes. Cool eggs immediately in cold water to prevent further cooking.
2. Soften gelatine in 1 can of the consommé in a small sauce pan. Stir over low heat until gelatine is dissolved. Add remaining consommé, wine, vinegar and salt. Set aside.
3. Pour boiling water over tarragon leaves. Drain leaves and plunge in ice water.
4. Beat pâté with heavy cream until smooth.

Put mixture in a pastry bag fitted with small star tip.
5. Spoon 1 tablespoon gelatine mixture into 6 oval molds or custard cups. Refrigerate 5 minutes or until gelatine is just set, not firm. Arrange 2 tarragon leaves on gelatine in each mold. Pipe liver pâté in a design around tarragon leaves. Carefully cover with a thin layer of gelatine. Chill until gelatine is set.
6. Peel eggs. Place 1 egg in the center of each mold or custard cup on top of gelatine. Pour remaining gelatine mixture around the eggs to cover them.
7. Refrigerate molds. If there is any gelatine left, pour into a shallow pan and refrigerate with eggs.
8. Unmold eggs onto individual serving dishes. Chop any remaining gelatine and place around eggs. Garnish with parsley.
9. Makes 6 servings.

GARLIC EGGS

2 cloves garlic
12 filets of anchovy
6 capers
3 tablespoons olive oil
1 teaspoon wine vinegar
½ teaspoon salt
⅛ teaspoon freshly ground black pepper
6 hard cooked eggs

1. Crush garlic cloves. Add anchovies and capers and mash together to make a paste. Stir in oil, vinegar, salt and pepper.
2. Peel eggs and cut in quarters. Cover eggs with sauce.
3. Makes 4 to 6 servings.

STUFFED EGGS

4 hard cooked eggs
2 tablespoons crumbled Roquefort cheese
1 teaspoon prepared mustard
1 teaspoon snipped chives
½ teaspoon rosemary
2 tablespoons mayonnaise
Salt and pepper
Paprika

1. Peel eggs. Split lengthwise and remove yolks.
2. Combine yolks with cheese, mustard, chives, rosemary and mayonnaise. Blend well. Season to taste with salt and pepper.
3. Use mixture to fill egg whites. Sprinkle a bit of paprika on top of each egg.
4. Makes 8 filled egg halves.

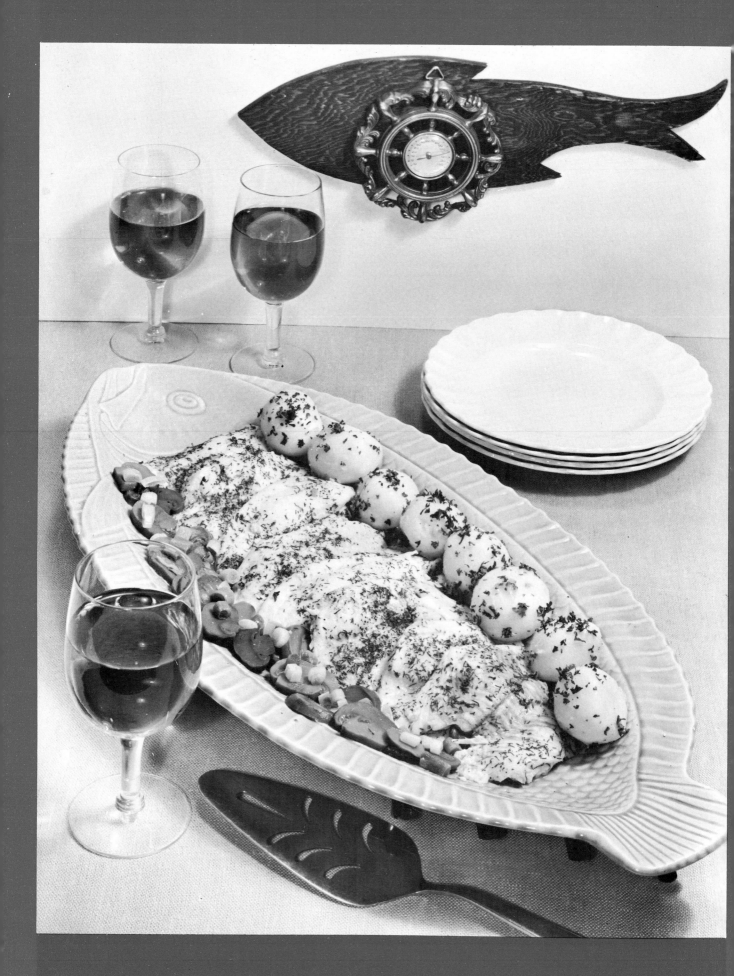

Fish and Shellfish

France is a country lapped by oceans on three sides and crossed by a multitude of rivers, both big and small. This means there is a plentiful supply of fish and shellfish, enough to please everyone's taste. They are the proud possessors of several varieties of oysters, which come from the ocean so delightfully seasoned that they need only a squirt of lemon to please the most jaded palate. Here in America the mussel is all but ignored but in France it becomes a gourmet's delight.

Because fish is so abundant and varied, the French have evolved many ways of cooking it. A simple piece of freshly caught, fried or broiled fish is delicious, cooked to perfection, but they have gone a step farther to concoct fish dishes poached or baked in wine sauces. Simple filets are topped with delightful cream and mushroom sauces. Cold poached fish, topped with mayonnaise, is a summer's delight. And best of all, the great fish dish that everyone raves about, the combination of many fishes, called bouillabaisse.

VERMOUTH-POACHED FISH FILETS
(shown opposite)

- 1 bunch scallions
- 1½ pounds fish filets, flounder, sole or perch
- 1 teaspoon salt
- Grind of fresh pepper
- 1 teaspoon dried dill weed or tarragon
- Dry vermouth
- ¼ cup toasted slivered almonds

1. Heat oven to 350°F.
2. Trim scallions. Slice white bulbs and 3 inches of green stalks. Spread scallions in a shallow, buttered baking dish. Arrange fish filets in a single layer over scallions. Sprinkle with salt, pepper and dill or tarragon. Pour enough vermouth into baking dish to just cover filets.
3. Cover with a lid or a piece of aluminum foil. Bake 15 minutes. Remove lid and bake 5 minutes longer or until fish flakes easily when tested with a fork.
4. Scatter almonds over surface just before serving.
5. Makes 4 servings.

FISH FILETS

- 2 tablespoons finely chopped onion
- 1 medium carrot, cleaned and chopped
- 1 lemon, sliced
- Pinch of thyme
- 1 small bay leaf
- 1 teaspoon salt
- ¼ teaspoon pepper
- 1 to 1½ pounds fish filets
- 1 cup dry white wine
- 2 tablespoons vermouth
- 1 tablespoon chopped parsley

1. Heat oven to 400°F.
2. Place onion, carrot, lemon, thyme, bay leaf, salt and pepper in a greased shallow baking dish. Place filets on top of vegetables. Combine wine and vermouth and pour over fish.

3. Bake 20 minutes or until fish flakes easily when tested with a fork.
4. Sprinkle with parsley and serve with juices in baking dish.
5. Makes 4 to 6 servings.

ALMOND FISH FILETS

- 1 medium onion, sliced
- 1 bay leaf
- 4 fish filets
- ¼ teaspoon salt
- Grind of fresh pepper
- Pinch of thyme
- ¼ cup blanched slivered almonds
- 1 tablespoon salad oil
- 1 small onion, grated
- 1 teaspoon grated lemon peel
- 1 tablespoon snipped parsley
- 1 tablespoon white wine
- 1 chicken bouillon cube
- ¼ cup boiling water

1. Heat oven to 350°F.
2. Place onion slices and bay leaf in a shallow baking dish. Season fish filets with salt, pepper and thyme. Place on top of onion slices.
3. In a small skillet, brown almonds lightly in hot oil. Add onion and cook about 1 minute. Stir in lemon rind, parsley and wine. Dissolve bouillon cube in boiling water and add to sauce. Blend thoroughly and pour over fish.
4. Bake 15 to 20 minutes or until fish flakes easily when tested with a fork.
5. Makes 4 servings.

FISH DUGLÈRE

- 4 fish filets
- 1 teaspoon salt
  Grind of fresh pepper
- 5 tablespoons butter or margarine, divided
- 1 medium onion, chopped
- 1 clove garlic
- 4 ripe tomatoes, peeled and chopped
- 1 tablespoon snipped parsley
- ¼ cup dry white wine
- ½ cup water
- 1 tablespoon flour

1. Season filets with salt and pepper. Melt 3 tablespoons of butter in a large skillet. Add onions and garlic and cook gently until onions are soft.
2. Place filets in pan. Arrange tomatoes and parsley over fish. Add wine and water. Cover with a circle of waxed paper, cut to fit within pan, with a hole in the center. Cover tightly and simmer over medium low heat about 8 minutes or until fish flakes easily when tested with a fork.
3. Remove fish to a hot platter. Boil liquid until it is reduced to ⅓ its original quantity. Remove garlic.
4. Cream together flour and remaining 2 tablespoons butter. Stir into mixture in skillet and cook, stirring, until mixture comes to a boil and is thickened. Pour sauce over fish.
5. Makes 4 servings.

SOLE BELLE AURORE

- 6 filets of sole or flounder
- 3 tablespoons butter
- 1 tablespoon minced onion
- ½ cup clam juice
  Pinch of salt
  Grind of fresh pepper
- ½ cup non-dairy powdered cream
- 3 tablespoons flour
- 1 cup boiling water
- ¼ cup minced parsley

1. Halve the filets lengthwise; roll and tie with thread or secure with toothpicks.
2. Melt butter in a skillet over medium heat. Add onion and cook just until very lightly browned. Add filets and cook until lightly browned.
3. Add clam juice, salt and pepper. Bring just to the boil. Lower heat and simmer 10 minutes or until filets flake easily when tested with a fork.
4. Remove fish to a shallow casserole. Combine powdered cream and flour. Blend into

hot liquid in skillet. Blend in boiling water. Cook over medium heat, stirring constantly, until mixture thickens. Stir in parsley and pour sauce over fish in casserole.
5. Preheat broiler. Place casserole under broiler and brown lightly.
6. Makes 6 servings.

FILETS DE SOLE VÉRONIQUE

- 6 filets of sole, about ¼-pound each
- 2 tablespoons butter
- 2 tablespoons chopped onion
- 1 teaspoon salt
- ⅛ teaspoon pepper
- ¾ cup dry white wine, divided
- 1 tablespoon softened butter
- 4 teaspoons flour
- ⅓ cup instant non-fat dry milk
- 1 cup seedless green grapes

1. Heat oven to 350°F.
2. Pat sole dry with paper toweling. Spread bottom of a shallow casserole with butter. Sprinkle onion in bottom of dish. Season sole with salt and pepper. Roll each filet and skewer with toothpicks. Place in casserole on top of onion. Pour ½ cup wine over fish.
3. Cover the casserole with a piece of waxed paper, cut to fit down over the top of the fish. Bake 20 minutes or until fish flakes easily when tested with a fork.
4. Remove filets and place on a heat-proof platter and keep warm. Remove toothpicks.
5. Drain liquid from fish into a small saucepan. Work together the softened butter and flour into a paste. Stir into the fish stock and cook over medium heat, stirring, until mixture is smooth. Stir in dry milk and remaining ¼ cup wine. Cook, stirring constantly, until thickened.
6. Pour sauce over filets on the heat-proof platter. Arrange grapes around fish filets. Place under preheated broiler and broil about 1 minute or until the sauce bubbles.
7. Makes 6 servings.

Filet of Sole Véronique is a dish any cook would be proud to serve. Sole, poached in white wine and garnished with grapes, makes a company dinner.

American Dairy Association

FILET OF SOLE IN WHITE WINE

1 bottle (7½ ounces) clam juice
½ cup dry white wine
½ bay leaf
6 whole peppercorns
½ teaspoon salt
Sprig of parsley
1 clove garlic, split
Water
2 pounds filet of sole
Lemon juice
2 tablespoons butter
2 tablespoons flour

1. Combine clam juice, wine, bay leaf, peppercorns, salt, parsley, garlic and ½ cup water in a saucepan. Bring to a boil. Reduce heat and simmer, uncovered, 15 minutes.
2. Heat oven to 350°F.
3. Sprinkle filets with lemon juice. Fold each filet into thirds. Arrange in a single layer in a shallow baking dish.
4. Strain clam mixture over filets. Cover dish tightly with aluminum foil.
5. Bake 15 minutes or until fish flakes easily when tested with a fork.
6. Carefully remove filets to a warm serving platter. Keep warm. Reserve 1 cup of the liquid from the baking dish.
7. Melt butter in a saucepan. Stir in flour. Remove from heat and stir in fish liquid. Return to heat and cook over medium heat, stirring constantly, until smooth and thickened. Taste for seasoning. Add a little lemon juice if needed.
8. Serve with poached fish.
9. Makes 6 servings.

BAKED SOLE MOUSSE

3 cups cooked flaked sole or flounder
(about 1½ pounds)
3 egg whites, slightly beaten
1 teaspoon salt
½ teaspoon paprika
Grind of fresh pepper
Non-dairy powdered cream
1½ cups boiling water
2 cans (4 ounces each) sliced mushrooms, drained
3 tablespoons butter or margarine
2 tablespoons water

1. Heat oven to 350°F.
2. Combine cooked flaked fish, beaten egg whites, salt, paprika, pepper, 1½ cups non-dairy powdered cream and boiling wa-

ter. Mix well. Pour mixture into a lightly buttered 1½-quart fish mold or casserole. Place mold in a pan of hot water. Bake 45 to 50 minutes or until mixture is set.
3. Sauté well drained mushrooms in butter in a small skillet. Combine 2 tablespoons non-dairy powdered cream with 2 tablespoons water. Stir into mushrooms and bring just to the boil.
4. Unmold mousse on a hot serving platter. Serve with mushroom sauce.
5. Makes 6 to 8 servings.

SOLE IN MOUSSELINE SAUCE

6 filets of sole
Salt
Pepper
½ cup dry white wine
3 egg yolks
Dash cayenne pepper
½ cup butter
¼ cup heavy cream

1. Heat oven to 400°F.
2. Wipe filets with paper toweling. Sprinkle with salt and pepper and roll up each filet. Secure with toothpicks.
3. Heat wine in a skillet with a dash of salt. Add sole, cover and simmer slowly for about 5 minutes, or until fish is opaque. Remove sole to a baking dish.
4. Boil down wine to 2 tablespoonsful; strain into blender container. Add egg yolks, a pinch of salt and cayenne pepper. Turn blender on for a few seconds. Heat butter until it is foaming hot. Turn on blender, remove cover and slowly pour in butter. Turn sauce out of blender and cool slightly. Whip cream until stiff and fold into cooled sauce. Spoon over poached filets.
5. Bake 10 minutes or until thoroughly heated.
6. Makes 6 servings.

Note: To prepare sauce without a blender, combine egg yolks, reduced wine, salt and cayenne pepper in a small saucepan. Cook over hot, *not boiling,* water, stirring constantly until slightly thickened. Melt butter and beat in a little at a time, beating constantly with a wire whisk. Then cool and fold in whipped cream.

SALMON SAINT-JACQUES

1 can (1 pound) salmon
1 cup light cream
2 tablespoons dry white wine
3 tablespoons butter or margarine
2 tablespoons minced onion
3 tablespoons flour
½ teaspoon salt
⅛ teaspoon pepper
1 teaspoon Ac'cent
1 egg yolk, beaten
1 teaspoon snipped parsley
¾ cup fine bread crumbs
2 tablespoons melted butter or margarine
2 tablespoons grated Parmesan cheese

1. Heat oven to 425°F.
2. Drain salmon. Combine salmon liquid, cream and wine. Set aside.
3. Melt butter in a saucepan; add onion and cook until transparent. Stir in flour, salt, pepper and Ac'cent. Gradually stir in reserved salmon liquid mixture. Cook, stirring constantly, until mixture thickens and comes to a boil.
4. Stir a small amount of hot mixture into beaten egg yolk. Return to mixture in saucepan. Cook over low heat, stirring constantly, for 1 minute. Remove from heat.
5. Fold in salmon and parsley. Spoon mixture into 4 individual baking dishes. Combine bread crumbs, butter and Parmesan cheese. Sprinkle over top of salmon.
6. Bake 5 minutes or until crumbs are lightly browned.
7. Makes 4 servings.

FISH STEAKS IN WHITE WINE

6 tablespoons butter, divided
4 salmon or swordfish steaks
1 cup dry white wine or sherry
Salt and pepper
2 teaspoons chopped parsley
1 teaspoon lemon juice

1. Melt 4 tablespoons butter in a skillet over medium heat. When foam subsides, add salmon steaks and brown lightly on both sides.
2. Add wine and season with salt and pepper. Cook quickly until about three-fourths of the liquid is absorbed. When fish flakes easily with a fork, it is done.
3. Remove to a hot serving platter. Blend together 2 tablespoons butter, parsley and lemon juice. Spread over fish and serve immediately.
4. Makes 4 servings.

SUMMER FISH STEAKS

1 tablespoon olive oil
1 to 1½ pounds sword fish or salmon steaks, cut in 4 to 6 pieces.
4 tomatoes, peeled and chopped
Pinch of fennel
Pinch of thyme
1 small bay leaf
1 clove garlic, crushed
4 peppercorns
½ teaspoon salt
¼ teaspoon saffron
1 cup dry white wine
1 lemon, cut in thin slices

1. Heat oil in a large skillet. Tip skillet so oil covers bottom of pan.
2. Place fish steaks in skillet. Add tomatoes, fennel, thyme, bay leaf, garlic, peppercorns, salt and saffron. Pour wine over the top.
3. Bring mixture to a boil. Cover and simmer over low heat 10 minutes or until fish flakes easily when tested with a fork. *Do not overcook.*
4. Cool fish in cooking liquid. Chill until cold.
5. Serve fish cold with 4 to 6 tablespoons of cooking liquid. Garnish with thin slices of lemon.
6. Makes 4 to 6 servings.

SEAFOOD MÉDITERANNÉE

½ cup olive oil
3 cloves garlic, minced
6 small rock lobster tails, cut in thirds
1 teaspoon oregano
1½ teaspoons salt
½ teaspoon pepper
1 can (1 pound) Italian plum tomatoes
1 cup dry white wine
2 bay leaves
1½ dozen cherrystone clams, scrubbed
1 pound shrimp, cleaned and deveined
1 cup snipped parsley

1. Heat olive oil in a Dutch oven. Add garlic and cook, stirring, for 1 minute. Add lobster pieces and cook, stirring, for 3 minutes.
2. Add oregano, salt, pepper, tomatoes, wine and bay leaves. Blend thoroughly and bring to a boil. Cover and simmer 5 minutes.
3. Add clams, shrimp, and parsley. Bring mixture to a boil. Reduce heat, cover, and cook 5 minutes or until shrimp are cooked and the clams are open.
4. Serve in soup bowls with French bread.
5. Makes 4 to 6 servings.

BOUILLABAISSE MARSEILLAISE

- 1 pound cleaned red snapper
- 1 pound perch, cleaned
- 1 pound cod
- 1 pound eel
- 1½ pounds striped bass
- 2½ pounds mackerel
- 2 medium sized lobsters or 4 lobster tails
- 3 large leeks, cleaned and cut in chunks
- 2 medium onions, chopped
- 1 carrot, peeled and chopped
- 1 pound fresh tomatoes, peeled and chopped
- 2 cloves garlic, crushed
- 2 tablespoons snipped parsley
- 1 teaspoon saffron
- 1 bay leaf
  - Pinch thyme
  - Pinch chopped fresh fennel
  - Grated rind of ½ orange
- 1 teaspoon salt
  - Dash of pepper
  - Water
- ½ cup olive oil

1. Cut snapper, perch, cod, eel, bass and mackerel into 1-inch slices. Cut lobsters in half, remove vein. Cut tail section into chunks, including shell. Crack lobster claws and break into sections.
2. In a large kettle combine leeks, onions, carrot, tomatoes, garlic, parsley, saffron, bay leaf, thyme, fennel, orange rind, salt and pepper. Cover mixture with water. Bring to a boil and simmer 5 minutes. Add fish, except perch and cod. Pour olive oil over top and add more water, if needed, to cover. Bring to a boil and boil rapidly for 8 minutes.
3. Add perch and cod. Boil rapidly 8 more minutes.
4. You may serve the soup and fish separately. Or serve both together in large soup bowls, with lots of French bread.
5. Makes 10 to 12 servings.

CHAFING DISH CRAB MEAT

- 3 tablespoons butter
- 4 large mushrooms, sliced
- 2 teaspoons finely chopped shallots
- 2 tablespoons tomato paste
- 1¼ cups heavy cream, divided
- 1 pound fresh, canned or frozen lump crab meat, picked over but not broken up
  - Salt and pepper
- 2 egg yolks
- 1 teaspoon snipped parsley
- 1 teaspoon snipped chives
  - Pinch of tarragon
- ¼ cup cognac
  - Hot cooked rice

1. Have ingredients all measured out and ready on a tray if preparing this in a chafing dish at the table.
2. Melt butter in chafing dish or electric skillet. Add mushrooms and cook about 5 minutes, stirring.
3. Add shallots and cook until liquid from mushrooms has disappeared. Stir in tomato paste and cook a few minutes.
4. Stir in 1 cup cream and cook, stirring constantly, until mixture begins to simmer and is well blended.
5. Add crab meat. Season to taste with salt and pepper. Stir gently and heat well.
6. Beat together the egg yolks and ¼ cup cream. Stir this mixture slowly into crab meat mixture. Add parsley, chives and tarragon. Heat, stirring constantly, until mixture is hot. *Do not boil.*
7. Stir in cognac. Serve immediately over hot cooked rice or keep warm over hot water if serving for a buffet.
8. Makes 6 servings.

CRAB MEAT EN RAMEKIN

- 2 tablespoons butter or margarine
- 2 tablespoons flour
- 1 tablespoon prepared mustard
- ½ teaspoon Worcestershire sauce
  - Few drops Tabasco
- ¼ teaspoon nutmeg
- ½ cup milk
- ½ cup heavy cream
- 2 egg yolks, slightly beaten
- ¼ cup dry white wine
- 3 cups picked over crab meat
  - Buttered bread crumbs

1. Heat oven to 400°F.
2. Melt butter in a heavy saucepan. Stir in flour and cook 1 minute, stirring constantly. Remove from heat.
3. Stir in mustard, Worcestershire sauce, Tabasco and nutmeg. Stir in milk and

cream. Cook over low heat, stirring constantly, until mixture is smooth and thickened.

4. Stir a little of the hot sauce into beaten egg yolks. Return egg mixture to remaining sauce and cook over very low heat 1 minute.

5. Fold in wine and crab meat. Fill 4 to 6 ramekins with crab meat mixture. Top with buttered bread crumbs.

6. Bake 10 minutes or until heated through and lightly browned on top.

7. Makes 4 to 6 servings.

SHRIMP AU GRATIN

2 pounds shrimp, shelled and cleaned
2 cups dry white wine
½ cup butter, divided
1 pound fresh mushrooms, chopped
¼ cup chopped onion
¼ cup flour
¼ cup heavy cream
1 teaspoon salt
¼ teaspoon pepper
1 cup crushed saltines

1. Combine shrimp and wine in a saucepan and simmer gently about 5 minutes, or until shrimp are no longer translucent. Drain shrimp, reserving hot wine.

2. Melt ¼ cup butter in a saucepan. Cook mushrooms and onion in hot butter until lightly browned. Blend in flour. Remove from heat and slowly add 2 cups of the hot wine in which shrimp were cooked. Cook over low heat, stirring constantly, until smooth and thick. Stir in cream. Season with salt and pepper.

3. Add shrimp to hot sauce. Divide mixture into 8 individual ramekins. Sprinkle crushed saltines over the top. Use remaining butter to dot top of each ramekin.

4. Preheat broiler. Place ramekins about 4 inches from source of heat and cook until lightly browned on top.

5. Makes 8 servings.

QUENELLES WITH SEAFOOD SAUCE

6 frozen pastry shells or toast shells
1 can (14½ ounces) lobster bisque
½ can water
1 can (4 ounces) shrimp, drained
½ teaspoon salt
    Grind of fresh black pepper
**1 can (10¾ ounces) Quenelles de Brochet
    (Pike Dumplings)**
1 teaspoon lemon juice

1. Bake patty shells according to directions on package.

2. If you prefer toast shells, trim crust from slices of bread. Fit slices of bread into cupcake pans. Brush surface with melted butter. Toast in a moderately hot oven (375° F.) 10 to 15 minutes or until lightly browned. Cool in pan and remove carefully.

3. Combine lobster bisque and water. Beat with a rotary beater until smooth. Heat to the boiling point. Add shrimp, salt and pepper. Cut quenelles in halves and add to sauce. Heat thoroughly, but do not boil. Stir very carefully so that quenelles will hold their shape. Fold in lemon juice.

4. Serve piping hot in pastry shells or toast shells.

5. Makes 4 servings.

MUSSELS IN WINE

3 dozen mussels
1 cup dry white wine
1 cup heavy cream
1 medium onion, finely chopped
¼ cup snipped parsley
2 tablespoons butter
½ teaspoon salt
¼ teaspoon cayenne pepper

1. Check mussels, discarding any that are not tightly closed. Scrub well under cold running water to remove sand, seaweed and barnacles. A stiff brush or steel wool works very nicely. With a sharp knife, trim off beard around the edges. Place mussels in a large bowl and cover with cold water. Let stand 1 to 2 hours.

2. Drain mussels. Put in a large kettle with the wine, cream, onion, parsley, butter, salt and cayenne pepper.

3. Cover tightly and bring to a boil. Continue cooking for 3 minutes or until flesh of mussels turn white.

4. Serve mussels covered with juice in large flat soup bowls. Serve with French bread to mop up the juice.

5. Makes 4 servings.

ROCK LOBSTER À LA BORDELAISE

¼ cup butter or margarine, divided
2 medium carrots, peeled and diced
1 small onion, chopped
4 rock lobster tails (4 to 6 ounces each)
1 tablespoon olive oil
½ teaspoon salt
  Pinch of cayenne pepper
½ cup dry white wine
3 tablespoons tomato paste
2 tablespoons bottled clam juice
1 bouillon cube

1. Melt 2 tablespoons butter in a small saucepan. Add carrots and onions and simmer over low flame about 20 minutes, stirring
2. Cut lobster tails in 2-inch pieces.
3. Heat olive oil and 1 tablespoon butter in a heavy skillet. Add lobster pieces and cook over high heat, stirring, until lobster shells turn red. Add onion mixture, salt, cayenne pepper, wine, tomato paste, clam juice and bouillon cube. Bring to a boil. Cover and cook over medium heat 10 minutes.
4. Remove lobster from skillet to a heated serving dish and keep warm.
5. Simmer sauce left in skillet until it is reduced to about half its original volume. Remove skillet from heat. Add remaining tablespoon of butter in small bits, stirring until butter is melted and sauce is well blended. Pour sauce over lobster.
6. Makes 4 servings.

SOUTH AFRICAN ROCK LOBSTER THERMIDOR (shown opposite)

2 packages (9 ounces each) rock lobster tails
  Boiling water
1 tablespoon whole pickling spice
¼ cup butter or margarine
⅓ cup flour
1 can (10½ ounces) condensed chicken broth
¾ cup heavy cream
2 tablespoons sherry
1 tablespoon brandy
2 cans (4 ounces each) button mushrooms, drained
  Salt and pepper
¼ cup grated Parmesan cheese

1. Drop rock lobster tails into a large pot of boiling water to which pickling spice has been added. When water comes back to a boil, remove lobster and drench in cold water.
2. When lobster tails are cool, cut away un-

derside membrane of each tail and remove meat. Reserve shells. Dice lobster meat.
3. Melt butter in a saucepan over medium heat. Stir in flour and cook 1 minute. Remove from heat.
4. Gradually stir in chicken broth and cream. Add sherry and brandy. Cook over low heat, stirring constantly, until sauce comes to a boil and thickens.
5. Remove from heat and fold in mushrooms and diced lobster meat. Season to taste with salt and pepper.
6. Reheat thoroughly. Spoon mixture into reserved lobster shells. Sprinkle with Parmesan cheese.
7. Preheat broiling compartment. Broil lobster tails, about 4 inches from source of heat, until golden brown.
8. Makes 8 servings.

ROCK LOBSTER IN WHITE WINE SAUCE

8 rock lobster tails (4 ounces each)
  Boiling water
  Salt
4 tablespoons butter
4 tablespoons flour
2 cups milk
½ cup heavy cream
2 packages (3 ounces each) cream cheese
1 jar (3 ounces) pimiento, chopped
2 tablespoons snipped parsley
2 tablespoons scraped onion
½ teaspoon salt
1 teaspoon paprika
2 egg yolks, slightly beaten
¼ cup dry white wine
  Hot cooked spaghetti

1. Drop frozen rock lobster tails into boiling salted water. When water comes back to a boil, cook for 2 minutes. Drain immediately and drench with cold water. Remove meat from shells and cut in small pieces.
2. Melt butter in a saucepan over low heat. Stir in flour and cook 1 minute. Remove from heat and slowly stir in milk and cream. Cook, stirring constantly, until sauce comes to a boil and thickens.
3. Mash cream cheese with a fork. Stir into hot sauce. Add pimiento, parsley, onion, salt and paprika.
4. Stir a little of the hot sauce into beaten egg yolks. Return mixture to sauce in saucepan. Cook over low heat, stirring constantly, for 1 minute.
5. Stir in wine and lobster. Heat thoroughly before serving over spaghetti.
6. Makes 6 servings.

SEAFOOD CRÊPES

1 cup plus 2 tablespoons sifted flour
Pinch of salt
3 eggs, beaten
1½ cups milk
1 tablespoon melted butter or margarine
1½ tablespoons cognac
Butter
Crab or Tuna Filling

1. Combine flour and salt in a bowl. Beat eggs and milk together. Stir into flour mixture and beat until smooth. This can be done on low speed of a mixer or with a wire whisk. Stir in melted butter and cognac. Let mixture stand for 2 hours before cooking.
2. Heat a small frying pan, about 5¼ inches in diameter across the bottom, over medium high heat.
3. When skillet is hot, add ½ teaspoon butter and swirl around pan to cover sides and bottom. Pour in 1 full tablespoon batter. Rotate and tilt pan quickly to spread batter over bottom of skillet. This must be done quickly before batter has a chance to set.
4. Cook crêpe about 1 minute or until it is set and brown on one side. Loosen sides with spatula and flip crêpe over quickly with the fingers. Lightly brown second side. The second side will not brown as nicely as the first side, so it is usually turned inside when it is rolled around a filling.
5. Make crêpes and stack in a pile as they are baked. They may be used immediately, or made early in the day and filled just before serving. They may also be frozen, with a piece of waxed paper between each crêpe.
6. Fill with desired filling and procede as in given recipe.
7. Makes 20 to 24 5½-inch crêpes, or less if crêpes are larger.

CRAB FILLING

¼ cup butter or margarine
¼ cup flour
1½ cups milk
¼ cup dry sherry
½ cup chicken broth or bouillon
Salt
Pepper
1 egg yolk, beaten
½ cup heavy cream, divided
2 cups king crab meat, canned or frozen
1 can (3 ounces) chopped mushrooms, drained

1. Melt butter in a saucepan over medium heat. Blend in flour. Remove from heat and stir in milk, sherry and chicken broth. Cook over medium heat, stirring constantly, until smooth and thickened. Season to taste with salt and pepper.
2. Pour a little of cooked mixture over beaten egg. Return egg mixture to remaining sauce. Stir in ¼ cup cream. Cook over low heat 1 minute.
3. Reserve ½ cup of this sauce. Add crab meat and mushrooms to remaining sauce. Fill crêpes with crab mixture and roll up. Place fold side down in a heat-proof shallow baking dish.
4. Whip remaining ¼ cup cream. Fold into ½ cup of the reserved sauce. Spread mixture over crêpes.
5. Heat broiler. Run mixture under heat just long enough to brown lightly and glaze top of crêpes.
6. Makes 6 servings.

TUNA FILLING

½ cup butter or margarine, softened
3 egg yolks
⅓ cup boiling water
2 tablespoons lemon juice
Dash cayenne pepper
2 cans (6½ to 7 ounces each) chunk style tuna, drained
1 tablespoon minced parsley
½ cup grated Swiss cheese.

1. Soften the butter in top of a double boiler. Gradually beat in egg yolks and water. Place over hot water and cook, beating with a wire whisk, until mixture begins to thicken. When thick and smooth remove from heat.
2. Blend in lemon juice and cayenne pepper. Fold in tuna and parsley.
3. Heat oven to 400°F.
4. Spoon tuna filling in center of each crêpe. Roll up and placed folded side down in a shallow baking dish. Sprinkle with cheese.
5. Bake 10 to 15 minutes or until heated through.
6. Makes 6 servings.

COQUILLES ST. JACQUES PARISIENNE

1 cup dry white wine
½ teaspoon salt
  Grind of fresh pepper
½ bay leaf
2 tablespoons minced shallots or green onions
1 pound sea scallops
½ pound fresh mushrooms, sliced
  Water
  Butter
4 tablespoons flour
¾ cup milk
2 egg yolks, beaten
½ cup heavy cream
¼ cup grated Swiss cheese

1. Combine wine, salt, pepper, bay leaf and shallots in a stainless steel or enameled saucepan. Bring to a boil and simmer 5 minutes.
2. Add scallops and mushrooms and enough water to just cover scallops. Bring to a boil. Cover, lower heat and simmer 5 minutes. Remove scallops and mushrooms and set aside.
3. Boil liquid down rapidly until it is reduced to 1 cup. Remove bay leaf.
4. Melt 3 tablespoons butter in a saucepan. Stir in flour. Remove from heat and slowly stir in the hot scallop liquid and the milk. Return to heat and cook, stirring constantly, until mixture boils and is smooth and thickened.
5. Beat together egg yolks and cream. Beat some of the hot sauce into egg yolks. Return to mixture in saucepan and cook over low heat, stirring constantly, for 1 minute. Season to taste with salt and pepper.
6. Cut scallops into small pieces. Fold into sauce with mushrooms. Butter scallop shells or small individual casseroles. Fill shells with scallop mixture. Sprinkle cheese over top of shells. Dot tops with 1 tablespoon of butter.
7. Preheat broiler.
8. Place on broiler rack and broil about 7 inches from source of heat until sauce is bubbly and the top is lightly browned.
9. Makes 4 to 6 servings.

FISH SOUP-STEW

¼ cup olive oil, divided
1 large onion, chopped
3 cloves garlic, minced
1 leek, well cleaned and chopped
3 celery stalks, finely chopped
1 tablespoon leaf saffron
½ teaspoon thyme
1 bay leaf
1 can (1 pound 1 ounce) peeled Italian tomatoes with basil
1 large tomato, peeled and chopped
1 cup dry white wine
2 cups water
  Salt and pepper
1 teaspoon fennel seeds, crushed
2 pounds firm-fleshed fish (bass, carp or sea bass) cut into large serving pieces
2 dozen raw mussels, scrubbed and cleaned
2 dozen clams, washed
1 tablespoon anise liquer
¼ cup finely snipped parsley

1. Heat 2 tablespoons olive oil in a large heavy kettle. Add the onion, garlic, leek, celery and saffron. Cook, stirring, until limp but not browned.
2. Add thyme, bay leaf, tomatoes, wine, water, salt, pepper and fennel. Bring to a boil and simmer, uncovered, 45 minutes.
3. Add fish, mussels and clams. Cover. Bring to a high boil and cook 20 minutes. Season to taste with salt and pepper.
4. Stir in remaining olive oil, liqueur and parsley. Serve immediately with toasted French bread.
5. Makes 4 servings as a main dish.

Poultry

Pot-au-Feu freely translated means "Pot on the Fire" and is one of the best known French dishes. Pot-au-Feu is an easily assembled hearty stew-soup that simmers by itself for several hours. The simplicity of this famed dish comes as a surprise to the many people who think all French dishes are apt to be long and complicated.

Traditionally, a marmite or a large, tall straight-sided stock pot is used. Some people insist that it must be made of tinned copper, while others say that enameled cast iron or earthenware is the only kind of pot that gives the proper results. Actually, any large covered pot may be used, as long as it's reasonably heavy. Since it must accommodate a piece of beef, some sausage and a chicken, as well as an assortment of vegetables, it should measure 6 to 8 quarts. If you don't have a pot large enough, cook the meats and vegetables separately, using some of the stock from the meats for cooking the vegetables.

The service of this dish is a thing the French and the devotées of French cooking love to discuss. One group says that the broth created during the cooking is the only part worth eating, while those on the other side of the fence contend that it's the meat and vegetables that are worth waiting for. The best way to serve it is to have the bouillon for a first course and follow it with the meat and vegetables.

If you have any leftover bouillon, save it. This will provide the stock for many other good French dishes. It can be frozen and then used as needed.

POT–AU–FEU WITH ARTICHOKES

(shown opposite)

1½ **pounds eye round of beef, tied**
4 **marrow bones**
1 **veal knuckle, split**
1 **carrot, coarsely chopped**
1 **onion, coarsely chopped**
1 **tablespoon salt**
6 **parsley sprigs**
1 **bay leaf**
½ **teaspoon thyme**
4 **cloves garlic**
8 **peppercorns**
  Water
3½ **pound chicken, cleaned and trussed**
1 **pound Polish sausage**
6 **medium carrots, peeled and halved**
6 **medium potatoes, peeled**
6 **medium artichokes**
  Salt

1. In a very large pot combine beef, bones, knuckle, chopped carrot, onion and salt. Place parsley, bay leaf, thyme, garlic and peppercorns in a small piece of cheesecloth and tie it tightly. (This is called a bouquet garni.) Add to pot. Add enough water to cover. Bring to a boil slowly. Cover and simmer over low heat 1½ hours, skimming off foam occasionally.
2. Remove beef and bouquet garni. Set aside. Remove and discard bones and coarsely chopped vegetables from cooking liquid.
3. Return beef and bouquet garni to stock. Add chicken and sausage. Bring to a boil and simmer 15 minutes, skimming off foam occasionally.
4. Add carrots and potatoes. Cover and simmer about 45 minutes or until chicken and vegetables are tender.
5. While this is cooking, wash artichokes and cut in half. Cut off stem at base. Trim tips of leaves and cut off about 1 inch from tops of artichokes. Place artichokes in a sepa-

rate pot. Add 2 to 3 inches of the stock in which meat is cooking. Cover and boil gently 30 to 40 minutes, or until base can be pierced easily with a fork.
6. Lift meats and vegetables from cooking stocks and arrange in serving dish. Combine stocks from meat and artichokes; skim off fat and season to taste with salt.
7. Serve stock in soup dishes as a first course. Serve meat and vegetables with mustard or horseradish, if desired.
8. Makes 6 servings.

POT–AU–FEU

3 **pounds lean brisket of beef**
¼ **pound salt pork**
1 **onion stuck with 2 cloves**
3 **leeks, well washed and cut in chunks**
1 **stalk celery, cut in chunks**
9 **carrots, peeled and halved**
1 **turnip peeled and cut in chunks**
  Sprig of parsley
1 **teaspoon thyme**
1 **tablespoon salt**
3½ **pound chicken, cleaned and trussed**
6 **potatoes, peeled**
1 **small head cabbage, cut into 6 sections**

1. In a very large pot put brisket, salt pork, onion stuck with cloves, leeks, celery, 6 carrot halves, turnip, parsley and thyme. Add enough water to cover. Bring to a boil over high heat. Add salt and cook gently over low heat for 1½ hours.
2. Add chicken and continue cooking 30 minutes.
3. Add potatoes, cabbage and remaining carrots. Continue cooking about 30 minutes or until chicken and vegetables are tender.
4. Serve the pot-au-feu in large soup plates, giving each person some broth, meat, vegetables and chicken. Serve with plenty of crusty French bread.
5. Makes 6 servings.

California Artichoke Advisory Board

CHICKEN AND GARLIC

⅓ cup olive oil or salad oil
4 stalks celery, cut into thin strips
6 sprigs parsley
1 teaspoon tarragon
2 whole clusters garlic
1 broiler-fryer, cut in quarters
  Salt
  Freshly ground black pepper
  Nutmeg
⅓ cup brandy

1. Heat oven to 375°F.
2. Pour olive oil into a casserole that has a very tightly fitting cover. Add celery, parsley and tarragon.
3. Separate garlic into cloves and peel. Cloves of garlic will peel easily if each one is placed on a board and pressed hard with the side of a knife or rapped smartly with the flat side of a cleaver. Do not smash garlic. Add garlic cloves to casserole.
4. Sprinkle chicken pieces with salt, pepper and nutmeg. Place chicken in casserole, turning each piece of chicken in the oil and vegetables. Add brandy.
5. Cover top of casserole with a piece of heavy-duty aluminum foil, pressing it down tightly on sides. Place lid on top.
6. Roast 1½ hours.
7. Open casserole just at serving time. Serve with slices of French bread fried in butter or oil, or pieces of toast. Spread garlic cloves and vegetables on each piece of bread or toast and cover with some of liquid in bottom of casserole.
8. Makes 4 servings.

CHICKEN MAXIMILIAN

2 broiler-fryer chickens, cut in quarters
1½ teaspoons salt
1 teaspoon paprika
¼ cup soft type margarine
2 tablespoons slivered orange rind
1½ cups orange juice
2 teaspoons instant minced onion
½ teaspoon ginger
½ teaspoon dried tarragon
4 teaspoons cornstarch
1 avocado

1. Sprinkle chicken quarters on both sides with salt and paprika.
2. Heat margarine in a large skillet over medium high heat. Add chicken quarters a few at a time and brown well on both sides.

Chicken takes on a fabulous taste when it is turned into Coq au Vin. Simmered to a turn with tiny onions, mushrooms and wine, it is delicious.

California Wine Institute

Remove chicken quarters as they get browned.
3. Return chicken to skillet. Add orange rind and juice, minced onion, ginger and tarragon. Cover and simmer, 20 to 25 minutes.
4. Remove chicken and place on a hot platter.
5. Blend cornstarch with a little cold water. Stir into sauce in skillet. Cook, stirring constantly, until mixture thickens and comes to a boil.
6. Peel and cut avocado in wedges. Arrange around chicken. Pour a little sauce on chicken and avocado. Serve remaining sauce with chicken.
7. Makes 8 servings.

COQ AU VIN

4 slices bacon
¼ cup butter or margarine
2 broiler-fryers, cut in quarters
16 small white onions
16 large mushrooms
2 cloves garlic, minced
1 bunch scallions, cleaned and cut up
¼ cup flour
3 cups dry red table wine
2 chicken bouillon cubes dissolved in
1 cup boiling water
2 teaspoons salt
¼ teaspoon pepper
½ teaspoon thyme
1 bay leaf

1. Cut bacon in small pieces. Place in Dutch oven over medium heat. Cook until bacon is crispy. Remove bacon pieces and reserve.
2. Place butter in Dutch oven with bacon fat. Brown chicken pieces well on all sides. Remove chicken pieces and reserve.
3. Peel onions, but leave whole. Clean mushrooms and leave whole. Place onions and mushrooms in hot drippings in Dutch oven and brown lightly. Remove onions and mushrooms.
4. Pour off drippings in pan, leaving about 2 tablespoonsful in pan. Add garlic and green onion. Cook over medium heat until onion is limp. Stir in flour and cook over medium heat about 2 minutes, stirring constantly, until flour is lightly browned. Remove from heat and stir in wine and chicken bouillon. Return to heat and cook, stirring, until mixture comes to a boil.
5. Season with salt, pepper and thyme. Add bay leaf. Add bacon bits, chicken pieces, onion and mushrooms. Cover tightly and simmer 30 to 45 minutes or until chicken is tender. Remove bay leaf.
6. Makes 8 servings.

BAKED CHICKEN CONTINENTALE

    2 broiler-fryer chickens, quartered
    2 teaspoons Ac'cent
  1½ teaspoons salt
    ½ cup margarine, softened
    1 clove garlic, crushed
    1 cup fine dry bread crumbs
    ½ cup grated Parmesan cheese
    ¼ cup chopped parsley
    1 teaspoon tarragon, thyme or rosemary
    ½ teaspoon dry mustard

1. Heat oven to 375°F.
2. Sprinkle chicken quarters on both sides with Ac'cent and salt. Combine softened margarine and garlic.
3. On a piece of waxed paper, combine remaining ingredients.
4. Spread chicken quarters on both sides with margarine-garlic mixture; dip in bread crumb mixture to coat well. Place in a baking pan.
5. Bake 1 hour or until chicken is tender.
6. Makes 8 servings.

TWIN CHICKENS ORANGE

    2 whole broiler-fryer chickens
    1 teaspoon salt, divided
    4 oranges
    3 sprigs of tarragon
    1 garlic clove, cut in half
    4 tablespoons sugar
    ¼ cup red wine vinegar
    2 cups chicken bouillon
    4 peppercorns
    1 tablespoon cornstarch

1. Heat oven to 375°F.
2. Sprinkle cavity of each chicken with ½ teaspoon salt. Hook wing tips into back.
3. Remove peel of 1 orange with a vegetable peeler, cutting peel into long strips. Reserve for sauce. Squeeze juice from this and 3 remaining oranges. Reserve juice for sauce. Cut 2 of the squeezed oranges into small chunks. Fill body cavities of chicken with orange sections and 1 sprig of tarragon each. Tie legs together with strings, then tie legs and tail together. Rub with garlic.
4. Place chickens in a shallow, open roasting pan. Roast 30 minutes per pound.
5. While chickens are cooking, prepare the sauce. Stir sugar and vinegar together in a saucepan. Bring to a boil, stirring until sugar is dissolved. Reduce heat and simmer about 5 minutes or until mixture thickens slightly. Add bouillon, remaining sprig of tarragon, peppercorns and salt to taste. Bring to a boil and simmer 10 minutes. Add orange juice. Add orange peel.

6. Pour sauce over chickens during the last half hour of roasting. Baste frequently.
7. Remove chickens to a heated serving platter. Remove cavity fillings and discard. Stir a little water into cornstarch. Stir mixture into orange sauce in pan. Bring mixture to a boil, stirring, until thick and clear.
8. Serve sauce with roast chicken.
9. Makes 8 servings.

POULET AU POT HENRI IV
(shown opposite)

    1 whole 3-pound broiler-fryer chicken
    2 cups water
  1½ teaspoons salt
    ½ teaspoon dried tarragon
    ½ teaspoon dried thyme
    2 sprigs parsley
    1 bay leaf
    6 peppercorns
    4 carrots, scraped and cut in 1½-inch pieces
    2 white turnips, pared and sliced
    4 leeks or 8 scallions, root and coarse green part removed, cut in 3-inch pieces

1. Place chicken in a large kettle. Add water, salt, tarragon, thyme, parsley, bay leaf and peppercorns. Bring to a boil. Reduce heat, cover and simmer 30 minutes.
2. Add carrots, turnips and leeks. Simmer, covered, another 30 minutes.
3. Remove chicken to a serving dish. Remove vegetables and place around chicken. Keep chicken and vegetables warm while making Lemon Sauce.
4. Makes 4 servings.

LEMON SAUCE

    1 tablespoon butter
    1 tablespoon flour
  1½ cups strained chicken stock from boiled chicken
    2 egg yolks
    ½ cup heavy cream
  1½ tablespoons lemon juice

1. Melt butter in a saucepan. Blend in flour.
2. Remove from heat and slowly stir in chicken stock, blending well.
3. Return to heat and cook, stirring constantly, until mixture comes to a boil.
4. Beat together egg yolks, cream and lemon juice. Pour a small amount of the hot mixture into egg mixture. Return to hot mixture in saucepan. Cook over low heat until sauce is thoroughly heated and slightly thickened.
5. Spoon a little sauce over chicken. Serve remainder in sauce dish.
6. Makes 2¼ cups sauce.

National Broiler Council

BAKED CHICKEN

- ¼ cup butter or margarine
- 1 broiler-fryer, cut in serving pieces
- 1 medium onion, chopped
- ½ pound fresh mushrooms, sliced
- 1 can (10 ounces) condensed cream of mushroom soup
- ¾ cup dry sherry
- 1 tablespoon chopped parsley
- 1 teaspoon salt
- 1 teaspoon paprika
- Grind of fresh pepper
- 1 or 2 lemon slices

1. Heat oven to 350°F.
2. Melt butter in a large skillet over medium heat. Add chicken pieces and brown slowly on both sides. Remove from skillet and place in a shallow baking dish.
3. Add onions and mushrooms to butter in skillet and cook until limp, but not browned. Stir in soup, sherry, parsley, salt, paprika, pepper and lemon slices. Pour over chicken in casserole.
4. Bake 1 hour or until chicken is tender.
5. Makes 4 servings.

CHICKEN WITH EGGPLANT

- 1 broiler-fryer chicken, cut in serving pieces
- Paprika
- 2 teaspoons salt, divided
- ¼ teaspoon pepper
- 2 tablespoons butter or margarine
- ½ cup chicken bouillon
- 1 clove garlic
- 1 medium eggplant, peeled and diced
- 4 scallions, cut in small pieces
- 2 tomatoes, peeled and diced
- ¼ teaspoon thyme
- 1 tablespoon parsley

1. Sprinkle chicken pieces with paprika and 1 teaspoon of the salt and pepper.
2. Melt butter in a large skillet over medium-high heat. Place chicken pieces in skillet, skin side down, and brown lightly on both sides. Remove chicken from skillet.
3. Add bouillon and simmer a few minutes, scraping brown particles from bottom of skillet. Return chicken to skillet. Add garlic, eggplant, scallions and tomatoes. Sprinkle with remaining salt, thyme and parsley. Cover and simmer 30 minutes or until chicken is tender.
4. Remove garlic clove before serving.
5. Makes 4 servings.

CHICKEN WATERZOIE

- 2 broiler-fryer chickens cut in serving pieces
- 1¾ cups water, divided
- ½ cup dry white table wine
- 1 bay leaf
- 1 onion, stuck with 2 cloves
- 1 stalk celery
- 1½ teaspoons salt
- ⅛ teaspoon pepper
- ⅛ teaspoon thyme
- 3 tablespoons flour
- 2 egg yolks
- 2 tablespoons lemon juice
- 1 teaspoon sugar
- Parsley

1. Put chicken in a large pot. Add 1½ cups water, white wine, bay leaf, onion, celery, salt, pepper and thyme. Cover tightly and bring to a boil. Reduce heat and simmer 45 minutes to 1 hour or until chicken is tender.
2. Remove chicken and strain broth. Measure 2 cups of the broth into the pot. Combine remaining ¼ cup water and the flour to make a paste. Stir into broth in pot. Bring to a boil, stirring constantly.
3. Beat egg yolks, lemon juice and sugar together in a small bowl. Stir in a small amount of the hot mixture. Then gradually return to hot broth, stirring constantly. Heat but do not boil. Add chicken pieces and heat but do not boil.
4. Turn into serving dish and garnish with parsley.
5. Makes 8 servings.

CHICKEN TARRAGON

- 1 broiler-fryer, cut in serving pieces
- 1 tablespoon seasoned salt
- ½ teaspoon freshly ground black pepper
- Dash of paprika
- ¼ cup butter or margarine
- 1 medium onion, thinly sliced
- ½ pound fresh mushrooms, sliced
- 1 teaspoon tarragon

1. Sprinkle chicken pieces with blended salt, pepper and paprika.
2. Melt butter in a large skillet over medium low heat. Add chicken pieces and brown slowly on all sides, 15 to 25 minutes. Remove chicken.
3. Add onions and mushrooms to skillet and cook until tender but not browned. Return chicken to skillet. Sprinkle with tarragon.
4. Cover tightly and simmer about 20 minutes, or until chicken is tender.
5. Makes 4 servings.

CHICKEN VÉRONIQUE

2 broiler-fryer chickens, cut in serving pieces
Salt
Paprika
½ cup butter or margarine, divided
1 onion, finely chopped
1 clove garlic, minced
¼ pound mushrooms, sliced
4 tablespoons flour
1 tablespoon sugar
2 cups chicken bouillon
2 tablespoons lemon juice
1 cup white seedless grapes

1. Sprinkle chicken pieces with salt and paprika.
2. Melt ¼ cup butter in skillet over medium heat. Add chicken and brown well on all sides. Remove chicken.
3. Add remaining ¼ cup butter to the skillet. Add onion and garlic and cook over low heat 5 minutes, stirring occasionally. Add mushrooms and cook 2 minutes.
4. Blend in flour and sugar. Add chicken bouillon and lemon juice. Cook, stirring constantly, until mixture comes to a boil and is thickened.
5. Add chicken pieces. Cover tightly. Lower heat and simmer 30 minutes or until chicken is tender. Add grapes the last 5 minutes.
6. Arrange chicken on a warmed serving platter and pour sauce over the top.
7. Makes 6 servings.

GINGER GLAZED CHICKEN

1 can (6 ounces) frozen orange juice concentrate, thawed, undiluted
¼ cup water
2 tablespoons soy sauce
¼ teaspoon pepper
1 teaspoon salt
1 garlic clove, crushed
2 tablespoons slivered candied ginger
1 broiler-fryer, cut in serving pieces

1. Combine orange juice, water, soy sauce, pepper, salt, garlic and candied ginger. Place chicken pieces in a shallow dish. Pour orange juice mixture over top. Let stand in refrigerator about 3 hours or overnight, turning occasionally.
2. Heat oven to 375°F.
3. Remove chicken from orange sauce and place in a baking pan. Bake about 45 minutes, brushing frequently with orange sauce mixture, until tender.
4. Heat remaining sauce and serve with chicken.
5. Makes 4 servings.

CHICKEN PILAF PROVENÇAL

4 tablespoons olive oil, divided
2 tablespoons butter
2 broiler-fryers, cut in serving pieces
1 tablespoon flour
2½ cups chicken broth or bouillon
1 teaspoon salt
30 cloves garlic, peeled
¾ cup long-grain rice

1. Heat 2 tablespoons olive oil and the butter in a heavy Dutch oven. Add chicken pieces and brown thoroughly on all sides. Remove chicken.
2. Stir in flour and blend. Slowly stir in chicken broth, salt and garlic cloves. Bring to a boil, stirring constantly.
3. Return chicken to Dutch oven. Lower heat, cover and simmer 45 minutes.
4. While chicken is cooking, fry rice in the remaining 2 tablespoons olive oil, until rice is opaque. When chicken has cooked 45 minutes, add rice, easing down into broth in Dutch oven. Cover and simmer 20 minutes longer.
5. Serve chicken and rice together.
6. Makes 6 servings.

POULET MASCOTTE

2 tablespoons olive oil
1 tablespoon butter
1 3-pound chicken, cut in serving pieces
12 tiny new potatoes, peeled
1 can (14 ounces) artichoke hearts, drained and cut into halves
1 teaspoon salt
¼ teaspoon white pepper
½ teaspoon crumbled thyme or rosemary
2 tablespoons snipped parsley

1. Heat olive oil and butter in a large skillet over medium high heat. When butter has stopped foaming, add chicken pieces and brown well on both sides. Remove chicken pieces.
2. Add potatoes and brown well on all sides. Remove potatoes.
3. Add artichoke hearts to skillet and brown on both sides.
4. Return chicken and potatoes to skillet with artichoke hearts. Add salt, pepper and thyme. Cover tightly and simmer over low heat about 20 minutes. Remove cover, increase heat slightly and cook 10 to 15 minutes or until chicken and potatoes are tender.
5. Remove chicken and vegetables to a warm serving platter and sprinkle parsley.
6. Makes 4 servings.

WINE-TARRAGON CHICKEN

1 broiler fryer, cut in serving pieces
1¼ cups dry white wine, divided
1 teaspoon dried tarragon
¼ cup butter or margarine
½ teaspoon salt
⅛ teaspoon pepper
1 tablespoon flour

1. Arrange chicken pieces in a 9-inch square baking dish. Combine 1 cup wine and tarragon. Pour over chicken and refrigerate, covered, several hours or overnight.
2. Drain; reserving marinade. Pat chicken pieces dry with paper toweling.
3. Heat butter in a skillet over medium heat. Add chicken pieces and brown well on all sides. Remove chicken pieces as they brown. Pour off all but 2 tablespoons of the drippings in the skillet.
4. Return chicken to skillet. Sprinkle with salt and pepper. Add ¼ cup of the reserved marinade. Cover and simmer 25 to 30 minutes or until chicken is tender.
5. Combine flour with remaining ¼ cup white wine to make a smooth mixture.
6. Remove chicken to a heated serving platter. Pour remaining marinade into skillet. Add flour-wine mixture. Bring to a boil, stirring constantly. Reduce heat and simmer a few minutes longer. Pour sauce over chicken.
7. Makes 4 servings.

CHICKEN IN HERBS AND WHITE WINE

2 whole chicken breasts
Flour
½ cup butter or margarine
½ teaspoon salt
Grind of fresh pepper
1 tablespoon tarragon
¾ cup dry white wine, divided
3 tablespoons snipped parsley

1. Have butcher split and bone chicken breasts. Place between 2 pieces of waxed paper and pound as flat as possible with a pounder or flat side of a heavy cleaver.
2. Dust breasts lightly with flour. Melt butter in a skillet over medium high heat. Add chicken breasts and brown lightly on both sides. Add salt, pepper, tarragon and ½ cup wine. Simmer breasts, uncovered, 5 or 10 minutes, or until tender. Place breasts on a warm serving platter.

3. Add parsley and remaining ¼ cup wine. Simmer over high heat, stirring, until sauce is reduced a little. Taste and add additional salt and pepper if necessary. Pour sauce over chicken breasts.
4. Makes 4 servings.

OVEN-BROWNED ROQUEFORT CHICKEN

6 chicken pieces, breasts or whole legs
3 tablespoons flour
1½ teaspoons salt, divided
¼ teaspoon freshly ground pepper
1 teaspoon rosemary
4 tablespoons butter or margarine
⅔ cup dairy sour cream
2 teaspoons chopped chives
½ cup crumbled Roquefort cheese, packed
2 teaspoons grated lemon rind
2 tablespoons lemon juice
¼ cup slivered blanched almonds

1. Wipe chicken pieces with a damp paper towel. Combine flour, 1 teaspoon salt, pepper, and rosemary in a paper bag. Shake chicken pieces in flour mixture, coating each piece well.
2. Heat butter in a heavy skillet over medium heat. Brown chicken well on all sides. Remove to a shallow baking dish.
3. Heat oven to 350°F.
4. Blend together sour cream, remaining salt, chives, Roquefort cheese, lemon rind and juice. Spread mixture over chicken in baking dish.
5. Bake 30 minutes. Sprinkle almonds over top of chicken. Continue baking 10 to 15 minutes or until almonds are browned and chicken is tender.
6. Makes 6 servings.

CHICKEN BREASTS CHAUD-FROID
(shown opposite)

3 large chicken breasts, split
Water
1 teaspoon salt
1 stalk celery, with leaves, cut in 2-inch pieces
1 carrot, cut in 2-inch pieces
1 sprig parsley
4 whole peppercorns
2 tablespoons butter or margarine
2 tablespoons flour
2 cups chicken broth
2 envelopes unflavored gelatine
1 egg yolk
¼ cup cream
Truffles or ripe olives

1. Place chicken breasts in a large saucepan. Add 2 cups water, salt, celery, carrot, parsley and peppercorns. Cover and simmer 30 minutes or until chicken breasts are tender. Remove chicken breasts and refrigerate until thoroughly chilled. Strain stock into another saucepan. Boil, uncovered, until stock is reduced to 2 cups.
2. Melt butter in a saucepan. Blend in flour. Remove from heat and gradually stir in reserved 2 cups of chicken broth. Cook, stirring constantly, until mixture thickens and comes to a boil. Simmer 5 minutes over very low heat.
3. Soften gelatine in cold water. Stir softened gelatine into hot mixture until dissolved. Remove from heat.
4. Beat egg yolk with cream. Blend a little of the hot sauce into egg yolk. Return mixture to hot sauce. Cook over low heat, stirring

constantly, for 2 minutes. *Do not boil.* Remove from heat and chill until slightly thickened.
5. Remove skin from cold chicken breasts and place chicken on a cake rack over a shallow pan.
6. Spoon slightly thickened sauce over chicken breasts. If all of sauce runs off chicken, it is not thick enough and should be chilled a few more minutes. If sauce forms thick patches on chicken, it is too thick. This can be remedied by heating it slightly to thin it a little, then chilled again. Sauce will become firm quickly on the cold chicken.
7. Press pieces of truffles or olives into glaze to make flower or other design in center of each chicken breast. Place in refrigerator until ready to serve.
8. Makes 6 servings.

CHICKEN BREASTS SUPREME

6 whole chicken breasts
2 teaspoons Ac'cent
Salt and pepper
¾ cup butter or margarine, divided
¼ cup finely chopped onion
2 tablespoons finely chopped parsley
½ teaspoon rosemary
½ teaspoon basil
1½ cups packaged stuffing mix
½ cup boiling water

1. Heat oven to 350°F.
2. Cut chicken breasts in half and remove bones. Cut through thickest part of each half breast to form a pocket. Sprinkle with Ac'cent, salt and pepper.
3. Melt ½ cup butter in a saucepan. Add onion and cook until onion is tender but not brown. Remove from heat. Stir in herbs and stuffing mix. Add boiling water and mix well.
4. Fill pockets in chicken breast with stuffing mix. Secure with skewers.
5. Place chicken on a rack in a shallow baking pan. Melt remaining butter and brush over chicken breasts.
6. Bake about 1 hour or until chicken is tender.
7. Serve with Supreme Sauce.
8. Makes 12 servings.

SUPREME SAUCE

3 tablespoons butter or margarine
3 tablespoons flour
2 chicken bouillon cubes
1¾ cups boiling water
½ cup heavy cream
2 egg yolks
½ teaspoon paprika
2 teaspoons lemon juice
2 tablespoons finely chopped truffles, optional

1. Melt butter in a saucepan. Blend in flour and cook over medium heat 30 seconds. Remove from heat.
2. Add bouillon cubes to boiling water and stir until dissolved. Stir into flour-butter mixture.
3. Return to heat and cook, stirring constantly, until mixture thickens and comes to a boil.
4. Beat together heavy cream and egg yolks. Stir a small amount of the hot mixture into egg yolks and blend well. Return egg mixture to saucepan. Cook over low heat, stir-ring constantly, just until mixture comes to a boil. Do not boil.
5. Stir in paprika, lemon juice and truffles.
6. Serve with Chicken Breasts Supreme.
7. Makes about 2¼ cups sauce.

CHICKEN À LA VALLÉE D'AUGE

4 whole broiler-fryer chicken breasts
¼ cup butter or margarine
1 teaspoon salt
⅛ teaspoon pepper
⅓ cup Calvados or applejack
6 shallots or scallions, minced
1 tablespoon chopped parsley
¼ teaspoon dried thyme
¼ teaspoon rosemary
½ cup dry white table wine or apple cider
½ cup heavy cream

1. Cut chicken breasts in half and remove bones if desired. Melt butter in a large skillet over medium low heat. Add chicken breasts and cook until lightly browned, 15 to 20 minutes.
2. Add salt and pepper. Warm Calvados in a small saucepan and pour over chicken. Ignite with a match and allow Calvados to burn out.
3. Add shallots, parsley, thyme, rosemary and white wine. Cover tightly and simmer over low heat, 15 to 25 minutes or until chicken is tender.
4. Remove chicken breasts and place on a heated platter. Add heavy cream to sauce in pan and blend well. Stir and heat to serving temperature, but do not boil.
5. Sauce may be poured over chicken or served separately.
6. Makes 8 servings.

CHICKEN IN COGNAC-CREAM

2 whole chicken breasts
1 egg
Water
Flour
Fine dry bread crumbs
Salt
Pepper
6 tablespoons butter
3 tablespoons warm cognac
1 cup cream
2 egg yolks, beaten

1. Have butcher split and bone chicken breasts. Place breasts between 2 pieces of

waxed paper and pound as flat as possible with the side of a heavy cleaver.

2. Beat egg with 1 tablespoon water in a flat dish. Dip flattened chicken breasts in flour, then in beaten egg and finally in bread crumbs. Sprinkle with salt and pepper. Chill breasts in refrigerator at least 2 hours.

3. Heat butter in a skillet over high heat to a point where it is bubbling, but not smoking. Brown chicken breasts quickly on both sides. Cook an additional minute or so on each side, or until tender. Carefully pour over warm cognac. Ignite with a match and allow to burn out. Remove chicken breasts to a warm serving platter.

4. Beat together cream and egg yolks. Reduce heat under skillet. Stir in cream and egg yolk mixture. Cook, stirring constantly, until mixture is slightly thickened. *Do not boil.* Taste and add salt and pepper if necessary. Pour sauce over chicken.

5. Makes 4 servings.

CHICKEN BREASTS ARGENTEUIL

4 whole chicken breasts
Soft type margarine
Salt
Pepper
Tarragon
2 packages (10 ounces each) frozen asparagus, defrosted
3 egg yolks
2 tablespoons lemon juice
¼ teaspoon dry mustard

1. Heat oven to 375°F.
2. Have butcher bone and remove skins from each chicken breast. Cut each breast in half. Place each half between 2 pieces of aluminum foil and pound with the flat side of cleaver or rolling pin. Spread inside of each chicken breast with margarine and sprinkle lightly with salt, pepper and tarragon. Place 3 or 4 asparagus spears crosswise in center of each breast and fold ends over. Fasten with skewer or wooden picks. Place fold side down in a shallow baking pan. Spread tops of chicken breasts with margarine.
3. Bake 45 minutes, or until chicken is tender and lightly browned.
4. When chicken is almost done, combine egg yolks, lemon juice, ¼ teaspoon salt and dry mustard in the top of a double boiler. Add ½ cup soft type margarine. Place over hot,

not boiling, water and cook, stirring with a wire whisk until sauce thickens. Remove from heat and serve over chicken breasts.

5. Makes 8 servings.

TURKEY-ALMOND CRÊPES

1 cup plus 2 tablespoons sifted flour
Pinch of salt
3 eggs, beaten
1½ cups milk
1 tablespoon melted butter or margarine
1½ tablespoons brandy
Butter

1. Combine flour and salt in a bowl. Beat eggs and milk together. Stir into flour mixture and beat until smooth. This can be done on low speed of an electric mixer or with a wire wisk. Stir in melted butter and brandy. Let mixture stand for 2 hours before cooking.
2. Heat a small crêpe pan, 5½ to 6 inches in diameter across the bottom, over medium high heat.
3. When skillet is hot add ½ teaspoon butter and swirl around pan to cover sides and bottom. Pour in 1 full tablespoon batter. Rotate and tilt pan quickly to spread batter over bottom of skillet. This must be done before batter has a chance to set.
4. Cook crêpe about 1 minute or until it is set and browned lightly on the bottom. Loosen sides with a spatula and flip crêpe over quickly with the fingers. Brown lightly on second side. The second side will not brown as nicely as the first side, so it is usually turned inside when it is rolled around a filling.
5. Make crêpes and stack in a pile as they are baked. They may be used immediately or made early in the day and filled just before serving. They may also be frozen with a piece of waxed paper between each crêpe.
6. Fill with Turkey Almond Filling and proceed as in given recipe.
7. Makes 18 to 24 crêpes, depending on size.

TURKEY-ALMOND FILLING

4 tablespoons butter or margarine
4 tablespoons flour
2 cups turkey or chicken broth
1 teaspoon tarragon
1 teaspoon salt
2 tablespoons brandy
1 cup heavy cream
3 egg yolks
2½ to 3 cups turkey chunks
¾ cup toasted, salted almonds
½ cup grated Parmesan cheese

1. Melt butter in a saucepan. Stir in flour and cook 1 minute. Remove from heat and slowly stir in turkey broth, blending well. Return to heat and cook, stirring constantly, until smooth and thick. Stir in tarragon, salt and brandy.
2. Beat together cream and egg yolks. Stir a little of the hot sauce into the egg yolks, beating well. Return egg mixture to sauce in saucepan. Cook over medium heat, stirring constantly, about 2 minutes. *Do not boil.*
3. Combine half of the sauce with the turkey chunks. Keep warm.
4. Heat oven to 450°F.
5. Stir the almonds into turkey mixture. Divide mixture among crêpes and roll up. Place, fold side down, in a shallow baking dish. Combine remaining sauce with cheese. Pour over top of crêpes in pan.
6. Bake 5 to 10 minutes or until sauce is bubbly and mixture is browned on the top.
7. Makes 6 to 8 servings.

ORANGE DUCKLING AU VIN

6 whole oranges
⅔ cup port wine
2 ready-to-cook ducklings, 4½ to 5 pounds each
3 teaspoons salt
2 onions, sliced into rings
1¼ cups orange juice
1½ tablespoons sugar
1½ teaspoons lemon juice
⅔ cup chicken consommé

1. Heat oven to 475°F.
2. Peel 5 oranges and slice into thick cartwheel slices. Pour wine over slices and set aside.
3. Rinse ducks. Drain thoroughly and wipe dry inside and out with paper toweling. Rub cavities of each duck with salt. Cut remaining unpeeled orange into quarters. Place 2

quarters in each cavity. Remove fat from neck opening. Secure skin to back with skewer, cutting away extra skin. Cut away tail and most excess skin from cavity. Tie legs together. Fold wing tips back on the wings. Deeply prick entire surface of duck with a fork. Spread onion rings over bottom of a large shallow roasting pan. Place ducks, breast side up, on top. Roast 30 minutes. Reduce heat to 350°F. Remove ducks from pan. Drain off all fat. Place ducks on their sides and roast 25 minutes. Turn ducks on other side and roast 25 minutes. Return to breast-up position and roast about 30 minutes. Baste twice with ¾ cup of the orange juice during last 30 minutes of roasting.
4. While ducks are roasting, combine sugar and lemon juice in a large skillet. Cook over medium heat, stirring constantly, until mixture begins to caramelize and turns golden brown. Remove from heat. Immediately stir in ½ cup orange juice and consommé. Cook over high heat, stirring constantly, until caramel melts. Boil mixture about 5 minutes or until liquid is reduced to about ⅓ cup. Set aside.
5. Remove ducks from roasting pan, draining juice in cavities into roasting pan. Remove orange quarters from duck and discard. Strain drippings into a deep bowl. Return ducks to pan and place in oven, with the heat turned off, to keep warm.
6. Carefully skim all fat from drippings. Drain wine from orange slices and add wine and ¾ cup drippings to reserved caramel mixture in skillet. Boil briskly 5 minutes or until reduced to about ¾ cup.
7. To serve, cut ducks into quarters with duck shears or kitchen scissors. Cover each piece with a small amount of sauce. Serve each piece with a marinated orange section and remaining sauce.
8. Makes 8 servings.

POTTED DUCKLING

4½ to 5 pound duckling
Salt
Freshly ground black pepper
3 leeks
2 tablespoons flour
2 large carrots, peeled and sliced
2 white turnips, peeled and cubed
1 clove garlic, minced
½ cup dry white wine
1 cup canned, peeled tomatoes
½ cup frozen green peas
¼ cup chopped parsley

1. Heat oven to 500°F.
2. With poultry shears cut duck into 4 serving pieces. Cut away as much of the fat from around edges of duck as possible. Sprinkle with salt and pepper.
3. Heat a large skillet over high heat. Add duck pieces, fat side down, and cook quickly until well browned. Pour off fat from skillet. Turn duck over and brown other side.
4. Place duck in a heavy casserole. Add neck and gizzard. Bake, uncovered, 20 minutes. Pour off fat as it accumulates.
5. Clean leeks and split in half lengthwise. Rinse under cold running water to remove all sand. Shake out moisture and cut in pieces, all except the very top tough part of leek.
6. Place casserole on top of range over moderate heat. Let cook a few minutes. Add leeks. Sprinkle with flour and stir well. Add carrots, turnips and garlic. Add wine and tomatoes. Bring to a boil. Lower heat, cover tightly, and simmer about 40 minutes or until duck is tender. Add peas the last few minutes of cooking.
7. Sprinkle with parsley and serve.
8. Makes 4 servings.

WINE-GLAZED DUCK

    1 duckling
    Salt
    Paprika
    2 tablespoons grated onion
    1 cup dry red wine, divided
    ⅓ cup brown sugar, firmly packed
    ⅓ cup granulated sugar
    1 tablespoon cornstarch
    ¼ teaspoon salt
    1 teaspoon grated orange peel

1. Have your butcher cut duckling into quarters. Trim off all excess fat.
2. Heat oven to 400°F.
3. Place duckling pieces in a shallow baking pan. Roast, uncovered, 30 minutes. Remove from oven and drain off all fat in the pan.
4. Season duckling with salt and paprika. Sprinkle with grated onion. Pour ¼ cup wine in bottom of the pan. Cover pan with a piece of aluminum foil. Continue roasting until duckling is tender, about 40 to 45 minutes.
5. Combine sugars, cornstarch, salt, orange peel and remaining ¾ cup wine in a saucepan. Cook over medium heat until mixture comes to a boil.
6. Remove duckling from oven. Pour wine

sauce over top of duckling. Roast, uncovered, about 10 minutes longer, or until duck is nicely glazed. Baste frequently with liquid in bottom of pan.
7. Makes 4 servings.

GAME BIRDS L'ORANGE

    6 partridges or small game birds
    Salt and Pepper
    Salt pork or bacon
    6 to 8 oranges
    3 tablespoons butter or margarine
    3 green onions, minced
    ¾ teaspoon dried tarragon
    6 tablespoons currant jelly
    ¼ teaspoon dry mustard

1. Heat oven to 425°F.
2. With string, tie legs and wings close to body of each bird. Season with salt and pepper. Completely cover breast of each bird with slices of salt pork or bacon. Tie tightly in place with string. Place birds on a rack in a shallow, open roasting pan. Roast birds 30 minutes.
3. While birds are roasting prepare sauce. Wash oranges. With a vegetable peeler or a zester remove very thin orange colored top of the rind from one orange, shred into fine pieces with scissors to make 3 tablespoonsful of rind. Reserve.
4. Section 3 or 4 oranges to make about 1½ cups drained orange sections. To section, cut off peel in a circular motion, cutting deep enough to remove white membrane. Go over fruit again to remove any remaining white membrane. Cut along side of each dividing membrane from outside to middle of core. Remove section by section, over a bowl, to hold juice. Drain sections and measure juice. Squeeze juice from enough additional oranges to measure 1¼ cups orange juice. Reserve juice and sections.
5. In a large skillet melt butter over medium heat. Add onion and tarragon and cook about 4 minutes, stirring. Add orange juice, shredded peel, currant jelly, dry mustard and salt. Stir and bring to a boil.
6. Remove birds from oven. Remove strings and salt pork. Place birds in skillet. Cover tightly and simmer gently 15 to 20 minutes, turning birds occasionally.
7. Remove birds to a warm serving platter. Add orange sections to sauce. Heat quickly and serve with birds.
8. Makes 6 servings.

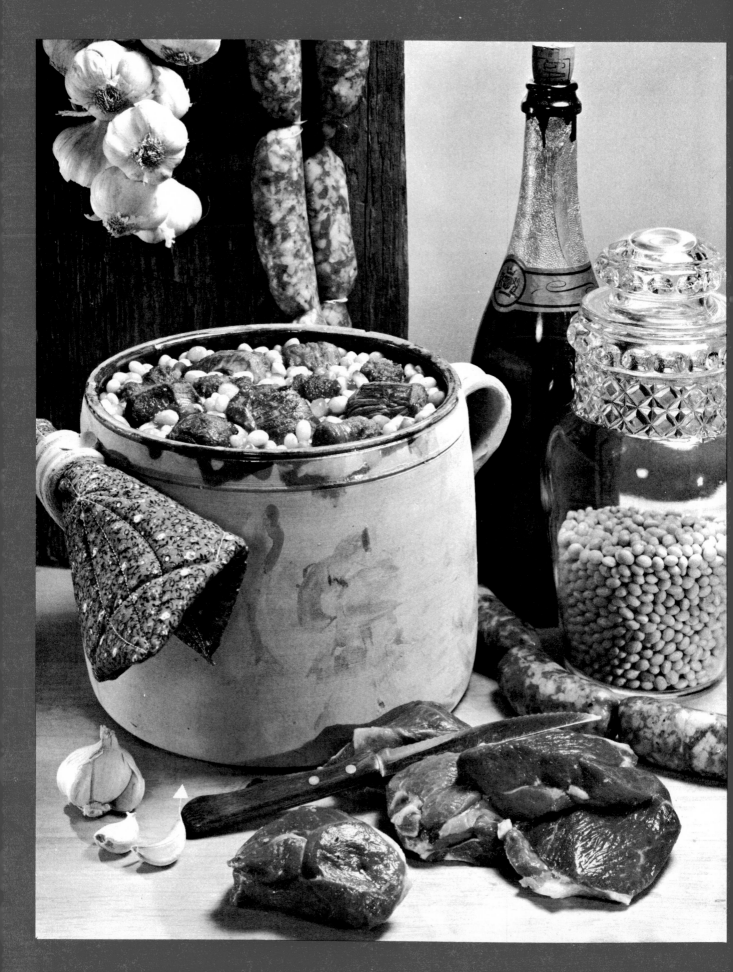

Meats

What is a cassoulet? It's a combination of beans and meats cooked in a rich broth in an earthenware utensil which at one time was known as the "Cassole d'issel".

There are various theories concerning a cassoulet and of course many variations. Some people would never make cassoulet without including preserved goose, others prefer duck. Some swear that the golden crust that forms on the surface must be broken several times during the baking and that this crust then becomes a part of the cassoulet. But no matter what the school of thought, it will usually contain pork, lamb, sausages and beans.

Here are 3 variations. Once you have tried these, you will probably want to go on and invent your own cassoulet.

WINE CASSOULET

1 pound white pea or navy beans
Water
½ pound salt pork, cut in slices
1½ pounds boneless lamb shoulder, cut in cubes
4 large pork chops
½ pound pork sausages
2 large onions, chopped
1 can (8 ounces) tomato sauce
½ cup dry red wine
3 cloves garlic, finely chopped
¼ cup chopped parsley
1 teaspoon thyme
1 bay leaf
Salt and pepper to taste

1. Wash and pick over beans, discarding hulls and imperfect beans. Put in a container and cover with water. Let stand overnight.
2. Drain beans. Place in a large saucepan and cover with cold water. Bring to a boil and then simmer slowly for about 1 hour, or until beans are tender. Drain beans and reserve liquid.
3. In a large skillet, fry salt pork until some of the fat has cooked out. Remove salt pork. Brown lamb, pork chops and sausages in pork fat. Drain thoroughly on paper towels.
4. Cut pork chops and salt pork into 1 inch pieces. Slice sausage.
5. Drain all but 2 tablespoons of the fat from skillet. Add onions and cook until onions are limp but not browned. Add tomato sauce, wine, garlic, parsley and seasonings. Combine tomato mixture with drained beans.
6. In a large casserole alternate layers of beans and meats, ending with a layer of beans. Pour reserved bean liquid over all ingredients, just enough to cover.
7. Heat oven to 350°F. Bake 1½ hours or until meats are tender.
8. Makes 8 servings.

QUICK CASSOULET

3 cans white beans
4 tablespoons salad oil
1 large onion, chopped
3 cloves garlic, minced
1 tablespoon chili sauce
½ teaspoon thyme
4 bacon slices, cut in pieces
3 lamb steaks
3 pork chops
1 pound Italian or garlic sausage
1 cup beef bouillon
½ cup dry bread crumbs

1. Heat oven to 350°F.
2. Drain beans and place in a large casserole.
3. Heat oil in a skillet. Add onion and garlic and cook until onion is tender but not browned. Add to beans with chili sauce and thyme.
4. Fry bacon in the skillet until almost done. Remove pieces of bacon and put in casserole. Brown lamb steaks and pork chops in bacon fat in skillet. Remove lamb and pork and cut meat in cubes. Add to bean mixture.
5. Prick sausage all over with a fork. Place in a skillet and cover with water. Bring to a boil and simmer 30 minutes. Remove and cut in slices. Add to bean mixture.
6. Toss bean mixture lightly. Pour beef bouillon over top.
7. Bake 30 minutes or until bubbly and piping hot. Sprinkle bread crumbs over top and bake an additional 5 minutes.
8. Makes about 6 to 8 servings.

Note: If you have leftover duck or goose, use in place of one of the meats.

CLASSIC CASSOULET

5 cups white beans
4 ounces salt pork
1 bay leaf
3 sprigs parsley
1 teaspoon thyme
4 peppercorns
2 carrots, scraped and halved
1 whole onion
8 cloves
2 teaspoons salt
2 pound boned pork loin, cubed (keep the bones)
1½ pound boned shoulder lamb, cubed (keep the bones)
2 onions, chopped
2 cloves garlic, chopped
1 cup tomato purée
Beef bouillon
1 pound garlic sausage, either French style or hot Italian sausage
1 cup very fine bread crumbs, from crusty French bread if possible
Freshly ground black pepper

1. Pick over beans, discarding hulls and imperfect beans. Wash and place in a deep bowl. Add water to cover and let soak overnight.
2. Cover salt pork with water. Bring to a boil and simmer 5 minutes. Drain and dice.
3. Put beans in a Dutch oven or heavy heat-proof casserole. Add enough water to cover. Add salt pork. Tie bay leaf, parsley thyme and peppercorns in a small piece of cheesecloth (bouquet garni). Add to beans with carrots, whole onion stuck with the cloves and salt.
4. Bring to a boil. Reduce heat, cover, and simmer gently about 1 to 1½ hours or until beans are just tender. Do not overcook. Remove bouquet garni, carrots and onion.
5. While beans are cooking prepare meat. Brown the pork and lamb cubes and bones in a large skillet or Dutch oven. Add chopped onions and garlic and cook 2 minutes. Stir in tomato purée. Cover and simmer about 1 hour, or until meat is tender. During cooking time, add beef bouillon as needed.
6. Prick sausage all over with a fork. Place in a skillet and cover with water. Bring to a boil and simmer 1 hour. Drain and cut in slices about ½ inch thick.
7. When meat is done, remove bones. Combine meat mixture with cooked beans. Taste and add salt and pepper if necessary. Add more beef bouillon if mixture is too dry.
8. Preheat oven to 375°F.
9. In a deep casserole place layers of the bean and meat mixture with slices of sausage between. Top layers with sausage slices. Combine bread crumbs with a good grind of pepper. Sprinkle over top.
10. Bake 1 to 1½ hours. As bread crust bakes and dries out on top of casserole, push it gently down into the casserole. When casserole is bubbling hot, it is ready to serve.
11. Makes about 12 servings.

CHOUCROUTE GARNIE

3 pounds sauerkraut
½ pound salt pork, sliced
1 large onion, thinly sliced
1 large Polish or Italian sausage, cut into 2-inch pieces
1 pound smoked loin of pork
1 bay leaf
¼ teaspoon thyme
1 teaspoon freshly ground black pepper
6 juniper berries, optional
2 cups dry white wine or beer
2 cups water
12 medium potatoes, peeled and boiled
12 frankfurters

1. Place sauerkraut in a deep bowl. Fill bowl with cold water and let stand a few minutes. Drain off water. Wash sauerkraut in bowl in more running water. Drain and squeeze out as much water as possible. Set aside.
2. Brown salt pork pieces in a large Dutch oven. When pork is browned and there is some fat in bottom of Dutch oven, add the onion, sausage and loin of pork. Brown meat and sausage on all sides. Remove meat and reserve.
3. Add sauerkraut to pan with bay leaf, thyme, pepper and juniper berries. Add wine or beer and water. Cover pan and simmer about 3 hours, stirring occasionally. Add more liquid, if necessary, to keep top of sauerkraut covered.
4. Return sausage and pork to Dutch oven. Cover tightly and simmer about 45 minutes.
5. Add potatoes and frankfurters. Cover and simmer about 15 minutes or just until potatoes and frankfurters are heated through.
6. To serve: Place sauerkraut in center of a large heated platter. Cut pork into thin slices and arrange on sauerkraut. Surround with sausage, potatoes and frankfurters.
7. Serve with a variety of mustards and either dry white wine or beer.
8. Makes 6 to 8 servings.

ROAST FRESH HAM

1 fresh ham, 6 to 8 pounds, boned and tied
1 bottle dry red wine
2 to 3 cloves garlic, crushed
1 onion, thinly sliced
1 bay leaf
½ teaspoon ground cloves
¼ teaspoon ground ginger
¼ teaspoon nutmeg
1 tablespoon salt
1 teaspoon crushed rosemary
½ cup golden raisins
½ cup pine nuts
  Tabasco

1. Place meat in a deep bowl or earthenware casserole. Combine remaining ingredients and pour over ham. Cover and let stand in refrigerator 3 days, turn occasionally.
2. On the day ham is to be cooked, remove from refrigerator and let stand in marinade at room temperature for several hours.
3. Heat oven to 325°F.
4. Remove ham from marinade and pat dry with paper toweling. Place on a rack in a shallow roasting pan. Insert meat thermometer in thickest part of ham.
5. Roast 25 to 30 minutes per pound of meat, or until a meat thermometer registers well done. Baste frequently with the marinade during cooking time.
6. Remove ham to a heated serving platter.
7. Skim fat from hot marinade. Strain into a saucepan. If sauce has cooked down too much, add a little more red wine. Season to taste with salt and pepper. Add raisins, pine nuts and a dash of Tabasco. Serve with sliced ham.

SAUSAGE IN WINE

1½ pounds pork sausage
¼ cup water
¾ cup dry white wine
1 tablespoon butter
1 tablespoon flour
1 cup beef bouillon
1 egg yolk, beaten
1 tablespoon lemon juice

1. Place sausage in a large skillet. Add water. Cover and simmer 5 minutes. Drain off water and continue cooking 10 minutes or until sausage is well browned on all sides.
2. Pour fat off skillet. Add wine and cook until wine is reduced to half the original volume.
3. Meanwhile, melt butter in a small saucepan. Stir in flour. Stir in bouillon and cook, stirring constantly, until thickened.
4. Remove sausage to a heated serving dish and keep warm. Stir reduced wine into bouillon mixture. Stir a small amount of the hot mixture into beaten egg yolk. Return mixture to saucepan. Stir in lemon juice. Cook over very low heat, stirring constantly, for 1 minute. Taste and season.
5. Pour sauce over sausage and serve.
6. Makes 4 servings.

PORK CHOPS IN VERMOUTH

¼ cup flour
1 teaspoon salt
½ teaspoon thyme
¼ teaspoon pepper
6 pork chops, cut ½ inch thick
2 tablespoons butter
2 tablespoons salad oil
½ cup dry vermouth or dry white wine

1. Combine flour, salt, thyme and pepper. Cut as much fat from pork chops as possible. Dust pork chops with flour mixture.
2. Heat butter and oil in a heavy skillet over medium heat. Add pork chops and cook until golden brown on both sides. Drain off every bit of fat from the skillet. Add vermouth. Cover and simmer about 30 minutes or until pork chops are tender.
3. Add more wine during cooking time, if necessary, to keep chops from sticking.
4. Makes 6 servings.

PORK CHOPS AND OLIVES MARSALA

¼ cup flour
1 teaspoon salt
¼ teaspoon pepper
4 shoulder pork chops, about ¾ inch thick
1 clove garlic, halved
3 tablespoons salad oil
½ cup water
½ cup marsala wine
½ cup sliced pimiento-stuffed olives
2 tablespoons chopped parsley

1. Combine flour, salt and pepper. Rub pork chops with garlic and dredge in flour.
2. Heat oil in a skillet. Brown pork chops well on both sides. Drain off excess fat.
3. Pour water over meat. Reduce heat. Cover tightly and simmer 30 minutes.
4. Add wine and olives and continue cooking 30 minutes or until chops are tender.
5. Sprinkle parsley on top just before serving.
6. Makes 4 servings.

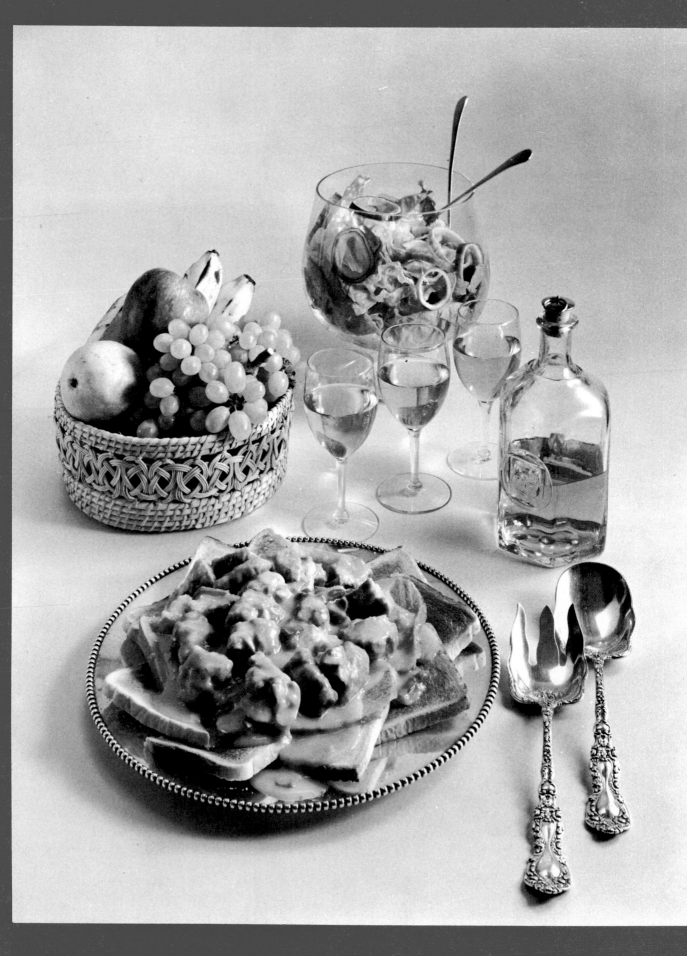

PAUPIETTES AU PÂTÉ

8 veal scallops
Salt
Freshly ground black pepper
1 can (4½ ounces) smoked liver pâté, chilled
¼ cup butter or margarine
2 tablespoons brandy
1 clove garlic, chopped
1 onion, chopped
½ cup dry white wine
2 tablespoons snipped parsley

1. Place veal slices between 2 pieces of aluminum foil. Pound until very thin with a pounder or the flat side of a cleaver. Sprinkle with salt and pepper.
2. Open can and remove pâté carefully. Cut pâté into 8 equal sized strips. Place strips of pâté on slices of veal. Roll veal around pate. Tie rolls with string.
3. Melt butter in a skillet. When foam subsides, add veal and cook gently until golden brown on all sides.
4. Warm brandy. Pour over veal and ignite with a match. Allow flames to burn out. Add garlic, onion and wine. Cover and simmer over low heat about 30 minutes or until veal rolls are tender.
5. Remove veal rolls to serving platter, scrape up juices in bottom of pan and pour over veal.
6. Serve with mushrooms, artichoke hearts and canned French petit pois.
7. Makes 6 to 8 servings.

◀ SHERRIED SWEETBREADS AND HAM (shown opposite)

2 quarts water
2 tablespoons lemon juice
2 tablespoons salt
3 pairs veal sweetbreads, about 3 pounds
4 tablespoons butter
1 green pepper, sliced
1 large onion, minced
¼ cup flour
¼ teaspoon pepper
1 cup non-dairy powdered cream
2 cups boiling chicken broth or bouillon
¼ cup sherry
6 slices cooked ham, heated
Buttered toast points

1. In a large kettle combine water, lemon juice and salt. Bring to a boil. Add sweetbreads, reduce heat and simmer 20 minutes. Drain and plunge in cold water. Let stand a few minutes. Hold sweetbreads under cold water and remove membrane and veins. Cut sweetbreads into bite-sized pieces.
2. Melt butter in a heavy saucepan over medium heat. Add green pepper and onion; cook until tender and very lightly browned. Blend in flour and pepper.
3. Remove from heat. Add powdered cream and then boiling chicken broth. Beat with a wire whisk to blend. Cook over moderately high heat, stirring constantly, until mixture comes to a boil and is thickened. Stir in sweetbreads and sherry. Heat thoroughly.
4. Serve piping hot over slices of cooked ham. Garnish with buttered toast points.
5. Makes 6 servings.

VEAL ITALIENNE

8 very thin veal cutlets
4 thin slices Gruyère or Swiss cheese
4 thin slices prosciutto
Salt
Freshly ground black pepper
Flour
2 tablespoons butter
3 tablespoons olive oil
½ cup dry white wine
½ cup chicken bouillon

1. Have butcher flatten veal until it is ⅛ to ¹⁄₁₆ inch thick.
2. Place a slice of cheese and a slice of prosciutto on 4 pieces of veal. Top with remaining 4 slices of veal. Press edges of veal together to seal, or fasten securely with toothpicks.
3. Season with salt and pepper. Dip in flour and shake off excess flour.
4. Melt butter and oil in a skillet over medium high heat. When the foam subsides, add veal and cook, two at a time, turning gently, until well browned on both sides. Remove veal to a heated platter.
5. Discard most of fat from skillet, leaving a thin film on the bottom. Pour in wine and bouillon and bring to a boil, stirring up any browned bits of veal on bottom of pan.
6. Return veal to pan. Reduce heat, cover tightly and simmer about 20 minutes, or until veal is tender. Turn veal over once during cooking period.
7. Remove veal to a heated serving platter and pour sauce over the top.
8. Makes 4 servings.

VEAL SCALLOPS MARSALA

1½ pounds veal scallops
　Flour
3 tablespoons butter or margarine
3 tablespoons salad oil
　Salt and pepper
　Marsala wine
¼ cup chopped parsley

1. Ask butcher to pound scallops paper thin. If butcher does not pound them thin enough, do it at home. Place each scallop between 2 pieces of waxed paper and pound with the flat side of a cleaver, a meat pounder or any heavy flat object.
2. Dust scallops with flour. Melt butter in large skillet, add oil and heat. Brown scallops quickly.
3. Cover with Marsala and continue cooking until the wine is reduced to half. Turn scallops once during cooking.
4. When wine is reduced and the meat is tender, remove meat to hot platter and add ¼ cup Marsala to the pan.
5. Bring to a boil, add parsley and pour over the veal.
6. Serve with hot cooked rice, if desired.
7. Makes 4 servings.

CÔTÉ DE VEAU QUERCYNOISE

6 to 8 veal chops, about 1 inch thick
　Salt and pepper
¼ cup butter
¼ cup olive oil
1½ cups chicken broth
1 clove garlic, minced
1 can (5 to 10 ounces) cepès or chanterelles, (wild French mushrooms)

1. Roll ends of chops. Fasten ends with skewers. Sprinkle both sides of the chops with salt and pepper.
2. Heat butter and olive oil in a skillet over medium heat until foam begins to subside. Add chops and cook until golden brown on both sides. Continue cooking until chops are cooked to the desired degree of doneness. Remove chops to a hot platter and keep warm.
3. Add chicken broth and garlic to pan drippings, stir to remove browned bits from bottom of pan.
4. Wash mushrooms under running water. Drain and blot dry. Slice. Add mushrooms to sauce and cook briskly for 5 minutes. Pour mixture over chops. Serve immediately.
5. Makes 6 to 8 servings.

VEAL SCALLOPS JARNAC

12 veal scallops
　Flour
6 tablespoons butter
2 tablespoons salad oil
½ teaspoon salt
½ teaspoon freshly ground pepper
1 teaspoon tarragon
3 tablespoons warm cognac
¾ cup heavy cream
2 egg yolks, beaten

1. Sprinkle the veal scallops very lightly with flour.
2. Heat butter and salad oil in a skillet over high heat. Quickly cook the veal, turning several times, until browned on both sides. Reduce heat and add the salt, pepper and tarragon.
3. Pour the warm cognac over top of veal. Ignite with a match and allow flames to burn out. Remove scallops to a platter.
4. Beat together the cream and egg yolks. Reduce heat under skillet to very low. Add cream mixture to skillet and cook, stirring constantly, until mixture begins to thicken. Serve sauce with the veal scallops.
5. Makes 6 servings.

VEAL ROULADES

18 veal scallops
　pound ground ham
3 cloves garlic crushed
3 tablespoons snipped parsley
1 teaspoon rosemary
　Sprinkle of nutmeg
　Salt and pepper
6 strips of bacon
　Salad oil
⅔ cup white wine
1 bay leaf

1. Place veal between 2 pieces of waxed paper. Pound with a pounder or the flat side of a heavy cleaver.
2. Combine ham, garlic, parsley, rosemary, nutmeg and salt and pepper to taste. Divide this mixture evenly on top of each veal slice. Roll up and tie firmly with heavy string.
3. Cut bacon strips in pieces. Cook in heavy skillet until bacon is crisp and fat is rendered out. Remove bits of bacon. Brown veal rolls in hot bacon fat on all sides. Add salad oil, if needed, during browning time.
4. Add wine, bay leaf and bacon bits. Cover tightly and simmer over low heat 1 hour or until veal is tender.
5. Remove string before serving. Serve with sauce over each roulade.
6. Makes 6 to 8 servings.

VEAL CHOPS WITH MUSHROOMS

    4 loin veal chops, about 1¼ inches thick
⅓ cup butter or margarine
½ pound mushrooms, sliced
    2 tablespoons lemon juice
½ cup sliced onion
½ clove garlic, crushed
¼ cup flour
    1 teaspoon salt
⅛ teaspoon freshly ground pepper
    1 can (10½ ounces) condensed beef
        bouillon
⅔ cup dry white wine
    1 teaspoon chopped fresh tarragon leaves
½ teaspoon snipped chives

1. Trim excess fat from chops. Roll up ends of chops and fasten with wooden picks.
2. Melt butter in a skillet over medium high heat. Brown chops on both sides. Remove chops and set aside.
3. Sprinkle mushroom slices with lemon juice. Place in the skillet with onion and garlic. Cook, stirring, until golden, about 5 minutes. Remove mushrooms and onions and set aside.
4. Stir flour, salt and pepper into drippings in the skillet. Gradually stir in bouillon and wine. Add tarragon and chives. Bring to a boil, stirring constantly.
5. Add chops and cooked vegetables. Cover and simmer over low heat 30 minutes or until chops are tender.
6. To serve, remove chops to a heated serving platter. Remove picks from chops. Serve with gravy and vegetables.
7. Makes 4 servings.

VEAL CHOPS

    6 veal chops, cut ½ inch thick
        Flour
¼ cup salad oil
¼ cup butter or margarine
    6 cloves garlic
    2 medium bay leaves
½ teaspoon thyme
        Salt and pepper
    2 tablespoons red wine vinegar
½ cup chicken bouillon
¼ cup water

1. Dredge chops lightly on all sides with flour. Heat oil and butter in a skillet large enough to hold all the chops. Brown chops lightly on both sides.
2. Scatter garlic cloves around chops. Place a piece of bay leaf on top of each chop. Add thyme, salt and pepper. Cover tightly

and simmer chops 30 minutes or until tender and the sauce in skillet is syrupy. Remove chops to a hot serving platter and keep warm.
3. Stir vinegar into skillet and cook over high heat until it has evaporated. Stir in bouillon and water and simmer, stirring, about 5 minutes. Taste and add salt and pepper if desired. Pour sauce over chops.
4. Makes 6 servings.

VEAL MARENGO

    2 pounds boneless shoulder of veal
1½ tablespoons olive oil
    1 clove garlic, minced
    10 small white onions, peeled
½ pound mushrooms, sliced
1¼ teaspoons salt
¼ teaspoon freshly ground black pepper
1½ tablespoons flour
    1 can (8 ounces) tomato sauce
½ cup dry white wine
    1 cup canned chicken broth
        Bouquet garni

1. Cut veal into 1½-inch cubes. Heat olive oil in a skillet with the garlic. Brown veal in hot oil, cooking only enough pieces at a time to cover the bottom of skillet. Remove veal and place in a casserole.
2. Brown onions in hot olive oil in skillet. Remove onions and place over veal.
3. Add mushrooms and brown lightly and quickly. Remove mushrooms and place over top of veal.
4. Stir salt, pepper and flour into remaining oil in skillet. Add tomato sauce, wine and broth. Cook, stirring constantly, until smooth and slightly thickened. Pour over veal in casserole.
5. Add the bouquet garni consisting of a small stalk of celery with leaves, 2 sprigs of parsley a bay leaf and a bit of thyme. Tie together with stem of the parsley or tie up in a small piece of cheesecloth.
6. Heat oven to 325°F.
7. Cover casserole with a lid or heavy duty aluminum foil. Bake 1¼ hours or until veal is tender.
8. Remove bouquet garni and discard.
9. Makes 6 servings.

63

VEAL IN CREAM

½ cup butter or margarine, divided
1 onion, chopped
2 cloves garlic, minced
2 pounds boneless veal shoulder, cut in 1½-inch cubes
2 cups strong chicken bouillon
1 teaspoon salt
Freshly ground black pepper
1½ cups heavy cream
1 pound mushrooms, cut in halves
¼ cup cognac

1. Melt ¼ cup butter in a heavy skillet. Add onion and garlic and cook until limp but not browned.
2. Add veal and cook, stirring until veal loses its pink color. Do not brown. Add bouillon, salt and pepper. Cover and simmer gently 1½ hours.
3. Add cream and simmer uncovered about 30 minutes. Stir occasionally.
4. Melt remaining butter in a skillet. Add mushrooms and cook about 3 minutes. Add mushrooms to veal mixture and simmer 15 minutes longer.
5. Stir in cognac and heat before serving.
6. Makes 6 servings.

BRAISED SHOULDER OF VEAL

4 pounds veal shoulder
2 cloves garlic
4 tablespoons butter
1 teaspoon salt
1 teaspoon freshly ground pepper
1 cup bouillon
1 cup dry white wine
1 teaspoon tarragon
1 onion
½ bay leaf

1. Have butcher bone, roll and tie veal shoulder. Be sure to take the bones also.
2. Make small incisions in the meat with a sharp knife and insert thin slivers of garlic.
3. Melt butter in Dutch oven over medium high heat. Add veal and brown well on all sides, turning often.
4. Sprinkle with salt and pepper. Add bouillon, white wine, tarragon, onion and bay leaf. Add the veal bones.
5. Cover and simmer gently about 2 hours or until veal is tender.
6. Remove veal to a hot serving platter. Remove strings and slice. Skim fat from juices in the pan. Remove onion, bay leaf and bones. Serve sauce with veal.
7. Makes 4 to 6 servings.

BLANQUETTE DE VEAU

1½ pound shoulder of veal
1 quart water
1 tablespoon salt
⅛ teaspoon powdered thyme
1 bay leaf
1 sprig parsley
12 small white onions
6 carrots, scraped and quartered
2 tablespoons butter or margarine
2 tablespoons flour
2 tablespoons lemon juice
2 egg yolks
½ teaspoon Tabasco
Chopped parsley

1. Have veal cut into 1¼-inch cubes. Put in a deep saucepan with water, salt, thyme, bay leaf and parsley. Cover and simmer 1 hour, or until meat is almost tender.
2. Add onions and carrots and continue cooking until meat and vegetables are tender. Drain off stock and add enough water to make 2 cups liquid.
3. Melt butter in a saucepan. Stir in flour. Slowly stir in hot stock from veal. Cook, stirring constantly, until thickened.
4. Combine lemon juice and slightly beaten egg yolks. Stir about 1 cup of the hot sauce slowly into egg yolk mixture. Return to remaining sauce in saucepan. Cook over low heat until slightly thickened, *do not boil.* Stir in Tabasco.
5. Add sauce to veal and vegetables and heat but do not boil.
6. Arrange on a heated serving dish. Sprinkle with parsley. Serve with cooked rice or noodles.
7. Makes 6 servings.

SAUTEÉD CALVES' LIVER

4 slices calves' liver, cut ⅜-inch thick
Salt and pepper
¼ cup flour
2 tablespoons butter
2 tablespoons salad oil

1. Have butcher remove filament from slices of liver.
2. Sprinkle with salt and pepper. Dredge with flour and shake off excess flour.
3. Heat butter and oil in skillet until butter foam subsides and it just begins to turn brown. Place liver in skillet and cook 2 to 3 minutes. Turn liver and cook 2 to 3 minutes on second side.
4. Liver is done when its juices run a very pale pink when slice is pricked with a fork.
5. Makes 4 servings.

VEAL KIDNEYS IN RED WINE

4 veal kidneys
10 mushrooms
4 tablespoons butter
4 green onions, cleaned and chopped
Salt and pepper
½ cup red wine

1. Slice kidneys in thin slices and remove hard core and excess fat.
2. Clean and slice mushrooms.
3. Melt butter in a heavy skillet over medium high heat. Add kidney and cook quickly until nicely browned on both sides.
4. Add mushrooms and green onions and cook about 5 minutes, stirring.
5. Sprinkle with salt and pepper and add red wine. Cook 4 to 5 minutes or until kidneys are tender and ingredients blended. Taste and add more seasoning if necessary.
6. Serve on buttered toast or fried bread.
7. Makes 4 to 6 servings.

KIDNEY AND MUSHROOM SAUTÉ

6 veal kidneys
6 tablespoons butter
½ pound small whole mushrooms
6 tablespoons flour
1 cup non-dairy powdered cream
2 cups hot beef broth
¼ cup sherry
Salt and pepper to taste

1. Trim kidneys by removing fat and the thin filament surrounding kidneys. Cut into slices.
2. Melt butter in a skillet over very high heat. When foam from butter subsides a little, add kidneys and cook very quickly, about 3 minutes. Remove kidneys to a chafing dish or casserole. Reduce heat a little and cook mushrooms until lightly browned on all sides. Remove to chafing dish.
3. Add flour to liquid in skillet, blending with a wire whisk; cook and stir 1 minute, but do not brown.
4. Remove from heat and stir in cream and hot beef broth all at once. Beat with wire whisk to blend.
5. Cook over moderately high heat, stirring constantly, until sauce comes to a boil and thickens. Blend in sherry and seasonings.
6. Pour over kidneys and mushrooms and heat gently, but do not boil. Serve from chafiing dish or casserole.
7. Makes 8 servings.

LIVER JULIENNE

1 pound calves' liver
Flour
Salt and pepper
Paprika
2 tablespoons olive oil
2 tablespoons butter
1 clove garlic, minced
½ cup dry white wine
2 tablespoons snipped parsley
¾ cup dairy sour cream

1. Cut liver into thin strips about ½-inch thick. Dredge with flour seasoned with salt, pepper and a little paprika.
2. Heat oil and butter in a large skillet just until foam from butter begins to subside. Add strips of liver and garlic and cook very quickly, turning so that all the liver strips become browned and cooked. This should take about 2 to 4 minutes.
3. Remove liver to a hot platter and keep warm.
4. Pour off most of fat from skillet. Add wine and parsley and cook, stirring, so that brown bits are stirred up from bottom of pan. Add sour cream and heat but *do not boil.* Taste and add more seasoning if desired.
5. Return liver strips to pan and stir well. Serve with buttered noodles or hot cooked rice if desired.
6. Makes 4 servings.

CALVES' BRAINS BEURRE NOIR

2 calves' brains
1 teaspoon salt
1 onion stuck with 1 clove
1 bay leaf
Pinch of thyme
4 peppercorns
2 tablespoons butter
2 tablespoons vinegar

1. Soak brains in cold water for 2 hours. Remove thin outer skin as gently as possible, without tearing the flesh. Cover with cold water and soak for 3 hours. Drain.
2. Place brains in a large saucepan. Cover with cold water. Add salt, onion, bay leaf, thyme and peppercorns. Cover and bring to a boil. Lower heat and simmer 20 minutes. Set aside and keep warm.
3. In a small skillet melt butter and cook until butter is dark brown. Arrange brains on a heated serving dish and pour butter over.
4. Put vinegar in skillet and cook briskly. Pour over brains. Serve at once.
5. Makes 4 servings.

CALVES' BRAINS SAUTÉ

2 calves' brains
1 teaspoon salt
1 onion, stuck with 1 clove
1 bay leaf
Pinch of thyme
4 peppercorns
2 tablespoons flour
¼ cup butter, divided
6 thin slices lemon
1 tablespoon snipped parsley

1. Soak brains in cold water for 2 hours. Remove thin outer skin as gently as possible without tearing the flesh. Cover with cold water and soak for 3 hours. Drain.
2. Place brains in a large saucepan. Cover with cold water. Add salt, onion, bay leaf, thyme and peppercorns. Cover and bring to a boil. Lower heat and simmer 20 minutes. Drain.
3. Cut brains into slices ½-inch thick. Dredge slices with flour.
4. Melt 2 tablespoons of the butter in a large skillet. Add brains and cook for 10 minutes or until well browned on both sides. Remove brains to heated serving dish and keep warm.
5. In a small skillet heat remaining butter until it is medium brown in color. Pour over brains. Serve with lemon slices and sprinkle with parsley.
6. Makes 4 servings.

VEAL CUTLETS À L'EVELYN

2 to 3 tablespoons salad oil
8 small veal cutlets, trimmed of tendons
Salt and pepper
½ teaspoon paprika
1 scallion, cleaned and chopped
Pinch of marjoram or oregano
2 tablespoons chopped onion
2 tablespoons chopped parsley, divided
1 clove garlic, crushed
Water
½ cup cream
3 tablespoons brandy
2 to 3 tablespoons port, sherry or Madeira
2 egg yolks, well beaten

1. Heat oil in a large skillet over medium high heat. Sprinkle veal with salt, pepper and paprika. Sauté in oil until golden brown on both sides.
2. Add scallion, marjoram, onion, 1 table-spoon parsley and garlic. Cover and simmer about 10 minutes, or until veal is tender. Add a little water if mixture looks dry.
3. Remove veal to a warm serving plate.
4. Combine cream, brandy, port and well beaten egg yolks. Stir into skillet. Place over very low heat and cook, stirring constantly, until slightly thickened and heated through. Pour over veal and sprinkle with remaining tablespoon of parsley.
5. Makes 5 to 6 servings.

MOLDED VEAL

(shown opposite)

2 envelopes unflavored gelatine
1½ cups water
2 cans (10½ ounces each) condensed beef consommé
2 tablespoons lemon juice
1 jar (2 ounces) pimientos, sliced, drained
2½ cups cooked veal, cut into bite-sized pieces
¾ cup thinly sliced celery
1 jar (11 ounces) mixed pickles, drained
2 hard cooked eggs, sliced

1. Soften gelatine in ½ cup cold water. Heat remaining water with 1 can beef consomme. Add gelatine and stir until dissolved. Add lemon juice and remaining consomme.
2. Measure out ⅓ cup of the consommé mixture and put in electric blender. Add pimientos and blend until smooth. Pour into 1½-quart mold. Refrigerate until set.
3. Chill remaining consommé mixture until it mounds slightly when dropped from a spoon. Stir in veal, celery and ¾ cup of the pickles, chopped. Spoon into the mold on top of pimiento mixture. Chill until thoroughly set.
4. At serving time, unmold onto serving dish. Garnish with egg slices and remaining pickles.
5. Makes 8 to 10 servings as a first course, 6 servings as a main course.

National Biscuit Co.

The French manner of roasting lamb differs from the American because our meat experts have found that lower oven temperatures result in less meat loss and juicier roasts. Hence, these recipes are "American style"—that is, roasted in a slow oven. However, if you wish to be truly French, prepare roast lamb as follows:

If you are fond of the flavor of garlic, make several incisions in the top of the lamb and insert a thin sliver of garlic in each incision. Put the meat in a very hot oven, 450° F., and sear for 15 minutes. Reduce heat to 350° F. and continue roasting until meat is of desired degree of doneness. For medium rare leg of lamb, it will take about 12 minutes per pound. For well done it will take about 15 minutes per pound.

ROAST LEG OF LAMB WITH SPICY WINE SAUCE

(shown opposite)

1 cup dry red wine
¼ cup salad oil
1 onion, coarsely chopped
2 cloves garlic, minced
½ teaspoon Tabasco
Salt
1 leg of lamb
Stewed Tomatoes

1. Combine wine, oil, onion, garlic, Tabasco and salt to taste. Place lamb in a glass or enameled-ware pan just large enough to hold it. Pour wine mixture over the top. Cover and let stand in the refrigerator 6 hours or overnight. Turn meat occasionally.
2. Heat oven to 325°F.
3. Remove lamb and pat dry with paper toweling. Place on a rack in a shallow roasting pan. Insert a meat thermometer into heavy part of leg, being careful not to touch the bone.
4. Roast meat about 25 minutes per pound or to the desired degree of doneness. Lamb should be pink in the center when it is eaten. Baste lamb occasionally with the wine marinade.
5. Serve with Stewed Tomatoes.
6. Makes 6 to 8 servings.

STEWED TOMATOES

2 tablespoons butter
2 cloves garlic, crushed
1 small onion, thinly sliced
2 cans (2 pounds 3 ounces each) plum tomatoes, drained and juice reserved
1 tablespoon sugar
1 teaspoon salt
Freshly ground pepper

1. Melt butter in a medium saucepan. Add garlic and onion and cook until limp but not browned.
2. Add reserved tomato juice and boil until reduced to 1⅔ cups.
3. Add tomatoes, sugar, salt and pepper to taste. Heat to serving temperature.
4. Makes 6 to 8 servings.

LEG OF LAMB IN PASTRY

3 lamb kidneys
Butter or margarine
Madeira
¼ pound mushrooms, cleaned and chopped
¾ teaspoon salt
½ teaspoon rosemary
¼ teaspoon thyme
¼ teaspoon tarragon
4 to 4½ pound leg of lamb, boned
1 package pie crust mix
1 egg yolk
2 tablespoons flour
1½ tablespoons red currant jelly

1. Remove fat and white veins from kidneys. Wash and pat dry with paper towels. Cut kidneys into tiny pieces.
2. Melt 3 tablespoons butter in a skillet over medium high heat. Add kidneys and cook until golden brown. Stir in 1 tablespoon Madeira, mushrooms, salt, rosemary, thyme and tarragon. Remove from heat and let stand.
3. Heat oven to 425°F.
4. Lay leg of lamb flat. Cut off most of the fat. Place kidney mixture in center of lamb. Roll up lamb and fasten with skewers or tie with string. Place on a rack in a shallow roasting pan. Rub the top with softened butter. Insert meat thermometer into thickest part of meat, not into the stuffing.
5. Roast about 60 minutes or until the meat thermometer registers 150°F.
6. Prepare pie crust mix, following directions on package. On a lightly floured board, roll pastry out into a 15- by 12-inch oval.
7. Remove roast from oven. Place roast in a clean, shallow roasting pan without a rack. Remove thermometer and skewers or cut off strings. Reserve first roasting pan.
8. Lay pastry over lamb in roasting pan. Press pastry against meat and tuck underneath to cover roast completely. Beat egg yolk with 1 teaspoon of water and brush over top of pastry.
9. Bake 15 to 20 minutes or until pastry is golden brown.
10. While meat is cooking, add 1 cup of water

Recipe continues on next page

to drippings in first roasting pan. Heat, stirring to loosen browned bits in bottom. Strain mixture and let stand a few minutes. Skim off as much fat as possible.

11. Melt 2 tablespoons butter in a small saucepan. Stir in flour and cook, stirring constantly, until slightly browned. Stir in strained drippings. Cook over medium heat, stirring constantly, until smooth and thickened. Stir in 3 tablespoons Madeira and red currant jelly. Heat thoroughly.

12. Remove lamb from roasting pan and place on carving board. Cut in slices and serve with gravy.

13. Makes 8 servings.

LEG OF LAMB WITH WHITE BEANS

    1 pound dried pea beans
    Water
  ¼ cup butter or margarine
    2 cloves garlic
    2 pounds onions, thinly sliced
    Seasoned salt
  ½ teaspoon salt
  ¼ teaspoon freshly ground pepper
    1 teaspoon rosemary, divided
    2 cans (1 pound each) Italian plum tomatoes
    1 leg of lamb, about 6½ to 7 pounds

1. Place beans in a large kettle. Cover with water. Bring to a boil over high heat and simmer 2 minutes. Remove from heat, cover and let stand about 1 hour.

2. Return beans to heat. Bring to a boil. Reduce heat and simmer covered about 1 hour or until beans are tender. Check liquid during cooking period, adding water if necessary. Drain beans.

3. Heat oven to 325°F.

4. Heat butter in a large skillet. Crush 1 clove of the garlic and add to hot butter. Add onions and cook until golden brown, stirring occasionally.

5. In the bottom of a shallow roasting pan combine cooked beans, onion mixture, 2 teaspoons seasoned salt, salt, pepper, ½ teaspoon rosemary and tomatoes. Blend thoroughly.

6. Split remaining clove of garlic and rub over entire surface of lamb. Sprinkle lamb with seasoned salt and remaining rosemary. Place lamb on top of beans. Insert a meat thermometer into heavy part of leg, being careful that it does not touch the bone.

7. Roast, uncovered, 3 to 3½ hours or until

meat thermometer registers medium well done.

8. Remove lamb to carving board. Turn beans into a serving dish. Serve slices of lamb with beans.

9. Makes 10 servings.

BRAISED STUFFED SHOULDER OF LAMB
(shown opposite)

    5 pound boned and rolled lamb shoulder
    3 tablespoons salad oil, divided
  ¼ cup finely chopped onion
  12 saltine crackers, finely rolled
    2 teaspoons grated lemon rind
    1 teaspoon mint flakes, crushed
  ½ teaspoon salt
  ¼ teaspoon freshly ground black pepper
    1 egg, slightly beaten
    4 ounces boiled ham, cut in julienne strips
  ½ cup apple juice
    1 can (10½ ounces) condensed beef consommé
    2 cups cherry tomatoes
    2 tablespoons flour
    Cold water

1. Unroll meat, wipe with a damp cloth.

2. Heat 2 tablespoons oil in a Dutch oven. Add onion and cook until soft but not browned. Scrape onion and oil into a mixing bowl. Add crackers, lemon rind, mint flakes, salt and pepper. Add egg and blend lightly.

3. Spread stuffing mixture on meat. Spread ham strips out over top of stuffing. Roll up and tie securely.

4. Heat remaining tablespoon of oil in the Dutch oven. Brown lamb slowly on all sides. Add apple juice and half the can of consommé. Refrigerate remaining consommé for other use.

5. Heat oven to 325°F.

6. Cover Dutch oven and place in oven. Cook 2 to 2½ hours or until lamb is done. Add cherry tomatoes the last 10 minutes of cooking.

7. Transfer meat and tomatoes to a heated serving platter. Remove strings from meat and discard.

8. Blend flour with enough water to make a smooth paste. Add to meat juices in Dutch oven. Cook, stirring, until mixture comes to a boil. Simmer 2 minutes. Serve gravy with lamb.

9. Makes about 8 servings.

Beef

Beef Bourguignonne is probably one of the most famous of all French dishes. You can have it almost anywhere in the world and you can make the best one of all in your own home.

There are probably as many variations of Beef Bourguignonne as there are different ways of spelling its name. The meat may be cooked in one big piece, and then sliced for serving, or cut into cubes before cooking. Cut into cubes, it is tastier and generally preferred by most people.

Simply, it is beef cooked in red wine. The spices and herbs can vary, it can be cooked with or without vegetables, or in a number of combinations. It is best cooked in large quantities for a long period of time. Beef Bourguignonne is good the first day, but even better when reheated. It also takes well to the freezer, so freeze the leftovers and have them several weeks later.

BOEUF BOURGUIGNONNE

5 pounds beef chuck or round, cut into 1½-inch pieces
1 tablespoon Ac'cent
1 tablespoon salt
¼ teaspoon pepper
½ pound salt pork
2 medium onions, chopped
1 clove garlic, minced
3 cups dry red wine
1 bay leaf
¼ cup chopped parsley
1 teaspoon thyme
1 pound mushrooms, cleaned and sliced
3 tablespoons flour

1. Sprinkle beef with combined Ac'cent, salt and pepper.
2. Cut salt pork into small cubes. Heat an oven-proof casserole or Dutch oven over medium high heat. Add salt pork pieces and cook until golden brown. Remove pieces of salt pork. Add beef to hot fat, a few pieces at a time; brown well on all sides and remove.
3. Add onion and cook until onion is tender but not browned. Return salt pork and beef to Dutch oven. Add garlic, wine, bay leaf, parsley and thyme. Cover and simmer about 3 hours or until meat is tender. Add additional wine if necessary during cooking time.
4. Add mushrooms during the last 15 minutes of the cooking time.
5. Combine flour with a little cold water to make a smooth paste. Stir into hot mixture and cook, stirring constantly, until mixture is thickened.
6. Makes 12 servings.

OVEN-BAKED BEEF BOURGUIGNONNE

4 pounds beef rump or beef chuck
⅓ cup warm cognac
2 whole onions, each stuck with 2 cloves
2 cloves garlic
1 teaspoon thyme
½ bay leaf
4 cups dry red wine
1 tablespoon salt
1 teaspoon freshly ground black pepper
1 slice orange
2 tablespoons butter
18 small white onions, peeled

1. Have the beef rump tied. If there is very little fat on the outside, have the butcher tie on several pieces of beef suet.
2. Heat a Dutch oven over medium-high heat. Add beef and brown thoroughly on all sides. Pour warm cognac over beef and ignite with a match. Allow flames to burn out.
3. Heat oven to 300°F.
4. Add 2 cloved onions, garlic, thyme, bay leaf, dry red wine, salt, pepper and orange slice. Bring to a boil on top of the range.
5. Cover Dutch oven and bake about 2 hours. Turn once or twice during cooking period.
6. Melt butter in a skillet. Add white onions and brown on all sides. Add to beef in Dutch oven. Cook 30 minutes more or until beef is tender.
7. Remove beef and onions to a hot serving platter. Cook down liquid in Dutch oven. Strain and serve with slices of the beef.
8. Makes 8 to 10 servings.

 Beef Bourguignonne has become as much a part of our American cooking as of the French. It is a savory dish combining beef cubes, wine and herbs.

Ac'cent

POT ROAST PROVENÇAL

5 pounds eye round of beef, tied
12 to 14 whole pimiento-stuffed green olives
3 to 4 large cloves garlic, slivered
1 medium onion, sliced
1 stalk celery, cut into chunks
1 large bay leaf
4 whole cloves
1 tablespoon sugar
1 teaspoon Ac'cent
¼ teaspoon savory
¼ teaspoon peppercorns
¼ teaspoon salt
1½ cups dry red wine
2 tablespoons salad oil
1½ pounds peeled new potatoes
4 carrots, cut into 2-inch sticks
1 cup diced tomatoes
Water
1 tablespoon flour

1. Stick a sharp pointed knife into the fat side of the meat, every inch or so, then wiggle it to make a hole. Put an olive and a sliver or two of garlic into each hole. Place meat in a large bowl. Add onion, celery, bay leaf, cloves, sugar, Ac'cent, savory, peppercorns, salt and any remaining garlic or olives. Pour wine over the beef. Let stand in the refrigerator overnight. Turn occasionally.
2. Remove beef and reserve marinade. Pat meat dry with paper toweling. Heat salad oil in a large Dutch oven. Add beef and brown slowly on all sides. Pour off any excess fat. Add marinade to beef. Cover tightly and simmer 3 to 3½ hours.
3. Add potatoes, carrots and tomatoes the last 30 minutes of cooking time. Cover and continue simmering until meat and vegetables are tender.
4. Remove meat to a hot serving platter. Remove vegetables with a slotted spoon and place around pot roast.
5. Strain liquid in pan and measure. Add enough water to make 2 cups. Return liquid to Dutch oven.
6. Blend flour with 2 tablespoons cold water. Stir into liquid and bring to a boil. Cook 1 minute, stirring constantly. Serve with beef.
7. Makes 6 to 8 servings.

Pot Roast Provencal may well become a favorite in your home. Made with garlic, herbs and wine, it has the extra added fillip of stuffed green olives.

Spanish Olive Commission

BOEUF À LA MODE

2 tablespoons butter or margarine
4 pound beef rump roast, rolled and tied
¼ cup chopped onion
2 cups dry white wine
½ cup hot water
1½ teaspoons salt
½ teaspoon thyme
¼ teaspoon freshly ground pepper
3 whole cloves
½ bay l
Spri
12 small whne onions, peeled
6 medium carrots, pared and quartered lengthwise
2 tablespoons flour

1. Melt butter over medium-high heat in a Dutch oven. Add beef and brown well on all sides. This should take about 30 minutes. During last few minutes of browning, add chopped onion.
2. Add wine, water, salt, thyme, pepper, cloves, bay leaf and parsley. Bring to a boil. Reduce heat and simmer, covered, 2½ hours.
3. Add whole onions and carrots. Cover and simmer 1 hour or just until beef is fork tender.
4. Remove beef to a heated serving platter. Lift out vegetables with a slotted spoon and place around beef. Keep warm.
5. Skim off excess fat from top of cooking liquid. Combine ¼ cup cold water with the flour. Gradually stir into liquid in Dutch oven. Bring to a boil and cook, stirring constantly, until mixture is smooth and thickened. Strain gravy and serve with meat and vegetables.
6. Makes 8 to 10 servings.

BEEF BOURGUIGNONNE MARINER

3 pounds beef chuck or top round, cut into 2-inch cubes
1 small onion, sliced
2 cups red wine
1 small bay leaf
4 sprigs parsley
Pinch of thyme
2 tablespoons salad oil
½ teaspoon salt
¼ teaspoon freshly ground black pepper
1 small carrot, sliced
1 clove garlic, crushed
3 tablespoons butter or margarine, divided
1 tablespoon flour
½ cup beef consommé
¼ pound salt pork, diced
24 small white onions, peeled
½ pound whole fresh mushrooms

1. In a deep bowl combine beef, sliced onion, wine, bay leaf, parsley, thyme, oil, salt, pepper, carrot and garlic. Let stand at least 4 hours, turning occasionally. Remove beef and pat dry with paper towels. Strain marinade and reserve for later use.
2. Heat 2 tablespoons butter in a Dutch oven. Add beef and brown well on all sides. Remove beef and stir in flour. Cook, stirring constantly, for about 2 minutes. Stir in consommé and marinade. Return beef to pan and bring to a boil. Cover and simmer about 2 hours.
3. While beef is cooking, heat remaining 1 tablespoon butter in a small skillet. Add salt pork and white onions. Cook over medium heat about 10 minutes, or until pork and onions are golden brown. Scrape salt pork bits, onions and fat in pan into Dutch oven with meat. Add mushrooms. Cover and simmer 45 minutes or until meat is fork tender.
4. Serve with plain boiled potatoes.
5. Makes 6 to 8 servings.

CARBONNADES FLAMANDE

2 pounds dry onions
Butter
3 pounds chuck or round steak, cut in cubes
Flour
Salt and pepper
3 cloves garlic
1 cup beer

1. Peel and slice onions. Melt about 4 tablespoons butter in a Dutch oven. Cook onion until soft and lightly browned. Remove onion.
2. Dust chuck cubes with a little flour. Melt 4 tablespoons butter in Dutch oven. Add

cubes and brown over high heat. Return onion to Dutch oven.
3. Season with salt and pepper. Add garlic and beer.
4. Cover tightly and simmer about 1¼ hours or until beef is tender.
5. Mix together 2 tablespoons flour with 2 tablespoons cold water to make a paste. Drop into sauce in small pieces. Cook, stirring, until sauce thickens slightly and comes to a boil. Taste and add more salt and pepper if desired.
6. Makes 6 servings.

DAUBE PROVENÇALE

5 pound rump of beef
3 or 4 slices salt pork
2 pig's feet or 1 calf's foot
2 bay leaves
8 cloves garlic
1 whole clove
1 strip orange peel
1 teaspoon rosemary
Several sprigs parsley
1 tablespoon salt
2 teaspoons freshly ground black pepper
Red wine
Cooked macaroni

1. Place beef in a large bowl or casserole. Add salt pork, pig's feet, bay leaves, garlic, clove, orange peel, rosemary, parsley, salt and pepper. Cover meat with red wine. Cover bowl with aluminum foil and let stand for at least 24 hours.
2. Place meat and marinating ingredients in a heavy casserole or Dutch oven.
3. Heat oven to 200°F.
4. Cook about 6 hours or until meat is tender.
5. Remove meat to a hot serving platter. Let stand for about 15 minutes before slicing.
6. Skim excess fat off liquid in pan. Strain sauce and serve part of it with cooked macaroni, a traditional accompaniment for this dish.
7. This is excellent served cold. Strain the sauce and let it cool. Slice the meat and arrange on a serving platter. Cover with sauce. Place in refrigerator and allow the sauce to jell over slices of meat.
8. Makes 8 to 10 servings.

BEEF TENDERLOIN

1 whole beef tenderloin, 4 to 6 pounds
Salad oil
Garlic

1. Heat oven to 450°F.
2. Remove surface fat and connective tissue from beef tenderloin. Place on a rack in a shallow roasting pan. Turn narrow end of tenderloin under to make the roast an even thickness.
3. Rub top of meat with cut clove of garlic. Brush with oil or cover top with strips of suet.
4. Insert a meat thermometer into the center of the thickest part of the meat.
5. Roast 45 to 60 minutes or until meat thermometer registers rare.
6. Cut in slices about 1-inch thick and serve with wine or mushroom sauce.
7. Makes 8 to 10 servings.

FILET DE BOEUF, DUC DE ROQUEFORT

½ **cup celery, coarsley chopped**
1 **small onion, sliced**
1 **bay leaf, crumbled**
¼ **teaspoon dried rosemary**
3½ **to 4 pound filet of beef**
Butter
Salt
Pepper
2 **tablespoons cognac**
3 **cups sifted flour**
½ **cup shortening**
Ice water
½ **pound Roquefort cheese**
1 **egg yolk**
1 **tablespoon milk**
1 **cup veal stock or chicken bouillon**
1 **truffle, minced (optional)**

1. Heat oven to 450°F.
2. Place celery, onion, bay leaf and rosemary in the bottom of a baking pan.
3. Cover filet with a generous coating of butter. Sprinkle with salt and freshly ground black pepper. Place on top of celery mixture in baking pan. Bake 30 minutes.
4. Remove filet from oven. Warm cognac and pour over top of filet. Ignite with a match and allow flames to burn out. Let meat stand in pan and cool completely while preparing pastry covering.
5. Sift together flour and 1 teaspoon salt into a mixing bowl. Cut in shortening with a pastry blender or two knives to the consistency of cornmeal. Add about 4 tablespoons ice water, or enough to make the dough stick together. Shape into a ball, wrap in waxed paper and chill.
6. On a lightly floured board, roll dough into a rectangle about ⅛-inch thick.

7. Remove filet from pan, leaving vegetables in pan. Force Roquefort cheese through a sieve and mix it into a paste. Spread cheese over top and sides of filet.
8. Place filet on center of pastry. Wrap pastry around filet, trimming edges as needed. Secure ends with a bit of cold water.
9. Place filet on a baking sheet. Beat together egg yolk and milk. Brush top of pastry with egg yolk mixture.
10. Bake 15 minutes or until pastry is nicely browned.
11. While filet is baking, remove as much fat as possible from top of vegetables in roasting pan. Add veal stock and place over medium heat. Simmer, stirring constantly to bring up all browned bits of meat from bottom of pan. Strain mixture into a saucepan.
12. Chop truffle and add to sauce. Let simmer about 15 minutes to blend flavors. Stir in 1 tablespoon softened butter just before serving.
13. Remove filet to a heated serving platter. Cut in generous slices and serve with truffle sauce.
14. Makes about 6 to 8 servings.

BEEF SCALLOP FLAMBÉ

1½ **pound filet of beef**
4 **tablespoons butter**
2 **tablespoons salad oil**
¼ **cup cognac**
Salt and pepper
¼ **cup chopped shallots**
½ **cup finely snipped parsley**
2 **tablespoons Worcestershire sauce**
2 **tablespoons chili sauce**
3 **tablespoons Madeira**

1. Cut filet of beef in thin slices similar to veal slices used in veal scallopini.
2. Heat butter and oil in a heavy skillet over very high heat. Add scallops and fry very quickly, to brown on both sides. This should take about 2 minutes. Warm the cognac. Pour over meat and ignite with a match. Let flames burn out. Season to taste with salt and pepper. Remove to a hot serving platter. Keep warm.
3. Pour most of the fat out of skillet. Add shallots, parsley, Worcestershire sauce, chili sauce and Madeira. Bring to a boil and simmer 2 minutes. Season to taste. Pour over beef on platter.
4. Makes 4 to 6 servings.

In France the beef carcass is cut in a different manner than here at home. French butchers follow muscle separations for cutting the carcass while American butchers cut cross grain, leaving the bones on in many cases. Because the cuts are different, it may help to explain some of the names you will see on French menus or in some of the recipes.

Entrecote: A steak cut from the rib roast section, similar to our rib or club steak.

Rumsteck: Cut from the end of the rump.

Contre Filet: A steak cut from the loin of beef. This particular piece of meat is usually left on in American markets and sold as part of a Porterhouse or T-Bone steak.

In France the whole filet of beef is removed from the animal and cut into three different parts. In America you will occasionally find filets on sale; however, usually you will have to put in a special order to the butcher.
   1. The large end, or the sirloin end, is considered the least tender in France and is called Bifteck.
   2. The middle section is cut into steaks about 2 inches thick and called Chauteaubriand. A 1-inch steak cut from this section becomes a filet.
   3. The skinny end of the filet or that found in the T-bone section is cut into Tournedos and wrapped in salt pork strips or slices of bacon. The even smaller end is cut into Filet Mignon, and is considered the most tender.

BEEF WELLINGTON

1 recipe pastry
1 whole beef tenderloin, 4 to 6 pounds
1 clove garlic, halved
Salt and pepper
4 pieces suet or 6 strips bacon
Forcemeat Filling or Chicken Liver Pâté
3 to 4 truffles, optional
1 egg, lightly beaten
Sauce Madeira

1. Prepare pastry (recipe follows).
2. Heat oven to 450°F.
3. Rub the filet all over with the cut side of garlic. Sprinkle with salt and pepper. Cover with suet or bacon strips, securing with string if necessary. Place on rack in roasting pan. Insert meat thermometer into thickest part of filet.
4. Roast 45 to 50 minutes or until meat thermometer registers rare.
5. Cool meat slightly. Remove suet and place meat in refrigerator until final preparation.
6. Heat oven to 425°F.
7. On a lightly floured board roll pastry into an 18-by 18-inch square or large enough to enclose beef.
8. Lay beef along one edge of pastry. Cover with forcemeat or pâté. Cut truffles in halves and place along the top in a line. Lift pastry up over beef, overlapping it under meat and sealing edges. Trim off a few small ends of pastry for garnish. Brush edges with beaten egg to seal.

9. Carefully place beef on baking sheet, sealed edge down.
10. Cut decorative shapes from pastry trimmings and arrange down center of pastry. Brush all over with beaten egg.
11. Bake about 30 minutes or until pastry is cooked and lightly browned.
12. Remove carefully with two broad spatulas to a hot serving platter. Cut in fairly thick crosswise slices and serve plain or with Sauce Madeira.
13. Makes 10 to 12 servings.

PASTRY

4 cups flour
1 teaspoon salt
½ cup butter
½ cup shortening
1 egg, lightly beaten
Ice water

1. Place the flour, salt, butter and shortening in a mixing bowl. Blend together with a pastry blender or fingertips until mixture resembles large bread crumbs. Add egg and enough ice water to make mixture form a ball. Wrap in waxed paper and chill in refrigerator.
2. This should be made in advance and can be made the day before final preparation.

Beef Wellington is a classic French dish for a very, very special occasion. Tenderloin of beef is covered with forcemeat or pâté and baked in a crust.

FORCEMEAT

¼ cup butter or margarine
¼ cup chopped onion
½ cup chopped mushrooms
¼ cup cognac
½ pound finely ground veal
½ pound finely ground pork
1 egg, lightly beaten
¼ cup heavy cream
¼ cup chopped parsley
1 teaspoon salt
¼ teaspoon basil
¼ teaspoon thyme
¼ teaspoon rosemary
⅛ teaspoon ground allspice
⅛ teaspoon pepper

1. Melt butter in a small saucepan. Add onion and cook until onion is tender but not browned. Stir in mushrooms and cognac and cook over medium heat 5 to 10 minutes.
2. Turn mixture into a large bowl. Add remaining ingredients and mix lightly but thoroughly.
3. Cover and refrigerate until ready to use.

SAUCE MADEIRA

2 tablespoons butter or margarine
2 tablespoons finely chopped shallots
1½ cups canned beef gravy
2 tablespoons lemon juice
¼ cup Madeira

1. Melt the butter in a small saucepan over medium heat. Add shallots and cook until tender but not browned.
2. Add gravy and lemon juice and bring to a boil. Stir in Madeira and heat thoroughly.
3. Makes 1½ cups sauce.

CHICKEN LIVER PÂTÉ

6 tablespoons butter
¼ cup chopped shallots
2 cloves garlic, finely chopped
1 pound chicken livers
¼ cup cognac or Madeira
4 thin slices ham, diced
Salt and pepper

1. Melt butter in a heavy skillet over medium heat. Add shallots and garlic and cook until tender but not browned.
2. Turn heat to high. Add chicken livers and cook quickly until browned on all sides. Add cognac and stir to scrape up browned particles from bottom of skillet.

3. Add diced ham and simmer 2 minutes. Cool.
4. Turn mixture out onto a chopping board and chop very fine or put mixture through a meat grinder. Add salt and pepper to taste.

FONDUE BOURGUIGNONNE

1 cup butter
1 cup salad oil
Sauces
2½ pound filet of beef, well trimmed and cut into ½-inch cubes

1. Place butter and oil in fondue pan. Place over medium heat and heat to 375°F.
2. Place fondue pan on stand over canned heat flame. Keep oil sizzling hot during cooking time.
3. On the table place bowls of as many different dipping sauces as desired.
4. Serve each person a plate containing raw chunks of beef. Give each person 2 forks, one two-pronged fondue fork and one dinner fork. Pierce a chunk of meat with the fondue fork. Hold meat in the hot oil and brown according to taste; rare, medium or well done will take from 10 to 30 seconds.
5. Transfer meat to dinner fork, dip cooked meat into a sauce of choice and eat. Meanwhile, spear another cube of meat with fondue fork and place in hot oil.
6. Makes 6 to 8 servings.

BÉARNAISE SAUCE

¼ cup tarragon vinegar
¼ cup dry white wine or dry Vermouth
2 teaspoons tarragon leaves
1 tablespoon chopped shallots
½ cup butter or margarine
1 egg
¼ teaspoon salt
Pinch of cayenne

1. Combine vinegar, wine, tarragon leaves and shallots in a small stainless steel or earthenware saucepan. Cook over low heat until mixture is reduced to 2 tablespoons. Remove from heat, cool slightly.
2. Melt butter in the top of a double boiler over hot, not boiling water. Be sure that the bottom of the double boiler does not touch the water.
3. Add egg, salt, cayenne and reduced liquid. Beat with a wire whisk until mixture is smooth and thick.
4. Remove from hot water at once.
5. Makes ¾ cup sauce.

BLENDER BÉARNAISE SAUCE

2 tablespoons dry white wine
1 tablespoon tarragon vinegar
2 teaspoons dried tarragon
2 teaspoons minced shallots
½ cup butter
3 egg yolks
¼ teaspoon pepper
2 tablespoons lemon juice
¼ teaspoon salt

1. In a small saucepan combine the wine, vinegar, tarragon and shallots. Bring to boil and cook rapidly until almost all the liquid disappears.
2. In a small saucepan heat the butter until it is bubbling, but do not brown.
3. In the container of an electric blender place the egg yolks, pepper, lemon juice and salt. Cover the container and flick the motor on and off at high speed.
4. Remove cover, turn motor on high and gradually add the bubbling butter. Add the herb mixture, cover and blend very quickly on high speed.
5. Makes about 1 cup sauce.

MUSTARD SAUCE

¼ cup prepared mustard
¼ cup mayonnaise
1 clove garlic, crushed
¼ teaspoon Tabasco

1. Combine all ingredients. Refrigerate until ready to serve.
2. Makes about ½ cup sauce.

TOMATO-MUSHROOM SAUCE

⅔ cup catsup
2 tablespoons chopped cooked or canned mushrooms
¼ teaspoon Tabasco

1. Combine all ingredients. Refrigerate until ready to serve.
2. Makes about ½ cup sauce.

SAUCE SMETANE

¾ cup dairy sour cream
1 to 2 tablespoons grated horseradish
Salt and pepper

1. Combine the sour cream with the prepared horseradish. Season to taste with salt and pepper. There is a wide difference among various prepared horseradish sauces — some are mild whereas others are very strong — so taste often while preparing

sauce. Refrigerate until ready to serve.
2. Makes about ¾ cup sauce.

TOURNEDOS

6 tournedos wrapped with bacon
Olive oil
Finely chopped garlic
Finely chopped parsley
1 cup dry white wine
Salt and pepper
6 slices fried bread (preferably French bread)

1. Place tournedos in an ovenproof glass pie dish. Top with enough oil to moisten each steak. Sprinkle with garlic and parsley. Let stand in the refrigerator 24 hours.
2. Heat a heavy skillet over very high heat. Sear tournedos quickly in hot skillet on both sides. Dribble in wine, a little at a time, so that the tournedos will go on cooking and not drown in the wine. When tournedos are done to your liking, remove and place each one on a slice of fried bread.
3. Serve with sauce from skillet.
4. Makes 6 servings.

STEAK DIANE

4 sirloin strip steaks, cut ½-inch thick
Salt
Freshly ground black pepper
1 teaspoon dry mustard
¼ cup butter
3 tablespoons lemon juice
2 teaspoons snipped chives
1 teaspoon Worcestershire sauce

1. With a meat mallet or the bottom of a heavy saucepan, pound steaks to ⅓ inch thickness. Sprinkle one side of each steak with salt, pepper and ⅛ teaspoon dry mustard. Pound mixture into meat. Repeat with other side of meat.
2. Melt butter in skillet over medium high heat.
3. When butter is very hot add steaks and cook 2 minutes on each side. Remove steak to a hot serving platter.
4. Add lemon juice, chives and Worcestershire sauce to drippings in skillet. Bring to boil. Pour over meat.
5. Makes 4 servings.

Note: For a very special party touch, Steak Diane may be prepared at the dinner table in a chafing dish or electric skillet.

QUICK WINE STEAKS

1 package (1 ounce) beef gravy mix
1 cup beef bouillon
1 cup dry red wine
1 tablespoon red currant jelly
6 thin, tender steaks, cut just less than ½ inch thick
1 teaspoon salt
¼ teaspoon pepper
¼ cup butter or margarine

1. Prepare beef gravy mix according to directions on the package, using 1 cup beef bouillon. Stir in wine and jelly. Heat and stir until jelly dissolves.
2. Sprinkle steaks with salt and pepper.
3. Heat butter in a large, heavy skillet over high heat. Brown steaks very quickly in hot butter. Pour wine sauce over steaks and cook over high heat 3 to 4 minutes, or until steaks are cooked to desired degree of doneness.
4. Makes 6 servings.

FRENCH STEAKS

2 tablespoons butter
1½ tablespoons salad oil
2 pounds beef steak, ¾ to 1 inch thick
½ cup beef bouillon or dry red wine
2 tablespoons softened butter

1. Put butter and oil in a heavy skillet over high heat. When the butter has foamed and begins to subside it is right for the steak.
2. Cut steak in 4 pieces, or use 4 cuts of small steak. Fry steak on one side 3 to 4 minutes. Turn steak and brown on other side 3 to 4 minutes, depending on desired degree of doneness. Test for doneness by cutting a small incision in the steak.
3. Remove steak to a hot platter and season with salt and pepper. Keep warm.
4. Pour fat out of skillet. Add bouillon or dry red wine and cook over high heat. Scrape up brown bits from bottom of the pan and boil until liquid is reduced almost to a syrup. Remove from heat and stir in butter until it has melted. Pour sauce over steak.
5. Makes 4 servings.

PEPPER STEAK

3 pound boneless sirloin steak
3 tablespoons whole peppercorns
1 tablespoon salad oil
2 tablespoons butter, divided
½ cup dry red wine
2 tablespoons brandy
1 teaspoon salt

1. Wipe steak with a damp paper towel. Place peppercorns on a board and crush with a rolling pin, or crush in a mortar and pestle. Pat crushed peppercorns on both sides of steak, so that they stick to steak.
2. Heat a large, heavy skillet over high heat. Add oil and 1 tablespoon butter. When foam begins to subside, add steak. Brown on both sides, about 2 minutes on each side. Reduce heat to medium and cook about 8 minutes on each side for medium rare. Make a small slit in steak to check for doneness, and cook to your own taste.
3. Remove steak to a hot serving platter and keep warm.
4. Add remaining butter, wine, brandy and salt to skillet. Simmer, stirring, about 3 minutes. Pour sauce over steak.
5. Makes 6 servings.

BEEF ROULADES WITH ROQUEFORT
(shown opposite)

6 cubed beef steaks, about 1½ pounds
1 teaspoon salt
¼ teaspoon pepper
½ cup crumbled Roquefort cheese, packed
1 can (3 ounces) mushroom pieces
1 tablespoon minced onion
2 tablespoons flour
2 tablespoons shortening
1 can (12 ounces) vegetable juice cocktail
1 tablespoon Worcestershire sauce

1. Sprinkle steaks with half of the salt, pepper and Roquefort cheese.
2. Drain mushrooms, reserving juice. Combine mushrooms, onion and remaining salt and pepper. Sprinkle mixture over Roquefort cheese on steaks.
3. Roll up steaks and fasten securely with wooden picks. Dredge rolls in flour.
4. Heat shortening in a large skillet over medium heat. Brown rolls well on all sides in hot fat. Pour off as much fat as possible from the skillet.
5. Combine juice drained from mushrooms,

vegetable juice cocktail and Worcestershire sauce. Pour mixture around beef. Cover skillet tightly and cook over low heat 40 minutes or until tender.

6. Remove roulades to a heated platter. Stir remaining Roquefort cheese into sauce in pan. Cook, stirring to bring up browned bits from bottom of pan, until sauce is blended. Pour sauce over roulades.

7. Makes 6 servings.

BEEF ROULADES

2½ **pounds round steak**
¾ **pound ground pork**
1 **teaspoon poultry seasoning**
¾ **teaspoon salt**
½ **clove garlic, crushed**
2 **tablespoons finely chopped onion**
¼ **cup soft white bread crumbs**
8 **slices bacon**
3 **tablespoons butter or margarine**
8 **small white onions, peeled**
⅓ **cup flour**
1 **can (10 ounces) beef bouillon**
2½ **cups dry red wine**
1½ **pounds fresh mushrooms**
1 **bay leaf**

1. Cut round steak into 8 equal-sized pieces, ⅛ inch thick.

2. Combine ground pork, poultry seasoning, salt, garlic, onion and bread crumbs. Toss lightly.

3. Place about 2 tablespoons of mixture on each piece of beef. Roll up. Wrap each roll with a slice of bacon and tie with heavy thread.

4. Melt butter in a Dutch oven over medium high heat. Brown beef rolls on all sides in hot butter. Remove meat from Dutch oven. Add onion and brown lightly all over. Remove onion. Remove Dutch oven from heat.

5. Stir in flour. Gradually stir in bouillon and wine. Return to medium heat and cook, stirring constantly, until mixture comes to a boil. Return meat and onion to Dutch oven. Add mushrooms and bay leaf. Simmer over low heat 1½ to 2 hours, or until meat is tender. If sauce gets too thick during cooking time, thin with a little more red wine.

6. Before serving, remove thread from beef roulades. Serve with onions and mushrooms and gravy from pan.

7. Makes 4 to 6 servings.

To someone visiting France for the first time, it comes as a surprise to find that French people adore hamburgers. Their hamburgers are made from lean beef and mixed with a variety of other ingredients. They are usually pan-fried, much as steak, and finished off with a sauce.

However, a popular innovation from America is hamburger quick lunch counters and restaurants. The French enjoy a quick hamburger on a bun, with a cup of coffee or a soft drink, much as we do here. But most Frenchmen do not pick up a hamburger and bun in the hands, as we do, but leave it on the plate and eat it with fork and knife. The favorite in Paris is a hamburger with a fried egg on top, which may account for the use of knife and fork!

FRENCH HAMBURGER

¼ cup finely minced onion
  Butter
1½ pounds ground lean beef
1½ teaspoons salt
⅛ teaspoon pepper
⅛ teaspoon thyme
1 egg, lightly beaten
  Flour
1 tablespoon salad oil
½ cup beef bouillon or dry red wine or white wine

1. Cook onion in about 2 tablespoons butter until tender but not browned. Scrape onion and butter into a mixing bowl.
2. Add beef, salt, pepper, thyme and egg. Mix lightly to blend thoroughly. Form into patties about ¾ inch thick.
3. Just before cooking, dust patties lightly with flour.
4. Place 1 tablespoon butter and salad oil in skillet over high heat. When foam begins to subside, add patties and fry 2 to 3 minutes on each side, or longer if well done meat is preferred.
5. Remove patties and place on a warm serving platter. Keep warm.
6. Pour off all fat from skillet. Add liquid and boil rapidly, scraping brown bits from bottom of pan. When liquid is reduced almost to a syrup remove from heat. Stir in about 2 tablespoons softened butter. Pour sauce over hamburgers.
7. Makes 4 to 6 servings.

WINE BURGERS

1 pound ground chuck
½ cup dry red wine, divided
1 teaspoon salt
⅛ teaspoon pepper
2 tablespoons snipped parsley
2 tablespoons snipped chives

1. Combine chuck, ¼ cup red wine, salt and pepper. Mix lightly. Shape into 4 patties.

2. Heat butter in a skillet over medium high heat. Fry patties on both sides to the desired degree of doneness. Remove patties and place on heated serving dish.
3. Pour off fat from skillet. Add remaining wine, parsley and chives. Cook over high heat about 1 minute, stirring up browned bits from bottom of pan. Pour sauce over patties.
4. Makes 4 servings.

GROUND STEAK PARISIAN

2½ pounds ground lean beef
  Salt and pepper
⅔ cup crumbled Roquefort cheese
¼ cup butter
½ pound mushrooms, sliced
1¼ cups dry red wine

1. Season beef lightly with salt and pepper. Mix lightly. Divide into 12 oval patties. Divide Roquefort cheese evenly on 6 of the patties. Place remaining patties on top of cheese and seal edges.
2. Melt 2 tablespoons butter in a skillet. Add mushrooms and brown lightly. Remove mushrooms.
3. Add remaining butter to skillet. Brown meat patties on both sides in hot butter.
4. Return mushrooms to skillet. Add wine and simmer, uncovered, 5 minutes, basting meat constantly. Serve immediately.
5. Makes 6 servings.

SUZETTE'S MEATBALLS

1 cup fresh bread crumbs
2 tablespoons milk
  Butter
2 onions, chopped
1½ pounds chuck, ground twice
2 egg yolks
1 teaspoon curry powder
¼ teaspoon sage or thyme
¼ teaspoon mace
¼ teaspoon marjoram or oregano
¼ teaspoon tarragon or basil
  Salt and pepper
  Dry bread crumbs
2½ cups dairy sour cream
1 teaspoon lemon juice
  Chopped dill or parsley

1. Combine fresh bread crumbs and milk and set aside.
2. Melt 4 tablespoons butter in a small skillet. Add onion and sauté until golden brown.
3. In a mixing bowl combine ground chuck, egg yolks and cooked onion. Squeeze any excess milk from bread crumbs and add crumbs to meat. Add seasonings. Mix thoroughly with your hands. Shape mixture into small even balls. Press a small lump of firm butter into center of each ball. Roll balls in dry bread crumbs. Pat well in hands so the crumbs will stick. Chill for 30 minutes so that crumbs will stick to the meatballs a little better.
4. Melt 4 tablespoons of butter in a large skillet. Add meat balls and cook until golden brown on all sides and cooked through. Remove meatballs to a hot serving dish and keep warm.
5. Pour off almost all the fat from the skillet. Stir in the sour cream, lemon juice and chopped dill. Heat, scraping bits from bottom of skillet, but do not boil. Taste for seasoning. Pour sauce over meatballs.
6. Makes about 6 servings.

STEAK TARTARE

1 pound sirloin or round steak
½ cup finely chopped green onion
4 egg yolks
  Minced onions
  Capers
  Chopped parsley
  Salt
  Freshly ground black pepper
  Pumpernickel or rye bread

1. Have butcher remove all fat from meat and have meat put through the grinder twice.

2. Place meat in a bowl, add green onion and toss lightly with a fork.
3. Divide meat and pile lightly on 4 serving plates. Make an indentation in the center and slip in a raw egg yolk. Garnish with minced onion, capers and parsley.
4. Serve with salt, freshly ground black pepper and thinly sliced pumpernickel or rye bread.
5. Makes 4 servings.

MUSHROOM WINE BURGERS

1 pound ground chuck
¼ cup cream
¼ cup milk
1 tablespoon minced onion
1 teaspoon salt
¼ teaspoon pepper
2 tablespoons butter or margarine
2 tablespoons flour
½ cup beef bouillon
½ cup red dinner wine
1 teaspoon Worcestershire sauce
2 tablespoons chopped parsley
1 can (4 ounces) sliced mushrooms
3 or 4 slices toast

1. Combine chuck, cream, milk, onion, salt and pepper. Toss lightly with a fork. Shape into 3 or 4 thick patties.
2. Pan fry patties in hot butter in a skillet just until browned on both sides. Remove patties and keep warm.
3. Add flour to the drippings in the skillet. Stir in bouillon and wine. Cook, stirring constantly, until mixture boils and thickens. Add Worcestershire sauce, parsley and mushrooms with liquid. Season to taste with salt and pepper.
4. Return patties to sauce and simmer until meat is cooked to the desired degree of doneness.
5. Place meat patties on toast and pour sauce over the top.
6. Makes 3 or 4 servings.

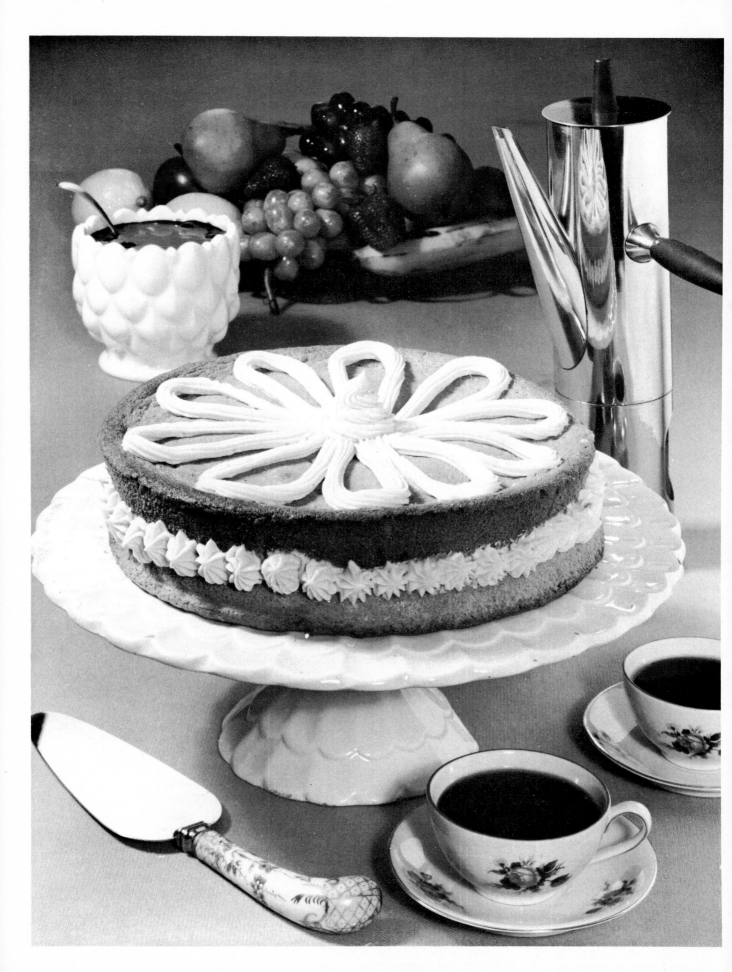

Desserts

When it comes to desserts, the French have a reputation for some of the best in the world. Nothing is more tempting than a tray of luscious French pastry made up of cream puffs, Napoleons and cream-filled or fruit-topped tarts. The French are famous for dessert soufflés, high and puffy, served piping hot and often laced with flavorful liquors. Flaming desserts rate high for restaurant fare, but Cherries Jubilee and flaming Crepes Suzettes can also be made at home.

However, do not dream blissfully of having gorgeous desserts like this every night of the week. You will find that most French people eat fruit and cheese for dessert at home and if they have anything sweet it is likely to be a simple pudding. Fancy French pastries are usually bought at the bakery which even in small towns has a wondrous display of the baker's art. Flaming desserts are reserved for dining out or for very special occasions.

ROUE AUX MARRONS
(shown opposite)

6 eggs
1½ cups sugar, divided
1 cup sifted flour
Butter
½ teaspoon almond extract
1 teaspoon grated lemon rind
1 cup confectioners' sugar
2 tablespoons kirsch
1 can (15¾ ounces) unsweetened chestnut purée
Water
2 squares (2 ounces) unsweetened chocolate
2 tablespoons rum
2 teaspoons grated orange rind.

1. Break eggs into a mixing bowl and let stand until they reach room temperature.
2. Heat oven to 350°F.
3. Grease the bottoms of 2 9-inch layer cake pans. Cut 2 9-inch circles of waxed paper. Place in bottom of pans and grease waxed paper.
4. With an electric mixer beat eggs until foamy. Gradually beat in 1 cup sugar, 2 tablespoonsful at a time. Beat until mixture resembles whipped cream and holds soft peaks. Sift flour over top of eggs and fold in carefully with a rubber scraper. Fold in ¼ cup melted butter, almond extract and lemon rind.
5. Divide batter between 2 prepared pans. Bake 25 to 30 minutes or until top springs back when lightly touched in the center with the fingers. Loosen edges of cake layers with a sharp knife and turn out on a cake rack to cool. Remove waxed paper before cooling. Cool thoroughly before frosting.
6. Cream ½ cup butter until light and fluffy. Gradually stir in confectioners' sugar, kirsch and chestnut purée. Beat until smooth and shiny. Spread half the filling over the top of one layer. Top with second layer. Put remaining frosting in pastry bag. Garnish top and sides of cake with frosting,

as shown.

7. Combine water and ½ cup sugar in a saucepan and boil for 5 minutes. Add chocolate and stir until chocolate is melted. Cool sauce. Stir in rum and orange rind.
8. To serve, cut cake in serving pieces. Pass sauce to pour over top of cake.
9. Makes one 9-inch cake.

VACHERIN

6 egg whites
2 cups sugar
¼ teaspoon salt
1½ teaspoons lemon juice
2 pints vanilla ice cream, softened
1 cup heavy cream
½ cup diced marrons glace (preserved chestnuts)

1. Heat oven to 275°F.
2. Draw 2 circles, each 9 inches in diameter, on heavy brown paper. Place the paper on a baking sheet.
3. Beat egg whites until stiff. Gradually beat in combined sugar and salt. Add lemon juice alternately with last ½ cup of the sugar. Continue beating until mixture is very stiff and glossy.
4. Divide egg white mixture between the circles on brown paper, spreading it out to the edges of the circles, and smoothing the surface.
5. Bake 1 hour and 15 minutes. Remove from oven and let cool on brown paper.
6. Slip a long thin spatula between the meringue and paper to loosen without breaking. Place one layer on a flat cake plate or tray. Spread with 1 pint softened ice cream. Whip cream until stiff and spread half of cream over ice cream. Sprinkle with half the marrons. Repeat, using second layer, ice cream, whipped cream and maroons.
7. Set Vacherin in freezer until ready to serve. Do not hold for more than 1 hour. Use a thin, sharp knife to cut into wedge-shaped pieces.

BÛCHE DE NOËL

4 eggs, separated
1⅔ cups sugar, divided
½ teaspoon vanilla
1 cup sifted cake flour
½ teaspoon baking powder
¼ teaspoon salt
3 tablespoons rum, divided
⅓ cup water
2 egg yolks
½ cup butter or margarine, softened
1½ squares unsweetened chocolate, melted
1 teaspoon instant coffee powder

1. Heat oven to 375°F.
2. Grease the bottom of a 15½- by 10½- by 1-inch jelly roll pan. Dust the greased surface with flour. Shake off excess flour.
3. Beat the egg yolks until thick and lemon colored. Gradually add ½ cup sugar, beating constantly. Stir in vanilla.
4. In large mixer bowl, beat the egg whites until soft peaks form. Gradually add ½ cup sugar, beating until egg whites stand in stiff peaks.
5. Gently fold egg yolk mixture into egg white mixture. Sift together flour, baking powder and salt. Sift over top of egg mixture and fold in gently.
6. Spread mixture evenly in prepared jelly roll pan. Bake 10 to 12 minutes or until top springs back when lightly touched.
7. Loosen edges of cake. Immediately turn out onto a kitchen towel that has been liberally sprinkled with confectioners' sugar. Sprinkle cake evenly with 2 tablespoons rum. Roll up cake and towel, starting at long side. Cool.
8. In a small saucepan combine ⅔ cup sugar and water. Bring to a boil and cook to 240°F. on a candy thermometer or to the soft ball stage.
9. In a small mixing bowl, beat egg yolks until thick and lemon colored. Very gradually add the hot syrup, beating constantly. Continue beating until mixture is completely cool. Beat in the softened butter, 1 tablespoonful at a time. Add chocolate and remaining rum and instant coffee powder. Continue beating until thick.
10. Unroll cake. Spread evenly with half of the filling. Roll cake up starting at long side. Cut a 4-inch piece from end of roll, cutting on the diagonal. On a serving platter, place 4-inch piece along side of large roll, at an angle to look like a tree branch. Frost with remaining filling. Mark frosting with tines of fork to resemble bark on a tree.

GÉNOISE HÉLÈNE

4 eggs
½ cup sugar
1½ teaspoons vanilla, divided
Dash of salt
1 cup sifted cake flour
½ cup butter, melted and cooled
1 can (1 pound 13 ounces) pear halves
½ cup apricot preserves
1 package (6 ounces) semi-sweet chocolate pieces
2 cups dairy sour cream, divided
¼ cup confectioners' sugar
¼ teaspoon grated nutmeg

1. Heat oven to 350°F.
2. Generously butter the bottom of two 8-inch round cake pans. Dust with flour. Set aside.
3. Place eggs, sugar, 1 teaspoon vanilla and salt in a mixing bowl which can be set in a larger bowl filled with hot water. Beat until very light and fluffy and doubled in volume (about 5 minutes with an electric mixer).
4. Remove bowl from water and continue beating until stiff peaks form and mixture is glossy (about 10 minutes on high speed with an electric mixer).
5. Sift one third of the flour over batter and very gently fold into the mixture. Repeat with second third of the flour and then last third of flour. Very carefully fold in melted butter.
6. Divide batter in half between the two prepared cake pans. Bake 35 to 40 minutes or until top springs back when touched lightly with fingers.
7. Remove from oven and cool on wire racks for 5 minutes. Turn out of pans onto racks to cool completely.
8. Drain pears, reserving syrup. In a small bowl mix together ¼ cup of the syrup with the apricot preserves. Set aside for glaze.
9. Melt chocolate pieces over hot water. Cool slightly. Stir in 1 cup of the sour cream until well blended. Set aside for glaze.
10. To assemble genoise, split each cake layer in half, crosswise. Place bottom half of a layer on a cake plate. Spread with a thin coating of the apricot glaze. Spread with 3 tablespoons of the chocolate-sour cream mixture. Add top half of layer and repeat coating of glaze and chocolate. Repeat with second layer, spreading some glaze and chocolate mixture on top and sides of cake. Place in refrigerator to chill.
11. In a chilled bowl, with chilled beaters, beat remaining cup of sour cream until doubled

in volume. This will take about 5 minutes. Fold in confectioners' sugar, ½ teaspoon vanilla and nutmeg.

12. Remove cake from refrigerator. Arrange 6 pear halves, cut side down, on top of génoise with narrow ends towards center. Fill in center and between pears with sour cream mixture. Chill about ½ hour before serving.

13. Dice remaining pears. Fold into remaining sour cream mixture and serve as a sauce with the génoise.

14. Makes 12 servings.

COUQUES

½ cup warm water (105-115°F)
1 package or cake yeast, active dry or compressed
2¼ cups unsifted flour, divided
½ cup butter or margarine, melted
3 eggs, beaten
¼ cup sugar
½ teaspoon salt
2 cans (1 pound each) pear halves, drained
¼ cup dark brown sugar, firmly packed
¼ cup butter or margarine
½ teaspoon cinnamon
½ teaspoon nutmeg
Whipped cream

1. Measure warm water into a large warm bowl. Sprinkle or crumble in yeast; stir until dissolved. Stir in ½ cup flour. Cover and let rise in a warm place, free from draft, about 30 minutes.

2. Blend in 1½ cups flour, ½ cup melted butter, eggs, sugar and salt. Beat until well blended. Cover and let rise in a warm place, free from draft, until doubled in bulk, about 1 hour.

3. Stir batter down. Cover and refrigerate at least 2 hours.

4. Grease twelve 10-ounce deep pie dishes. Place about ¼ cup batter in each dish. Using well floured hands, pat mixture around dishes, bringing it about 1 inch up the side of each dish. Place a pear half, cut side up, in each dish.

5. Combine remaining ¼ cup flour, and brown sugar in a small bowl. Cut in butter with a pastry blender or two knives. Stir in cinnamon and nutmeg. Sprinkle mixture over top of pears.

6. Let rise, uncovered, free from draft, about 30 minutes.

7. Heat oven to 375°F.

8. Bake about 15 minutes, or until done.

9. Remove from dishes and serve warm topped with whipped cream.

10. Makes 12 couques.

ROQUEFORT CHEESE CAKE

1 tablespoon butter or margarine, softened
⅓ cup packaged cereal crumbs
2 tablespoons flour
½ cup sugar, divided
5 packages (3 ounces each) cream cheese, softened to room temperature
½ cup crumbled Roquefort cheese, packed
3 eggs, separated
½ cup dairy sour cream
Dash of salt
2 teaspoons grated lemon rind
Strawberry Glaze

1. With softened butter, thoroughly butter sides and bottom of a 9-inch spring form pan. Sprinkle buttered surface with cereal crumbs.

2. Heat oven to 325°F.

3. In a bowl combine flour and half the sugar. Add cream cheese and Roquefort cheese and beat until smooth and fluffy.

4. Beat egg yolks until light. Blend the eggs into the cheese mixture. Stir in sour cream, salt and lemon rind.

5. Beat egg whites until soft peaks form. Gradually beat in remaining sugar; continue beating until stiff. Fold egg whites into cheese mixture. Pour into pan.

6. Bake 45 to 60 minutes or until cake is firm in the center. Turn off heat. Let stand in oven for 45 minutes.

7. Cool at room temperature and then chill.

8. Cover top with Strawberry Glaze. Loosen sides of pan and place on serving dish.

9. Makes 8 servings.

STRAWBERRY GLAZE

1 pint strawberries, washed and sliced
⅓ cup strawberry jelly
1 tablespoon cornstarch
¼ teaspoon cinnamon
⅓ cup water

1. Crush ½ cup of the sliced berries. In a saucepan combine crushed berries, jelly, cornstarch, cinnamon and water. Cook over low heat, stirring constantly, until mixture is smooth and clear. Strain sauce and cool slightly.

2. Arrange remaining berries over top of cheesecake. Spoon cooled mixture over top of berries, coating them evenly.

3. Chill at least 1 hour before serving.

GÂTEAU MARIGNAN

    Water
**2 packagaes or cakes yeast, active dry or
    compressed**
2 cups unsifted flour
4 eggs, slightly beaten
    Sugar
½ teaspoon salt
⅔ cup margarine, softened
1 jar (10 ounces) strawberry jelly
1½ cups heavy cream
2 cups sliced fresh strawberries

1. Measure ½ cup warm (105-115°F) water into a small warm bowl. Sprinkle or crumble in yeast. Stir until dissolved.
2. Place flour in a large bowl. Add eggs and dissolved yeast. Beat for 2 minutes.
3. Cover bowl and let rise in a warm place free from draft, about ½ hour or until bubbly and doubled in bulk.
4. Stir down. Add 1 tablespoon sugar, salt and softened margarine. Beat until well mixed and dough is elastic when dropped from a spoon, about 4 minutes. Turn into a well greased 3-quart ring mold. Let rise in a warm place, free from draft, about ½ hour or until doubled in bulk.
5. Heat oven to 450°F.
6. Bake 10 to 12 minutes or until done. Cool a few minutes, then turn out of ring mold and cool.
7. Form a basket by cutting inner ring from top of cake. Cut this thin ring in half for handles.
8. Melt jelly with 1 tablespoon water in a small saucepan. Brush over cake and handles.
9. Place handles on cake across the center at an angle so that they support each other like handles on a basket. Use toothpicks for added support if necessary.
10. Whip cream until stiff. Add 2 tablespoons sugar and beat just until well blended. Fold in strawberries.
11. Place cake on a serving platter. Fill center with cream mixture. Serve immediately.

GÂTEAU AUX CERISES

**2 packages (3 ounces each) cream cheese,
    softened**
¼ cup butter or margarine
½ cup sugar
2 teaspoons grated orange peel
1 teaspoon salt
3 eggs
    Water
**1 package or cake yeast, active dry or
    compressed**
2¼ cups unsifted flour
½ cup orange marmalade
1 can (1 pound) cherry pie filling
    Vanilla ice cream

1. Cream together cream cheese and butter until light and fluffy. Add sugar, grated orange peel, salt and eggs. Beat until very well blended.
2. Measure ¼ cup warm (105-115°F) water into a small warm bowl. Sprinkle or crumble in yeast. Stir until dissolved.
3. Add yeast and flour to cream cheese mixture. Beat until very well blended.
4. Cover top of bowl. Let rise in a warm place, free from draft, about 1 hour or until doubled in bulk.
5. Beat batter down and spoon into a greased 6½-cup ring mold. Let rise in a warm place, free from draft, about 1 hour or until doubled in bulk.
6. Heat oven to 375°F.
7. Bake ring 20 to 25 minutes or until done. Cool. When cold turn out onto a serving plate.
8. Combine orange marmalade and 1 tablespoon water. Cook over medium heat until marmalade becomes thin and begins to boil. Brush on cake.
9. Combine cherry pie filling and ½ cup water. Stir until blended.
10. Fill center of the cake with vanilla ice cream. Top with cherry sauce.

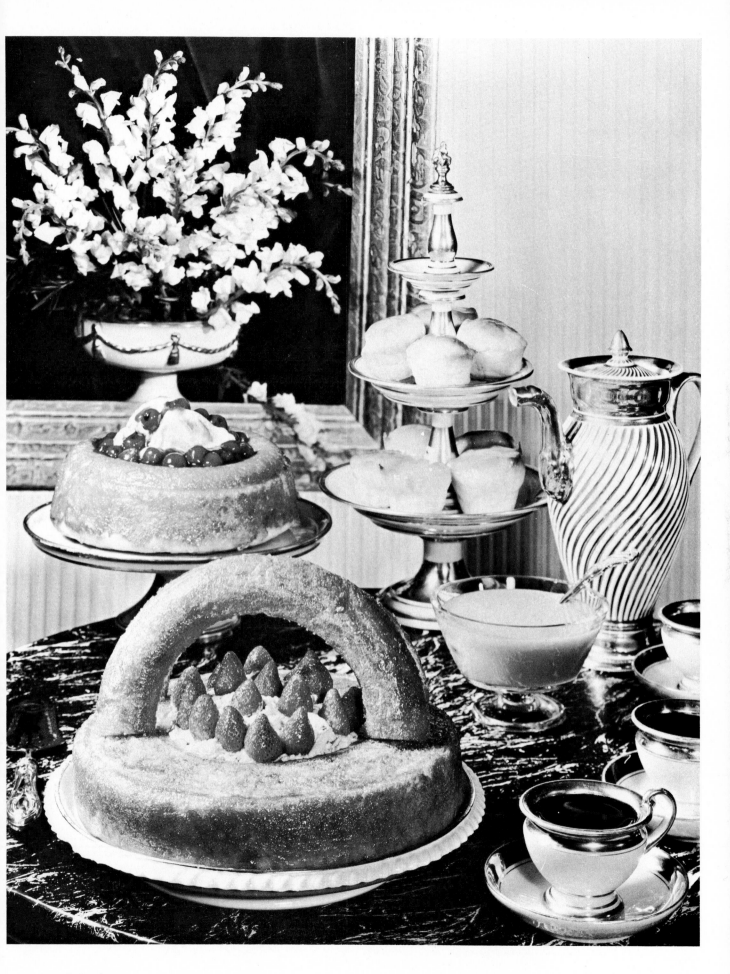

BABA AU RHUM

¼ cup milk
¼ cup warm water (105-115°F.)
1 package or cake yeast, active dry or
  compressed
¼ cup butter or margarine, softened
¼ cup sugar
3 eggs
2 cups unsifted flour
Rum Sauce

1. Put milk in a small saucepan and heat just until bubbles appear around edge of pan. Cool to lukewarm.
2. Measure warm water into large warm mixer bowl. Sprinkle or crumble in yeast. Stir until dissolved. Add milk, butter, sugar, eggs and flour. Blend at low speed of electric mixer for one minute, then beat 2 minutes at medium speed. Scrape down sides of bowl. Cover bowl and let rise in a warm place, free from draft, for 30 minutes.
3. Beat batter down with a wooden spoon. Spoon mixture into a greased 9-inch ring mold. Cover and let rise in a warm place, free from draft, until doubled in bulk.
4. Heat oven to 350°F.
5. Bake ring mold 30 minutes or until done.
6. Immediately prick surface with a fork, before removing from pan. Slowly pour rum sauce over cake. After syrup in absorbed, turn cake out on a serving plate.

RUM SAUCE

½ cup sugar
⅓ cup water
¼ cup rum

1. Combine sugar and water in a small saucepan. Bring to a boil.
2. Remove from heat and stir in rum. Pour over Baba.

Puff Paste

The pride and joy of every pastry chef and home baker is puff paste. It is the basis for many mouthwatering delicacies on the French pastry tray in a good restaurant. It can be fashioned into circles and filled with cream or jams. Pieces folded in half are filled with fruit or jams. Tiny shells can be filled with custard or berries. Of course the favorite of all, strips of delicate puffed pastry sandwiched together with custard, are Napoleons, or "little cakes of a thousand layers".

Puff paste is not easy to make, but is certainly well worth the effort if you have the time and the will. The secret of puff paste is the layering of butter between layers of pastry which as it is turned and folded incorporates air between the layers. When the pastry is placed in a hot oven, the trapped air expands and makes the pastry flaky and delicate. The making of puff paste is time consuming, because it must rest and chill between rollings and turnings. But the main secret is to prevent the butter from breaking through the pastry as you are turning and rolling. Your first attempt may be utter disaster, but if you persevere you will become an expert and be able to produce the finest of all French pastry.

PUFF PASTE (PÂTÉ FEUILLETÉ)

4 cups unsifted flour
½ teaspoon salt
1 pound sweet butter, chilled
1 cup ice water

1. Mix together flour and salt in a large bowl. Cut ½ pound of the butter into small pieces and add to flour mixture. Chill remaining butter. With a pastry blender, cut butter into flour until mixture is like coarse cornmeal.
2. Add ice water to flour mixture, stirring lightly with a fork. Stir just until mixture is blended. Shape into a ball. Wrap in foil or waxed paper and chill for 30 minutes.
3. Put dough on a lightly floured board and using a floured rolling pin roll dough into a rectangle about ½ inch thick.
4. Dot center third of dough with bits of remaining chilled butter. Fold over both ends of dough to cover butter in center. Press edges together to seal in as much air as possible. Wrap in waxed paper and chill in refrigerator about 20 minutes.
5. Place dough on a lightly floured board and roll into a rectangle about ½ inch thick. Roll lightly to be sure that none of the butter pops through the dough while rolling. Turn the rectangle so that it is horizontal, then fold dough into thirds, crosswise again. Roll dough out to ¼-inch thickness and fold in thirds again. Wrap lightly in waxed paper and chill in refrigerator 10 to 20 minutes.
6. Roll dough, turn and fold twice more as in Step 5, being sure to chill between rolling.
7. Dough may now be used immediately or chilled in the refrigerator over night. Dough will keep well in refrigerator for several days.
8. Puff paste can be made into many shapes and has many uses. Probably the best known are Pastry Shells and Napoleons.

PASTRY SHELLS

1. Roll out puff paste on a lightly floured board to ¼-inch thickness. Cut in 2-inch circles with a floured cutter, plain or fluted. Cut the center from half the circles to make rings. Brush the edges of the whole circles with water and place a ring on top of each. Press each circle and ring gently together and put them on a baking sheet covered with a double thickness of brown paper. Brush the rings with beaten egg and replace the tiny circle cutouts lightly in each ring. Chill in the refrigerator for 30 minutes.
2. Heat oven to 425°F. Bake 20 to 25 minutes or until puffed and golden brown.
3. When cool, remove the tops and fill shells with fresh berries, custard or jam. (Cut in larger circles, they can be used as a main course, filled with creamed chicken or crab meat.)

NAPOLEONS

    1 recipe Puff Paste
    1 package (3⅝ ounces) vanilla pudding
        and pie filling mix
 1½ cups milk
   ½ cup heavy cream
      Confectioners' sugar

1. Heat oven to 425°F.
2. Divide puff paste in half. Return half of pastry to refrigerator and use for other sweets. Carefully divide the pastry in thirds. On a floured board, lightly roll one third of the dough into a 12-inch square. Place carefully on a baking sheet that is covered with two thicknesses of brown paper.
3. Prick top of pastry generously with a fork and chill about 10 minutes.
4. Bake 20 to 25 minutes or until pastry is dry and golden brown.
5. Carefully remove to a flat surface and bake remaining thirds of dough in the same manner. You will now have three rectangles of baked pastry.
6. Cook pudding according to directions on package, using 1½ cups milk. Cover top of pudding with a piece of waxed paper and chill in the refrigerator.
7. When pudding is chilled, whip cream until stiff. Fold cream into chilled pudding and blend until mixture is smooth.
8. Place 1 pastry rectangle on baking sheet. Cover with half of pudding mixture. Cover with second pastry rectangle and spread with remaining pudding. Top with third pastry rectangle and sprinkle with confectioners' sugar.
9. Refrigerate for 1 hour. With a very sharp knife, cut it in thirds crosswise. Cut each third into 6 slices.
10. Makes 18 small napoleons.

MINARETS

   ½ cup butter or margarine
    1 cup boiling water
   ½ teaspoon salt
    1 cup sifted flour
    4 eggs
    1 package (6 ounces) semi-sweet chocolate
        morsels
    6 tablespoons evaporated milk
    1 package (8 ounces) cream cheese
   ¼ cup sugar
    2 teaspoons vanilla

1. Heat oven to 400°F.
2. In a medium sized, heavy saucepan, heat butter with boiling water over high heat, stirring occasionally, until butter is melted.
3. Turn heat to low. Add salt and flour all at once. Stir vigorously over low heat, until mixture leaves side of pan in a smooth compact ball. Remove from heat.
4. Add eggs, one at a time, beating with a wooden spoon until smooth after each addition. Continue beating until mixture has a satin-like sheen.
5. For base of each minaret, spoon 8 mounds of the mixture on a greased baking sheet, using about 2 tablespoons of the mixture for each. For top of each minaret, spoon 8 mounds of the mixture onto baking sheet, using about 1 teaspoon mixture for each.
6. Bake small puffs about 20 to 25 minutes. Bake large puffs about 40 to 45 minutes or until puffed and lightly browned.
7. Remove from baking sheets and cool.
8. Melt semi-sweet chocolate morsels over hot, not boiling water. Remove from heat and cool slightly.
9. Gradually add evaporated milk to cream cheese and blend until smooth. Stir in sugar and vanilla. Stir in melted chocolate. Chill until mixture is of spooning consistency.
10. Cut puffs in half. Spoon filling into bottom half of large puffs. Place large puff tops on filling hollow side up. Spoon in more filling. Fill small puffs and place on top.
11. Place in freezer and freeze until ready to serve. Sprinkle with confectioners' sugar before serving.
12. Makes 8 servings.

FRENCH CHEESECAKE PUFF

¼ **cup butter or margarine**
½ **cup hot water**
¼ **teaspoon salt**
2 **tablespoons sugar**
Pinch of cinnamon
½ **cup sifted flour**
2 **eggs**
1 **cup creamed cottage cheese**
½ **cup sugar**
¼ **cup heavy cream**
Grated rind of 1 lemon
Juice of 1 lemon

1. Heat oven to 400°F.
2. Place butter, hot water, salt, sugar and cinnamon in a medium saucepan. Bring to a boil over high heat.
3. Turn heat to low. Dump in flour all at once and stir vigorously until mixture leaves sides of pan and becomes a smooth, compact ball.
4. Remove from heat and beat in eggs, one at a time, until smooth. Continue beating with a spoon until mixture is smooth and shiny.
5. Grease a baking sheet. Spread mixture out on baking sheet into a circle about 10 inches in diameter. Mound mixture around edge of circle to make an edge that will puff up during baking.
6. Press cottage cheese through a sieve to make a smooth mixture. Stir in sugar, cream, lemon rind and juice. Pour mixture into center of circle.
7. Bake about 35 minutes or until mixture is puffed up and lightly browned.
8. Serve warm.
9. Makes 6 to 8 servings.

CHOCOLATE ECLAIRS

1 **cup water**
½ **cup butter or margarine**
¼ **teaspoon salt**
1 **cup sifted flour**
4 **large eggs**
Chocolate Nut Filling

1. Heat oven to 400°F.
2. In a large saucepan bring water, butter and salt to a boil. Add flour all at once and cook over medium heat, stirring constantly, until mixture leaves sides of pan and forms a ball of dough.
3. Remove from heat and stir in eggs one at a time, beating well after each addition. Continue beating until mixture is smooth and glossy.
4. Separate dough into egg-size balls. Place on greased baking sheet. Using spoons, stroke and stretch each ball into an eclair-shaped rod about 4 inches long.
5. Bake 30 to 35 minutes or until eclairs are puffed up and lightly browned. Remove from oven and turn off heat. Make a slit in the side of each puff to allow steam to escape. Return to oven and let stand about 10 minutes with oven door ajar.
6. Remove from baking sheet and cool on wire rack.
7. When cool, cut eclair shells in half lengthwise. Remove any moist dough in center. Fill with Chocolate Nut Filling. Dust tops with confectioners' sugar if desired.
8. Makes about 12 large eclairs.

CHOCOLATE NUT FILLING

1 **package (3⅝ ounces) chocolate nut pudding**
1 **cup heavy cream**
1 **cup milk**

1. Prepare pudding according to package directions, using heavy cream and milk.
2. Cool. Use to fill eclairs.

ELEGANT CREAM PUFFS

½ **cup water**
¼ **cup butter or margarine**
¼ **teaspoon salt**
½ **cup sifted flour**
2 **large eggs or 3 small eggs**
Sour Cream Filling
Chocolate Glaze

1. Heat oven to 400°F.
2. In a large saucepan bring water, butter and salt to a boil. Add flour all at once and cook over medium heat, stirring constantly, until mixture leaves sides of pan and forms a ball of dough.
3. Remove from heat and stir in eggs, one at a time, beating well after each addition. Continue beating until mixture is smooth and glossy.
4. Mound batter on a greased baking sheet into 6 mounds at least 2 inches apart.
5. Bake 30 to 35 minutes or until puffs are high and lightly browned. Remove from oven and turn off heat. Make a slit in the side of each puff to allow steam to escape. Return to oven and let stand about 10 minutes with oven door ajar.
6. Remove from baking sheet and cool on wire rack.
7. To serve, split puffs in half. Scoop out any moist dough in center. Fill with Sour Cream Filling and top with Chocolate Glaze.
8. Makes 6 large puffs.

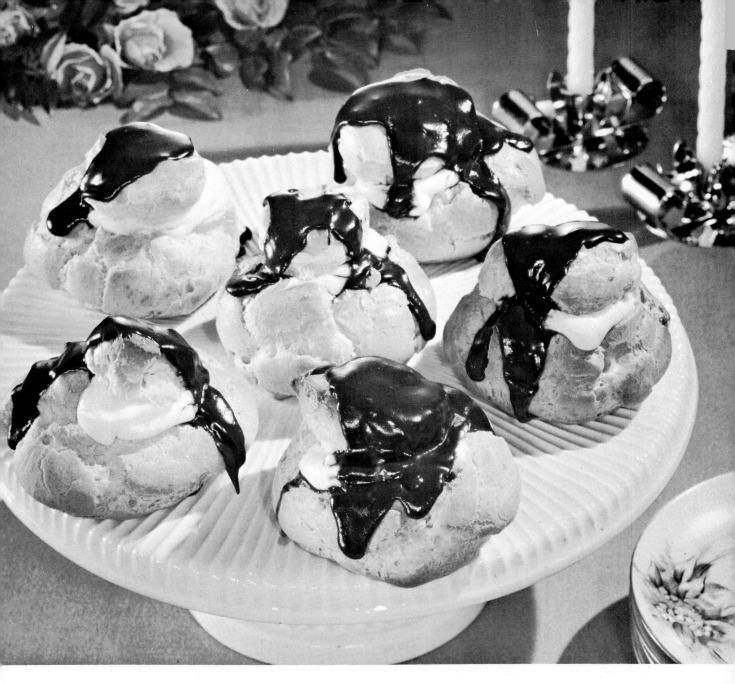

SOUR CREAM FILLING

½ cup sugar
⅓ cup sifted flour
1½ cups milk
2 eggs, slightly beaten
1 tablespoon butter
½ teaspoon vanilla
1 cup dairy sour cream

1. In a large heavy saucepan combine sugar and flour. Slowly stir in milk. Cook over medium heat, stirring constantly, until mixture comes to a boil. Remove from heat.
2. Stir a small amount of the hot milk into beaten eggs. Return egg mixture to milk in saucepan and stir well. Cook over low heat, stirring constantly, until mixture comes to a boil. Remove from heat immediately.
3. Stir in butter and vanilla. Turn mixture into a bowl. Cover the surface of the custard by pressing a piece of waxed paper directly on the surface of the pudding. Chill in the refrigerator.
4. When mixture is cooled, beat with a rotary beater until fluffy. Fold in sour cream. Use to fill cream puffs.

CHOCOLATE GLAZE

¼ cup cocoa
½ cup confectioners' sugar
¼ cup milk

1. In a small bowl, combine cocoa and confectioners' sugar. Blend in milk. Stir until mixture is smooth. Drizzle over top of filled cream puffs.
2. Chill puffs until ready to serve.

PETIT FOURS

2¼ cups sifted cake flour
1 cup sugar
2 teaspoons baking powder
1 teaspoon salt
½ cup margarine, softened
1 teaspoon vanilla
2 eggs
¾ cup milk, divided
1 jar apricot or pineapple preserves
Confectioners' Sugar Icing

1. Heat oven to 350°F.
2. Grease the bottom of a 15½- by 10½- by 2-inch jelly roll pan. Cover with a sheet of waxed paper. Grease top of paper.
3. Sift together flour, sugar, baking powder and salt into the large bowl of an electric mixer. Add margarine, vanilla, eggs and ½ cup milk. Beat 2 minutes at medium speed, scraping sides and bottom of bowl constantly with a rubber scraper.
4. Add remaining milk and beat 2 minutes longer. Scrape bowl occasionally.
5. Pour into prepared pan, spreading dough out evenly.
6. Bake about 25 minutes or until cake springs back when touched lightly with the fingers.
7. Remove from oven and cool slightly. Turn out onto a cake rack and remove waxed paper. Cool.
8. Cut cake into fancy shapes. Use cookie cutter for 2½-inch rounds or cut out 2-inch squares. Cut rectangles about 2½- by 1½-inches. Arrange pieces in pairs, flat sides together.
9. Spread bottom piece with preserves, then press top into place gently. Frost with confectioners' sugar icing. Top with finely chopped nuts, chocolate or colored sprinkles.
10. Makes 16 petit fours.

CONFECTIONERS' SUGAR ICING

½ cup margarine, softened
Salt
½ teaspoon vanilla
2 cups confectioners' sugar
2 to 3 tablespoons hot milk

1. In the small bowl of an electric mixer combine margarine, pinch of salt, vanilla and confectioners' sugar. Add about 1 tablespoon hot milk. Beat at high speed about 10 minutes, gradually adding more milk until of smooth spreading consistency.
2. Makes about 1 cup icing.

ELEGANT PARTY ECLAIRS

½ cup water
¼ cup margarine or butter
⅛ teaspoon salt
½ cup sifted flour
2 eggs
Chocolate Filling
Confectioners' sugar

1. Heat oven to 400°F.
2. In a saucepan combine water, margarine and salt. Bring to a boil. Remove from heat and add flour all at once. Cook over low heat, stirring constantly, until mixture leaves the sides of the pan and forms a ball.
3. Remove from heat. Add eggs, one at a time, beating until smooth and glossy after each addition.
4. Fit a pastry bag with a number 7 plain tube. Fill pastry bag with mixture. Press out eclairs, about 2 inches long, onto a greased baking sheet. Leave about 2 inches of space between each eclair.
5. Bake 15 to 20 minutes or until golden brown and crisp.
6. Remove from oven and cool slightly. Cut a slice from top of each eclair and carefully remove dough or filament inside. Cool.
7. To serve, fill with with Chocolate Filling and dust tops with confectioners' sugar.
8. Makes about 27 tiny eclairs.

CHOCOLATE FILLING

⅔ cup sweetened condensed milk
1 square unsweetened chocolate
⅛ teaspoon salt
¼ cup water
¼ teaspoon vanilla
½ cup heavy cream, whipped

1. Combine milk, chocolate and salt in top of a double boiler. Cook over rapidly boiling water until chocolate melts. Continue cooking, stirring constantly, until mixture is very thick, about 5 minutes. Gradually stir in water, keeping mixture smooth. Continue cooking, stirring constantly, until mixture thickens again.
2. Remove from heat and stir in vanilla. Refrigerate until ready to fill eclairs.
3. Before filling eclairs, fold whipped cream into chocolate mixture.
4. Makes about 1⅓ cups filling.

French pastries and more! A handsome array of Petit Fours, Elegant Party Eclairs, Easy "French" Pastries, Chocolate Mousse and Mincemeat crêpes.

The Borden Co.

CHOCOLATE MOUSSE

2 teaspoons unflavored gelatine
Cold water
1 can (15 ounces) sweetened condensed milk
3 squares unsweetened chocolate
3 eggs, separated
1 teaspoon vanilla
2 tablespoons cognac

1. Soften gelatine in ¼ cup cold water.
2. In top part of double boiler combine sweetened condensed milk and chocolate. Cook over boiling water until chocolate melts. Continue cooking, stirring, until mixture is smooth and very thick, about 5 minutes. Gradually stir in ½ cup water, keeping mixture smooth.
3. Beat egg yolks slightly. Stir a small amount of the hot mixture into egg yolks. Return egg mixture to top of double boiler. Cook over hot water, stirring constantly, until mixture is smooth and thick, about 5 minutes.
4. Remove from heat and stir in softened gelatine, vanilla and cognac. Stir until gelatine is dissolved. Cool to room temperature.
5. Beat egg whites until they stand in stiff peaks. When chocolate mixture mounds slightly when dropped from a spoon, fold in egg whites.
6. Pour mixture into a 5-cup mold which has been very lightly oiled.
7. Refrigerate about 3 hours or until firm.
8. Unmold on a serving dish and serve with whipped cream, if desired.
9. Makes about 6 servings.

EASY "FRENCH" PASTRIES

1 package (9½ ounces) flaky refrigerator biscuits
1 can (15 ounces) sweetened condensed milk
⅓ cup lemon juice
½ teaspoon vanilla
½ teaspoon almond extract
Canned fruit such as apricot halves or canned cherry pie filling, or fresh fruit such as strawberries or blueberries.
1 jar currant jelly, optional

1. Heat oven to 375°F.
2. Open packaged biscuits according to package directions. Carefully split each biscuit in half crosswise.
3. Press each biscuit half into a tiny tart pan, about 2½-inch diameter, to make pastry shell. Press a small piece of aluminum foil over top of shell and fill with dried beans or peas. Place shells on a baking sheet.

4. Bake 8 minutes. Remove from oven. Remove foil and beans from each shell. Return shells to oven and bake about 5 minutes longer or until inside of shells are slightly brown and firm.
5. Remove from oven and cool slightly. Take shells from pans and cool thoroughly before filling.
6. In a mixing bowl combine sweetened condensed milk, lemon juice, vanilla and almond extract. Stir until well blended and thickened. Spoon mixture into cooled shells. Refrigerate 30 minutes or longer.
7. Top each pastry with either canned or fresh fruit. If desired, melt currant jelly over low heat and dribble a little on top of each pastry for a pretty glaze. Refrigerate until ready to serve.
8. Makes 20 tarts.

MINCEMEAT CRÊPES

5 tablespoons sifted flour
½ teaspoon sugar
¼ teaspoon salt
2 eggs
1 cup milk
Salad oil
Confectioners' sugar
1 package (9 ounces) condensed mincemeat
¾ cup water
1 cup orange juice
3 tablespoons Grand Marnier, divided

1. In a medium-sized mixing bowl blend flour, sugar and salt. In another bowl beat eggs slightly and then beat in milk. Pour egg mixture into flour mixture and beat with a wire whisk until thoroughly blended. Let stand at least 1 hour.
2. Heat a small skillet, about 5½-inch diameter bottom, over medium high heat. Brush with a light coat of salad oil. Pour in about 1 tablespoon batter, tilting pan to cover entire bottom. Cook until lightly browned. Loosen edge slightly with thin spatula, pick up edges with fingers and flip crêpe over on other side. Remove crêpes and stack in a pile, sprinkling each one with a little confectioners' sugar to keep from sticking.
3. Crumble mincemeat into a small saucepan. Add water and stir over medium heat until lumps are broken. Bring to a brisk boil and boil 1 minute.
4. Pour mixture into a chafing dish or skillet. Add orange juice and 2 tablespoons Grand Marnier. Heat. Turn each crêpe into the sauce and fold in quarters, using a fork and

a spoon. When all the crêpes are folded and turned, warm the remaining Grand Marnier. Pour carefully over crêpes and ignite with a match. Spoon sauce over crêpes while it is flaming.

5. Serve immediatley on heated dessert dishes.
6. Makes 6 servings of 2 crêpes each.

DESSERT CRÊPES

1 cup plus 2 tablespoons sifted flour
4 tablespoons sugar
Pinch of salt
3 eggs, beaten
1½ cups milk
1 tablespoon melted butter
1½ tablespoons cognac

1. Combine flour, sugar and salt in a bowl. Beat together the eggs and milk. Stir into flour mixture and beat until smooth. This can be done on low speed of a mixer or with a wire whisk. Stir in melted butter and cognac. Let mixture stand for at least 2 hours before cooking.
2. Heat a small skillet, about 5½-inches diameter across the bottom, over medium high heat.
3. When skillet is hot add ½ teaspoon butter and swirl around pan to cover sides and bottom.
4. Pour in 1 full tablespoon batter. Rotate and tilt pan very quickly to spread batter over bottom of skillet. This must be done before batter has a chance to set.
5. Cook crêpe about 1 minute, or until it is set and browned on one side. Loosen sides with spatula and flip crêpe over quickly with the fingers. Lightly brown second side. The second will not brown as nicely as the first side, so it is usually turned inside when it is rolled or folded.
6. Roll crêpes, fold them into quarters, or stack them on top of each other. They may be served immediately with a sprinkle of confectioners' sugar, fresh fruit or a sauce. They may also be used in other dishes such as Crêpes Suzette.
7. Makes 20 to 24 crêpes.

CRÊPES SUZETTE

6 lumps sugar
1 orange
½ cup butter
1 tablespoon lemon juice
¼ cup Curacao or Cointreau
¼ cup Grand Marnier
1 receipe dessert crêpes
½ cup warm brandy

1. Rub sugar lumps on the skin of the orange until they are covered with the aromatic oil. Crush the lumps and blend well with the butter. Squeeze the juice from the orange and reserve.
2. In a chafing dish or flat skillet melt the butter and sugar mixture. Add orange juice, lemon juice, Curacao and Grand Marnier. Bring mixture to a boil.
3. One by one place the crêpes in the sauce, spoon the sauce over them so they are moistened on both sides, and fold in quarters.
4. Pour warm brandy carefully over crêpes. Ignite with a match.
5. Serve crêpes on heated plates while sauce is still blazing.
6. Makes 6 to 8 servings.

CRÊPES DIRECTOIRES

6 bananas
½ cup finely chopped almonds
12 dessert crêpes
6 tablespoons butter
4 tablespoons sugar
¼ cup Grand Marnier
⅓ cup warm cognac

1. Heat oven to 350°F.
2. Bake bananas in their skins 18 to 20 minutes.
3. Split banana peel and remove bananas. Split in half, lengthwise.
4. Sprinkle chopped almonds over top of crêpes. Roll a crêpe around each banana half.
5. Melt butter and sugar in a chafing dish or large flat skillet. When mixuture starts to caramelize, add crêpes. Then add Grand Marnier and heat crêpes in sauce.
6. Carefully pour on cognac. Ignite with a match and spoon syrup over top of crêpes.
7. Serve on warm dessert plates with sauce over top.
8. Makes 6 servings.

CRÊPES AUX FRAISES

1 package (9 ounces) cream cheese
1 cup dairy sour cream
3 boxes (10 ounces each) frozen
  strawberries, defrosted
3 tablespoons butter
3 tablespoons grated orange rind
2 tablespoons lemon juice
3 tablespoons Cointreau
3 tablespoons brandy
18 to 20 dessert crêpes

1. Heat oven to 350°F.
2. Cream together cheese and sour cream until light and smooth. Set aside.
3. Press strawberries through a sieve to remove the seeds. Put pulp in a saucepan, add the butter, orange rind and lemon juice. Bring to a boil and boil 1 minute. Set aside.
4. Spread each crêpe with part of the cream cheese mixture. Roll up and place side by side in a shallow casserole. Do not stack crêpes.
5. Add Cointreau and brandy to strawberry sauce. Spoon a small amount of the sauce over crêpes in the casserole.

6. Bake 15 minutes. Serve with remaining heated strawberry sauce.
7. Makes 6 to 8 servings.

FRENCH LEMON WAFERS

½ cup butter or margarine
½ cup sugar
2 teaspoons grated lemon peel
1 tablespoon lemon juice
⅛ teaspoon salt
3 unbeaten egg whites
1 cup sifted flour

1. Heat oven to 400°F.
2. Cream together butter, sugar, lemon peel, juice and salt until light and fluffy.
3. Add egg whites alternately with the flour, beating well after each addition.
4. Force mixture through a pastry tube or drop by teaspoonsful about 1 inch apart on greased baking sheets.
5. Bake about 10 minutes until or edges are lightly browned.
6. Remove from baking sheets and cool on wire racks.
7. Makes about 3½ dozen wafers.

CRÊPES JUBILEE
(shown opposite)

1 can (1 pound 5 ounces) cherry pie filling, divided
4 tablespoons kirschwasser
1 recipe desert crêpes

1. Combine 1 cup cherry pie filling with 2 tablespoons of the kirschwasser. Spread 1 heaping teaspoon of the pie filling mixture on one side of a crêpe and roll up. Repeat with remaining crêpes.
2. Place rolled crêpes in a 9½- to 10-inch flat crêpe pan or a large heat-proof platter. Pour remaining pie filling around rolled crêpes. Place crêpe pan or platter on an alcohol burner stand.
3. Heat remaining 2 tablespoons kirschwasser. Pour carefully over crêpes and ignite with a match. Allow flames to burn out.
4. Serve crêpes with sauce immediately.
5. Makes about 10 servings.

ALMOND WAFERS

¾ cup butter or margarine, softened
1½ cups sugar, divided
1 teaspoon grated lemon rind
2 egg yolks
1½ cups sifted flour
⅛ teaspoon almond flavoring
1 cup blanched, sliced almonds
¼ teaspoon nutmeg
1 egg white
1 tablespoon water

1. Heat oven to 375°F.
2. Cream butter with 1 cup sugar and lemon rind until light and fluffy. Beat in egg yolks, one at a time. Stir in almond flavoring. Add flour and stir until well blended. Chill dough until firm.
3. Combine almonds with remaining sugar and nutmeg. Beat egg white with water until foamy.
4. With the fingers, shape dough into ½-inch balls. Place on greased baking sheets. Flatten balls with the bottom of a glass that has been dipped in sugar. Brush top of cookies with egg white. Sprinkle almond mixture on top of cookies.
5. Bake 8 to 10 minutes or until edges are lightly browned.
6. Remove to wire racks to cool.
7. Makes about 5 dozen wafers.

MADELEINES

¾ cup sweet butter
2 eggs
¾ cup sugar
½ teaspoon grated lemon rind
½ teaspoon vanilla extract
1 cup unsifted flour

1. Put butter in a small, deep saucepan. Heat slowly until foam on top of butter disappears and there is a light brown sediment on the bottom of the pan. Remove from heat and skim off any brown bits on top of butter. Carefully pour off clear butter, leaving sediment in pan. Set butter aside.
2. Heat oven to 450°F.
3. Put eggs, sugar and lemon rind in a flat mixing bowl, and stir just until blended. Place bowl over a saucepan containing hot water. Water should not touch the bottom of the bowl nor should it boil. Place saucepan over low heat until egg mixture is lukewarm.
4. Remove bowl from hot water and beat with an electric mixer at high speed until light, fluffy and tripled in volume. Add vanilla.
5. Fold in flour and butter carefully. Do not beat.
6. Butter ¾-inch madeleine pans. Fill two-thirds full with batter.
7. Bake 7 to 8 minutes or until golden brown. Let stand about 2 minutes. Turn out of pans. Butter pans again, refill with batter and bake. Repeat until all batter is used.
8. Serve madeleines upside down to show the fluted pattern.
9. Makes about 40 madeleines.

The dessert flan is a tart or open-faced pie, consisting of a straight-sided pastry shell and a sweet fruit filling, plain or with a custard base. The fruit is arranged attractively and covered with a clear glaze.

Pastry for a flan is usually richer and "shorter" than the crust for an American pie. It is high in butter or shortening content, often contains sugar, and occasionally an egg. It is sometimes hard to work with, but it is easy to patch up, and when it is filled, no one will ever see the patches.

A flan ring is merely a ring of metal, usually aluminum, that is placed on a baking sheet. After baking, the ring is removed and the shell stands alone since the crust is usually much thicker than our pie crust. If you do not have a flan ring, here are directions for making one: Tear off a strip of heavy-duty aluminum foil 17 inches long. Divide in half to make two 17-inch strips. Fold each to form a 1¼-inch strip, then join ends to form a 9-inch circle. Remove foil ring before serving.

FLAN PASTRY

1 cup sifted flour
1 egg yolk
1 tablespoon sugar
½ cup slightly softened butter
Grated rind of 1 lemon
Pinch of salt
Ice water

1. Sift flour into a mixing bowl. Make a well in center of flour and add egg yolk, sugar, butter cut into small pieces, lemon rind and salt. Mix ingredients in center into a paste with fingers. Quickly work in the flour, adding a very little ice water, if needed, to moisten the dough so that it can be gathered together into a ball.
2. Wrap dough in waxed paper and chill in refrigerator for at least an hour.
3. When dough is well chilled, place on a lightly floured board. Flour rolling pin and roll dough lightly from the center out to the edge. Lift dough and turn occasionally, flouring bottom if necessary to keep it from sticking. Roll dough into a circle about 2" larger than pan.
4. Place dough very carefully in pan. Either roll it gently over a rolling pin and place over top of pan, or fold dough in half, then in half again. Unroll or unfold over pan.
5. Press dough gently into bottom of pan and fit carefully around edges without pulling it. Press dough against sides to make it stick. Make a small decorative edge around top of pan with dough. If dough breaks, take small pieces of dough and press down over breaks.
6. Some recipes call for filling to be placed in unbaked shell. Refrigerate shell while making filling.
7. To make a baked shell, line the dough with a piece of aluminum foil. Fill with dried beans or rice. Bake in hot oven (400°F.) 10 minutes. Reduce heat to moderate (350°F.) and bake 10 minutes. Remove shell from oven, take out foil and beans. Prick bottom of shell with fork. Return shell to oven and bake 5 to 10 minutes or until shell is baked and lightly browned. Remove ring. Cool before filling.
8. Makes 1 9-inch shell.

STRAWBERRY FLAN

⅓ cup sugar
¼ cup cornstarch
¼ teaspoon salt
1¾ cups milk
2 eggs, beaten
¼ teaspoon grated lemon rind
¼ teaspoon vanilla
1 9-inch baked flan shell
2 pints fresh strawberries
⅓ cup red currant jelly

1. Mix together sugar, cornstarch and salt in a heavy saucepan. Slowly blend in milk. Cook over medium heat, stirring constantly, until mixture thickens and boils for 30 seconds.
2. Stir a small amount of the hot mixture into beaten eggs. Return egg mixture to saucepan. Cook over low heat, stirring constantly, until very thick and smooth.
3. Remove from heat and stir in lemon rind and vanilla. Cool. Press a piece of waxed paper directly on surface of custard to prevent skin forming. Chill in refrigerator.
4. Spread chilled custard filling in tart shell. Clean and hull berries. Place berries as close together on surface of custard as possible.
5. Put jelly in a small saucepan and heat until melted. Spoon over strawberries. Chill.
6. Makes 8 servings.

A Strawberry Flan is so pretty that it is a shame to cut it. But do—you will find the pastry covered with a rich custard and topped off with strawberries.

California Strawberry Advisory Board

PEACH FLAN

Whipped topping mix (enough to make 2 cups)
½ cup cold milk
½ cup sugar
2 cups cottage cheese
1½ teaspoons vanilla
½ cup chopped almonds
1 can (1 pound 13 ounces) sliced peaches
1 9 inch baked flan shell
1 tablespoon cornstarch
2 teaspoons lemon juice
⅛ teaspoon mace

1. Combine whipped topping and milk. Beat until topping stands in a stiff peaks. Gradually add sugar and blend well.
2. Put cottage cheese in blender and blend until smooth. If you do not have a blender, put cottage cheese through a fine sieve.
3. Fold cottage cheese, vanilla and almonds into whipped topping.
4. Drain peaches and save syrup. Cut slices in half lengthwise.
5. Put half of the whipped topping mixture into baked flan shell. Arrange half the peaches over filling. Spoon remaining topping mixture over peaches. Arrange remaining peaches on the top in an attractive pattern. Chill thoroughly.
6. Measure 1 cup peach syrup into a saucepan. Add cornstarch, lemon juice and mace and blend well.
7. Cook over medium heat, stirring constantly, until syrup thickens. Cool. Spoon glaze over peaches on top of flan. Chill 2 to 3 more hours before serving.
8. Makes 1 9-inch flan.

PEACH-PLUM FLAN

Sugar
⅓ cup flour
¼ teaspoon salt
2 cups milk
2 egg yolks, beaten
2 tablespoons butter
1 teaspoon vanilla
1 9-inch baked flan shell
1 tablespoon water
1 cup diced red plums
½ teaspoon lemon juice
2 fresh peaches, peeled and sliced or
1 package (12 ounces) frozen sliced peaches, thawed and drained

1. In a heavy saucepan mix together ⅔ cup sugar, flour and salt. Gradually stir in milk.

Cook over medium heat, stirring constantly, until mixture boils. Boil 1 minute and remove from heat. Stir a small amount of hot mixture into egg yolks. Return egg yolk mixture to hot cooked mixture and blend well. Cook over low heat, stirring constantly, just to the boiling point.
2. Remove from heat and stir in butter and vanilla. Cool slightly. Pour into baked flan or pie shell. Chill in the refrigerator.
3. In a small saucepan combine ¼ cup sugar and 1 tablespoon water. Bring to a boil. Add plums and simmer until mixture thickens, stirring often.
4. Remove from heat and stir in lemon juice. Put mixture through a sieve and cool.
5. Arrange peach slices on top of cooled filling in flan shell. Pour plum mixture over top of peaches. Chill before serving.
6. Makes 6 to 8 servings.

UPSIDE DOWN APPLE TART (TARTE TATIN)

8 medium cooking apples
1 cup sugar, divided
1 teaspoon cinnamon (optional)
½ cup melted butter or margarine
½ recipe flan pastry

1. Heat oven to 400°F.
2. Peel, core and quarter apples. Cut each apple quarter in half. Toss in a bowl with ½ cup sugar and the cinnamon. Turn apples into a 10-inch deep cake pan or shallow casserole.
3. Sprinkle top of apples with remaining sugar and pour melted butter over the top.
4. Roll out dough into a circle to fit top of pan. Place over top of apples. Allow edges of dough to fall inside of pan.
5. Bake about 45 minutes or until apples are tender.
6. Invert tart onto serving dish immediately.
7. Serve warm with whipped cream, if desired.
8. Makes 8 servings.

AMERICAN FRENCH FRUIT TART

1 ²⁄₃ cups vanilla wafer crumbs
1 tablespoon instant coffee powder
¼ cup butter or margarine, melted
5 egg yolks
¾ cup sugar
3 tablespoons flour
2 cups milk
1 teaspoon vanilla extract
  Fresh peaches, pared and sliced
  Fresh strawberries, hulled and washed
  Fresh blueberries
½ cup red currant jelly

1. Heat oven to 375°F.
2. Combine vanilla crumbs and instant coffee powder. Stir in melted butter and mix well. Pour crumb mixture into a 9-inch pie plate. Press crumbs firmly against bottom and sides, using an 8-inch pie plate.
3. Bake 8 minutes. Cool.
4. Beat egg yolks and sugar together until thick and lemon colored. Slowly beat in flour until well blended.
5. Scald milk with vanilla added. Stir into egg mixture. Return egg mixture to saucepan. Cook over medium heat, stirring constantly, until custard thickens and comes to a boil. Simmer 1 minute.
6. Pour custard into a bowl. Cover the surface of the custard with a circle of waxed paper to prevent a skin forming on top of custard. Cool thoroughly.
7. Spoon custard mixture into pie shell. Top custard with fresh fruit in desired pattern.
8. Melt red currant jelly in a saucepan over low heat. Brush melted jelly over fruit to glaze. Refrigerate until ready to serve.
9. Makes 8 servings.

COUPE AUX MARRONS

18 champagne biscuits or French lady fingers
  Vanilla ice cream
  Chopped marrons in syrup

1. Arrange 3 champagne biscuits in each individual dessert dish. Place a scoop of vanilla ice cream in each dish. Top with about 1 ½ tablespoons of marrons in syrup.
2. Makes about 6 servings.

BAVAROIS AUX FRAISES

1 envelope unflavored gelatine
½ cup sugar
  Dash of salt
2 eggs, separated
1 ¼ cups milk
1 pint fresh strawberries, sliced
1 teaspoon vanilla
1 cup heavy cream, whipped

1. Combine gelatine, sugar and salt in a saucepan. Beat together egg yolks and milk. Stir into sugar mixture in saucepan.
2. Place over low heat and cook, stirring constantly, until mixture is thick enough to coat a metal spoon. Cool.
3. Add strawberries and vanilla. Chill until mixture mounds slightly when dropped from a spoon.
4. Beat egg whites until stiff but not dry. Fold in gelatine mixture and whipped cream. Pour into a 1 ½-quart mold. Chill until firm.
5. Unmold on a serving plate and garnish with strawberries, if desired.
6. Makes 6 servings.

STRAWBERRY SOUR CREAM BISQUE

1 pint fresh strawberries, cleaned and thinly sliced
1 quart dairy sour cream
1 cup sugar
½ cup almond macaroon crumbs
1 teaspoon vanilla
  Dash of salt

1. In a bowl combine strawberries, sour cream, sugar, macaroon crumbs, vanilla and salt.
2. Turn mixture into individual molds, small paper cups or refrigerator trays.
3. Place in freezing compartment and freeze until firm.
4. Before serving, remove from freezer and let stand in the refrigerator or at room temperature about 15 or 20 minutes before serving.
5. Makes 8 servings.

CHARLOTTE RUSSE

12 lady fingers
2 envelopes unflavored gelatine
1 cup sugar, divided
¼ teaspoon salt
4 eggs, separated
2½ cups milk
2 tablespoons brandy
1 cup heavy cream, whipped

1. Split lady fingers in halves. Cut a small sliver off one end of each and discard. Stand upright around sides of an 8-inch spring form pan. Set aside.
2. Combine gelatine, ½ cup sugar and salt in a saucepan. Beat together egg yolks and milk. Stir into gelatine mixture. Cook over low heat, stirring constantly, until gelatine is dissolved, about 5 minutes.
3. Remove from heat and add brandy. Chill until mixture mounds slightly when dropped from a spoon.
4. Beat egg whites until stiff but not dry. Gradually add remaining ½ cup sugar and beat until very stiff.
5. Fold gelatine mixture into egg whites. Fold whipped cream into mixture.
6. Carefully pour mixture into prepared pan. Chill in refrigerator until firm.
7. To unmold, release spring and remove sides of mold carefully. Place on a serving plate and garnish with additional whipped cream, if desired.
8. Makes 12 servings.

SHERRY CREAM MOLD

2 envelopes unflavored gelatine
1½ cups milk
¾ cup sugar
¼ teaspoon salt
4 eggs, separated
½ cup sweet sherry
1½ cups heavy cream
Ladyfingers, split in half lengthwise

1. Sprinkle gelatine over top of milk in top part of double boiler. Let stand a few minutes to soften gelatine.
2. Place over water that is just simmering. Stir in sugar, salt and beaten egg yolks. Cook, stirring occasionally, until mixture coats a metal spoon.
3. Remove from heat and blend in sherry. Fill bottom of double boiler with ice water. Place top of double boiler in ice water to hasten chilling.

4. Beat egg whites until they stand in soft peaks. Beat cream until stiff.
5. When egg yolk mixture has thickened slightly, fold mixture into beaten egg whites. Then fold in cream.
6. Lightly butter the sides of a 2-quart mold. Arrange ladyfinger halves around edge of mold. If necessary, trim top edge with sharp knife or scissors until level with top of mold. Turn custard mixture into mold.
7. Chill in refrigerator 3 or 4 hours or overnight.
8. When ready to serve, loosen around sides with a thin bladed knife and invert on a serving plate. Lift off mold.
9. Makes 10 servings.

STRAWBERRY CUSTARD PIE
(shown opposite)

1 package (3¾ ounces) vanilla pudding and pie filling mix
1 baked 10-inch pie shell, cooled
8 ladyfingers, split
1 pint strawberries
1 jar (10 ounces) red currant jelly
2 teaspoons water
Whipped cream or prepared whipped topping

1. Prepare pie filling mix as directed on package. Cool for 5 minutes, stirring twice, to prevent a skin from forming. Pour filling into pie shell. Cool to room temperature.
2. Place ladyfinger halves, cut side down, over top of pie filling. Hull strawberries and cut in half. Arrange berry halves, cut side down, in circles over top of ladyfingers, placing halves close together.
3. Heat jelly with water until softened. Blend until smooth. Cool; then spoon over berries. Chill.
4. Just before serving, border pie with prepared whipped topping or whipped cream.

CAFE BRÛLOT DIABOLIQUE

6 lumps sugar
8 whole cloves
1 stick cinnamon, about 1 inch long
1 lemon peel, cut into strips
4 ounces cognac
4 cups hot, very strong coffee

1. Place all ingredients except coffee in a chafing dish. Do not stir. Ignite cognac with a match and stir carefully until ingredients are well blended.
2. Slowly pour in hot coffee and continue to stir.
3. To serve, ladle into demitasse cups.
4. Makes about 10 demitasse cup servings.

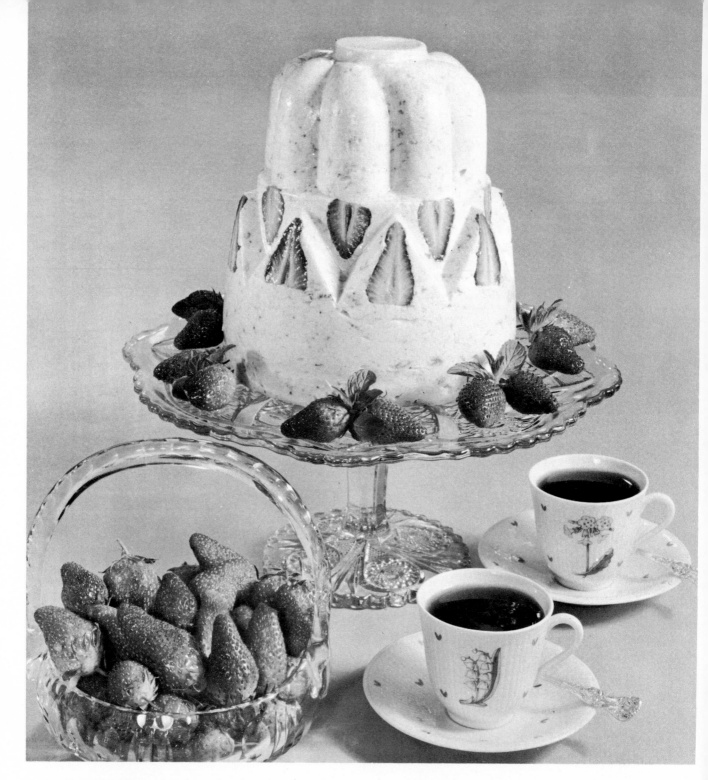

STRAWBERRY BAVARIAN CREAM

    3 envelopes unflavored gelatine
    1 cup cold water
    1 cup sugar
  ¼ teaspoon salt
    2 cups mashed strawberries, juice and pulp
    2 tablespoons lemon juice
    2 cups heavy cream, whipped

1. Sprinkle gelatine on cold water in a 2½-quart saucepan to soften. Place over low heat, cook stirring constantly, until gelatine is dissolved. Remove from heat.

2. Add sugar and salt and stir until sugar is dissolved. Stir in mashed strawberries and lemon juice. Chill until mixture is the consistency of unbeaten egg whites.

3. Fold in heavy whipped cream. Turn mixture into a 2-quart mold. Chill until firm. When ready to serve, unmold on a serving plate. Garnish with fresh strawberries and mint leaves if desired.

4. Makes 8 to 10 servings.

BAVARIAN CREAM

2 envelopes unflavored gelatine
1 cup sugar, divided
¼ teaspoon salt
4 eggs, separated
2½ cups milk
1 teaspoon vanilla
2 cups heavy cream, whipped

1. Combine gelatine, ½ cup sugar and salt in a deep saucepan. Beat together egg yolks and milk. Stir into gelatine mixture. Place saucepan over low heat, cook, stirring constantly, until gelatine is dissolved. This will take about 5 minutes.
2. Remove from heat and add vanilla.
3. Place saucepan in refrigerator and chill until mixture mounds slightly when dropped from a spoon.
4. Beat egg whites until stiff, but not dry. Gradually add remaining ½ cup sugar and beat until very stiff.
5. Lightly place egg whites on top of gelatine mixture. With a rubber scraper, fold egg whites into gelatine mixture. Fold in whipped cream.
6. Turn mixture into a 10-cup mold. Place in refrigerator and chill until firm.
7. Unmold onto a chilled serving plate. Serve plain or with any desired fresh fruit.
8. Makes 8 to 10 servings.

BRANDIED COFFEE JELLY

2 envelopes unflavored gelatine
⅔ cup sugar
4 tablespoons instant coffee powder
¼ teaspoon salt
Water
4 tablespoons brandy

1. Combine gelatine, sugar, instant coffee powder and salt in a saucepan. Add 1 cup water. Place over low heat and cook, stirring constantly, until gelatine and sugar are dissolved. Remove from heat.
2. Add 2½ cups water and brandy. Pour into a 4-cup mold, 8 stemmed glasses or a serving dish. Chill until firm.
3. Unmold and garnish with whipped cream if desired.
4. Makes 8 servings.

COCONUT CREAM WITH STRAWBERRY RUM SAUCE

2 cups light cream, divided
2 envelopes unflavored gelatine
¼ cup cold water
1 cup sugar
2 cups flaked coconut
1½ teaspoons almond extract
3 cups heavy cream, whipped
Strawberry Rum Sauce

1. Put 1½ cups light cream in a saucepan. Bring just to a boil.
2. Sprinkle gelatine over remaining light cream, combined with cold water. Let stand a few minutes to soften.
3. Add softened gelatine and sugar to hot cream. Stir until sugar and gelatine are thoroughly dissolved.
4. Cool to lukewarm. Stir in coconut and almond extract. Fold in whipped cream. Turn mixture into a 2-quart mold. Chill until firm.
5. At serving time, unmold on a platter and serve with Strawberry Rum Sauce.
6. Makes 10 servings.

STRAWBERRY RUM SAUCE

½ cup sugar
2 pints strawberries, cleaned and halved
1⅓ cups water
¼ cup lemon juice
2 tablespoons cornstarch
3 tablespoons light rum

1. Combine sugar and strawberries. Let mixture stand several hours.
2. Drain and reserve syrup.
3. In a saucepan combine ⅔ cup of the strawberry syrup, water, lemon juice and cornstarch. Add strawberries and rum. Bring to a boil slowly, and boil ½ minute.
4. Chill and serve with Coconut Cream.

OEUFS À LA NEIGE

1 quart milk
Sugar
1 teaspoon vanilla
6 eggs, separated
½ teaspoon cornstarch
Salt
2 tablespoons rum or cognac

1. Pour milk into a skillet and bring to a boil over medium heat. Add 6 tablespoons sugar and vanilla. Stir to dissolve sugar.
2. Beat the egg whites until stiff. Gradually beat in 6 tablespoons sugar, cornstarch and a pinch of salt. Beat until mixture stands in stiff peaks.
3. Scoop up egg whites with two large spoons, shaping into egg-shaped ovals. Drop a few at a time into milk mixture, just barely simmering. Cook about 30 seconds on one side, then turn over with a slotted spoon. Cook second side for 30 seconds.
4. Drain egg shapes, which should be firm to the touch, on paper toweling. Repeat cooking until all egg whites are used.
5. Beat egg yolks until light and lemon colored. Gradually add some of the hot milk, stirring constantly. Pour beaten eggs and remaining milk mixture into a heavy saucepan. Cook over low heat, stirring constantly, until custard coats a metal spoon.
6. Remove from heat and stir in rum or cognac. Strain custard mixture into a wide shallow serving dish. Cover top of custard with egg shapes. Chill.
7. Put ½ cup sugar in a small heavy skillet. Cook over low heat, stirring constantly, until sugar melts and becomes light brown in color. Do not let the mixture burn.
8. Immediately pour the hot caramel syrup over the top of the egg whites. Chill.
9. Makes about 10 servings.

VANILLA MOUSSE WITH STRAWBERRY SAUCE

(shown opposite)

1½ cups milk
1½ cup sugar, divided
2 eggs, separated
2 envelopes unflavored gelatine
Water
1 tablespoon vanilla
1 pint heavy cream, whipped
1 pint fresh strawberries
1 tablespoon cornstarch
½ cup lemon juice
2 tablespoons butter

1. Combine milk and 1 cup sugar in top of double boiler. Place over low heat and heat just until bubbles form around edge of milk.
2. Beat egg yolks in a bowl. Gradually stir in hot milk. Return mixture to double boiler. Cook over hot water, stirring occasionally, until mixture coats a metal spoon.
3. Soften gelatine in ½ cup water.
4. Remove custard from heat. Stir in softened gelatine and continue stirring until gelatine is dissolved. Stir in vanilla.
5. Fill bottom of double boiler with ice water. Place top part in the ice water. Cool until custard mounds when dropped from a spoon. Beat with a rotary beater until light and frothy.
6. Beat egg whites until stiff but not dry. Fold into custard mixture.
7. Fold cream into custard mixture. Turn mixture into a 2-quart mold. Chill until set.
8. Clean and hull berries. Reserve 1 cup of the best berries for garnish. Force the remaining through a food mill or blend in an electric blender. Put through a strainer to remove seeds.
9. Combine the remaining ½ cup sugar with cornstarch in a medium saucepan. Gradually stir in 1 cup water.
10. Cook over medium heat, stirring, until sauce thickens and boils for ½ minute.
11. Remove from heat and stir in lemon juice, butter and puréed strawberries. Chill sauce.
12. To serve, unmold mousse onto a serving platter. Garnish with whole strawberries. Pipe a row of whipped cream around bottom of mold, if desired. Serve with cooked, chilled strawberry sauce.
13. Makes 8 to 10 servings.

California Strawberry Advisory Board

STRAWBERRY SOUFFLÉ

1 pint fresh strawberries
1¼ cup sugar, divided
1 envelope unflavored gelatine
4 eggs, separated
⅛ teaspoon salt
1 cup heavy cream, whipped
Brandied Strawberry Sauce

1. Fold a long strip of waxed paper or aluminum foil so that it is about 4 inches wide and long enough to extend around the outside of a 1½-quart soufflé dish. Lightly brush one side of the strip with oil. Fasten the strip, oiled side in, around top of soufflé dish. It can be tied with string or clipped together with paper clips.
2. Clean and crush strawberries. Force berries though a food mill or sieve. There should be about 1⅓ cups purée. Stir ½ cup sugar into the purée.
3. Remove ¼ cup sweetened purée. Sprinkle gelatine over top and let it stand to soften.
4. Combine egg yolks with ½ cup sugar in top of double boiler. Cook over boiling water, stirring, until mixture is thickened. Add gelatine mixture and stir until gelatine is dissolved.
5. Remove from hot water and cool. Blend in remaining strawberry purée.
6. Beat egg whites and salt until foamy. Gradually add remaining ¼ cup sugar and contine beating until mixture is shiny and holds stiff peaks. Fold in whipped cream. Gently fold in strawberry mixture.
7. Turn mixture into prepared soufflé dish. Chill until firm.
8. Remove collar and serve with Brandied Strawberry Sauce.
9. Makes 6 servings.

Cold Strawberry Soufflé is picture pretty, high and handsome in its serving dish. Served with Brandied Strawberry Sauce, every bite is truly heavenly!

California Strawberry Advisory Board

BRANDIED STRAWBERRY SAUCE

1 pint fresh strawberries
1 cup sugar
2 tablespoons cornstarch
2 tablespoons lemon juice
2 tablespoons cognac

1. Clean and crush strawberries.
2. In a saucepan combine sugar and cornstarch. Stir in lemon juice and crushed strawberries. Cook over medium heat, stirring, until sauce is thickened and clear.
3. Cool slightly. Stir in cognac. Chill well before serving with Strawberry Soufflé.
4. Makes about 1½ cups sauce.

SOUFFLÉ AUX MARRONS

2 tablespoons butter
2 tablespoons flour
1 cup milk
1 cup chestnut puree, unsweetened
½ cup sugar
2 squares unsweetened chocolate, melted
4 eggs, separated
1 teaspoon vanilla

1. Heat oven to 375°F.
2. Butter heavily the bottom and sides of a 1½-quart soufflé dish. Sprinkle butter-coated surface with granulated sugar. Shake out excess sugar.
3. Melt butter in a saucepan. Stir in flour. Remove from heat.
4. Put milk, chestnut purée and sugar in a bowl and beat with a rotary beater until smooth and well blended. Gradually stir chestnut mixture into the flour mixture.
5. Cook over low heat, stirring constantly, until thickened. Stir melted chocolate into chestnut mixture and remove from heat.
6. Beat egg yolks. Gradually stir hot chestnut sauce into egg yolks and stir until smooth. Cool.
7. Beat egg whites until stiff but not dry. Fold egg whites and vanilla into chestnut mixture. Pour mixture into prepared soufflé dish.
8. Place soufflé dish in a pan and add hot water to ½-inch depth in pan. Bake 40 to 45 minutes or until soufflé has risen and is set.
9. Serve immediately.
10. Makes 6 to 8 servings.

VANILLA SOUFFLÉ

3 tablespoons butter
3 tablespoons flour
¾ cup warm milk
¼ cup sugar
  Pinch of salt
4 egg yolks, well beaten
1 teaspoon vanilla
5 egg whites, stiffly beaten

1. Heat oven to 375°F.
2. Melt butter in a saucepan. Remove from heat and stir in flour. Return to heat and cook over low heat 1 minute. Remove from heat.
3. Add milk gradually and stir until smooth. Stir in sugar and salt.
4. Cook over low heat, stirring constantly, until mixture comes to a boil and is smooth and thickened. Remove from heat and stir quickly into beaten egg yolks. Stir until well blended. Stir in vanilla.
5. Add half the beaten egg whites to the custard mixture and fold in lightly but thoroughly. Be sure the mixture is blended evenly. Do not stir, as this will lose the air incorporated in the egg whites and the soufflé will not rise.
6. Add remaining egg whites and fold in quickly. A few patches of egg whites in the mixture will not matter, if the first incorporation has been complete.
7. Butter a 1½-quart straight-sided soufflé dish. Dust with sugar, until it is well coated. Shake out excess sugar.
8. Turn mixture into prepared soufflé dish. Bake 25 to 28 minutes. Remove from oven and serve immediately with whipped cream or sauce, if desired. It is also excellent served alone with no sauce.
9. Makes 4 servings. (It will make 6 servings, but not if every one loves soufflé.)

Variations

Almond Soufflé: Substitute almond extract for the vanilla extract. Stir in ½ cup blanched, grated almonds before folding in the egg whites.

Coffee Soufflé: Use half very strong coffee and half milk in place of all milk.

Lemon Soufflé: Omit the vanilla. Stir in the juice and grated rind of 1 lemon before folding in the egg whites.

Liqueur Soufflé: Omit the vanilla. Stir in ¼ cup Grand Marnier, Benedictine, Cointreau or Maraschino before folding in the egg whites.

Nut Soufflé: Stir 1 cup finely chopped nuts into custard mixture before folding in the egg whites.

SOUFFLÉ GLACÉ À L'ORANGE

⅔ cup crumbled macaroons
6 tablespoons Cointreau, divided
3 eggs
  Sugar
⅛ teaspoon salt
2 tablespoons dry white wine
1 tablespoon chopped marrons, in syrup
2 teaspoons toasted ground filberts
3 cups heavy cream
¼ cup sifted confectioners' sugar
10 orange shells (see note)
4 egg whites
¼ teaspoon cream of tartar
  Sauce Bernadotte

1. Soak crumbled macaroons in 4 tablespoons Cointreau. Set aside.
2. Beat eggs in top of double boiler until very light. Gradually beat in ⅓ cup sugar, salt and dry white wine. Cook over hot, not boiling water, beating with a wire whisk until very fluffy and thick, about 5 to 6 minutes. Immediately turn into a large bowl and continue beating with the whisk until cold.
3. Gently fold in macaroon mixture, marrons and ground filberts. Beat cream just until stiff and fold into cooked custard. Sift confectioners' sugar over top and fold in. Carefully add remaining Cointreau.
4. Spoon mixture into orange shells. Place in freezer and freeze until firm. If you are going to use these at a much later time, they should be wrapped in moisture-vapor proof wrapping.
5. Heat oven to 475°F.
6. Beat egg whites until frothy; add cream of tartar and beat to soft peaks. Gradually beat in ½ cup sugar. Continue beating until egg whites are very stiff but not dry. Remove orange shells from freezer. Spread meringue quickly all over top of filling. Place on a baking pan and bake 2 to 3 minutes or until meringue is lightly browned.
7. Serve immediately with Sauce Bernadotte.
8. Makes 10 servings.

Note: To make orange cups, wash large navel oranges. Cut ¼ to ⅓ from top of each orange. Carefully ream juice from oranges, keeping shells intact. Remove pulp from inside shells with a small spoon, being careful not to pierce skin. Scallops edges of orange cups if desired. Refrigerate before filling.

SAUCE BERNADOTTE

½ cup sugar
1 tablespoon cornstarch
Pinch of salt
2 cups orange juice
1 tablespoon butter
2 teaspoons grated orange peel
2 egg yolks, beaten
½ cup finely chopped fresh orange sections,
   well drained (from orange cups)
1 cup heavy cream, whipped
¼ cup Grand Marnier

1. Combine sugar, cornstarch and salt in a saucepan. Blend in orange juice. Add butter. Bring to a boil over medium heat, stirring constantly, and boil 1 minute. Add grated orange peel.
2. Blend some of the hot mixture into the beaten egg yolks. Return mixture to saucepan. Cook over low heat 1 minute.
3. Fold in orange sections. Turn into a bowl and chill until cold.
4. Fold in whipped cream and Grand Marnier. Serve chilled with Soufflé Glacé a l'Orange.
5. Makes 3¾ cups sauce.

OMELET SOUFFLÉ

8 eggs, separated
½ cup sugar
⅓ cup cognac or rum

1. Heat oven to 375°F.
2. Beat egg yolks until light and lemon-colored. Gradually beat in sugar. Stir in Cognac.
3. Beat egg whites until they stand in stiff peaks. Fold ⅓ of the egg whites into yolk mixture until they are well blended. Fold in remaining egg whites gently without losing too much air.
4. Heat a heavy metal skillet with an oven proof handle. Use a 10-inch aluminum omelet skillet if you have one. When skillet is hot, butter it well and sprinkle with granulated sugar. Pour soufflé mixture into skillet.
5. Bake 15 minutes. Remove from oven, sprinkle with granulated sugar and serve at once.
6. If desired, sprinkle with 2 tablespoons warm Cognac and ignite with a match before serving.
7. Makes about 6 servings.

CRÈME BRÛLÉE

6 eggs
⅔ cup sugar
½ teaspoon salt
2 cups milk
2 cups heavy cream
1 teaspoon vanilla
¾ cup firmly packed light brown sugar

1. Heat oven to 350°F.
2. Beat eggs slightly. Beat in sugar and salt. Add milk and cream gradually, stirring constantly. Add vanilla.
3. Pour mixture into a shallow 1½-quart baking dish. Place casserole in a shallow pan of hot water.
4. Bake about 60 minutes or until a knife inserted in the center comes out clean.
5. Cool. Chill custard in refrigerator.
6. Preheat broiling compartment with racks removed.
7. Carefully sift brown sugar over top of custard to about ¼-inch thickness, leaving center uncovered, if desired.
8. Set custard on broiler rack about 3 inches from source of heat. Broil about 4 minutes, or until sugar carmelizes and forms a crust. Watch carefully because the sugar burns very quickly.
9. Chill in refrigerator before serving.
10. Makes 10 servings.

Note: This can be baked in 6 individual serving dishes. In which case, use only 4 eggs and bake 35 to 40 minutes, or until a knife inserted in the center comes out clean.

MOCK CRÈME BRÛLÉE

2 packages (3½ ounces each) vanilla pudding and pie filling mix
3 cups milk
1 cup cream
½ cup brown sugar, firmly packed
½ cup chopped pecans

1. Cook pudding as directed on package using 3 cups milk and 1 cup cream. Cool slightly.
2. Pour pudding into a shallow 1½-quart baking dish. Chill thoroughly.
3. Preheat broiler compartment without rack. Sprinkle brown sugar evenly over surface of pudding. Sprinkle pecans over top of sugar. Place pudding on broiler rack, 5 inches from source of heat, and broil 4 to 5 minutes or until brown sugar melts and becomes bubbly. Watch carefully so that it does not burn.
4. Makes 8 servings.

POTS DE LA CRÈME AU CHOCOLAT

3 squares unsweetened chocolate
3 cups milk
⅔ cup sugar
¼ teaspoon salt
5 egg yolks, beaten
½ teaspoon vanilla
Heavy cream

1. Cut chocolate squares into small pieces, or shave it into curls with a vegetable peeler. Combine with milk in a saucepan. Cook over very low heat, stirring, until chocolate has melted. Add sugar and salt and continue cooking until mixture is smooth.
2. Remove from heat and slowly stir into beaten egg yolks. Return mixture to saucepan and cook over very low heat, stirrring constantly, until mixture thickens.
3. Remove from heat and stir in vanilla. Pour into custard cups or covered French china pots. Chill.
4. Serve with thick, heavy cream.
5. Makes 6 servings.

CARAMEL TOPPED EGG NOG CUSTARD

½ cup sugar
2½ cups canned egg nog
2 eggs
¼ teaspoon salt
2 tablespoons rum, optional

1. Heat oven to 325°F.
2. In a small heavy skillet, heat sugar over low heat until it melts and turns into a light, golden brown syrup. Stir constantly while sugar is melting. Pour about 1 tablespoonful of the hot syrup into five 5-ounce custard cups. Let cool.
3. In a medium-sized saucepan, scald egg nog.
4. Beat eggs with salt. Slowly stir hot egg nog into beaten eggs. Stir in rum, if desired. Pour mixture over syrup in custard cups. Set cups in a baking pan. Pour warm water into pan to depth of 1 inch.
5. Bake 1 hour and 30 minutes or until a knife inserted ½ inch from edge of custard cup comes out clean. Remove from oven and remove cups from hot water. Let cool at room temperature.
6. Chill in refrigerator about 2 hours or until well chilled. At serving time, carefully insert a knife around side of cup to loosen custard; invert cups over dessert dishes and quickly turn out custards and caramel syrup.
7. Makes 5 servings.

PEARS HÉLÈNE
(shown opposite)

6 small fresh pears
2 cups sugar, divided
Water
1 teaspoon vanilla
½ cup light corn syrup
Dash of salt
2 squares (2 ounces) semi-sweet chocolate
½ cup light cream
1 tablespoon butter
1 quart vanilla ice cream

1. Peel pears. Cut in half lengthwise and core. Combine 1½ cups sugar, 1½ cups water and vanilla in a large saucepan. Bring to a boil, stirring until sugar is dissolved.
2. Add pear halves to sugar mixture and simmer gently about 8 minutes, or just until pears are tender. Transfer fruit and juice to a dish and chill in the refrigerator.
3. Combine corn syrup, remaining sugar, 2 tablespoons water and salt in a saucepan. Bring to a boil and stir until sugar is dissolved. Bring to a full rolling boil and boil 3 minutes. Remove from heat. Add chocolate and stir until melted. Stir in cream and butter. Beat with rotary beater until smooth.
4. To serve, drain pears and arrange 2 halves in each dessert dish. Cover with a large serving of ice cream. Pour warm or chilled chocolate syrup over the top, as desired.
5. Makes 6 servings.

CHAMPAGNE FRUIT CUP

  1 can (11 ounces) mandarin orange sections,
    chilled
  1 can (1 pound) Queen Anne cherries, pitted
    and chilled
  1 cup halved, seeded grapes
  1 cup diced, unpeeled red apple
    Chilled champagne

1. Drain mandarin orange sections and cherries. Combine with grapes and apples. Chill.
2. At serving time spoon into saucer shaped champagne or sherbert glasses. Fill glasses with chilled champagne.
3. Makes 8 to 10 servings.

FRAISES À LA CRÈME
AU PETIT-LAIT
(STRAWBERRIES WITH FRENCH
BUTTERMILK CREAM)

  1 quart buttermilk
  1 pint heavy cream
  1¼ cups sugar
  1 teaspoon vanilla
  2 pints fresh strawberries
  ¼ cup confectioners' sugar

1. Blend together buttermilk, cream, sugar and vanilla. Pour into freezing trays and freeze until firm.
2. Clean strawberries and cut in half. Sprinkle with confectioners' sugar and chill 15 minutes.
3. Beat the frozen buttermilk cream until smooth. Serve with chilled strawberries.
4. Makes 6 servings.

SHERRY BAKED PEARS

  ½ cup sherry
  ½ cup water
  ½ cup brown sugar
  2 tablespoons fresh lemon juice
  3 tablespoons butter or margarine
  4 fresh pears

1. Heat oven to 350°F.
2. Combine sherry, water, sugar, lemon juice and butter in a small saucepan. Simmer over medium heat about 5 minutes.
3. While sauce is cooking, halve, pare and core pears. Arrange pears in a baking dish. Pour sherry sauce over pears. Cover dish.
4. Bake about 35 to 40 minutes or until pears are tender.
5. Serve warm or chilled, plain or with whipped or sour cream, if desired.
6. Makes 4 servings.

STRAWBERRIES AND CHAMPAGNE

  4 pints fresh strawberries
  ⅔ cup sugar
  ½ cup cognac
    Chilled champagne

1. Clean and hull strawberries. Sprinkle with sugar and cognac. Cover and chill several hours.
2. Spoon strawberries into dessert glasses. Pour champagne over berries.
3. Makes 8 servings.

Note: Champagne is also excellent with other fresh fruits such as raspberries or sliced fresh peaches.

VINTAGE BAKED APPLES

  6 baking apples
  ¼ cup brown sugar, firmly packed
  ¾ cup port
  6 whole cloves
  1 stick cinnamon, about 3 inches
  1 tablespoon lemon juice

1. Heat oven to 375°F.
2. Core apples and pare down about ¼ way from stem. Place apples in a baking dish.
3. Combine remaining ingredients in a saucepan. Bring to a boil and simmer about 5 minutes. Pour sauce over apples.
4. Bake about 45 minutes or until apples are tender. Baste occasionally with sauce in bottom of baking dish.
5. Serve warm or chilled, plain or with cream.
6. Makes 6 servings.

ORANGE ORIENTAL

  3 large oranges
  2 cups sugar
  1 cup water
    Candied violets (optional)

1. With a vegetable peeler remove just the outer orange rind from the oranges. Cut rind in slivers and place in a saucepan with sugar and water. Place over medium heat and simmer until slivers are tender.
2. Peel oranges until all of the white part of the rind is removed. Cut oranges in half crosswise. Place in a serving dish.
3. Pour hot sugar syrup over oranges. Refrigerate until thoroughly chilled.
4. Garnish with candied violets before servings, if desired.
5. Makes 6 servings.

WINE-BUTTER GLAZED PEACHES

    3 tablespoons butter
    2 tablespoons lemon juice
    6 small ripe peaches, peeled
    ⅓ cup brown sugar
    ⅓ cup rosé wine
    ½ cup heavy cream

1. Melt butter in a large skillet over medium heat. Add lemon juice and peaches. Turn peaches over and over to coat with butter.

2. Sprinkle with brown sugar and add wine to pan.

3. Poach over low heat, turning often, about 15 minutes or until peaches are heated through and lightly glazed.

4. Push peaches to one side and stir in cream. Bring just to the boil. Lower heat and simmer several minutes.

5. Serve peaches warm with some of the wine-cream sauce.

6. Makes 6 servings.

Famous French Cookery

Glossary of Terms

AU GRATIN: Gratin is the brown coating on food formed by broiling or baking in the oven. Au gratin has come to mean a method of preparing food in a sauce whose surface is covered with butter, bread crumbs or grated cheese and baked or broiled until lightly browned.

BATTER: A mixture of flour, liquid, and other ingredients, used as a basis for cakes, fritters, coating or pancakes. Its consistency may range from a thin liquid to a stiff, thick one, depending on the proportions of the ingredients.

BASTE: To moisten food while it is cooking, by spooning on melted fat, pan juices, wine or any other liquid.

BEAT: To mix ingredients together making a smooth batter, using a wire whisk, spoon, electric mixer or rotary beater.

BEATING EGG WHITES: To incorporate as much air as possible into the egg whites as you beat, thus increasing their volume. They can be beaten with a wire whisk, electric mixer or rotary beater.

BEATING EGG WHITES STIFF: Egg whites should stand in peaks, drooping over a bit. Surface should still be moist and glossy.

BEATING EGG WHITES VERY STIFF: Egg whites should stand in upright peaks, without drooping. Surface of egg whites should be dry.

BLANCH: To plunge food into boiling water for the purpose of removing skins, as with almonds, or for partial precooking as when freezing foods.

BLEND: To combine two or more ingredients well, usually with a spoon or electric mixer.

BOIL: To cook food in a boiling liquid in which bubbles constantly rise to the surface and break. In a rapid boil, the bubbles are vigorous and rolling. In a medium boil, the bubbles are gentle. In a very slow boil, the liquid hardly moves and is called a simmer.

BONE: To remove bones from meat or fowl as directed in some recipes.

BOUQUET GARNI: A combination of parsley, thyme and bay leaf for flavoring soups, stews, sauces and braised meat dishes. If the herbs are fresh and in sprigs, the parsley is folded around them and they are tied together. If the herbs are dried, they are wrapped in a piece of cheesecloth and tied. The bundle is made so that the herbs can be removed easily before serving.

BRAISE: To brown well in a little hot fat, then adding a small amount of liquid and cooking in a tightly covered pan over very low heat until tender.

BREAD: To coat food with dry bread crumbs or cracker crumbs. The food is often dipped first into a liquid or a beaten egg to help the crumbs stick to the surface.

BROTH: The liquid in which meat, fish, poultry or vegetables, or a combination of them, have been cooked.

BROWN: To turn the surface of food brown in color by cooking in hot fat on top of the range or at high temperature in the oven or broiler.

BRUSH ON: To apply melted fat, salad oil, cream, beaten egg, etc. to the surface of food with a pastry brush or crumpled waxed paper.

CARAMELIZE: To melt granulated sugar in a large skillet over medium heat, stirring constantly until sugar turns into a golden nut brown syrup. This is used either to line a dessert mold or to add flavor or color to other mixtures.

CEPES: Members of the mushroom family, apparently native to France. They sometimes grow exceedingly large and have a most unusual texture and flavor. In America, they can be found canned and packed in brine or deep fat fried. They may be used for an hors d'oeuvre, entrée or vegetable course.

CHILL: To place in the refrigerator or over cracked ice until cold.

CHOP: To cut food into small pieces. Place food to be chopped on a wooden board, hold tip of a French knife close to the surface of the board with one hand, then move knife handle vigorously up and down on the food with the other hand. Repeat several times, until food is thoroughly chopped.

CLARIFY: To clear a liquid, such as soup, by adding slightly beaten egg white (and the egg shells, if desired). These coagulate the particles in the liquid, which are then strained out.

COAT A METAL SPOON: A term that describes the degree of thickness of a sauce or custard. To test, stir liquid with a metal spoon, hold spoon above the pan and allow it to drip. It should retain an even film or coating of the liquid. A spoon dipped into a custard should emerge with a fairly thick coating.

CODDLE: To cook slowly in a liquid heated to just below the boiling point.

COMBINE: To mix or blend together two or more ingredients.

CONDIMENT: Any seasoning added to food to enhance its flavor.

COOL: To let stand at room temperature until cool to the touch.

CREAM: To rub or work fat such as butter or margarine with sugar against the sides of a bowl until light and creamy. Or to use an electric mixer until mixture is soft and creamy.

CRISP: To make firm. Leafy vegetables such as lettuce are rinsed in water and chilled. Dry foods, such as bread and crackers, are heated in an oven at a very low temperature.

CROUTONS: Bread cut into ½-inch cubes, tossed in a little melted butter or margarine (with a bit of garlic if desired), then broiled or toasted in a 300° F. oven. Served as a garnish in soups or salads.

CRUMB: To break into small pieces. Fresh bread crumbs are made by pulling a piece of fresh bread into small, soft particles. Stale bread crumbs are made with dried out bread by crushing with a rolling pin or in a blender. Refrigerate stale crumbs and use to coat croquettes and other foods.

CRUSH: To pulverize by rolling with a rolling pin until consistency of coarse powder. Fruits are usually crushed by mashing until they lose their shape.

CUBE: To cut into small equal-sized pieces ¼- to ½-inch square.

CUT IN: To combine solid fat with flour in pastry making. Using two knives, scissor fashion, or a pastry blender, cut shortening into flour or flour mixture until flour-coated fat particles are of desired size.

DEGLAZE: To use browned bits in pan for au jus sauce. After meat has been roasted or browned in a skillet on top of the stove, all of the grease should be poured off. Liquid is then added to the pan and as it simmers, browned bits from the bottom are stirred up and incorporated with the sauce.

DEGREASE: To remove fat from a liquid. Let the liquid stand for a few minutes so that the fat will rise to the top. Tip the container slightly and skim the fat from the surface with a spoon. Wrap an ice cube in a piece of paper toweling, draw it over the surface to soak up any remaining fat. If time permits, refrigerate the liquid in its container until the fat congeals on the surface, thus making it simple to lift off.

DEVEIN: To remove the black or white vein running along the back of a shrimp. With a sharp knife, make a shallow cut along the vein line, then lift or scrape out the vein.

DICE: To cut into very small even cubes.

DISSOLVE: To mix a dry substance with a liquid until it dissolves; or to heat it until it melts.

DOT: To scatter small bits of butter or margarine over the surface of food.

DRAIN: To remove liquid by pouring food into a colander or strainer until the liquid has dripped out, or by tipping pan while holding lid in place so that just the liquid is poured off.

DREDGE: To coat food with flour, sugar, bread or cracker crumbs.

DUST: To sprinkle food lightly with sugar, flour or crumbs.

ESCALOPE: A thin slice of meat, usually veal, that has been flattened.

FILET: To remove flesh of fish, poultry or meat from the bone prior to cooking. A filet is thus a piece of fish, poultry or meat without bone. The term also refers to the tenderloin of beef. A filet mignon is a steak cut from the smaller end of a filet of beef.

FLAKE: To break into small pieces with a fork, as in cooked fish recipes.

FLAMBÉ: A French term meaning blazing.

FOIE GRAS: The liver of a goose or duck fattened in a special way. Some of the best ones in France weigh as much as four pounds apiece. Pure foie gras is packed in tins and is usually sold only to restaurants because it is quite expensive. Mixtures of foie gras with other kinds of livers and seasonings, sold as pâté de foie gras, are available in many supermarkets and are excellent.

FOLD: To incorporate a delicate mixture into a thicker, heavier one, as folding in beaten egg whites or whipped cream. Place egg whites or cream on top of heavier mixture. Pass a rubber spatula down through mixture and across bottom of pan or bowl, bring up some of the mixture and place on top of egg whites or cream. Repeat until egg whites or cream are evenly combined with mixture. This should be done quickly but gently.

FRY: To cook in a very small amount of hot fat.

GRATE: To rub food on a grater to produce fine, medium or coarse particles. When grating lemon or orange rind, grate only the colored part of the rind.

GREASE: To rub the surface of food or utensils lightly with butter, margarine, shortening or salad oil.

GRIND: To cut food into small particles with a food grinder.

JULIENNE: To cut food into thin, match-like strips.

KNEAD: To work dough by pressing it with the heels of the hands, folding, turning and pressing; usually applied to yeast dough and worked on a floured board. Yeast dough should be kneaded until it looks full and rounded, smooth, satiny and tightly stretched.

LARD: To insert small pieces of fat in lean meat for flavor or juiciness. Fat may be put in gashes in the meat or run through with a larding needle. Pieces of fat salt pork or bacon placed over meat may be substituted for larding. This prevents meat from drying out and bastes it while cooking.

MARINATE: To let food stand in a seasoned liquid to enhance its flavor or make it more tender.

MARROW: The fatty filling of beef leg-bones. This is considered a delicacy in many types of cookery. It is poached and used in sauces, garnitures and on crisp toast as canapés.

MASH: To soften and break down by using a masher, the back of a spoon, a fork, or by forcing through a sieve.

MELT: To change fat into a liquid state by heating.

MINCE: To cut or chop very fine, with a chopper or a French knife.

MOUND: A spoonful of a mixture dropped into another mixture. A mound forms a definite heap and does not blend into the original mixture.

PARBOIL: To boil in water or other liquid until partially cooked, preliminary to another form of cooking.

PARE: To remove the outer covering of fruit or vegetables with a knife or paring tool.

PEEL: To pull off the outer covering, as of bananas or oranges.

POACH: To cook food immersed in a liquid that is barely simmering.

PREHEAT: To heat an oven or broiler to a desired temperature before putting in food.

PUREE: To make solid foods into a mush. This may be done with a meat grinder, food mill, an electric blender, or by pushing through a sieve.

REDUCE: To boil down a liquid, reducing it in quantity and concentrating its taste. This is usually done when making a sauce and is a very important step.

ROUX: A mixture of fat and flour blended together over low heat—the first step in making all sauces in which flour is the thickening agent.

SAUTÉ: To fry lightly in a small amount of hot fat.

SCALD: To heat a liquid to just under the boiling point or to the point tiny bubbles appear around the edge of the saucepan. Also, to pour boiling water over food.

SCORE: To make shallow slits or gashes with a knife or fork on the surface of food.

SEAR: To brown the surface of food quickly, over high heat, as in a hot skillet.

SEASON: To add seasonings to one's own taste.

SEPARATE: To separate egg yolks from the whites.

SET: A condition in which liquids have congealed and retain their shape, usually referring to gelatin mixtures.

SHALLOTS: Delicately flavored members of the onion family, having the slightest hint of garlic. They are sold by the pound and keep fairly well. If you do not have shallots, the minced white part of green onions can be substituted very nicely.

SHRED: To cut or break in thin pieces.

SIFT: To put through a flour sifter or fine sieve.

SIMMER: To cook in a liquid at a temperature slightly below boiling.

SKEWER: To hold in place by means of metal or wooden skewers or toothpicks.

SKIM: To remove a substance, usually fat, from the surface of a liquid.

SLIVER: To cut or split into long thin pieces.

SNIP: To cut into small pieces with kitchen shears.

STEEP: To let stand in a hot liquid.

STEW: A thick combination of a variety of foods cooked in liquid at a low temperature for a long period of time.

STIR: To blend with a spoon in a circular motion, widening circles until all ingredients are well mixed.

STOCK: A liquid in which meat, poultry, fish, bones, vegetables and seasonings have been cooked for a long time.

THICKEN: To make a liquid more dense by adding flour, cornstarch or egg yolks.

TOSS: To mix lightly with two forks or a fork and spoon.

TRUFFLES: Called the "black diamonds of gastronomy". They are members of the fungus family and grow underground in one part of France, near a certain type of oak tree. They are usually hunted with the aid of a pig or dog. They are black, roughly shaped, somewhat crisp and have a most luxurious aroma. Truffles from Perigord, traditionally associated with classic French cookery, can be used in many ways and add distinction to many dishes. In America, they are available canned, whole, sliced or just the peelings.

TRUSS: To bind the wings and legs of a fowl before cooking.

UNMOLD: To remove from a mold. Dip a small pointed knife in warm water and run it around inner edges of mold. Dip mold just to rim in warm water for two to three seconds. Remove and shake gently to loosen gelatin. Cover top of mold with chilled, inverted serving plate. Turn plate and mold over together. Lift off mold carefully. If the contents stick, rub the mold gently with a hot, damp towel.

WHIP: To beat rapidly, usually with an electric mixer or rotary beater to incorporate air and increase volume.

INDEX